INSIDE

LATIN

AMERICA

By JOHN GUNTHER
Author of INSIDE EUROPE, INSIDE ASIA

HARPER & BROTHERS

NEW YORK AND LONDON 1941

1. **ARGENTINA.** This powerful nation lives on wheat and beef, considers itself to have a great imperial destiny, has lost 40 per cent of its trade through the war, and is inclined to be sniffish about its neighbors. A huge metropolis, Buenos Aires, controls the limitless *pampa*. The only country in the world that has, in effect, two Presidents. Culture and economics dominated by Europe. Politics dominated by the conservative land-owning oligarchy.

2. **BOLIVA** is a primitive mountain state in the high Andes, predominantly Indian. Important as a source of tin.

3. **BRAZIL.** This great country, bigger than the continental United States, friendly, colorful, and picturesque, a limitless reservoir of unexplored richness, is more vital to hemisphere defense than any other South American state. From Natal, on the Atlantic bulge, to Dakar in Africa is only 1,600 miles. Brazil is a dictatorship, largely benevolent, under Getulio Vargas.

4. **CHILE** is predominantly white. One of the pleasantest and most civilized of nations, it lives on copper and nitrates, and has been hard hit by the war and the economic crisis. Ruled by the only Popular Front government in the Americas.

5. In **COLOMBIA** senators write poems, a newspaper man is president, bootblacks quote Proust, and business men bewail the low price of coffee. The capital, Bogotá, 8,500 feet high in the Andes, is the "Athens" of Latin America.

6. **COSTA RICA.** This delightful small state is a well-run democracy under a President who is a doctor of medicine and who gets $268 a month salary. The army consists of 250 soldiers and a brass band.

7. **CUBA.** Here President Fulgencio Batista wrestles with problems of poverty and sugar. Quieter politically than in many years, and very close and friendly to the United States.

8. **DOMINICAN REPUBLIC.** The dictator, General Trujillo, calls hmself "The Benefactor of the Fatherland" and is one of the hardest-boiled citizens in the Americas. His country lives—or tries to live—on sugar.

9. **ECUADOR.** A charming country, full of churches and cocoa, that has had 12 presidents in 10 years. Note (10), the Galápagos Islands, which would be very useful to the United States as a naval air base.

11. **GUATEMALA.** Largely Indian. Bossed by General Ubico, who like Trujillo in the Dominican Republic is on the hard-boiled side, to put it mildly.

12. The **GUIANAS** are the most wretched and miserable areas in all Latin America. Unbelievably poor, unbelievably filthy. The U. S. has leased a base at Georgetown in British Guiana. Dutch Guiana is officially known as Surinam. In French Guiana, where disintegration has been rapid since the defeat of France, is the famous penal colony Devil's Island.

LATIN AMERICA

Scale of Miles
0   200   400   600   800   1000

Note: Stars (★) indicate location of U.S. naval and air bases

13. In **HAITI** the people speak French, admire Ex-President Vincent, and discuss voodoo—if you care to listen.

14. Small **HONDURAS** is one of the banana republics, virtually a colony of the United Fruit Company.

15. **MEXICO.** This magnificent country, 30 per cent Indian, 60 per cent mestizo, is more important to us than any other Latin American state, Brazil possibly excepted. As with China, its contemporary life—crowded with vital problems—derives from a tremendous ancient civilization. Here Cárdenas made a great land reform, expropriated foreign oil, pushed the revolution on. Here Avila Camacho attempts to steer a strong middle course.

16. **NICARAGUA.** A vivid little country, dominated by a vivid man, General Somoza.

17. **PANAMA.** This country has a Harvard-educated, youthful, ambitious, temperamental president; it lives mostly on the Canal Zone, (18) the ten-mile wide lifeline connecting the Atlantic and Pacific. Absolutely vital to U. S. A. defense. Within 30 miles of the Zone are Indians who live today as primitively as in the time of Cortés.

19. **PARAGUAY** is a remote and picturesque state, ruled by Argentine imperialism and a clique of young army officers.

20. In **PERU**, a country with a noble history, the government strives to perform a transition from the dictatorship era to constitutional rule. Peru is a classic example of economic imperialism by foreigners. Outsiders control almost everything.

21. **PUERTO RICO** has been a headache to the United States for 40 years. Its poverty is a disgrace to the Stars and Stripes. Now our chief defense bastion in the Caribbean.

22. **EL SALVADOR.** This sophisticated little country is ruled by a dictator who is a theosophist, General Martínez.

23. **TRINIDAD.** Here the United States acquired the most important of its new Caribbean bases from Great Britain. Note also **JAMAICA** (24) and **ANTIGUA** (25) which help to block the Atlantic entrance to the Panama Canal. A gap in this chain of bases is **MARTINIQUE** (26) which belongs to Vichy.

27. **URUGUAY.** The most democratic of Latin American states, sensibly run by a moderate government. Great attention to paternalism, cooperatives, and the like. Resembles Scandinavia in social progress.

28. In **VENEZUELA**, which is the greatest oil exporter in the world, retail prices are higher than in New York. Chief problem: substitution of a constitutional regime of the old Gómez tyranny.

For

ARCHIBALD MacLEISH

TABLE OF CONTENTS

Note—ix

Chapter

I. Inside Latin America—1

II. Fifth Column and Hemisphere Defense—16

III. Avila Camacho Succeeds Cárdenas—34

IV. Mexico: Land, Revolution, People—53

V. Cárdenas Days and Years—78

VI. Mexicans Left and Right—87

VII. Foreign Policy and Axis Influence in Mexico—107

VIII. Two Dictators on Top—118

IX. The Banana Republics—131

X. Panama: Country, Zone, and Defense—147

XI. Hail Colombia—160

XII. The High Cost of Venezuela—176

XIII. Ecuador on Edge—187

XIV. What Peru Is and Isn't—197

XV. Tin and Tintypes in Bolivia—219

XVI. Popular Front in Chile—234

XVII. Chile Getting Hot—260

XVIII. Paraguay Is Ruritania—271

XIX. The Argentine Complex—282

XX. Beef, Fifth Column, and Bases—301

XXI. These Are Argentinians—319

XXII. Uruguay, the Denmark of Latin America—335

XXIII. Getulio Vargas—350

XXIV. Behold Brazil—370

XXV. A Word About Commodities—391

XXVI. Brazilian Roll Call—400

XXVII. The Coming American "Imperialism"—411

XXVIII. Our Orphan Island—423

XXIX. Columbus Called It Hispaniola—436

XXX. Cuba's Batista—454

XXXI. What To Do About It—470

Acknowledgments and Bibliography—479

Index—483

Note

THIS book follows closely the pattern of *Inside Europe* and *Inside Asia*, to which it is an obvious companion. It attempts to give a picture of the political situation in each Latin American country, an appraisal of its personalities, and a survey of its more pressing problems. It is a job of reporting above all, as were *Inside Europe* and *Inside Asia*. If it includes brief historical passages this is because no one can grasp the contemporary realities of Latin America without some knowledge of the background, which is unfamiliar to most of us.

To write this book I traveled 18,938 miles by air and I don't know how many other miles by train, boat, and car. I had 31 different hops in the shining DC-3's and giant clippers of Pan-American Airways. There are twenty different republics in Latin America, and I visited all of them. Count them—twenty. I also paused briefly in Puerto Rico and Trinidad.

In German-trodden Europe today only eight independent states survive; in all the vastness of Asia only seven. So Latin America, with its twenty friendly republics, is an important repository of what political independence remains in this convulsed world.

My trip began in the west and ended in the east. First I saw the magnificent plateau of Mexico, and then the shaggy valleys of the five Central American states; I climbed the high Andes into Colombia and Ecuador, and descended sharply to sea-level in Peru; I climbed once more to the icy granite uplands of Peru and Bolivia, so unbelievably remote and primitive, and then coasted down to sea-level again in Chile. I flew over the Andes a fourth time to visit Argentina, the most powerful, the most nationalist, and the most difficult of Latin American states. Then

I turned north and found a kind of climax in the gigantic, sumptuous world of Brazil. Finally I flew through the Caribbean tropics —Trinidad, Haiti, Cuba, and so on—until I reached home.

I was lucky enough to see seventeen out of the twenty available Latin American Presidents or Acting Presidents, and I saw eighteen of the twenty Foreign Ministers. In each country I talked to countless journalists, scholars, men of affairs, business leaders, and politicians—in and out of office. And in each country I did what I could to see as much as possible of that very important individual, the man in the street.

The reader will perhaps be surprised—as I was surprised—to discover how widely the twenty countries differ. There are almost as many divergences in national character and political outlook as in Asia or Europe. Every country has its own special problems, and some are highly complex. In several respects Mexico is as foreign to us—and hence as "difficult"—as China, and politics in Chile for instance are more intricate than anything I ever found in Europe.

My first chapter is in the nature of a general survey. Then I attempt to point out the intimate and increasing importance of our southern neighbors to the United States. Latin America is our exposed frontier, the vulnerable back door to our continent. In discussing each country I allude of course to the major problems of inter-American relations, continental solidarity, and hemisphere defense, as well as the activities public and private of Fifth Columnism.

It has been difficult to choose a title for this book. *Inside Latin America* seems to me unwieldy and not precisely fitting. After all, it is hard to think of Mexico or Cuba as "Latin" countries. *Inside South America* is, however, even less fitting, since there are only ten countries in South America proper, and I am writing about twenty. My Indian friends would like me to call the book *Inside Indo-America*. But this would seem to exclude states like Uruguay which certainly have an Indian origin but have no

Indian problem now. *Inside Spanish America* would give the wrong connotation and besides is inaccurate since Brazil speaks Portuguese. One of my Argentine acquaintances suggested *Inside the Other Americas*, but I feel that this is too long. Nor could I very well use *Inside the Western Hemisphere Except for the United States and Canada.* So *Inside Latin America* it is.

J. G.

INSIDE LATIN AMERICA

Chapter I
Inside Latin America

~~~~~~

THE first thing to say about Latin America is that no such thing exists. The phrase "Latin America" as such has little meaning, it seems to me. What does exist are twenty independent and highly individual countries which differ from one another strikingly. It is true that all have the same racial, historical and geographical background, and that all speak a brand of Spanish except Brazil, which speaks Portuguese, and Haiti, which speaks Creole and French. Yet the differences between the twenty states are profound.

Take Uruguay and Paraguay, small countries within a hundred miles of each other. The contrast between them is incredibly sharp. Uruguay is one of the most advanced countries in the world, and Paraguay is one of the most primitive. Uruguay is like Denmark before Hitler—with a highly developed social conscience, state control of industry, paternalistic co-operatives, and an almost too pure political democracy. But Paraguay is like—Paraguay. It resembles nothing except itself. It is the one country in Latin America where the Indian has, as it were, absorbed the Spaniard, instead of vice versa. It never had the advantage of Uruguay's enlightenment, but let no one say it is without its own peculiar charms.

On the northern edge of South America lie the three "Bolívar" countries, Venezuela, Colombia, and Ecuador. But, though geography binds them close, they have differed radically since their deliverance from Spain. The story is that Venezuela became a barracks, Colombia a university, and Ecuador a monastery. There are other differences too. In wealthy Venezuela, which lives on oil, the cost of living is about 250 per cent higher than in New York City. But Ecuador, close by, is one of the poorest countries in the world.

Take Peru. It has its own special problems. One is transition

I

from years of military dictatorship to a moderately liberal constitutional government. Another is imperialism by outsiders. Peru
is a classic example of the "semi-colonial" state. Oil is owned by
Canada and the United States, minerals largely by the United
States, and cotton partly by Japanese and Germans. The British
control the railways, the Italians largely control banking, and
Americans and Germans divide the sugar.

Bolivia, next door, is a one-crop country—if you can call tin,
on which Bolivia lives, a crop. Its population is perhaps 90 per
cent Indian. But Chile, with which Bolivia has a common frontier,
is predominantly white. Bolivia is ruled by the tin merchants and
a military President. But, in sharp contrast, Chile is the home of
the only Popular Front government in the Americas. The Chileans
have thrown the army leaders out, and their administration is
strongly Leftist.

Take Argentina. It lives on wheat and beef, it considers itself
to have a distinct imperial destiny, and it is haughty to its neighbors. Politically it is fascinating if only for the fact that it has,
at the moment of writing, two Presidents. One is sick, one is well,
and they dislike each other. Argentina is dominated by a clique of
oligarchs and land-owning bull breeders who—by fantastic skul-
duggery—manage to keep political power from a majority of the
people.

Finally, there is Brazil, which is almost as different from Argentina as China is from Japan. The Brazilians are mild people on
the whole, colorful and picturesque; their great country—larger
than the continental United States—is a magnificent reservoir of
potential wealth. Brazil is a dictatorship, though Brazilians don't
like to hear you say so. But it is a dictatorship that has considerable roots in popular support, and is benevolent on the whole.

Of the twenty countries in Latin America at least two are pure,
unadulterated, and unashamed dictatorships, Guatemala and the
Dominican Republic. Perhaps oddly, United States relations with
these two are very cordial. A good many others are dictatorships

in fact, though they maintain a parliamentary façade, like Cuba, Honduras, Nicaragua. In others it is very difficult to draw the line between dictatorship and democracy: for instance, in Ecuador, Venezuela, Peru. About seven countries are democracies, more or less: Argentina, Mexico, Costa Rica, Colombia, Chile, Uruguay. The most democratic of all is probably Costa Rica.

North Americans[1] should not worry overmuch that so many countries in the hemisphere are not democracies, though we like to assume democratic as well as political solidarity in hemisphere relations. Our standards of political and social behavior are very different from those of Latin America. Let our neighbors be judged by their own standards, not ours—especially as the *trend* toward democracy is steadily increasing. We in the United States have been luckier. "Democracy" to a Latin American state means, as a rule, not a formal system of government but a desire to be let alone to work out its own destiny. It means, as a rule, not personal liberty for the citizen but political liberty for the state.

In the United States there is a good deal more talk of hemisphere solidarity, on the whole, than in Latin America itself. The national rivalries in the southern continent are still considerable enough to cause occasional bad blood. You will find more sympathy for the Pan-American ideal in Washington than, say, in Asunción or Bogotá. In Argentina especially one hears other Latin American states mentioned with contempt. I have heard Argentineans of the most sophisticated intelligence call Venezuelans "savages" and Brazilians "niggers." One eminent Argentine began conversation with me by saying, "Remember, we are not Caribbeans!" Another was chilled with horror that I should even contemplate visiting such a "barbarous" state as Paraguay.

But—a very important but—the national rivalries of Latin America, considerable as they may be, are as nothing compared to those of Europe. Our neighbor continent may be frontier-conscious, but it is not crucified by frontiers as Europe is. There

---

[1] This is what Latin Americans call United States citizens as a rule. In Argentina we are sometimes known as "Unidenses."

are no criss-crosses of power politics and nationalist tension on anything remotely like the scale of Europe or Asia. Tacna-Arica was a very mild kind of Alsace-Lorraine, and so was the Leticia area. Even though Peru and Ecuador are having a frontier dispute—the only serious one remaining on the continent—it is not likely to disrupt the hemisphere. And nationalist rivalries in Latin America are diminishing, not increasing. The reasons for this fortunate lack of *vital* intra-continental quarreling are several. One, the prevailing common language. Two, the polarizing power of the United States.

The fact that Latin America is not a single political unit but is on the contrary an exceedingly complex and intricate miscellany of twenty countries provides grave difficulties to United States policy. It is by no means easy to devise means and methods for dealing with twenty independent states on a common issue.

Another word—the fact that there are twenty different countries obviously serves to make broad generalizations about "Latin America," any sweeping statements about the continent as a whole, very dubious and risky, to say the least.

A Race with Race

Another main preliminary point I would make has to do with a delicate topic, that of race. I do not wish to offend any Latin American sensibilities—which are acutely developed—but it is impossible to write honestly about the hemisphere without touching on this ticklish question.

One of my Brazilian friends mentioned casually something very relevant. He said: "The great difference between North and South America is that you North Americans brought your wives with you."

What he meant, of course, is that the Pilgrim Fathers who migrated to New England were in large part frontiersmen and settlers, and many of them did bring wives. They came to America to stay, to raise families, to push westward, to create a new civilization based on their democratic instincts and puritan values. They had said good-by to Europe forever. They were cutting loose from the Europe that no longer gave them the physical or spiritual sustenance they needed. They came to America to build a *new* world—literally.

By contrast the majority of Spaniards and Portuguese—not all, but the majority—who journeyed to Latin America were soldiers, freebooters, adventurers, *conquistadores*. They came not to settle a continent but to loot it. They came not to get away from Europe but to return to Europe wealthy. They came to found colonies to attach to the old world, not to establish a new world. And in almost all countries they did interbreed with the aboriginal Indian population, with results that are conspicuous today.

Also the Spanish *conquistadores* imported negro slaves from Africa, who poured in by the hundred thousand. Along the coastal areas they mixed with whites and Indians. Meantime many Indians were killed off; in some countries they were virtually all killed off. The negroes were substitutes for these corpses, and were forced to do the hard work that the surviving enfeebled Indians could not do. We, in North America, also killed off Indians; we also imported negro slaves. But for a variety of reasons, mostly geographical, there was very little intermarriage in North America between Indian and negro. Nor did our whites mix with negroes as freely as did the Spaniards and Portuguese.

So in Latin America today we have a racial mélange of considerable complexity—exactly as we have in the United States, though ours is of a different kind. Everyone knows this. But the social and political implications are not so well known. It is something that many people are sensitive about. Statistics tell part of the story. There are about 120,000,000 people in the twenty countries of Latin America. Of these not more than about 25,000,000 are pure white, and most of these "whites" are clustered in two or three countries. There are about 15,000,000 pure negroes, mostly in the Caribbean area, and about 17,000,000 surviving pure

Indians, mostly in Mexico and the Andean highlands. All the rest are *mestizos* (of mixed blood)—some 63,000,000 people.[2]

In chemistry we learned that a mixture was an unstable compound. A key to much that happens in Latin America is the psychological instability that derives from a complex racial heritage.

By and large those countries which are purest white—Costa Rica, Chile, Argentina, Uruguay—are those which are the healthiest politically, and which are nearest to democracy. Argentina and Uruguay never had a negro problem, and they exterminated most of their Indians quickly—as the United States did.

It would be misleading to assert that race is a dominant issue in Latin America. I am merely stating that it is an important issue. It would be absurd to say that problems of race alone have contributed to the underdevelopment of some Latin American states. A good many other factors must be taken into consideration. One is climate. It is not easy to build a healthy state when the temperature is 85 and the humidity 90 the year around. Another is altitude. One cannot expect advanced political development from people who live perpetually at 12,500 feet, as in the sterile highlands of Peru or Bolivia. Another is religion. The Roman Catholic Church has played a great role in Latin American history, as we shall see. Another is economics. And so on.[3]

Historical Interlude

As everyone knows, Columbus discovered the World of the West—he thought it was the East of course—in 1492. Following him came a turbulent onrush of *conquistadores* who staked out vast empires as their own. Cortés subjugated Mexico in 1521 and Pizarro demolished the Incas in Peru in 1533. Pope Alexander VI was prevailed upon to divide the New World between Spain and Portugal, and the new continent emptied its golden lap into the hands of the greedy captains. The speed and biting comprehen-

---

[2] Figures from Carleton Beals, *America South*, p. 53.
[3] For further generalizations about *South* America, see Chapter XI below.

siveness of the Spanish conquests were bewildering. Fifty years after Columbus such stalwarts as Pedro de Alvarado and Pedro de Valdivia, with tiny handfuls of troops, had established the rule of Spain from Guatemala to Chile, over at least 8,000,000 unmapped square miles. They built cities, universities, monasteries; they looted, despoiled, prayed, governed. By 1600 about 200,000 Spaniards had come to Latin America. Not more. The number of Indians whom they conquered lies between 25,000,000 and 30,000,000.[4] It was the greatest *blitz* in history.

The three hundred years between 1521, roughly, and 1821 comprise what is called the Colonial Period. At the beginning the prodigious Spanish domains were divided into two Viceroyalties, that of New Spain (centering on Mexico) and that of Peru. The rule of Spain was dogmatic and absolute. Later each Viceroyalty split. That of New Granada, founded in 1718, took what is now Colombia, Venezuela, and Ecuador from the Viceroyalty of New Spain, which continued to include Mexico and Central America; and the Viceroyalty of La Plata (1776) took what is now Argentina and its contiguous territory from Peru. The Viceroys came out from Spain, and were supreme rulers responsible only to the Spanish crown, which usually gave them a free hand. The Viceroyalties were divided into districts called captaincies general— like Chile, Cuba, and so on—which are more or less the basis of national frontiers today.

During its three colonial centuries Latin America (except Brazil) was little more than a feudal appendage to feudal Spain. This is the overwhelming main point to make. The Spanish ruling class sucked power, wealth, prestige, out of the enfeebled colonies without hindrance or pause. The Spanish were divided into two classes: the *gachupines* (literally "men with spurs"), who were Spaniards born in Spain, and who came to Latin America tempo-

---

[4] Duncan Aikman's *All-American Front* describes brilliantly how the Spaniards in South America outpaced the British and other settlers in the United States.

rarily as officials, administrators, army officers, and so on; and the *creoles*, who were pure-blooded Spaniards born in Latin America. The *creoles*—landowners, merchants, intellectuals—were considered to be sharply inferior to the ruling *gachupines*. Presently a vast *mestizo* class grew up, as more and more Spaniards moved into the colonies and bred with Indians. The Indians themselves—those who were not slaughtered—were mostly peons working on the land, living practically like animals. The contrast to the democratic-minded North American colonies during the same period is very striking.

The weight of this colonial heritage presses Latin America heavily to this day. As for instance:

The Spanish rulers permitted no development of free speech or liberal institutions. From this derives much contemporary backwardness.

The Spanish ruling class starved education and neglected public health. Result: the illiteracy and lack of physical development of much of Latin America.

Spain did not permit any colony to trade with any other; all trade was exclusively the privilege of the mother country. As a result, intra-Latin American trade never developed strongly, and even today is rudimentary. Think—to push home the point—how different United States history would have been if Virginia had been forbidden to trade with Massachusetts, or New York with Pennsylvania.

Boundaries between the captaincies-general were often ill-defined, which has been the source of much contemporary political friction.

Most of the land was held by individual landowners in colossal feudal tracts. The small farmer never got a chance. Nor did the small businessman. No middle class grew up.

Then—in the early 1800's—came explosive change. The colonial system collapsed; revolutions blazed like torches all over Latin America, and were passed, as it were, by hand from one country to the next. Spanish power cracked up, partly because of the fermentation caused by the French and North American revolutions, partly because Napoleon's invasion of Spain weakened the mother country, partly because of the intolerable decadence of the local *gachupínes*. Most of the great Latin American revolutionaries were *creoles*. A series of brilliant chieftains—Sucre, San Martín, O'Higgins, and especially Bolívar—set South America free. The continent woke up, dizzy, shaken—and began to walk. Bolívar himself liberated five nations. Except Cuba and Panama, every hemisphere state was independent by 1825.

So the present period of republicanism, national independence and close relations with the United States began.

"Nothing Lasts But the Church"

Latin America was, it happened, colonized by two countries, Spain and Portugal, that never experienced the Reformation. Thus Catholicism in peculiarly undiluted form dominated it from the earliest days, and remains today a profound and tenacious influence.

The early *conquistadores* fought in the name of the cross, and baptized Indians by the tens of thousands. In every new settlement the clergy took a large share of the best land, and achieved an important vested interest in the community, socially, politically, economically. The great archbishops admitted allegiance only to the King of Spain. They ruled like princes. The clergy were their troops, and the Inquisition their Gestapo. The Church had no competition, since no other religion but Catholicism was permitted. It grew fabulously rich and fabulously decadent. In several countries the Church owned as much as *one-half* the total land; Paraguay, for instance, became practically a Jesuit colony. Nowhere did the clergy, secular or regular, bestow upon the people anything like proper recompense for their inordinate position, though an effort was made in education.

In almost every Latin American country clericalism became

a serious political problem as soon as independence was won. This was natural, since the Church—rightly or wrongly—was identified with the old order, and most of the revolutionaries, though they were often good Catholics, were anticlerical. So in most countries two political parties grew up, separated by the church issue. The conservatives stood by the Church, and the liberals were anticlerical. This cleavage has dominated political development in Latin America to this day.

"When anticlericalism takes on an antireligious color," wrote an anonymous contributor to *The Republics of South America*, published by the Oxford University Press, "the moral position of the Church is generally strengthened. Most South American statesmen who wish to suppress the Church underestimate their task, because they do not distinguish between clericalism and religion, or realize that to crush the one is to revive the other."

In Latin America today most countries, after a century of struggle, have disestablished the Church and separated Church and State. In several, however, Catholicism remains the official and exclusive religion of the nation, as in Brazil. Even if the Church is disestablished, it remains enormously important, if only through the economic power it wields by ownership of ecclesiastical properties, and in its control of education, which it guards zealously. Church influence extends to other fields also. For instance, even in Argentina divorce is still forbidden.

Not all members of the Latin American clergy are reactionaries, by any means; many are wise and liberal-minded men. But some high churchmen have sympathized with subversive forces, to put it mildly. The Archbishop of Durango, in Mexico, gave public benediction to the Cristeros, who were waging bloody civil war in 1927. Some of the upper clergy have definite Fascist sympathies, especially with that brand of Fascism identified with the Spanish Falange. The Archbishop of Porto Alegre, Brazil, once offered prayers to save "intrepid Italy" from humiliation, and to protect

"Fascist Rome."[5] Country by country we shall survey the relation of the church—and clericalism—to local politics.

Some Elements in Economics

Another general point to make in this preliminary survey has to do with economics. Most of the Latin American states live, as everyone knows, by the export of raw materials. Most of them, moreover, are basically one-crop or one-product countries.

> Ecuador lives mostly on cocoa.
> Brazil lives mostly on coffee.
> Bolivia lives mostly on tin.
> Venezuela lives mostly on oil.
> Honduras lives mostly on bananas.
> Cuba lives mostly on sugar.
> Chile lives mostly on copper and nitrates.
> Haiti lives mostly on coffee.
> Uruguay and Argentina live mostly on beef.

And so on.

Traditionally South American trade—though not Caribbean trade—has been geared intimately with Europe. This was natural, since Europe needed South American raw materials and paid for them with the manufactured goods that the hemisphere had to have. Also the United States competed drastically with most of Latin America; we produced the same kind of commodities—beef, cotton, wheat, and so on—that it did. So Europe bought what we would not buy. In 1938 Europe took 93 per cent of Latin America's meat, 86 per cent of its corn, 73 per cent of its wool, 74 per cent of its cotton, 66 per cent of its hides and skins.[6] Total Latin American exports in that year, the last for which full figures are available, were $1,834,000,000. Of these, Europe took 54.4 per cent. Total Latin American imports were $1,488,000,000. Of these, Europe provided 43.6 per cent.

But the impact of these figures may be misleading. Europe

[5] Text in *Latin America*, by Samuel Guy Inman, p. 296.
[6] Figures from an admirable pamphlet, *Look at Latin America*, by Joan Raushenbush, published by the Foreign Policy Association.

as a whole is Latin America's biggest customer, yes, but the United States—even if many of our exports compete—is of great importance nevertheless, and it is growing steadily. We sell more to Latin America than we buy, however, which is the core of the problem.[7] Latin America has a favorable balance of trade *vis-à-vis* Europe, but an unfavorable balance *vis-à-vis* the United States. In 1938 we took 30.5 per cent of total Latin American exports and provided 34.0 per cent of total Latin American imports. Our trade is heaviest in the Caribbean area and with Brazil. We are by far the largest buyers of Cuban and West Indian sugar, Brazilian coffee, and other tropical produce like bananas and cocoa which we do not produce ourselves.

The effect of the war on Latin American economy has been disastrous. We all know that Europe is blockaded by the war. But we do not realize that the obverse is also true, that Latin America is necessarily blockaded too, since Europe is. The British Fleet on the one hand, German raiders and submarines on the other, are a double barrier. When Europe cannot import goods, Latin America cannot export them. So Latin America has lost much of its biggest market. The Central European countries are cut off. France and Scandinavia and the Balkans are lost. Trade with Germany has virtually ceased. And the British are buying less than formerly, partly because of the acute shortage of shipping, partly out of necessity to conserve gold and sterling.

It is difficult in the extreme to procure accurate, up-to-the-minute statistics on the amount of loss. But it is said that the Dominican Republic has lost actually 60 per cent of its export trade, which was largely sugar to Great Britain; Haiti has lost about as much. Argentina's great beef-exporting industry has been damaged, and Argentine surpluses of wheat and corn are piling up. Brazil has suffered drastically. We have seen that in 1938 Europe took 54.4 per cent of total Latin American exports. It is reasonable to assume that at least two-thirds—probably more

[7] In the first months of 1941 this equation was reversed as a result of greatly increased purchases by the United States.

—of this trade with Europe has been lost. This rate of loss is serious enough. As the war goes on, as the blockade continues, it may become even more severe.

Political unrest is likely to follow economic hardship, as we well know. Political explosion is apt to follow economic disintegration, not merely among our southern neighbors but anywhere. If only for this reason, the struggle for economic survival in Latin America is of profound importance to the United States.

American exports to the Latin American countries have risen enormously since the war, inasmuch as Europe is cut off as a source of supply. As between September 1938, and December 1939, our exports rose 48.4 per cent. As between September 1939, and February 1940, they rose 53.8 per cent. Imports have risen also, though not quite so steeply. The percentage of rise between September 1939 and February 1940 is 32 per cent. This indicates that we are taking up some of the burden caused to Latin America by war and blockade. But there is much more that we must do, as this book will endeavor to explain.

A further word on German trade. I have said that it has ceased. For all practical purposes this is correct. But if Germany should win the war, German trade might quickly become dominant. Latin America would be a perfect reservoir for everything that a German Europe would need—petroleum, tobacco, coffee, wheat, beef, tin. And the Germans know well how to deal with this kind of reservoir.

Pre-war Germany, using the barter technique, built up an astonishing Latin American trade very rapidly. In 1938 Germany took 10.5 per cent of all Latin America's exports (for purposes of comparison, Great Britain took 16.8 per cent) and supplied 17.1 per cent of all imports (as against 11.1 per cent for Great Britain). Germany squeezed ahead of the United States as an exporter to both Chile and Brazil; its exports to Argentina doubled between 1930 and 1938, and its trade with Guatemala— to name one more state—increased 265 per cent in five years.

Fifth Columnism by Germany in Latin America fed heavily on the trade advance. The present collapse of German trade—perhaps only temporary—has seriously impeded subversive activity, which was often financed by local German firms.

Importance to the United States

Latin America counts heavily these days. It is of such vital importance to North America for a variety of reasons. First, our mounting trade, which in 1939 was worth $1,087,162,000. As a general rule United States imports from Latin America comprise roughly 22 per cent of our imports, a percentage not lightly to be disregarded. In 1939 our exports to Latin America were 17.9 per cent of our total export trade. Figures for 1941 will be much higher.

Second, direct American investments in Latin America—in such categories as mines, utilities, packing plants, petroleum, and the like—amount roughly to $2,840,000,000, which is about 40 per cent of all American investments abroad. Aside from direct investments, our loans are $1,610,331,794. These are hangovers from the lush days of the 1920's, and 77.2 per cent of them are wholly or partially in default. But, in theory at least, our total stake in Latin America is almost four and a half billion dollars.

Third, raw materials. Here the importance of the American Republics is profound. We cannot chew gum without Latin America—because Mexico and Guatemala provide the necessary chicle. We cannot play gramophone records without Latin America—because Brazil produces the necessary carnauba wax. If hemisphere trade were completely shut off, we would have no coffee for breakfast, very little cocoa, very few bananas. We might face serious shortages of bauxite, tungsten, manganese ore, and tin.

The United States army issued recently a list of fourteen "strategic materials" which are indispensable to the conduct of warfare and which we do not produce ourselves. We badly need—and will continue to need—stocks of these materials. They are:

Antimony	Nickel
Chromium	Quartz crystal
Coconut shell char (for gas masks)	Quinine
Ferrograde manganese	Rubber
Manila fiber	Silk
Mercury	Tin
Mica	Tungsten

The United States totally lacks these fourteen substances, but Latin America has surpluses of several and with proper development could produce them all, except silk. Our neighbors can furnish us with antimony (Mexico and Peru), manganese (Brazil and Cuba), mercury (Mexico), quartz crystal (Brazil), chromium (Cuba), mica (Peru and Chile), and tin and tungsten (Bolivia). Coconut shell char could certainly be produced in Latin America if we need it, and manila fiber is now being made experimentally in Costa Rica. Brazil was once the world's greatest producer of rubber, and an attempt is being made now to revive its rubber industry. Quinine can be grown in Ecuador.[8]

Should the war spread to the Far East and cut off the United States from its normal sources of rubber, quinine, hemp, and tin, we can only pray that Latin America will be a substitute. Nor should one forget that the southern continent is today a very important producer of copper, petroleum, wool, and foodstuffs, which are not included on our list of strategic shortages, but which might be highly useful in time of war. Or which might be very awkward in the hands of someone else.

Finally, political considerations. Latin America is, as I have said, our exposed southern frontier. But before discussing the strategy of hemisphere defense let us inspect one of the factors which make defense necessary—the German Fifth Column.

[8] See *Foreign Policy Reports* for August 1, 1939, and August 1, 1940, by Howard J. Trueblood.

Chapter II
Fifth Column and Hemisphere Defense

~~~~~~

B<span></span>Y FIFTH COLUMNISM I mean, of course, propaganda, espionage, and subversive activity by Germans. In some cases the
Germans are assisted by Japanese, and sometimes by Italians,
though the Italians are not active as a rule. Most Italians in Latin
America assimilate very quickly, as they do in the United States;
in a generation they become good Argentinean or Brazilian or
Peruvian nationals with small concern for the mother country.
I found, in fact, that many Italians—particularly in the Argentine—were definitely anti-Fascist.

But the Germans are quite a different matter. And there are a
great number of Germans in Latin America. They may have
become naturalized, but by German law they have double nationality, and are considered full citizens of the Reich no matter
how long they have lived away. In addition to Germans actually
born in Germany and now living in Latin America there are
many thousand sons or grandsons of German immigrants. Most
of the second-generation Germans are as German as their fathers,
and they may have deeper sympathies for Germany than for the
countries of which they are theoretically citizens.

Following are the approximate number of first- and second-
generation Germans in the South American states:

Peru	3,000	Paraguay	18,000
Ecuador	2,100	Bolivia	8,000
Colombia	3,000	Chile	85,000
Venezuela	4,000	Argentina	250,000
Uruguay	10,000	Brazil	830,000

If you count in folk of more remote German ancestry, the
figures mount greatly; for instance, at least two million people in
Brazil have *some* German blood. The Germans live as a rule in
closely packed enclaves (like the Valdivia district in Chile or

Santa Catharina in Brazil) ; they go to German schools and speak German from childhood; most are to all intents and purposes as German as people living in Leipzig or Köln. Their geographical concentration in various countries increases their potential power.

The German communities are efficiently organized everywhere, usually under the leadership of the local Reich embassy or consulate. Leading German business men—who are strongly entrenched in Latin America—may be prominent in the organization, either overtly or in secret. The community functions on Nazi party lines exactly as in Germany. There is a German school, with swastika boldly flying; then comes the Hitler Jugend, to which the youngsters are obliged to belong; then come Storm Troop units, which may be armed. In several countries the Germans for a long time used the Hitler salute and wore Nazi insignia and brown shirts. Nowadays such open stigmata are forbidden almost everywhere—following the revelation of Fifth Column methods in Europe during the war.

The German agitators function in several ways. First, they attempt to purchase local newspapers; in almost every Latin American capital there is at least one German-subsidized sheet. Also they distribute their official news service, *Transocean,* to all newspapers that will take it. Again, they distribute doctrine in the form of leaflets, news bulletins, and the like. In one small country, Paraguay—where hardly 50,000 people can read and write— German agents distributed 2,936 kilograms of printed matter in 1939—almost three tons! Again, the Germans may operate secret radio stations.

Second, the Fifth Column works by close contact with local, *native* political parties of Fascist complexion. Almost every Latin American country has a rudimentary Nazi or Fascist opposition party which is financed or controlled by the Germans. In several countries, notably Chile, these domestic Fascists have made serious trouble. In some cases—until the German invasion of Russia turned everything upside down—the Nazis played closely with the communists. Anything that kept the local political pot boiling was useful to their purpose.

Third, the Germans attempt to influence officials and especially army officers of the government in power. This may be done in various ways, by suave official hospitality or by covert bribery. Plenty of Latin American politicians—who, after all, resemble politicians on other continents—may be approached in this way. The Germans have plenty of money. They know how to use it— very nicely.

Fourth, German couriers move incessantly from country to country, binding the organizations together. Latin America is, moreover, their only easy route of entry to the United States, and German agents, documents, and cash reach objectives in North America by the Dakar-Natal-Rio-Lima-Panama route.

No one should think that the Latin Americans are not aware of the Fifth Column problem. They know its manifest danger. They are good patriots; they don't like subversive activity by anyone. They are highly nationalist themselves, and they don't want to become German slaves. Several countries, like Cuba and Brazil, have taken more stringent steps against Fifth Columnism than has the United States. Cuba forbids all propaganda hostile to democratic ideals; Brazil has closed all the German schools. But the Nazi organizations continue to maintain secret activity almost everywhere.

Sensible Latin Americans realize that they can never be better than inferiors in a German-dominated world, no matter what the Nazis may promise them. This is because of Race. They are mostly of mixed blood, and they have not forgotten Hitler's Aryan principles.

The German Airways

Very important is the network of German or German-dominated airlines in Latin America; these are the throbbing arteries of the Fifth Column. They are of profound political interest in that German pilots have been trained for years over South American terrain and know every inch of strategic territory. Big German transport planes are today operating within a few hundred miles of the Panama Canal, and if war should come between the United States and Germany this could be an unpleasant point—to put it mildly.

An Italian line, L.A.T.I., is the only direct link between the Axis and the Americas. It maintains an efficient service between Berlin, Rome, Dakar, and Natal, on the bulge of Brazil; it brings the Axis capitals within three days of Rio de Janeiro and four of Buenos Aires. It discharges cargoes of diplomats and printed matter; it flies back with spies, platinum, and diamonds.

German commercial aviation has recently been squeezed out of Peru and Bolivia and has been hampered elsewhere by a shortage of pilots, planes, and spare parts. But the Germans do everything they can to maintain their services. When, rarely a Nazi merchantman slips through the blockade and reaches some Brazilian or other Latin American port, it almost invariably brings new planes, motors, and other replacement material, for the local airlines. The Germans have had a hard fight in several countries to keep up a sure gasoline supply. Even so, in the summer of 1941 their lines were serving five out of the ten South American republics, and covered not less than 21,762 route miles. Last year they flew a total of 3,700,000 miles.

The main German or German-subsidized airlines are Sindicato Condor and its affiliated companies in Brazil. Condor, which flies 10,000 miles, is theoretically Brazilian—indeed it receives subsidies from the Brazilian government and is very powerful in the country—but it is controlled by Deutsche Lufthansa. Its big fleet of Junker planes are German; so are most of its pilots, even though they may have adopted Brazilian nationality. Condor operates an intricate network all over Brazil, and is linked to the Aeroposta Argentina which flies all the way to the Straits of Magellan. Westward Condor connected with Lloyd Aereo Boliviano—recently taken over by the Bolivian government—and with Lufthansa Peru, which was an outright German company. In

Ecuador the Germans control Sedta, which is important because of its proximity to the canal. For a complete account of the way the German airlines work, see "Wings for the Trojan Horse," by Melvin Hall and Walker Peck, in the January 1941 *Foreign Affairs*.

As to United States commercial aviation, Pan American Airways and its affiliated companies—like Panair do Brasil and the Avianca Company in Colombia—cover 40,578 miles in all Latin America, but only about 30,000 miles in South America itself where the Axis airways fly. In May 1941, Pan American-Grace Airways (the west-coast affiliate of Pan American) got permission from the Civil Aeronautics Board to initiate a service across South America from Peru to Brazil, which was the chief link—a link the Germans had—missing in the great Pan-American chain. Recently President Roosevelt assigned $8,000,000 to development of United States aviation in Latin America.

Sources of Temptation

Time and again I asked friends in Latin America *why* their compatriots were tempted by Naziism or Fascism, *why* they were sympathetic to totalitarian ideals. The question never failed to provoke agitated conversation. I got several answers.

First, in many countries the people became desperately fatigued by the inefficiency of "democracy" (Latin-American model), its ineptitude in practice, its corruption by military adventurers. They saw graft, bribery, red tape, nepotism—and blamed "democracy." Their lives were made miserable by incessant changes in government. In one year Chile had five Presidents. Ecuador has had twelve different administrations in ten years.

Second, in some countries—Mexico, for instance—many people were influenced toward pro-Germanism by atavistic dislike of the United States and resentment against England. In Brazil, strong anti-British feeling has existed since the blockade, by which the country was cut off from munitions it had bought from Germany.

Third, economic factors. German traders built up a powerful

position in most Latin American business communities. They came mostly as small merchants, setting out in business for themselves, not as agents for distant corporations as did so many American business men. The Germans came to stay; they learned the language; they married Latin Americans and adopted local customs; they were friendly, substantial, and incredibly efficient.

Fourth, feudalism. The landed oligarchs, often supported by church and army, are naturally conservative, and still believe that Fascism will protect their property and other interests.

Fifth, many Latin Americans feel that Germany may win the war; they want to be on good terms with the victor, and to play the winning side. They know they are virtually defenseless, and they are not sure how effectively the United States can help them. Therefore they hesitate to affront Germany, the colossus that might gobble them. This sentiment is particularly strong in army circles, though it diminished after the United States passed the Lease-Lend Bill.

Sixth, matters of psychology and temperament. Traditionally Latin Americans like the Strong Man, and for most of a century the continent was governed largely by despotism and violence. Many Latin Americans dislike this phase of their history; they are ashamed of it. Then Hitler came along and gave a kind of moral ideology to despotism and violence. He erected a system out of it—and Latin Americans love systems. As a result many of them are tempted to see Fascism as a kind of justification of their own historical past. They feel that Hitler gives them excuse for their own history and contemporary inclinations.

Falange Influence

In several countries the Spanish Falange organization has become a leading Fifth Column agency, particularly in the Caribbean area. The reasons are obvious: most Latin Americans speak Spanish; they have close cultural and emotional associations with Spain; the Roman Catholic Church is powerful as it is in Spain. After Franco's victory the influence of the Falange spread rapidly in the Americas, and the Germans—especially in those countries where they faced difficulties—naturally enough came to use the Falange as their "front."

The Falange operates throughout Latin America much as do the Nazis, through propaganda organizations in almost every country which are responsible to a central agency—in Spain— known as the "Falange Exterior." Steadily these organizations pursue an anti-North American policy, and in the autumn of 1940 an "Hispanidad Council" was created in Madrid with Ramón Serrano Suñer, Franco's brother-in-law and Foreign Minister, as head. It was frankly stated that this Council hoped to re-establish Spain's former influence over Latin America, and even that it was "a continuation of the Council of the Indies, which governed the one-time Empire" (New York *Times*, Nov. 8, 1940). The Council was given "jurisdiction over relations with Latin America and the Philippines, and . . . it was expected to co-ordinate its work with that of the external division of the Falange."

The Falange itself admits its hopes of a restoration of the Spanish colonial system, but cautiously cloaks its program in words emphasizing "cultural" and "spiritual" rather than direct political aims. One article of the official Falange program is the following: "We have the will to Empire. We affirm that the historic fulfillment of Spain's mission lies in Empire . . . In respect to the countries of South America our aim is for a uniformity of culture, of economic interests, and of power. Spain affirms her position as the spiritual axis of the Hispanic world."

In May 1941, a Spanish monarchist named the Marqués de Aguilar registered with the State Department as an agent for Catholic and Royalist groups. He said (New York *Times*, May 20, 1941) that Hitler and Franco signed a secret pact in October 1938 giving the Nazis power to direct Spanish and Falangist policies abroad. Eight thousand Falangistas have been sent to Latin America, according to the Marqués, to do propaganda for the Axis and to combat Pan-Americanism. The Falange, he said, is represented in every Spanish embassy and consulate.

Spanish newspapers, indeed, are indignant any time that Latin American military or naval officers visit the United States on official missions; they continually emphasize that Latin Americans are the brothers of Spain "by the grace of God"; they say that Latin America must "choose" between the United States and Mother Spain; they discourage the term "Latin American" and use "Spanish-American" instead; they woo the hemisphere with every "spiritual" means at their command.

But, looking at it from the other point of view, let us remember that a great many Latin Americans do not take their Hispanism too seriously. They came from Spain—yes. And there are several million Spanish *citizens* in Latin America. But, particularly among the youth and in the middle class, the Spanish heritage is not overly popular. The historical, cultural, and political influence of Spain on the continent is still conspicuous—this must be acknowledged freely—but on the whole it is probably diminishing, not increasing. The Falange by itself is not dangerously important. It counts mostly as a weapon of the Germans.

Evolution of Hemisphere Policy

Now let us retrace steps a little. The long-time basis of American policy toward Latin America is that comfortable dog-eared doctrine, the Monroe Doctrine, which was enunciated by President James Monroe in 1823, and which says that "the American continents . . . are henceforth not to be considered as subjects for future colonization by any European powers. . . . We owe it to candor . . . to declare that we should consider any attempt on their part to extend their system to any portion of this hemisphere as dangerous to our peace and safety."

The Monroe Doctrine was, indirectly at least, suggested to the United States by the British Foreign Minister, George Canning. The British were playing balance-of-power politics against the Holy Alliance; they were frightened that the French and Spanish might attempt to make trouble in Hispano-America, which had just achieved independence after the wars of liberation. Incidentally, another great cornerstone in American foreign policy, the Open Door, also came about partly through British influence. And John Hay, the Secretary of State who made the Open Door, was also one of the fathers of Pan-Americanism.

The Monroe Doctrine, originally and essentially, was based on American (and British) fear of the Holy Alliance in Europe. In striking similarity, the present concept of Pan-American solidarity is based on fear of the Rome-Berlin Axis—all over the world.

The Monroe Doctrine was a unilateral expression of policy by the United States; this has caused much headache and heartache. The Latin American republics were not consulted, and many of them have resented the Doctrine bitterly, in that it seemed to give us privileges at their expense. For years Latin American nationalists called it a cloak for North American imperialism, and so on. Mentioning it in polite society in Buenos Aires was like praising Bolshevism to the Pope; Argentina, in fact, still does not recognize officially that it exists. Yet, had it not been for the Doctrine and the power of the United States behind it, more than one hemisphere country might have lost its independence by this time.

Of course, we interpreted the Doctrine as the exigencies of the moment demanded. We did not protest when Great Britain took the Falkland Islands from Argentina in 1833 or Belize (British Honduras) from Central America a little later. Nor did we assist Chile and Peru when they fought a bitterly contested—and luckily victorious—war against Spain in 1866. We did, however, invoke the Doctrine when the French installed Maximilian as Emperor of Mexico, and—interestingly enough—against Great Britain in 1895 over a boundary dispute in Venezuela. The last time the Doctrine was formally enunciated was July 1940, when Secretary of State Hull warned the Axis powers that we would not tolerate any change in the status quo in the Caribbean.

But nowadays the Monroe Doctrine, as such, is seldom talked about. It has been, as they say, "continentalized," and has developed for all practical purposes into a joint, multilateral conception of hemisphere defense, with all the Latin American states freely co-operating.

Imperialismo Yanqui

First a paragraph or two on a departed period. In the 1840's the United States took Texas and California from Mexico, and in 1898 we fought Spain and liberated Cuba. During the intervening time North America paid scant attention to South; we were facing problems of domestic consolidation and expansion, with little energy to look anywhere but westward. But the immense physical power of the United States began to express itself. Latin Americans came to look on us with trepidation as the "Colossus of the North," and prominent Americans began to talk of our "manifest destiny" in the hemisphere.[1] And just before the turn of the century we started to indulge in some pretty fancy manifestations of imperialism. As for instance:

In 1895 Secretary of State Richard Olney stated in regard to our intervention in the British-Venezuelan boundary dispute, "Today the United States is practically sovereign on this continent, and its fiat is law upon the subjects to which it confines its interposition."

In 1898 Cuba became virtually an American protectorate and in the same year we annexed Puerto Rico, where our commercial penetration soon grew profoundly. By terms of the Platt Amendment (now abrogated) we assumed the right to intervene in Cuba, and we still keep a naval base at Guantánamo.

In 1903 Theodore Roosevelt waved the Big Stick and "took" Panama from Colombia so that we could build a canal across the Isthmus. When Colombia refused to cede us the necessary land, the United States simply fomented a Panamanian revolution,

[1] This phrase was made popular by Senator Charles Sumner of Massachusetts, who, oddly enough, was a granduncle of Undersecretary of State Sumner Welles, the chief architect of the contemporary Good Neighbor policy which reverses "Manifest Destiny" ideas. See Charles Wertenbaker, *A New Doctrine for the Americas,* p. 79.

recognized the new government, and set to work. As Roosevelt said forthrightly, "I took the Canal Zone and . . . while the debate goes on, the Canal does also."

In the next year Roosevelt announced a "corollary" to the Monroe Doctrine claiming for the United States the right to "international police power" in the Western Hemisphere in the event of "flagrant cases of wrong doing" (by any of the American republics), or an "impotence which results in a general loosening of the ties of civilized society."

In the decade 1900-1910 United States marines intervened in both Nicaragua and Cuba. Concurrently came the beginnings of "dollar diplomacy" as banks poured money into Latin America and looked to the State Department to protect their debts.

Under Woodrow Wilson we developed the policy of nonrecognition of governments that took power by revolutionary means. This served to freeze the status quo in many countries, since no revolution could possibly hope for success without our favor. Particularly in Central America, we came to dominate domestic politics.

In 1914 the United States navy bombarded and seized Veracruz in Mexico, and in 1916 the United States army crossed the Mexican frontier to chase Pancho Villa, whom it never caught. (Villa, of course, thoroughly deserved chastisement.)

In 1915 we intervened in force in Haiti, in 1916 in the Dominican Republic, and in 1926 in Nicaragua. These countries remained American protectorates in everything but name until the Good Neighbor policy in the 1930's set them free, more or less.

Latin America has by no means forgotten this expansionist record, which indeed includes some highly unpleasant episodes. On the other hand one should inspect the record—which was short-lived anyway—with balance and realism. Take the Canal. Our method of acquiring it was not too pretty perhaps, but possession of the Canal is indisputably essential to the security and well-being of the United States, and if we did not have it, we would wish mightily that we had.

No one should throw bricks at T.R. unless he can conceive of an alternative method that would have gained us the Canal with less fuss and bother.

How and Why of Good Neighborliness

The Good Neighbor policy as a deliberate, systematic, and integrated attempt to improve North American relations with Latin America is the creation of the Franklin D. Roosevelt administration under the competent far-seeing leadership of Cordell Hull and Sumner Welles. There had, of course, been isolated attempts at good neighborliness before. The Pan-American ideal is as old as Bolívar, who summoned a conference of the Western Hemisphere republics in Panama in 1826. Pan-American conferences have been held since 1889, and the State Department dropped the Olney interpretation of the Monroe Doctrine years ago. It was President Coolidge who sent Dwight Morrow to Mexico, and it was Secretary of State Stimson who withdrew the marines from Nicaragua.

But by and large the Good Neighbor policy, as we understand it today, is identified—correctly—with Roosevelt II and the New Deal. Mr. Hull has been its pilot, and Mr. Welles its organizer. The Roosevelt administration gave the lead to good neighborliness not merely out of natural benevolence or delight in holding hands. We did not do it for the sake of any dewy Brazilian eyes or rippling Cuban shoulders. We were not seduced into it. We did it out of imperative considerations of practical politics. Our Latin American relations needed the most drastic overhauling. We could not ignore the continent and pretend it did not exist. Nor could we bully it or physically take it over. Only one alternative remained—to be friends.

Of course this should work both ways. As I heard it said in Bogotá, "If you lend your neighbor your garden hose, you don't want him to cut it up with his lawn mower." The neighbor republics have responsibilities too.

A few years ago Mr. Welles spoke as follows:

The policy of the "good neighbor" is not a one-way policy. It is inherently reciprocal in its nature. If this Government, in its dealing with its American neighbors . . . treats them with scrupulous respect for their sovereignty, for their rights and the rights of their nations, . . . it has the right to expect similar respect . . . and equivalent consideration.—*Foreign Policy Reports,* Aug. 15, 1937.

A pleasantly cynical definition of the Good Neighbor policy is included, as if coming from a German source, in *Total Defense* by Joan Raushenbush and Clark Foreman: "In the past seven years there has been a so-oddly called 'Good Neighbor' policy, which means that the North American statesmen now make long speeches to the Latins, telling themselves that all their own sins are in the past tense." And of course the United States *does* gain concrete and selfish advantages by being a Good Neighbor, though this is not to say that the policy is hypocritical.

The first official use of the phrase came in President Roosevelt's 1933 inaugural address, when he said, "In the field of world policy, I would dedicate this nation to the policy of the good neighbor—the neighbor who resolutely respects himself and, because he does so, respects the rights of others." Then the United States carefully refrained from military intervention in Cuba when Machado fell, and we repealed the Platt Amendment.

Also in 1933 came the Pan-American conference at Montevideo, which set a landmark. Not only did Mr. Hull, hat in hand, call gently on all the other delegations; he announced specifically that "no government need fear any intervention on the part of the United States under the Roosevelt administration." This amounted to a complete reversal of American policy. The hemisphere looked up with somewhat skeptical attention, to see if we would mean what we said. So far, we have.

Next came a special conference at Buenos Aires in 1936,

which President Roosevelt himself attended, and which in effect converted the Monroe Doctrine into a collective pact. By this time no United States soldiers or marines remained anywhere in Latin America, and we pledged ourselves never to use force or to intervene in collecting debts. The Buenos Aires conference was capped by one at Lima in 1938, where—despite some Argentine grumbling—a "Declaration of the Principles of the Solidarity of America" was accepted by all the 21 republics. Machinery for consultation was set up, and each state promised co-operation to resist aggression.

The Lima machinery has been put in motion twice, at a special meeting of Foreign Ministers at Panama in September-October, 1939, immediately after the outbreak of war in Europe, and at the Havana Conference of July 1940, which marked the furthest development yet seen of intra-American co-operation. Panama established a permanent neutrality committee that meets in Rio de Janeiro, and an Inter-American Financial and Economic Advisory Committee in Washington, which has founded a Pan-American bank. Also it created a 300-mile neutrality zone in hemisphere waters, a somewhat dubious experiment, and warned belligerents to keep out. Protests, academic in character, have several times been sent to both Great Britain and Germany for violation of the zone.

The Havana Conference that followed in 1940 had, as everyone knows, fairly spectacular results. The conference—again the Argentines did some grumbling—unanimously approved the Act of Havana, whereby the American republics reserve the right to take over European colonies in the hemisphere if they are threatened by a non-American power. An emergency committee was established to make speedy action possible; moreover, if this committee cannot act quickly enough, any American republic "shall have the right to act in the manner which its own defense or that of the continent requires." This of course was a green light to the United States in the event that the Axis expressed designs on

Martinique, the Dutch West Indies, the Guianas, or other foreign territory in the Americas.

In the summer of 1940 Uruguay had a Fifth-Column scare. Promptly the United States dispatched a cruiser, the *Quincy*, to Montevideo, and the American minister to Uruguay announced that it is "the avowed policy of my government to co-operate fully, whenever such co-operation is desired, with all the other American republics in crushing all activities that arise from non-American sources and that imperil our political and economic freedom." Words could hardly be stronger. The Uruguay putsch collapsed.

Thus the Monroe Doctrine has gradually been converted into a Hemisphere Doctrine. Thus have the Americas—under United States leadership—grown closer together than ever in their history.

What About Hemisphere Defense?

If the Germans win the war and turn their attention to the United States, it is almost certain that Latin America will be their avenue of attack. Besides, Germany and its Axis partners are highly interested in Latin America *per se*. Otherwise the immense amount of energy and cash the Germans have sunk into the continent make no sense. Hitler told Hermann Rauschning, "We shall create a new Germany in South America . . . Mexico is a country that cries for a capable master. With the treasures of Mexican soil, Germany could be rich and great . . . We shall create a new Germany there [Brazil]. We shall find everything we need."

The defense problem facing the United States is triple. First, the imperative necessity of protecting the Caribbean area and that overwhelmingly vital link between Atlantic and Pacific, the Panama Canal. I discuss this in Chapters X and XXVII.

Second, defense of the continent against actual German invasion, which presumably would first strike Brazil. It should never be forgotten that Dakar, held by Vichy France, is only some 1,600 miles from Natal in Brazil, whereas from New York to Natal is

3,600 miles. Here our best technique of defense would be to persuade Brazil to grant us naval and air-base facilities at Natal or Recife. No bridge is useful unless it is open at both ends. If we plug one end of the Dakar-Natal bridge across the South Atlantic, it becomes useless to an aggressor.

Latin Americans, like everyone else in the world, are understandably jealous of their sovereignty. They have a perfectly natural reluctance to see North American armed forces installed in their precious territory. Yet some compromise might be reached whereby we would have the use of Latin American bases, with absolute sovereignty retained by the country involved or pooled in a joint hemisphere trusteeship. This perplexing problem of bases will follow us throughout this book. It is the most important technical issue in the Americas.

Third, defense against a domestic Nazi putsch in a key Latin American state like Uruguay, say, or Colombia. Suppose a local Fascist party, supported of course by German Fifth-Columnists, seizes the local government, sets up a Nazi-dominated administration, and pursues a policy hostile to the United States and the rest of the hemisphere. This, the Quisling method, is the one the Germans would probably prefer to use. They need not invade; they hardly need raise the swastika flag; they could pretend that the Fifth Column government represents a purely domestic turnabout, and that it is no business of the United States to interfere. Native politicians—like Laval—would ostensibly control the new government, which would in reality be a German puppet regime. The new Prime Minister might protest blandly that he remained a good friend of the United States, while he was secretly taking orders from the local German *Gauleiter* or embassy.

Such a development could be seriously embarrassing to the United States, it goes without saying. It would not be easy to dispatch troops or marines to such a distant point as, say, Santiago de Chile, in time to be effective. Moreover, we have foresworn the use of force in Latin American affairs in the interests of the Good Neighbor policy. Our military hand is paralyzed. If we should,

in some extreme and flagrant circumstance, be compelled to intervene, the rest of the continent would probably willingly support
our action, inasmuch as it would be to defend the continent as a
whole against foreign penetration. But anti-Americans would
rock the hemisphere with atavistic cries of Yankee imperialism.
Besides, military action might be difficult in itself. It would not be
easy to blast an unfriendly government out of some South American capital, persuade another government to take its place, and
support it by armed force.

The solution to this difficulty lies, of course, in close vigilance
to our political relations with every Latin American state, and
the maintenance of intimately cordial bonds with them. The problem should be diplomatic and political, not military. Our best
defense against the dangers of internal dissension or revolution
is to push the Good Neighbor policy steadily forward. An ounce of
prevention is worth a ton of bombs. The United States should
make itself the indispensable friend of every hemisphere country;
we should demonstrate this so effectively that any unfriendly
political development is inconceivable.

Finally, the future of Latin America depends largely on the
outcome of the European war. If Germany should win the war
hands down, all Latin America except the Caribbean area might
be lost to the United States. We could directly defend those areas
within immediate range of the Panama Canal, but to defend the
rest would be a gamble. The temptation to Latin America to play
the German game—no matter what the United States does—
would be almost irresistible. More than one country is on the fence
at this moment (though they don't admit it) waiting to see
whether Britain or Germany wins. They may *want* Britain to win
—emotionally—but if Germany is a clear-cut victor they will be
tempted to take the winning side whether they like Germany or
not, out of regard to their own security. They could not afford to
do otherwise. Also all the Latin American states watch with the
closest attention the evolution of United States policy. They are

waiting to see what we do. If we declare war on Germany, most will probably follow us. But the first line of defense of Latin America remains the British fleet.

So much by way of preface and generalization. We begin now a parade through twenty countries. First—Mexico!

Chapter III
Avila Camacho Succeeds Cárdenas

～～～～～～～～～～～～～～～～～～～～～～～～

MEET General Manuel Avila Camacho, the solidly built, uncommunicative soldier who has been President of Mexico since December 1940. He is a key figure in the expanding orbit of hemisphere policy, and his character and attributes demand close understanding. General Avila Camacho does not remotely resemble his predecessor, the enigmatic and mystically inclined Cárdenas. Nor is he what the uninformed would call a very "typical" Mexican. His country is alive with every conceivable pattern of color, raw drama, and brilliant overtones. But Avila Camacho is about as colorful as a slab of halibut. He is steady, cautious, and efficient. The key to his character is sobriety.

I met a Mexican friend who welcomed his lack of color with considerable relief.

"We've had enough Napoleons and fake Napoleons in this country. What we need now is stability and a sense of responsibility and hard work."

Manuel Avila Camacho[1] was born on April 24, 1898, in Teziutlán, a town in the state of Puebla. Here the Avila and Camacho families had lived for generations. Teziutlán was one of the first points in Mexico settled by the Spaniards, and one of its churches, La Dolorosa, dates from the conquest. One of the Avila sisters lives in a Teziutlán house four centuries old and still habitable. The atmosphere where Avila Camacho grew up is definitely conservative and very Spanish.

His forebears came from Spain at least two centuries ago. But in time the purity of the stock diminished, as was inevitable, and

---

[1] Avila is his father's name, what we in North America would call his "last" name. Camacho, the mother's name, is put last as is the general habit in Latin America. Usually a Latin American personage is known best by his father's name, which is the one in the middle. But Avila Camacho prefers to use both names.

the family today is typically *mestizo*, though nearer Spanish than Indian. Avila Camacho's grandparents and parents were folk of education and substance, leaders of the community, members of the bourgeois class. His father was a landowner, not very rich, not very poor. His mother—who died recently—was a remarkably strong character. One legend is that she asked to be buried standing up.

Young Manuel went to the Teziutlán private school, then to the local Colegio Preparatorio. He studied engineering; his ambition was to be a civil engineer. But in 1911 came the upheaval of the great Mexican revolution. This date cuts across the history of Mexico like a painted steel curtain. It is the event from which everything in subsequent Mexican politics derives. Thirty years later, the giant fact of this revolution—which I shall describe briefly in the next chapter—still dominates almost every phase of Mexican political and economic life. By the events of 1911, the dictatorship of Porfirio Díaz came to an end; Mexico erupted into one of the most sinuous revolutions in history, the fermentations of which persist to this day.

Every contemporary Mexican politician, if he is over 40, took part in the revolution or one of the subrevolutions within the revolution that came after 1911. Political life was out of the question without a revolutionary record. Nothing else mattered to any degree. All that counted was what side you took during the revolution and what you did. In dealing with any Mexican political personality, the inevitable first point to mention, the first pivot to stake out, is his relation to the revolution. In these Mexican chapters I shall have to reiterate this, time and again. Manuel Avila Camacho was no exception to the general rule. He was only 13 when the revolution broke out, but he joined it two years later, in 1913, at the ripe old age of 15.

Now—a point to make at once—his record was never blazingly distinguished. He rose rank by rank. He was a careful plodding officer more interested in problems of organization than in *pis-*

tolero histrionics. He was not remotely of the type of Pancho Villa or Zapata. In fact, when he became politically prominent later, he was nicknamed the "Unknown Soldier," since so few people knew his record. Yet his rise was rapid. He became a brigadier general in 1924, when he was 26 years old, the commander of a cavalry regiment in 1930, and the commander of the 29th military zone (the Isthmus of Tehuantepec) in 1932. By 1935 he was an executive officer of the War Department and soon he became Assistant Secretary of War. Promotion to the Secretaryship of War came in 1938, and he found himself a full-fledged cabinet minister. A year later he resigned to run for the presidency of the republic. He was elected President in July 1940, and inaugurated in December. He is still only 43 years old.

Few legends or anecdotes survive of Avila Camacho's early fighting days. But early in 1924, when he was chief of staff to General Cárdenas (who was then governor of the state of Michoacán and whom he succeeded as President of Mexico sixteen years later), he was forced to surrender to superior forces. His ammunition was exhausted; he had no choice. The opposing general offered amnesty to all officers who would promise to lay down their arms and never fight again. Avila refused. He was told that he would be executed forthwith. "I'm ready," he said stolidly. The opposing general hesitated, called him a blockhead, and then freed him because he admired his courage.

In 1938, when Avila Camacho was Minister of War, a revolt flared up in Tabasco. The government general asked for reinforcements, since the rebel forces, numbering 1,800 men, were pressing hard. Avila Camacho ordered an airplane. He flew to the camp of the rebel commander, not to his own subordinate. He walked up to the rebel general's headquarters and said, in effect, "What are you after? What do you want?" They talked half a day. The rebel merely wanted more land for his peasants. Avila picked him up in his plane, and flew with him to the headquarters of the government general who had asked for the reinforcements. Avila introduced them calmly—and the revolt was over.

How Avila Camacho Became President

The Avila Camacho election campaign and the election itself are among the most bizarre events in recent Latin American history. But first a paragraph of background.

General Lázaro Cárdenas, who has been justly called the greatest Mexican since Juárez, was President from 1934 to 1940. The Mexican constitution, unlike most of those in Latin America, strictly forbids re-election of a President. In most hemisphere states a president may not succeed himself, but may run again after an intervening term. One term at a time is the rule. About Cárdenas I shall write much in subsequent chapters; suffice it now to state that this extraordinary Indian, with his almost supernatural powers of intuition and kinship with the common people, turned Mexico very powerfully to the Left during his six years in office. The Cárdenas government expropriated foreign oil; it allied itself with the great Mexican labor federation, the C.T.M.; it pushed hard on land reform, and distributed more land to peasants than any administration in Mexican history; it was, in short, a government seeking to fulfill the social promises of the revolution. Cárdenas did not finish the job by any means. But he made a prodigious six-year effort.

The scramble to succeed Cárdenas began in 1938. I will neglect the minor candidates, who dropped out early. A major candidate, who came to represent the forces of the Right, was General Juan Andreu Almazán, a wealthy landowner and politician-officer. Almazán, an out-and-out conservative, was a kind of Hoover to Cárdenas' Roosevelt; if Cárdenas was the New Deal, he was the Liberty League. He typified everything that Cárdenas stood against. Around him clustered the surviving *hacendados* (estate owners), the Rightist bureaucracy, the oil barons, the high clergy, the predatory generals. But the Almazanistas had genuine support among the people also, exactly as have Republican leaders among the people of the United States. Many honest folk were tired of Cárdenas. They complained of the high cost of living and they

were sick of his reforms. The Almazán movement, organized in
the spring of 1940, became known as the P.R.U.M.—Party for
the Unification of the Mexican Revolution. Note that even Almazán called himself a "revolutionary." Every Mexican politician
must.

Meantime the campaign of Avila Camacho as government
candidate was getting under way. Early in 1938, when he was Assistant Secretary of War, General Rodrigo M. Quevedo, one of
the toughest officers in the Mexican army, sounded him out for
the job. Avila refused on the ground that other officers were senior
to him, and he suggested that the army back his immediate superior, General Andrés Figueroa, the War Minister. Then Figueroa
died suddenly after a brain operation. Quevedo, eager to be
president-maker and convinced that Avila Camacho was the sound-
est, stablest man in Mexico, again approached him. Again he
cautiously refused. But a little later, having heard too often the
voice of temptation, he succumbed. He approached various provincial governors and other key men, and announced his candidacy.

There are 33 different political parties in Mexico, all tolerated
provided that they register with the government; but the only one
that normally matters is the official government party, because this
is the one that counts the votes. The official party, the P.R.M.
(*Partido Revolucionario Mexicano*) adopted Avila Camacho as
its candidate in December 1939. This would automatically have
insured his election had not the Almazán forces put up such a fight.
Avila Camacho had the whole support of the government organization and party leaders. Also behind him were the C.T.M. (*Confederación de Trabajadores de México*), the powerful labor federation, the C.N.C. (*Confederación Nacional de Campesinos*),
the analogous peasants' organization, and—at the beginning—the
communist party. Avila started out as definitely a Leftist candidate, with the backing and co-operation of the Cárdenas machine.

Then began a curious and tantalizing game of Mexican hide
and seek. Avila Camacho was the Cárdenas candidate—so it was

assumed. The two men had been associates for years, and had respected one another from the time Avila had been Cárdenas' aide in 1924. They had a curious modus vivendi; neither would ask the other any embarrassing questions. One story is that when Cárdenas' mother died, Avila condoled with him as follows: "I cannot give you sympathy, because sympathy is useless in such an irreparable loss. But I can give you my own mother, to be yours." From that time until Avila's mother died in 1939, Cárdenas accepted her as a kind of adopted mother, and called her "Mamita."

But during the campaign Cárdenas gave no assistance whatever to Avila Camacho. He denied that he had anything to do with his nomination; he never officially supported him, and never conceded that he was "his" man. Cárdenas took the point of view that his sole duty was to insure a fair and free election. He re fused to assist Avila Camacho (who after all was pledged to continuation of his own work) with troops on election day; he retired absolutely from the struggle, saying only that democracy in Mexico must come to maturity, that the people must vote freely, and that the vote must be respected. This quixotic behavior by Cárdenas perplexed and finally enraged the Camachistas. The two men met only twice during the whole campaign. As late as June 1940, a month before the elections, no one knew where Cárdenas stood. As one of the Camacho supporters said to me, "That Cárdenas is a very, very, *very* funny Indian."

Cárdenas apparently had curious relations with Almazán (another of his generals) too. Before the campaign, he asked Almazán, when he was commander at Monterrey, if he were going to be a candidate. Almazán said, "Give me a month to decide." Cárdenas said, "If you run, you're out as a general." Almazán asked if the President would make their conversation public. Cárdenas replied, "Everything I do is public." His motive was simple. He did not dislike Almazán but he did not want him to run as an *army* candidate. His idea was to make the campaign as free and democratic as possible, devoid of army influence. It was the first election in Mexican history in which the opposition was permitted to run freely.

Meantime the Avila Camacho forces carried out their plans with great skill. They relied basically on the support of the Left. But they maintained a discreet flirtation with the Right too. Avila sought to take the middle of the road, to get votes from both sides. As soon as it was safe to do so—that is, as soon as he could dispense with Left support—he shrewdly went farther Right, in order to buy off Almazán supporters who were threatening revolution. Thus he won Rightist sympathy. He declared that neither radical labor elements nor communists would have any share in his government, and he formally stated that he was a "believer," i.e. a good Catholic—something sensational for a Mexican *político* to do.

The election itself took place on July 7, 1940. It was a weird performance. By Mexican law the first five voters to arrive at each polling station are the judges who count the votes. This system was designed as a safeguard, to insure that the government in power would not "fix" the balloting. But it never worked out that way; everyone would scramble to the polls to get there first, and then steal the ballots or prevent anyone else from voting. On July 7 not only did this happen with resultant rioting and much bloodshed, but there were few police on hand to maintain order. This was because Cárdenas, an idealist of idealists, wanted to prove that he was not attempting to influence the voting in any way. So what happened was that Almazán gunmen grabbed the ballot boxes and stole them and the Camachistas countered with what means they had. Each side commandeered the "judges," stole votes wholesale, and retired to count them privately. As a result, each side claimed victory. No neutral count ever occurred. The Almazanistas and Camachistas each added up the ballots in their possession, padded the figures nicely, and issued the "results."

Disinterested neutral observers are on the whole inclined to think that Avila Camacho won. But they concede that Almazán probably carried Mexico City and the larger towns, and they do not think that Avila got anything like the thumping victory he claimed—2,476,641 votes to 151,101. Probably he won only by a very narrow margin, if at all.

The Almazán leaders threatened revolution at once. Almazán himself left Mexico suddenly on a trip first to Havana and then to the United States. Possibly he hoped to get recognition from the Department of State. He did not get it. But he formally claimed victory and stated flatly in various announcements that he would take over the presidency in December, if necessary by force of arms. His followers appointed a "Provisional President," General Héctor F. López, who lived more or less openly in Mexico City with that title, and they attempted to form a rump congress on Installation Day, September 1; their deputies boycotted the official congress meeting and held a secret session of their own. So for a time Mexico had two Presidents (to say nothing of Almazán himself) and two "legislative" bodies, at least on paper. But the farce began to run down. Cárdenas watched affairs with patience and good humor, and Avila Camacho kept the support of the army, the labor unions, and the political machine. No one paid the slightest attention to "President" López—not even enough to arrest him. In Monterrey what might have been a serious revolt was quickly crushed, and petty disturbances took place. But the Almazanistas had lost their moment. Presently the agitation began to dwindle, and finally it ceased.

Almazán might have made a successful revolution at least twice: first, immediately after election day; second, on September 1 when Camacho was "installed." But he failed to move each time. One story is that he hesitated to take real action because he is a very wealthy man and his properties near Monterrey might have been confiscated. What really doomed him was his trip to the United States. No Mexican revolution can be directed from the boardwalk at Atlantic City; Mexicans like their leaders to *lead* them in person and if possible on horseback. Again, no Mexican revolution has much chance of success unless the United States supports it or is at least benevolently neutral. The State Department accepted the official story that Avila Camacho was the winner, and that was that. The last thing the United States wanted was counter-revolution or civil war in Mexico. When it was announced that Vice-President Wallace would attend Avila Camacho's inauguration, Almazán's last chance was gone.

So the "Unknown Soldier"—the stolid general who never talked unless he had something to say—became President of its Republic.

Profile at Twilight

I met General Avila Camacho in October 1940, when he was President-elect. The setting was several times duplicated in meetings with other Mexican *políticos*. With a friend I went at dusk to a white-walled house and waited outside a heavy tawny-oak door. First came careful scrutiny through a peephole. Then in the patio I met members of the General's retinue—some of the toughest-looking bodyguards I ever saw outside the movies. They seemed straight out of *Viva Villa*. They smoked, smiled, chatted. With them was the President's personal physician and his handsome 15-year-old adopted son.

The sharp Mexican twilight deepened, and it got chilly. I saw no telephone in the guardhouse. But a signal came to one of the bodyguards and, even though we were not announced we walked across the lawn to the terrace where the General was waiting, alone. His room was open to the lawn. Most of the Mexicans I met received me thus, half out of doors. Informality is complete. You wait with the guard until you are called, then you walk straight in. No secretaries, no telephones, no anterooms. And always (except around Cárdenas) the group of lounging, smiling, hard-eyed gunmen.

General Avila Camacho is a hefty, big-shouldered, big-jowled[2] man with the most impassive manner I ever met in a politician. He wore a suit of very bright brown tweeds and blue sports shoes. The story is that he has never given a quick answer to anything,

[2] One of his nicknames is *El Buchudo*, the Double-Chinned.

and that no one has ever succeeded in hurrying him. He talked fairly freely to me in response to direct questions, but I certainly agree that he is not a chatterbox.

He told me that he hoped to make a quick unofficial visit to Washington before his inauguration. He has never been in the United States (incidentally, he speaks no English), except for brief jaunts across the border in Texas and California, and he was anxious to meet our leading politicians, to exchange information with them and improve his knowledge of United States affairs. The trip never materialized, but later—in the spring of 1941— it was again said that he would come to Washington.

The General explained that he is a firm believer in hemisphere solidarity and Pan-American defense. He said, "It is my ambition to make relations between the United States and Mexico better than they have ever been before. Not merely to keep them good as they are at present. But to make them better."

He talked about Fifth Columnism briefly, saying that it was not important in Mexico, which is a highly doubtful point; he emphasized his determination to rule in a completely democratic manner; he said that he had worked himself up through long years of dutiful service, and that he still thought of himself as an engineer, an administrator.

Personal Life of the President

The President lives in a big white California-style stucco house at 145 Avenida Castillo de Chapultepec in a fashionable part of town. This has been his residence for many years; the property is his wife's. He works in the National Palace about three miles away on Zócalo Square, and as he enters each morning he may— if he chooses—gain inspiration from the marvelous Diego Rivera frescoes illuminating the stairway. The President goes to work in a new black Packard sedan, which bears no special insignia; it merely carries the regulation yellow and orange license plate, Number F 98-00. He does not like pomp or display.

Aside from the town house the President has a small ranch,

called Soledad (his wife's name), near that delightful town Cuernavaca, and he often spends week ends there, riding and resting. Also he maintains the house in Teziutlán where he was born, but seldom visits it. When he took power there was some curiosity as to whether he would move into the traditional residence of the President, Chapultepec Castle. But Cárdenas had refused to make use of any such pretentious establishment with its bitter memories of Díaz—though other Presidents have used it for official entertainment—and so far Avila Camacho has likewise avoided it. One story is that the new President may take over a small villa called Los Pinos, facing Chapultepec Park, which Cárdenas lived in.

General Avila Camacho, who has always been industrious, rises at 6:30 every day except Sunday. As a rule he rides half an hour for exercise, and then reads the papers at breakfast. His secretaries appear, and at a little after nine he drives to his office. As a rule (like Vargas in Brazil) he sees his cabinet ministers in pairs, two each day. He works till 2 or later, and then has a substantial lunch. Unlike most Mexicans, he hates to sleep by day, and only seldom takes a siesta. He returns to his office somewhere between 4 and 5, and keeps at work until 10 or later. Then he has a light supper, reads or walks a while, and goes to bed.

The President is normal and moderate in his habits and appetites. He must watch his waist line severely, and he eats carefully. He drinks little. He is fond of Cuban cigars, and likes to smoke those which President Batista of Cuba sends him. He is apt to chew gum when he is not smoking. He reads little except the local newspapers, though he receives the American magazine *Life* regularly. No one has ever seen him in a night club or cabaret. He doesn't dance or gamble. Sometimes he sees the new American movies, especially newsreels, in private shows at his house; he seldom goes publicly to the theater. He is fond of classical music; when he reads at home he has the phonograph or radio playing softly, and as a rule he listens to Bach or Beethoven as he falls asleep.

But the President's chief avocations are outdoor sports. He loves fishing, and he thinks that everyone should eat more fish, especially as the fishing industry has been much neglected in Mexico. Above all, he passionately admires horses. He rides all the time. He has a stable of about 50 thoroughbreds, and his favorite game is polo. Many well-known polo players are his friends and have been his guests; Tommy Hitchcock, for instance. When he plays polo he wants badly to win; his rating is three-goal.

Avila Camacho was never thought to have been a poor man—successful generals are seldom poor in Mexico—but when he became President he listed his total assets as only $7,410, and those of his wife at $13,700. He said he had no cash deposits. Much of his property is believed to be in his wife's name, like the house on Avenida Castillo.

His attitude toward religion is that of most Latin American men of affairs. He maintains a respectful attitude toward the Church, but leaves practical devotion to the women of the family. He has no anticlerical record, and during the campaign, as noted above, he made a sensation by announcing that he was a believer. He seldom goes to mass, and he favors religious freedom, religious tolerance. His aim is not to interfere with the Church, provided it stays within the law.

Shortly after his inauguration the Archbishop of Mexico, Luis Martínez, asked all Catholics to co-operate with him. He said, "I feel certain that freedom of conscience and religious peace, which made great progress in the Cárdenas administration, will not only continue in the new presidential period, but also will be consolidated and perfected . . . I particularly draw attention to the fact that General Avila Camacho is the only President of Mexico in many years who has declared publicly and emphatically that he is a Catholic and who has recognized that the Mexican people have certain spiritual needs that can be satisfied only by religious freedom."[3]

Most people like Avila Camacho. He is easy to work with—though in the strain of taking over the presidency he surprised

[3] New York *Times*, Dec. 5, 1940.

his secretaries by flashes of bad temper—and most of the people close to him, especially the younger officers, admire him greatly. They like his fair-mindedness and conciliatory attitude, and his skill as a negotiator. Ponderous as he seems to be, he has considerable capacity to arouse affection.

Family and Friends

Probably the greatest single influence on General Manuel Avila Camacho is his wife, whom he adores. Unlike many Mexican generals and politicians, he has strong family sense. Señora Avila Camacho, whose maiden name was Soledad Orozco, came from a town in Jalisco called Sayula, where the General met her during a revolution many years ago. They have two adopted sons, blond boys of 12 and 15. Señora Camacho is a typical woman of the Mexican upper middle class: strongly Spanish in orientation, buxom, conservative, a devout Catholic, a good manager and housewife. Once, during the election campaign, her husband was stricken in Lower California with tonsillitis. She hates airplanes, but at once she flew to join him in near-by Sonora. She is proud of his accomplishments, and ambitious for his career.

The most picturesque member of the Avila Camacho family is the elder brother, General Maximino Avila Camacho. This general, who was governor and undisputed boss of the state of Puebla for many years, is a gaudy and exuberant character—almost legendary, in fact. He seems to belong to the epoch of Villa and Zapata rather than to these staid days. Maximino is everything that his brother is not—flamboyant, impulsive, immensely rich, a dictator with great flair for the dramatic, a *caudillo* (chieftain) who made one of Mexico's most important states a kind of bizarre private preserve, and lined it with personality and gold.

Another brother, 34-year-old Captain Gabriel Avila Camacho, has recently been in trouble. Following a rowdy café squabble at dawn on April 3, 1941, Gabriel shot and killed a man named Manuel Cacho, the son of a well-known jeweler and an acquaintance of the President's. No politics was involved. Gabriel claimed that the episode was an accident. He was arrested and the police offered to release him when they learned who he was; but his brother, Avila Camacho, insisted that he be held for investigation and that "strict justice be observed."

Important Right-wing influences on the President are two ex-Presidents of Mexico, Abelardo Rodríguez and Emilio Portes Gil. Neither is in the cabinet, and it would be incorrect to say that they dominate the new administration or control the President behind the scenes; but they are among his closest friends and are of manifest weight in advising him. Both are wealthy; both were puppets of another former President, Plutarco Elías Calles; both are on the reactionary side. Both have men actually in the Avila Camacho cabinet: Rodríguez is represented by Francisco Xavier Gaxiola, the Minister of National Economy, and Portes Gil by the new Minister of Agriculture, Marte R. Gómez.

The American colony in Mexico City, comprised mostly of tough-fingered entrepreneurs and business men, were 90 per cent for Almazán during the campaign, because they hated Cárdenas and what he stood for much as their analogues in the United States hated Roosevelt. But when it became clear that Almazán was fading out, they shifted rather uneasily to Camacho's side. They admire his substantial appearance and his caution, and they hope that his administration will proceed more and more to the Right. The American ambassador to Mexico, the venerable Josephus Daniels, was—far from being on the Almazán side—intimately close to Cárdenas, as befitted an ambassador of the New Deal. Mr. Daniels did not know Avila Camacho well before he became President. Their relations are now cordial, and the President has several times been a guest at the American embassy.

The inner circle around Avila Camacho includes the following men: General Quevedo, who first suggested that he run for President; Miguel Alemán, who was his campaign manager and is now Minister of the Interior; his personal physician, Dr. Octavio Mondragón; General Gilberto Limón, the president of the Polo Association and a famous polo player; brother Maximino, of course;

the handsome American-educated José Navarro, who is his personal press representative; and Major Waldo Romo Castro, his private secretary for eleven years.

In the secretariat the two most important men are Jesús González Gallo, a bright-minded 36-year-old lawyer, and Colonel Maximino Ochoa Moreno, the chief military aide, who controls the President's appointments and has a great deal to say about promotions in the army. González, who speaks English, is a Jaliscan, a former senator, and a pleasant personality. Colonel Ochoa is a veteran of the campaigns against Pancho Villa, and an officer of the old school. He served as Mexican military attaché to Germany, and for a time he was called pro-German. He received a decoration from the German government when he lived in Berlin. Another secretary, Roberto Trauwitz Amezaga, is partly of German ancestry and studied in Germany. He is the President's customary interpreter in audiences with Americans, since his English is perfect.

One influence on Avila Camacho may conceivably be that of William Randolph Hearst. The aging publisher, who has enormous Mexican properties, visited Mexico City with his entourage early in 1941, and was royally received by the new President. In sharp contrast to his former attitude, Hearst wrote column after column fulsomely praising Mexico and its government. He fairly oozed over. When Hearst returned to the United States, he referred to previous expropriations of some of his property and said (New York *Herald Tribune*, April 1, 1941), "They were pretty decent about that. They didn't take any more than was right. After all, it is their country." Far cry from the Hearst attitude during other Mexican administrations!

Avila Camacho in the Saddle

One should not assume that the new President has swung completely to the Right or broken completely with the Cárdenas tradition. The situation is more subtle and complex than that. Avila Camacho needs Left support, and he based his campaign on his promise "to consolidate the gains of the Cárdenas regime." What he has done so far is to mend fences, smile at both sides, keep them from conflict, and take a middle course. Because he succeeds a radically Leftist President, his program—at the moment of writing at least—seems somewhat more Right than it really is. Essentially he is a *Center* man. Nevertheless, the Left is frightened. Some Leftists go so far as to think that he will be worse for them than Almazán.

Avila Camacho has kept on a good many Cárdenas men, which would seem to indicate some degree of continuity with his predecessor. For instance, the competent Eduardo Suárez remains Minister of *Hacienda* (Treasury). Ignacio García Téllez, very close to Cárdenas, was retained but shifted from the portfolio of the Interior to the Labor Ministry. A Cárdenas man, General Heriberto Jara, the chief of the P.R.M., became Minister of Marine. Another, General Blas Corral, stays on as Minister of War, and General Jesús de la Garza was promoted from Undersecretary to Minister of Communications. Dr. Gustavo Baz, who under Cárdenas was rector of the University, became Secretary of Public Welfare. Dr. Francisco Castillo Nájera, the ambassador to Washington—one of the highest jobs a Mexican can have—remains at his post.

But a good many changes did occur, and many Cárdenas men have less important jobs than before, even if they have been retained. Efraín Buenrostro was shifted from the Ministry of Economy to be manager of the National Petroleum Administration. Ramón Beteta retired from his vital watchpost as Undersecretary of Foreign Affairs to become Undersecretary in the Treasury. Dr. Xavier Icaza retired from the Supreme Court to assume a job in the Ministry of Education. And so on.

Normally in Mexico a new administration meant a complete shakeup and reshuffle. All the Ins went Out, and all the Outs came In. Avila Camacho did not make any such drastic housecleaning. As has been well said, he is one of the few Mexican Presidents who have striven deeply for national unity *after* an election. His moderation was particularly notable because Mexico was suffering acute pangs of economic as well as political discomfort. The war had cut off what oil exports remained. The railways were in collapse. In Yucatán people were starving. There was agrarian unrest almost everywhere.

Since his inauguration in December 1940, Avila's chief "Rightist" manifestations have been these:

1. He ordered that henceforth peasants be given individual title to the land they worked on the *ejidos* (communal farms), which may result in a serious modification of the Cárdenas land-reform system. He did not abolish the *ejidos*—no Mexican politician would dare do that—but he gave encouragement to the principle of private ownership.

2. He took the railways out of the hands of the Workers' Administration that had been managing them since 1938, hoping thus to remedy confusion and inefficiency. The railways are now controlled by the government, though labor has three seats out of seven on the board.

3. He proposed new petroleum legislation which allows private Mexican—but not foreign—capital to participate in the oil business under certain restrictions. Under Cárdenas petroleum had been nationalized.

4. He revised the labor code by forbidding illegal "outlaw" strikes, though he promised that previous labor gains would be safeguarded. He told the workers that they were in "duty bound to show more discipline, adopt a more moderate policy, and cooperate in the national life." The Left applauded him, though with trepidation, when he upset the Right by appearing personally at the national convention of the C.T.M.

On the ticklish matter of education and the Church Avila Camacho moved very slowly. By terms of the 1917 constitution, education is the exclusive function of the state; church schools are technically barred (though some exist covertly or under disguise), and the clergy hopes above all to have this ban lifted. It asserts that the government's textbooks are "communistic," and that the government schools are "ruining" the youth. Strong pressure was put on Avila to revise the Education Law, i.e. to give the Church more power. So far he has not done so. But the end of this story is not yet.

Some Avila measures which have met with more or less general approval are the following:

Restatement of the antigraft law, providing that every person accepting public office must declare his wealth on entering and leaving office.

Recommendation to amend the constitution so that presidential candidates must withdraw from the army or from public office six months before the election, instead of a year, as at present. The object is to avoid disruption of administration for the longer period.

A decree prohibiting army officers from belonging to the P.R.M., the government party.

A proposed constitutional amendment for permanent tenure of office by judges, who are now appointed for six-year terms, in order to wean the judiciary away from politics.

Proposals to lift government restrictions on credit in order to stimulate investment of private capital.

Various pronouncements affirming complete solidarity with the United States, the development of joint efforts in the realm of Pan-American solidarity, and co-operation in hemisphere defense.

Glimpsing the Future

When Avila Camacho began his term he was scarcely known to the common people. The stolid general had almost always been an administrator, a man behind the scenes. His extravagant brother Maximino had been much more conspicuous. Since his inauguration the President has become fairly popular, except on the extreme Left. People are saying, "After all, he is the President. That makes him important. Give him a chance."

Recently he unexpectedly attended a Ballet Russe performance in the great marble Palace of Fine Arts—one of his rare appearances of this sort. He was spontaneously cheered with *"¡Viva México, Viva Avila Camacho!"* from gallery to orchestra pit. No such demonstration had been heard for years. The President was deeply touched.

What people hope most is that Avila Camacho will use his six years in hard constructive work, without too much experimentation, without fireworks. Mexico has had enough of flamboyance, *confusionismo,* and political hair pulling. Friends of Avila Camacho hope that he will give the country the most prosaic administration in its history. Poetry is out.

Chapter IV
Mexico: Land, Revolution, People

〰〰〰〰〰〰〰〰〰〰〰〰〰〰〰〰〰〰〰〰〰

B EFORE I had been in Mexico[1] a week I knew I was visiting
one of the most attractive, provocative countries on earth. I
found that altitude and the bracing sunshine combined to produce
the most brilliant weather I had ever known. I saw Aztec villages
that have scarcely changed since Cortés; I flew over pyramids bigger than those in Egypt; I ate limes stuffed with coconut. I found
that Mexico is the country where the letter "x" is pronounced three
different ways, where an important provincial capital may be two
days on muleback from the nearest railroad, and where during
one civic riot the taxicabs charged mounted cavalry like tanks—
and won. I found that the great tragedy of Mexico is that the land
is so fabulously rich and the people so miserably poor.

Then I discovered that Mexico reminded me irresistibly of another country I am fond of—China.

This is no new discovery, of course. And I must ask forgiveness
of my Mexican friends for mentioning it; they do not like to be
compared to the Chinese, though I mean the comparison as a great
compliment. One distinguished Mexican journalist was nearly expelled from college not many years ago because he dared to allude
to the possibility of common origin of Mexicans and Chinese.

Indeed an obvious first impression in Mexico is that so many
Mexicans, especially Indians in the backward villages, *look* so
astoundingly like Chinese. Their short legs, cheekbones, even eyes,
are Mongoloid. And one theory of modern anthropologists—the
dominant theory nowadays—is that the American Indians, in
North as well as South America, came originally from the Asia
mainland. They were Mongoloid adventurers perhaps mixed with

[1] I know that Mexico properly should be México, just as Peru is properly
Perú and Panama Panamá. But I propose to omit accents on names so familiar
in English without them.

Polynesian strains who crossed the Pacific either by primitive canoes or overland by way of the Bering straits.

Henry B. Parkes begins his *History of Mexico*,[2] the best modern history of the country, with a vivid and suggestive picture:

Man probably originated in the tablelands of Asia. From this center his descendants, compelled by famine or drawn by the promises of discovery, spread outwards in a series of waves of migration. . . . A movement of peoples towards the east crossed the Bering Straits and colonized the two continents of America. Meanwhile another series of invading tribes followed each other to the west, overrunning Europe or northern Africa and skirting the coasts of the Mediterranean. . . . For many thousands of years this was the limit of their advance. Finally, in the year 1492 of the Christian Era, they began to cross the Atlantic, and the two streams of migration were then—at the opposite extremity of the globe from their starting-point—to meet and mingle. The history of their mingling is the history of Mexico and of the other Latin-American countries.

Mexicans today are by and large highly intelligent, like the Chinese; they are friendly and sensitive, with deep artistic impulses; they are steeped in fatalism, like the Chinese. Mexicans love rice, village festivals, highly spiced food, colorful costumes, fireworks, and multitudinous holidays, like the Chinese; they dislike waste, most foreigners, cowardice, and punctuality. Like the Chinese they derive from a tremendous ancient civilization, which later crumbled into decay. Their country was invaded and exploited by the white West, just as China was; it was also despoiled, like China, by corrupt provincial governors and war lords. In Mexico City, as in the treaty ports of China, you have "Old Mexican hands" like "Old China hands," that is, white foreigners who live on the country, pretend to despise it, suck wealth out of it, and love it profoundly. Much corruption exists in Mexico, as in

[2] *A History of Mexico.* By Henry Bamford Parkes. Boston, Houghton Mifflin Co. p. 3.

China; much frustrated idealism; much political ineptitude; and an enormous amount of confused hope.

Another and more important analogy: Mexico, like China, is a country dominated by a revolution. The Mexican revolution (the earliest of the great modern revolutions) came in 1911 as we have seen; it preceded the revolution of Dr. Sun Yat-sen by two years. The Mexican revolution, like that of China, has ebbed, flowed, rushed around corners, jumped dams, dried up, spread out into the fields, disappeared, and welled up again. No one can define precisely what it was, is, or will be; no one knows just where it's going. It is simply accepted, as the Chinese revolution is accepted, as the ruling political Fact of the nation. Nation and revolution are indissolubly one.

A final point: Mexican politics, like Chinese politics, are dominated by a single pervasive loosely knit political party. In China it is the Kuomintang, in Mexico the Party of the Mexican Revolution.

Some Illusions About Mexico

One illusion, stupid but widely held in the United States, is that no Mexican Presidents ever die in bed, that assassination always ends their terms. Nothing could be sillier. There are no fewer than seven former presidents of Mexico living comfortably in the country today:

> Emilio Portes Gil
> Abelardo Rodríguez
> Pascual Ortiz Rubio
> Plutarco Elías Calles
> Pedro Lascurain
> Lázaro Cárdenas
> Roque González Garza

Another illusion is that all Mexican administrations are overthrown by violence. This is likewise silly. It *is* true that Mexico is still in a revolutionary period, and minor forays, putsches, attempted coups d'état, and plain bandit raids do often occur. But no Mexican government has been turned *out of office* by a revolution since 1920 when Obregón ousted the ineffable Carranza. No successful "revolution" in the normal sense of the word has taken place for 21 years.

Another illusion is that all male Mexicans carry heavy-calibered guns, subsist exclusively on redhot chili, wear glistening sombreros, and look like a combination of Montezuma, Sitting Bull and Wallace Beery. Just go into the Ritz Bar in Mexico City any day at teatime and have a look.

But I should add—and freely admit—that a great many Mexicans do carry arms.

Cortés Certainly Started Something

Turn Mexico sideways and superimpose it on a map of the United States. Put the extreme northwestern tip of Lower California on San Francisco say. The peninsula of Yucatán will then just touch Lake Superior, Mexico City will lie somewhere in Kansas, and the Isthmus of Tehuantepec will be in Tennessee. It's not a small country. The distance, as a crow or Douglas flies, between San Diego, on the Mexican-California border, and the tip of Yucatán, is the same as that between San Diego and Tallahassee, Florida. The comparatively short hop between El Paso and Mexico City is as great as from Memphis to Albuquerque.

Of the total area of Mexico, a great part—well over 70 per cent —is jagged and desolate mountain. Along each coastline is a narrow belt, called the *tierra caliente* (torrid zone) ; then the mountains rise to form the massive interior plateau. Mexico is like some enormous knotty spinal column, with misshapen ribs and vertebrae protruding on all sides. When Cortés returned to Spain and was asked what the country looked like, he gave a description that has never been excelled by picking up a stiff piece of paper and crumpling it.

Mexico produces much of the world's oil, 33 per cent of its

silver, 2 per cent of its gold. Its mineral resources—including lead, mercury, antimony, and the like—are so vast and varied as to be literally boundless. One silver mine, Real del Monte, has been worked since the time of Montezuma, and is still the wealthiest in the world.[3] Oil fields exist, as yet only partially exploited, which are probably the richest on earth next to those in Venezuela. But Mexico, because of its precipitous geography and its pressing lack of water, produces very little *soil*—a commodity that can be as valuable as gold.

Do not think that Mexicans have had exclusive use of their country for their own profit. Far from it. The foreign "take" has been and is enormous, and the bitter proverb runs, "Mexico is the Stepmother of Mexicans." British investment in oil alone has been calculated—by the British—at $250,000,000, and that of the United States at about $150,000,000. Of course oil has been expropriated by Mexico since 1938; of this more anon. As to Mexico's silver, it is about 75 per cent owned by American capital; most of the other mines are under American or other foreign control. As to land, foreigners till recently owned 20 per cent of the total private land in the country; of this Americans held half. But since Cárdenas speeded up the land reform, Americans have lost about 10,000,000 acres of property. The total United States investment in Mexico is still in the neighborhood of $500,000,000, our largest stake in the hemisphere except Canada, Chile, and Cuba.

On Mexico's 763,944 square miles live about 19,000,000 people. In population Mexico is the second largest country (Brazil is of course first) in Latin America; the people are not particularly homogeneous. The cattle hand in Sonora, tall, muscular, born to the saddle, has little in common with the pure-blooded Tarascan Indian from Michoacán or the Maya sisal-picker on the hot, fetid coast of Yucatán. There are no accurate racial statistics. But a rough-and-ready calculation is that 10 per cent of Mexico is white,

[3] This mine still produces 10 per cent of the world's silver, according to *Fortune*, October, 1938. *Fortune* is my source for much of the statistical matter in this chapter.

30 per cent Indian, 60 per cent *mestizo*. There are very few negroes —fewer than in Texas, for instance, across the border.

Three great centripetal forces hold this red-white-brown mass together. The first is the historical fact of political unity under Spanish domination from 1521 to 1821. The second is the power over almost all ranks of the people of the Roman Catholic Church. The third is the Spanish language. Still, perhaps two million people, almost 10 per cent of the population, speak their native Indian tongues, with only a rudimentary knowledge of Castilian.

There are other common denominators. One is poverty. The national income is only $36 per head per year. Another is public health—or the lack of it. The death rate is said to be the second highest in the world, and an Indian child has only a 50-50 chance to reach his tenth birthday. A third is illiteracy, which is about 60 per cent.

Mexican History: Five-Minute Glimpse

Hernán Cortés, one of the most remarkable characters in history, landed with 632 men and 16 horses near what is now Veracruz in April, 1519. This greatest of the *conquistadores*, cruel and treacherous as he may have been, was possessed of fantastic courage and a rare quality of historical vision. He was more than a mere looter, even if he once said, "I come to get gold, not to till the soil like a peasant." Early in his assault on Mexico he deliberately ordered the destruction of his own fleet, so that no escape could be possible—an apocalyptic action, rarely matched in human annals. Cortés was a realist—witness his remark that "the Spaniards are troubled with a disease of the heart for which gold is a specific remedy." He was cold as ice, capable of cutting off the feet of one of his men as punishment. Yet he was also capable of great magnanimity. His relations with Montezuma and Montezuma's successor Cuauhtémoc form a record of political astuteness that is still breathtaking, as anyone who has read Prescott or Bernal Díaz knows. Above all, the full-flavored Cortés had interesting political ideas. He did not want to kill off Indians.

He wanted to make the Indians work for him. He was a free-booter—the entire Mexican adventure was in disobedience of orders—but his idea and ambition was to conquer and create a *state*.

Cortés crushed the Aztecs by 1521. They outnumbered the Spaniards enormously, and at times they fought fiercely; they were beaten not so much by the guns of the invaders as by their own mythology. Montezuma, a baffling character, thought that Cortés represented the returning Toltec god Quetzalcoatl, or Plumed Serpent. The Indians thought that the Spanish horses were centaurs, and that the Spanish guns were magical instruments that fired of their own volition. And Cortés traded sagaciously on opposition to the Aztecs by other Indian tribes whom the Aztecs had oppressed, like the Tlaxcalans.

One detail is irresistible. When Cortés reached the land of the Tabascans and defeated them, they gave him twenty young women, including Marina, who became his mistress and interpreter. The twenty girls were duly baptized (I quote Parkes), "since the Spaniards would not sleep with idolaters, and then distributed among the leaders of the party."[4] The children of these twenty Aztec women, by Spanish fathers, are the origin of Mexico's present *mestizo* population. From these twenty women derive something like 9,000,000 people, figuratively speaking. It is not too fanciful to suggest that they are the mothers of Mexico, and spiritually the mothers of most of the rest of Latin America. They symbolized a process that is with us to this day.

Before the Spanish conquest the Indians maintained a distinct and highly developed civilization, as everyone knows. Southern Mexico and Guatemala were populated largely by the Mayas, who founded a loose agrarian "empire" some centuries before our era. They were very advanced people, as their great ruins at Uxmal and Chichén Itzá show. We know very little about them, however, since Spanish priests destroyed all but three of their books—one of the wickedest acts in history—and these three are undecipher-

[4] See also *Mexico and Its Heritage*, by Ernest Gruening.

able. The Mayas, who reached their highest point in the sixth or seventh century A.D., invented several types of calendar, and devised the symbol zero; they were excellent craftsmen in pottery, silver, gold; their language had a vocabulary of 30,000 words; they were good architects and engineers. But by the tenth century their civilization began to decline; they fell victim to disintegration from within and to conquest from without by stronger tribes, like the Toltecs.

The Mayas were peaceable folk. The tribes who made successive waves of invasion from the north were much more warlike. After the thirteenth century the Aztecs conquered most of Central Mexico, and in 1325 they founded Tenochtitlán, which is the Mexico City of today. For 196 years, until the coming of Cortés, they held power there. The Aztecs were not as great artists as the Mayas, but they were formidable builders, as witness their aqueducts and pyramids. They had sensible ideas of education, community life and land ownership; they worshiped the elements as represented by a variety of ornate gods; their government was a loose federation of clans, with leadership vested in a kind of national council. They were addicted—the obverse side of the coin—to human sacrifice revolting in character and degree.

But listen to Stuart Chase[5] summarizing Mexican civilization in the thirteenth century:

In astronomy it was far in advance of Europe; in architectural ornament it was as great as the world has ever seen . . . in its conception of the rights of the individual it stood manifestly above the feudal conceptions of the Old World, so far indeed that the Spaniards could not understand its political philosophy; in its minor arts of weaving, metal working, jewelry, pottery, it challenged the best which the Eastern Hemisphere had to offer; its knowledge of plants and medicinal herbs was profound; it honored women, it loved flowers, and the writers of untrue books of history it put to death.

What a fusion the birth of Mexico—and of most of Latin

[5] *Mexico: A Study of Two Americas*, p. 57.

America—represents! The crusty flamboyance, the seething vigor, the fanatic bigotry of sixteenth-century Spain, and the passivity, the inchoate artistic impulses, the rooted adhesion to the sparse native soil, of the Indians. On the one side, Spanish pride, greed, and passionate conservatism; on the other side, Indian credulity, compactness, tenacity.

I cannot hope in a book of this scope to trace the course of Mexico under Spanish rule in any detail. In 1535 Mexico became the Viceroyalty of New Spain; two years later it was officially announced that the Indians were human beings, who possessed souls and could be converted.[6] Spanish officials, priests, adventurers and riffraff began to pour in. At the beginning several able and responsible Viceroys held power, and attempted to create the kind of colony Cortés projected, but their work quickly crumbled. The Church and the great landowners entrenched themselves; for a time the Church owned 50 per cent of all land in Mexico. The *gachupines* (Spanish-born Spaniards) and *creoles* (sons and descendants of Spanish immigrants—though the haughty *creoles* will dislike that word) struggled for power. Came decay, corruption, chaos. Education, public welfare, public health, were not merely neglected; they were forgotten. For instance, according to Parkes, the Spaniards built no roads in Mexico until about 1800. The *gachupíne* oligarchy, with the creoles close behind, milked the country dry. The people groaned and sulked, and revolutionary ferment began. Its first great leader was a priest, one of the noblest characters in Latin American history, Father Hidalgo. He was caught by the Spaniards and shot, but this George Washington of Mexico was not forgotten. In 1821, Mexico shook off Spanish rule, and became an independent state.

From 1821 to 1857 there is little to record, except a confusing record of abortive and successful revolutions, and the intermittent rule of a fabulous mountebank known as Santa Anna. In the 1850's came the revolution of Benito Juárez, who was a pure-blooded Zapotec Indian, the first pure Indian to rule Mexico since

[6] Parkes, *op. cit.*

Montezuma. The three greatest men in Mexican history, Cortés excepted, were pure or almost pure Indians, incidentally—Juárez, Porfirio Díaz (a great man whether you like him or not), and Lázaro Cárdenas. The Juárez revolution was interrupted by the fantastic Maximilian episode; then Juárez ruled again till he died in 1872. His achievements were striking not so much in themselves but for their augury of the future. Juárez was the first Mexican President to work for education, land reform, and the Indians; he attacked the Church and took advantage of an earlier law separating Church and State.

After Juárez came the Porfirio Díaz dictatorship, which except for one brief interval lasted from 1876 to 1911. Díaz was an Indian from the Mixtec area with only a trace of Spanish blood, but he was typically and overwhelmingly a westerner, a white, in his behavior patterns and accomplishments. What he did, in a word, was to establish political stability (by means of totally ruthless dictatorship—for instance, he had at least 10,000 people shot) and to open the country to foreign capital. Díaz wanted roads, railways, oil wells, textile factories. To obtain these, he practically gave his country away. He distributed not less than 134,000,000 acres, about 27 per cent of the total area of Mexico, to his friends.[7] Mexico became a virtual colony of the Díaz clique and foreign interests. But it achieved considerable material progress.

In 1911 the Díaz regime collapsed, mostly of its own sagging weight. Mexico entered a period of authentic revolution from which it has not yet emerged.

The first leader of the revolution, Francisco Madero, was a wealthy landowner of Spanish descent who did not bring to his mission anything like the strength of character it deserved. Madero was straw and putty compared to Díaz. But he forced him out, because Díaz had made life intolerable to the bulk of the Mexican people. At first the revolution was almost exclusively "political," though its slogan was *Tierra y Libertad*—"Land and Liberty." It

[7] Incidentally his widow is still alive and receives survivors of the *ancien régime* regularly. I have met his granddaughter sipping coffee in the Ritz bar.

was a revolution of Outs to replace Ins. Its profound social and collectivist implications developed later. It started out as a simple if drastic shift in political power; it ramified, as we know, into one of the complex evolutions of modern times.

Madero did not last long. He was tricked, betrayed, overthrown, and eventually shot by orders of a murderous drunkard named Victoriano Huerta, who succeeded him. This was probably the most unsavory interlude in Mexican history. Against Huerta rose three different leaders; a volcanic orgy of disturbance developed into civil war. To untangle the story of these bloody years, with their interplay of constantly shifting forces—even to draw the simplest diagram—would take pages. A cross-grained professorial gentleman named Venustiano Carranza assumed leadership of the revolution, though he was a conservative at heart, and a land-owner in pocketbook. In the north a picturesque bandit chieftain, Pancho Villa, who resembled Carranza about as much as a prickly pear resembles a boiled potato, roamed the country looting and plundering—but in the name of the revolution. Nearer Mexico City a third leader, Emiliano Zapata, a pure Morelos Indian, stalking across the sierras on his black stallion, inflamed the peasants with revolutionary forays. To see Zapata, to know almost everything about him, one needs only look at the Diego Rivera frescoes in Cuernavaca. It was Zapata, incidentally, who invented the phrase which years later came to have wide currency in Europe and America, "It is better to die on your feet than to live on your knees."

The civil wars ended in 1920, after Villa and Zapata revolted against Carranza. The most competent general in Mexican history, General Alvaro Obregón, then crushed Villa and overthrew Carranza. It is a pity to have to foreshorten so drastically the record of General Obregón, who represented the Juárez-Madero tradition; he attempted to lead Mexico back to tranquillity on the one hand, while keeping alight the principles of the revolution with the other—at least at first. Obregón was President from 1920 to 1924. In 1928 a young Catholic fanatic murdered him.

After Obregón Mexican politics become comparatively dull and tidy. There are two main trends to chronicle. The first is the swing to the Right—though such generalization is inconclusive—represented by President Plutarco Elías Calles, who succeeded Obregón, and the Calles puppets who came later. I call this a "swing to the Right"; yet Calles was the most anticlerical President in Mexican history, and one of his successors, Abelardo Rodríguez, did more for land reform than any President in years. But the Calles decade—roughly 1924 to 1934—was definitely Rightist from other points of view. After Calles came Cárdenas and the contrasting swing to the Left which persisted until 1940. Now Avila Camacho is turning to the Center.

In summary let us say this. The Mexican Revolution of 1911 was the first of the great modern revolutions. Its achievements are difficult to draw up, since Mexico is still in a state of flux, but several points deserve brief mention. The revolution, even under conservative Presidents, unleashed vast national and social forces; it gave political integration to the people, and Mexico—after arduous pangs—became a genuine national state. And it is the only country in Latin America with an advanced social-economic program, with definite collectivist aims, principles and accomplishments.

Another Word on Indians

Oddly enough, the chief element in the Indian problem is not, as one might have thought, *racial* assimilation. There is scarcely any racial bitterness in Mexico among the great masses of the people. Intermarriage goes on steadily, and the point has been made—though some authorities doubt it—that the country is becoming more Indian all the time, that the "Indianization of Mexico" is increasing.

The Indians by and large are the poorest members of the Mexican nation. Most of them—despite their biological vitality—are inert politically. They are the shoeless peasants in remote Aztec villages, the stooped peons who squat half hidden along the roads of Michoacán. They are the *pelados*—the illiterates who "know nothing, have nothing, and want nothing." Their masters are the priests—who let them dance in church. They drink fantastic quantities of *pulque*, a sourish alcoholic drink made of the maguey plant, and of *tequila*, stronger alcohol.

But their costumes—in Michoacán, for instance—are flashes of primitive color as unspoiled as a tanager's wing. Their weaving, pottery, and other handicrafts—particularly in a pure Indian state like Oaxaca—are a joy to behold. Many are of great endurance and physical courage. The story is told of the Yaquis—hard-fighting Indians from the north—that if you put a rope around a Yaqui's neck, squeeze it, and ask him to talk, all that he will answer is, "Pull!"

As I have noted, about 2,000,000 Indians, not quite 10 per cent of the population of Mexico, do not readily speak Spanish. There are not less than 54 different Indian languages, some of them—like Zapotec—of staggering difficulty. Chinese is as easy as tiddlywinks compared to Chinantec, say, in which a word may have seventy different forms.

What counts in Mexico is not racial assimilation of the submerged Indian mass, but social, political, and economic assimilation. For generations the Indians were considered outcasts and slaves. What people hope for nowadays is a program of irrigation, education, public health, rural electrification, and road building that will reach the Indian mass—after all, 45 per cent of the population—and incorporate it into the living structure of the state. The problem is to make *Mexicans* out of Indians.

Recently a congress deputy made a speech in Aztec. Not many could understand him, but the other deputies rose and cheered.

The Land and the Ejido

I stood along a road penetrating a cornfield not far from Mexico City. The corn, yellow and billowing in the wind, was taller than I am; it flowed evenly to the road, where a heavy fence made of gray lava rocks and a line of soaring maguey cactus stopped it.

In the sky, the blazing blue sky of Mexico, massive sunshiny clouds look like crysanthemums.

Here, the thirsty land of Mexico. Here, the corn on which Mexico lives, which gives life to the land.

Then a village. The main street is grassy, meandering through lanes of plaster houses colored pale blue, mauve, white, and a shade of pink that would be the pride of Elizabeth Arden if she had invented it. At one corner the inevitable church, filled with Aztec ornaments, and named for a saint *plus* an Aztec name. In the churchyard yellow petals are scattered over crowded graves; flying on ropes are triangles of colored tissue paper, punctured as if to make confetti.

We enter a house. No windows, no chimney. A single low-power electric light bulb hangs from the cracked ceiling. No other light. There are two rooms, both with beaten dirt floors; in the dark kitchen a charcoal fire is smoldering; in the "living" room are some rough wooden chairs, some religious pictures and family photographs, and a large bed—really a straw mat stretched on wooden posts and covered with a *serape* (blanket)—on which most of the family sleeps. Outside are pigs, chickens, and a burro. The children are shy, quiet, with good teeth and healthy smiles. The teeth are so good because the corn-meal *tortilla*, the staff of life in every Mexican village, is prepared with a powdering of limestone.

I asked the mother of the family, a squat, lustrous-eyed woman in her fifties, what she thought of politics. She answered, "If it pleases God and your good selves, any President will be welcome who improves our lot."

Then the village market, with its screaming variety of color. The neat, symmetrical piles of chili beans, spices, limes, cherries, eggs, apples, all laid out in precise, skillful designs. The heaps of brilliantly colored fruit and spices look like children's marbles in cardboard boxes. The market is noisy, fluid, and perfectly orderly. Sombreros of every conceivable size and shape of brim. Live pigs squealing and dead pigs in the shape of wineskins. Fluttering lanes of bright cotton textiles. Coal, wood, buttons. Many of the women have walked for miles. Market day is big business. But it is also a holiday. The women chatter, spit, sing, and relax.

From the market to an edifice at the end of the street is a span of two hundred yards. It is also a span of two centuries. The edifice is a school, one of the thousands of state schools that the revolution has spread over the country. Here spacious classrooms, modern desks in stamped metal, serious-minded young teachers. In the yard, in the very shadow of the gaunt deserted church, youngsters are listening to news on a loudspeaker or playing *Yanqui* basketball. What the villagers were proudest of was their new water supply. This had come the year before, and had transformed their lives.

The basic problem of Mexico is of course the land. The basic problem of the revolution is to make a successful land reform on *ejido* principles.

Literally *ejido* (pronounced é-*hee*-do) means "exit" or "way out." Its implications go back at least four hundred years to Aztec times, when clans owned land in common. This land usually lay on the outer edges of a village or tribal area; hence the term *ejido*, way out. The peasants worked the community area jointly; they pooled their resources and efforts, and shared the results. And it is this *ejido* system which the Mexican land reform attempts essentially to recreate. It resembles, as is obvious, such highly modern experiments as collective farming in the Soviet Union. Yet the inspiration for the Mexican procedure does not derive from Marxist doctrine. It is a throwback to the commun*al* (not commun*ist*) practice of the Aztecs.

But first a word on land in general. At least 65 per cent of the people of Mexico today—say 12,000,000 people—live by agriculture. Yet of the total land of Mexico only about 54 per cent has any agricultural use. All the rest is too mountainous or too arid for cultivation. And of this 54 per cent most has only very limited value, since it is forest or pasture land beyond the reach of irriga-

tion. Only 7.4 per cent of the total land of Mexico—a pitiably
small amount—is actually arable. And of this, only one half—
or 3.6 per cent of the total—is actually planted every year. The
other half is left fallow, for want of fertilizer.

When the Spaniards came they took all the best land as the
natural reward of conquest. Title was reserved to the Crown of
Spain; theoretically the settlers did not own the land, but held it
in trust. An institution known as the *encomienda* developed; this
was a kind of land grant giving a settler rights to exploit Indian
land and villages in return for "protecting the lives and property
of the Indians, maintaining political control for the Spanish crown;
and extending the influence of the Catholic Church."[8] At first the
encomiendas were assigned only for the lifetime of the colonist,
but later they were extended generation after generation. Thus
arose the most characteristic feature of Mexican life before the
revolution: the great *hacienda* (estate) maintained by a feudal
lord, where every kind of extravagance might take place, and
where hundreds or even thousands of Indian peons were serfs.
The *hacienda* became a self-sufficing and in effect self-governing
community, with churches, stables, shops, and so on within its
walled enclosure. Some *haciendas* reached fantastic size. One
family in Chihuahua, the Terrazas, owned thirty million acres,
which is the area of the state of Mississippi!

At first the Spanish conquerors permitted the Indian *ejidos* to
remain. But gradually—and inevitably—they were squeezed out.
The *hacendados* overran village after village, and so did the
prodigious ecclesiastical properties—which is one reason for Mexican anticlericalism. During the revolutions of the nineteenth century the church holdings were largely broken up, but private landowners—many of whom were absentees—continued to expand.
The system became feudalism in excelsis. Under Díaz it reached
its climax. Don Porfirio distributed not less than 134,000,000 acres

[8] From "The Land Problem in Mexico," by Charles H. Barber, in *Foreign
Agriculture*, published by the U. S. Department of Agriculture. This has been
my background for this section.

to the *hacendados*, as I have noted: one friend alone got 17,000,000 acres![9] Meantime the Indians lost their homes, their villages, their *ejidos*. Between 92 and 95 per cent of the heads of rural families in all Mexico had no land at all in 1910. The Indians became the most miserable kind of sharecroppers, or were forced upward into the barren mountains where they starved.

Then came the 1911 revolution. In 1915 Carranza issued a decree nullifying the seizure of all communal lands since 1856, and the new constitution of 1917, going much further, set out to break up the big estates. Its famous Article 27 stated that the Mexican *nation* retained ownership of all lands and waters in the national territory—including *sub*soil rights, which meant mines and oil—and that "the nation shall have at all times the right to impose on private property such limitations as the public interest may demand." This sentence is the cornerstone of the Mexican revolution.

The *ejido* system nowadays works more or less as follows. In theory each family is entitled to a share of the village land, as in Aztec times. Every person over 18 who lives in a community for more than a year may apply for a land grant; every person has a theoretical right to 4 hectares (about 10 acres) of irrigated land or its equivalent. In practice groups of 20 villagers petition for land together. The petition goes to the Mixed Agrarian Commission and to the governor of the province. The neighborhood is explored within a radius of seven kilometers to see what land is available. Then assignment is made, and according to law every expropriation is to be paid for. Also, as protection to the small land-owner, nothing may be taken from a property of less than 100 hectares of irrigated land. As to title, the situation is difficult to define accurately. In theory the title is in the name of an individual owner, but he may not sell his land or mortgage it. The *ejido* is considered the inalienable acquisition of the community.

From 1917 to the late 1920's the reform proceeded slowly. Then came Cárdenas. He organized an Ejidal Bank, to give

[9] Almost the size of South Carolina!

credit to the new farmers; he greatly accelerated the pace of distribution. From 1917 to date, approximately 55,000,000 acres—17 per cent of the total arable land of Mexico—have been expropriated and distributed to some 1,700,000 peasants. Hardly any of the great *haciendas* survive intact. Of this total at least half—perhaps 30,000,000 acres—were parceled out by Cárdenas in six years. Also he initiated the big-scale collective experiment at Laguna, a cotton-growing region near Torreón, where a $12,000,000 irrigation system is being built and land distributed to 32,000 workers. This was an attempt—so far only tentatively successful and still going on—"to recognize the economic and social basis, not of a single village but of an entire region."[10]

Cárdenas probably attempted too much. His scope and pace were too wide, too hurried. Inefficiency, bureaucratic delay, lack of funds, faulty education, produced confusion. Nevertheless, his effort to transform the agrarian system of Mexico in less than a decade, to abolish feudalism, to give the land of Mexico back to its own landless, was a stupendous undertaking.

I remember Cárdenas saying to me eloquently, "The Indian's conception of life depends on his having his own land. For the Indian, *land is life*. An Indian without land is an outcast. Ownership of land produces the harmony with environment which is essential to life in Mexico."

The political results of the land reform are worth careful note. Now that the peasants have their own property, the temptation to plunder is much diminished. The peasant feels that he has a personal stake in the development of the nation. He seeks to protect what he has. Therefore the impulse to revolutionary disturbance is greatly lessened, and the tendency to counter-revolution checked.

Church and Clericalism Versus State

I have mentioned the Church a good many times in this book so far, and I shall mention it often again. At this point

[10] *Foreign Policy Reports,* August 15, 1937.

let me sketch briefly the present status of the church conflict in Mexico.

Mexico was the first country in Latin America where the Church was disestablished. This occurred, as we know, before Juárez. Religious instruction is officially forbidden, and most teachers in the state schools, are fiercely, explosively anticlerical. Though severe anticlerical laws remain on the books, however, they are largely dead-letters. The churches are open for worship— I visited dozens of them—and priests are permitted to say mass. But priests do not appear on the streets in clerical garb, their *number* is heavily restricted. The government's main weapon in attacking the clergy was to reduce its numerical strength. For instance, in Mexico City, with a population of 1,029,000, at least 80 per cent Catholic, only about 25 priests are allowed—a manifest injustice to worshipers.

The story of the Mexican church dispute is gnarled and bitter. I give only the bare essential points. Church property was in theory nationalized in 1857, but the churches themselves were untouched. Under Díaz there came a strong clerical reaction; then the 1911 revolutionists sought to swing the clock back to Juárez, and the 1917 constitution provided for state control of education. No government dared to pass any serious enabling legislation, but the Church, affronted and fearful, refused to accept the constitution.

Then came the Calles period. This doughty President attacked the Church not merely from religious but from political motives; he knew that the Church was his foremost and implacable enemy. A fierce crisis rose. The fundamental question was whether Calles or the Church should hold effective political power over the nation. The Archbishop of Mexico City continued to reject the constitution, and Calles retaliated by putting stiff anticlerical laws into force. Priests, for instance, were forbidden any religious activity unless they registered with the government. The Church replied by going on strike, as it were; all the churches in Mexico shut down. Rebellions of fanatic Catholics, the Cristeros, had to be suppressed by force. Churches were burned and priests and nuns murdered. A compromise settlement—largely fostered by American ambassador Dwight Morrow—came in 1929. The government did not repeal its laws, and the priests finally consented to register. But in general restrictions against the Church were relaxed. People resumed going to mass.

Now, eleven years later, echoes of the conflict still rumble, but it has ceased to be a major issue. Cárdenas was responsible for much amelioration, and Avila Camacho promises to continue it.

Sketched in Petroleum[11]

The oil dispute, like the church conflict, is no longer considered by most Mexicans to be a really vital controversy. But it demands brief mention, if only because the 1938 expropriation of United States and British oil properties is the most drastic step yet taken by any Latin American government against private foreign interests. Basically the struggle for power was analogous to that in the quarrel over the Church: namely, who was boss in Mexico, the government or someone else.

The issue has roots far back. The great oil interests—especially the British-controlled Mexican Eagle Company, which controlled about 70 per cent of the nation's production—began commercial exploitation of oil early this century. The companies grew to have their own towns, their own armies; they were states within a state. They pumped millions of barrels of oil out of Mexico; yet during the Díaz period and until about 1917, they never paid one cent of royalty or even taxes to the Mexican government. They got their oil absolutely free. After 1917 the royalty was only 5 per cent.

This produced a passionate and understandable resentment among Mexicans. The revolutionists got busy, and the new constitution of 1917, as I have noted, nationalized the land and subsoil of the country. The companies were forced to reorganize, to pay more royalty, and, under Calles later, to accept "confirmatory

[11] For the background of this section I am largely indebted to Mr. Harry Block.

concessions." These provided that the basic ownership of Mexican oil was inalienably vested in the nation, and that concessions could be given only to Mexican citizens or to foreigners who agreed not to invoke the protection of their governments. All but 22 out of the 606 oil companies then operating in Mexico accepted the Calles laws—but with mounting bitterness. And these 22 controlled the bulk of production.

In 1937 the Mexican government, under Cárdenas, launched a full-dress investigation of the petroleum industry, as provided for by the labor law. Strikes flared up in the oil fields; tension crackled. The workers demanded better wages, better living conditions, and confirmation of their right of collective contract. The commission of investigation submitted its report to the Mexican Labor Board. It stated that the companies had earned average annual profits of 56,000,000 pesos for the previous three years, which represented a return of 17 per cent on the total fixed invested capital; that the cost of living in the oil zones had increased 89 per cent since 1934; and that the companies should forthwith increase their payment of wages and social benefits by 26,000,000 pesos ($7,200,000) per year. These recommendations were accepted by the Mexican government and upheld by the Supreme Court, and the oil companies were required to submit to them. A deadline was set for March 7, 1938.

The oil companies, their backs to the wall, protested fiercely and then began to bargain. They contested the Mexican figures—they still do—but they renewed an offer to pay 13,000,000 pesos (one half of what the Mexican government asked) in workers' benefits. President Cárdenas held a long series of conferences in a stormy atmosphere. People crowded the streets. The Mexicans claimed that the oil companies behaved in a manner unbecoming to the dignity of the nation. Cárdenas sent a message: "Tell the American ambassador that if our petroleum is an obstacle to the conservation of our national dignity, we will burn the oil wells." He said this when his colleagues were alarmed at what the United States might do.

On March 18—the deadline had been delayed—the companies agreed finally to pay the 26,000,000 pesos demanded, but they rejected stipulations about participation by labor in management of the industry. They refused a personal guarantee by Cárdenas that the additional wages would not exceed the 26,000,000 pesos named, which they feared was merely a taste of more to come. Cárdenas thereupon took the final irrevocable step. Citing authority from a 1936 Act that implemented Article 27 of the constitution, he decreed the expropriation of the companies, and nationalized their property.[12]

The reaction in the United States was, on the whole, not too severe. The oil companies got some backing from Washington, but not as much as they hoped for, though the U. S. Treasury stopped buying Mexican silver for a time. Mr. Hull said forthrightly that the United States did not question the right of the Mexican government to expropriate foreign property, but that it earnestly hoped and asked that fair compensation would be paid. Since that date at least one important expropriated company, Consolidated Oil (owned by the Sinclair interests), has accepted Mexican terms and is being paid back, partly in oil. Mexico agreed to give Sinclair $8,500,000 for his property, and Sinclair has stated that "all the terms of the contract have been scrupulously complied with." (New York *Herald Tribune*, January 5, 1941.)

But the British government protested vigorously and officially, and threatened retaliation in the form of British boycott of Mexican oil. The Mexican government claimed that Mexican Eagle was a corporation bound by local law, and that the British government had no right to interfere. Came a squabble over minor British claims of damages, not related to the oil dispute, dating from the revolution. Mexico paid up, asserting tartly that it

---

[12] Not all the companies were expropriated. In fact, only 17 were named in the decree. The Gulf-Mellon interests were, for instance, unaffected. But the expropriation included all the other dominant companies, especially Mexican Eagle (controlled by Royal Dutch Shell) and Standard of New Jersey.

always paid its bills, whereas the British had canceled payments on their war debt to the United States. The Mexicans withdrew their minister from London, and the British broke off diplomatic relations. Full relations are still—in the summer of 1941—suspended; the British have no minister in Mexico City, nor has Mexico in London.

After expropriation Mexican oil went through hard times. The Mexicans paid severely for their boldness. The expropriated companies refused, perhaps naturally, to buy Mexican oil, and markets dwindled. The oil accumulated, and Mexico had neither storage facilities nor tankers to handle it. So began a series of barter deals with Germany and later Japan. The war came, which cut off Mexican oil further. The industry might have collapsed had it not been for the rapidly expanding domestic Mexican market; in any case it suffered stringently. Threats of strikes and labor trouble continued, and in the spring of 1941 it was laboring under a huge deficit.

The American attitude to the expropriation marked a milestone in the development of hemisphere relations. Everywhere in Latin America it was considered a kind of hallmark of American sincerity in the Good Neighbor policy. We did *not* send marines to protect Standard Oil and the investments and dividends of American citizens. So, said people all the way from Havana to Tierra del Fuego, we really must be meaning what we say.

Late in August, 1941, just as this book goes to press, negotiations between Mexico, the State Department, and the companies for a settlement of the oil dispute seemed near completion. Mexico, it is thought, will make a token payment to the companies, and will receive a credit from the Export-Import bank for defense needs.

"At length Corruption, like a General Flood . . ."

Former President Cárdenas is reported to have said sadly once, "Whenever I put my hand in a basket I pull out a thief."

Let no one think that political corruption is anything peculiarly

Mexican. Reflect merely on the Harding administration in Washington and the case of Secretary Fall and Teapot Dome. Nor is corruption in Mexico more flagrant than it has been in China, say, or France—not to mention other Latin American states. There are countries in this hemisphere beside which Mexico is pale with virtue.

But graft or *mordida*—literally, "the bite"—plays a role in Mexican affairs. Partly it is an inheritance from colonial days, when you had to pay for all favors, political and otherwise. An interview with Díaz cost 3,000 pesos, Parkes' *History of Mexico* says. For years any provincial general who did not amass a fortune—by gouging it out of the peons—was considered not merely a fool, but crazy. A general would contrive—by giving favors—to get the concession, say, for building a new road. His troops would provide free labor; he would pad the bills enormously; he could graft hand over fist. About one candidate in a recent election the people cynically say, "By all means let him win, because he *already* has his fortune."

Many honest Presidents, like Cárdenas and Avila Camacho, hate corruption; they do what they can to stamp it out. But their hands are tied, because they must permit their subordinates some liberty of financial action, in order to *insure their loyalty*. This is very Chinese.

So many reasons exist for corruption that one can scarcely list them. First, poverty. A policeman gets 2.75 pesos (55 cents) a day—and as often as not must pay the sergeant for his job. Second, the lack of a permanent civil service. The middle class hardly exists, and almost the only way to get rich is to enter politics. Third, the tradition that Mexican politicians may serve only one term at a time. The reason for this was, of course, to prevent undue concentration of power, but its result is that the politicians grab all they can while the grabbing is good.

One Mexican friend explained to me vividly the difference between "honest" and "dishonest" graft. The honest grafter is one who cultivates his field, or office, or province, with some regard to the common benefit. All he takes is a reasonable share, as a kind of bonus for his managerial talent. The "dishonest" grafter takes everything he can get, and so destroys that on which he—as well as other folk—should feed.

One thing I noticed: almost every person I met in Mexico was uncomfortable as soon as the question of money came up.

What Mexico Needs

I asked four eminent Mexicans of different professions what the country needed most.

One was a musician. He answered, "Education and public health."

One, a professional soldier, said, "Steadfastness and organization."

The third was a high ranking jurist. He answered, "More sense of responsibility in public men."

The fourth was an ex-President of the republic. He said, "Capital, technicians, education, and hard work."

Chapter V

Cárdenas Days and Years

GENERAL LÁZARO CÁRDENAS Y DEL RÍO, about whom I have talked much in these pages, is out of office now. But the character and career of this most remarkable Mexican of modern times deserve further word.

Cárdenas is shaped something like a top—an enormous round chest tapers to a less conspicuous waist and slender hips. His hair is jet black, his eyes a pure olive green. He has thick red lips, from which comes his nickname—the Trumpeter. His manners are infinitely polite and gracious. He sits on the very edge of his chair, and—a curious point—keeps his small feet on tiptoe. He is very seldom angry; when he does lose his temper, his face flushes darkly, he remains absolutely silent for a moment, and then speaks in a strained, subdued voice.

His physical endurance is enormous, and he drives his secretaries crazy. They are afraid to sleep—especially when they are on the road with him—because they know he will be off at three or four in the morning, and they seldom know where he's going. He cannot stand to remain long in town; he is possessed by a necessity to be *close* to the people. He drinks mildly—a little beer in the evening—but never smokes. His appetites are healthy and normal. He takes no exercise. He seldom reads. His handwriting is close-packed, decisive, and illegible. His married life has been happy. His son, aged 10—who has an American tutoress—is named for the last Aztec emperor, Cuauhtémoc.

He lives entirely without ostentation, and even when he was President he almost never attended official functions. His caretaker in his Michoacán house is his former barber. When, as President, he lived at Los Pinos, the small lodge near Chapultepec Castle, he liked to point to his swimming pool. "It is my most economical investment," he would say. "I ask my guests to join me in a dip at 6 A.M., and no one ever accepts a second invitation to visit me."

He likes best to live at Eréndira, his property at Pátzcuaro, in the Tarascan province, Michoacán. Here he feels really at home; he has a small boat, and he loves to cruise on the high frigid waters of the lake. The house is named for a heroine in Tarascan legend; the Tarascans were a hardy tribe never conquered by the Aztecs. Cárdenas likes to saunter into the village, put up at a wonderful old hotel called the Ocampo, and eat his favorite native dishes—a kind of pork cooked with chilis, *chicharrón* (crisp pig's skin broiled until the fat disappears) and *chilaquiles*, a humble dish of tortillas diced and cooked with chili sauce.

A man of the camp, he has many friends, but if you ask five different people who are those closest to him, you get widely different answers. Almost everyone would include the Beteta brothers, Ramón, who is now Undersecretary of Finance, and Ignacio, who was the chief of his military staff; his chief private secretary, Agustín Leñero; the Mexican ambassador to Washington, D. Castillo Nájera; General Miguel Henríquez, a splendid officer who helped his campaigns greatly; and a former head of the labor department, Agustín Arroyo.

When I saw General Cárdenas—just before he gave up the presidency—the thing that impressed me most was his profound simplicity. He was almost naive. He does not often give interviews; in fact, he was the most elusive head of state I ever pursued. I should not have been able to see him at all except for the courteous help of Dr. Castillo Nájera and other friends. When finally I was received in the President's room in the National Palace, with its glossy floors and green leather chairs and the huge map of Mexico at one end, I found that Cárdenas was interviewing me, not vice versa.

He disconnected his two telephones to prevent interruptions, and then talked about the coming administration and his work for the land and the peasants. When I had asked my questions he said politely, *"¿Terminado?"* and I rose to go. But he mo-

tioned me to remain, and then went on to ask questions for half
an hour—about the presidential campaign in the United States,
about problems of American labor, about Japan's attitude to the
war in Europe, about agrarian problems in the Philippines. His
knowledge of world affairs was discerning. When I left, he said,
"You are young. Do good work for the world."

General Cárdenas was born in a village called Jiquilpán, in the
province of Michoacán, on April 21, 1897. His father was a
shopkeeper, a full-blooded Tarascan Indian, who died young. The
Cárdenas family was grindingly poor. Young Lázaro had a few
years of elementary education, and then set out to earn a living.
He worked in a printer's shop for a time, and picked up a few
pesos as assistant to the village jailer. Came the revolution. Young
Lázaro joined up—and took his solitary prisoner with him, the
legend says. This was in 1914, when he was 17.

His military career was rapid and fairly distinguished, though
he was never an inspired officer like his chief, General Obregón.
By 1920 he was a colonel, and by 1924, when the civil wars were
over, a general of brigade. Like all Mexican generals he was a
politician, but his honesty and powerful civic sense made him an
unusual type. Very unusual. He was an odd fellow, this big
Indian.

Once when he was stationed in the Tampico district an oil-
company go-between reputedly handed him an envelope contain-
ing 25,000 pesos, explaining that this was always given to the
local general for "protecting the properties." Cárdenas refused
the bribe, saying that the oil belonged to the people of Mexico—
and has hated the oil companies ever since. Once, after helping
to defeat the Escobar rebellion against Calles, he returned to the
military authorities 93,000 out of the 100,000 pesos that had been
given him for expenses of the campaign.[1] Other generals thought
him a simpleton—if they could bear to think.

[1] *The Reconquest of Mexico.* By Nathaniel and Sylvia Weyl, p. 94.

But Calles admired him, and his career advanced. He became successively governor of Michoacán, president of the National Revolutionary party (which he later transformed into the present P.R.M.) and Minister of the Interior. Then Calles picked him to be President of the Republic because he thought this unassuming and competent officer would do a good routine job without daring to threaten his own position behind the scenes. Calles had been *jefe máximo* (supreme chief) for ten years.

Calles got fooled. Within a year Cárdenas smoothly, gravely, quietly, threw him out. He performed this miracle by saying with conviction and authority, "*I* am the President of Mexico, and I intend to maintain the position the constitution gives me." He added, "I don't think the Congress will refuse support to any President who fulfills his obligations in good faith." The "simpleton" again!—who knew just what he was doing.

Then steadily Cárdenas gathered the reins of power in his own hands. His reforms—especially land distribution—got under way. The C.T.M. helped him greatly. Twice he had to squash rebellions, one made by the anticlerical Red Shirts of General Garrido Canábal in Tabasco, the other from the Right (the revolt of the reactionary General Cedillo in the north). Calles watched from California. He was too fatigued—and perhaps too patriotic in a way —to interfere.

Of the Cárdenas qualities and sources of power one may mention several. First is his instinctive kinship with the common people, and the way his aims, his ideals, have expressed the inarticulate aspiration of the Indian masses. Cárdenas is never so happy as when he sits on his haunches along a roadside, talking with the peasants for long hours. His travels in Mexico have been epochal, like those of Mr. Gandhi—whom he in some respects resembles—in India. When he was nominated for President in 1934, no one thought he would make an extensive campaign, since his election was assured by the backing of the government machine. But he set out and visited thousands of villages in all the 33 Mexican states. Probably he has seen more of Mexico with his own eyes than any other living Mexican.

He likes to travel alone, except for one aide-de-camp and a chauffeur. He never carries arms. Once, visiting Guadalajara a few years ago, he all but gave the local governor a nervous breakdown. He refused any escort, and thousands of Indians came in from the countryside to see him. The President of the Republic would sit on the curb, alone, unguarded, hearing complaints, adjusting grievances, listening. He once told Waldo Frank, "It is important that the people know I come among them without fear."

Once, when he was traveling in the north, someone fired at the olive presidential train. Cárdenas asked that the train be stopped and backed into the station. He got off, alone, unarmed, and walked into the station yard, to ask who had done the shooting, and why.

Recently Dr. W. Cameron Townsend, the head of the Indian language school in Morelos, heard steps at the door. There was Cárdenas and his young son. They had come unexpected and unannounced. Informally they spent the day together. Cárdenas sat in the front seat of Townsend's modest automobile and looked at the orange groves and water supply that his administration had given the village.

One of the defects sometimes noted in Cárdenas may derive from *too* close association with the Indians, *too* intimate an identification of his own career with theirs—that is, a certain groping quality, a certain naive tendency to rely purely on intuition rather than calculation, in tackling administrative problems.

Another quality that Cárdenas possessed as President—and still possesses—is, as is clear, his moral sense. His policies were more revolutionary than those of any President since Juárez; he touched thousands of people in that very sensitive spot, the pocketbook; yet he was never threatened or molested. One reason is that almost everyone conceded his absolute integrity and sense of justice.

Some years ago he dedicated a monument to Father Morelos near Cuernavaca. He noted the inscription, "To raise the moral standard of men is the greatest problem of nations." He was so impressed by this that he copied it on his country house at Palmira—a house which he subsequently gave to the nation as an agricultural school.

In Sonora a general once remonstrated with him for his incessant attention to detail, his 16-hour working day. The general said, "Don't wear yourself out. Tomorrow is another day. And tomorrow everyone will forget what you have done today." Cárdenas replied sternly, "The duty of a public official is to serve the people in every way he can, with no thought of reward, without even thought of appreciation."[2]

He hates cruelty and bloodshed. In his six years of office not one political execution took place, a record unique in Mexico. When General Cedillo was shot (on the field of battle) the officer who killed this troublesome rebel proudly asked for promotion. But Cárdenas was horrified at Cedillo's death, and he demoted the officer.

Another quality Cárdenas possesses is great peasant shrewdness. He seldom directly refuses anything to anybody. Nor does he ever attack anyone openly if he can possibly help it. During the 1940 election campaign he scrupulously avoided any disparagement of Almazán (who was one of his old comrades-in-arms) or of his supporters. On one occasion the Almazanistas issued a savage chapter-and-verse attack on Cárdenas' brother Dámaso, accusing

[2] One expression of Cárdenas' moral sense was a hatred of gambling; more than one prominent politician got rich on gambling concessions, and the poor— some of the rich too—were perpetually being fleeced. In older days big officials often recouped their losses out of the federal treasury! Cárdenas forbade all gambling in Mexico, even card playing in clubs and private homes. Of course the law was not strictly enforced.

him of corruption. The Mexico City newspapers didn't dare print this, whereupon Cárdenas calmly told them that they should do so.

Once a delegation of villagers accosted him when he was inspecting the Laredo highway near Tasquillo. They asked that the road be moved ten miles so that they would have the use of it. Mockingly Cárdenas remarked, "So you want the outside world to see your unkempt doorsteps, your dirty bedraggled streets . . . ?" The village elders swore that they would compel the citizenry to improve their habits. Cárdenas rejoined: "No. Do not compel. Simply persuade."

One story is that Cárdenas was so subtle-minded that he permitted Trotsky to come to Mexico merely in order to prove that he, Cárdenas, was not—as people were saying loosely at that time—a Stalinist! The allegation was ridiculous enough. Mexico broke off relations with the Soviet Union in 1929, and they have never been resumed.

As to defects, he had—and has—several, like most men in great positions. He knew he had only six years, and he tried to do things too fast. He never cared for problems of administration—he spent at least two-thirds of his time out of Mexico City—and he hated to delegate responsibility. He wanted to do everything himself—and much of the time his own entourage couldn't find him. He was secretive and vain (though perhaps not so much for himself as for the Mexican people) and he thought that he alone could adjust the grievances of 20,000,000 Mexicans. He perplexed his admirers by permitting equivocal responsibility in various departments; he liked to have *two* men in charge of each separate show. This was caused partly by his hatred of bureaucratic rigidity, partly by his deep inner belief that the best man would come out on top. Finally (like President Roosevelt) he was far too tolerant. He hated to get rid of friends even if they were manifestly incompetent.

His accomplishments—quite aside from the land reform, which is the most important of them—will, nevertheless, live in Mexican history.

First, he gave Mexico political stability and order of a kind not seen since Díaz, without any infringement whatever on civil liberties. There were no political prisoners, no suppressions of free speech, under Cárdenas. Associated with this was the new value on human life his regime inspired. Mexico had swarmed with bloodshed for savage year after savage year. Under Cárdenas, killing stopped.

Second, his education and public works program brought roads, schools, water supply, sanitation, to thousands of villages. He built more schools than all governments since 1911 combined. Coupled with this came a gradual elevation in the standard of living. More people began to drink beer instead of pulque, to wear blue overalls instead of cotton shirts, to wear shoes or sandals instead of going barefoot.

Third, he helped reduce the power of the army (as had Calles) by breaking up the old provincial armies and transferring recruits and troops from one part of Mexico to another. I heard it said that he had so shaken up the army—most of the higher officers disliked him—that no single general was sure of the support of more than two or three hundred men.

Above all, he gave the Mexican people a sense of national participation in affairs. He sought strenuously to uplift the masses, so that *they* could henceforth keep power, and themselves check the inroads of plunder and reaction.

The present situation—in the summer of 1941—is that Cárdenas has completely lived up to his promise to retire from politics. He has not made a single speech since his retirement from the presidency in December 1940, nor a single public appearance in Mexico City. President Avila Camacho, as I have indicated in Chapter III, has retained many Cárdenas men in the new administration. But Cárdenas himself is absolutely out.

This must be a wrench to him, since so much of his own work was incomplete, so much merely sketched out. Probably he hated intensely to leave office . . . But he felt with profound conviction that he must give the people an authentic example of democracy in practice, that he must set a precedent for the future by unconditional voluntary retirement.

Nevertheless, Lázaro Cárdenas remains the most important living Mexican.

Chapter VI
Mexicans Left and Right

~~~~~~

VICENTE LOMBARDO TOLEDANO, for years the boss of Mexican labor, wiry, handsome, magnetic, looks younger than his 47 years. He has dark tufts of hair jutting over his ears like Mephistopheles, and a sharp, businesslike, fast-working mind. He has been called "hot-eyed," of "diseased vanity," and suffering from "lack of balance." But none of these alleged characteristics appears when he receives the casual visitor.

Lombardo, who was born in Teziutlán (the same Puebla village that saw the birth of Avila Camacho) of partly Italian stock, is one of the most vivid personalities in Mexico. He came into the labor movement through a consuming interest in workers' education. He is no horny-handed workman himself, but a student, a teacher, an intellectual. He took a degree in law, taught law, and then became director of the National Preparatory School in Mexico City. He traveled widely—for a time he was a delegate to the International Labor Office in Geneva—and wrote several books, one a history of trade unionism in Mexico, one on the Indian languages of the Puebla district.

Do not think that this professor, this intellectual, this specialist in labor theory, is a dry-as-dust theoretician. Far from it. Lombardo is the best orator in Mexico, a first-class organizer, and as aggressive as any politician on the continent. For relaxation he goes hunting, and likes to shoot bear and ocelot. Like Cárdenas, with whom he has been closely associated, he is a tremendously hard worker, and frequently he puts in a 15- or 16-hour day. His offices are managed with efficiency and dispatch. When I called on him. I was unavoidably a few minutes late, and I was rebuked with a friendly—but pointed—glance at the clock.

I saw Lombardo during the 1940 election campaign, and like all Mexicans of the Left he was worried that Avila Camacho was going Right. But the C.T.M. did not attack Avila Camacho, because they preferred him to Almazán; nor did Camacho attack the C.T.M., because he needed Left support. Lombardo told me that Mexico in long perspective faced three great problems : (1) land reform, (2) education, (3) termination of foreign "imperialism." I asked him what kind of Mexico he wanted. He replied, "A democratic socialist state."

Lombardo Toledano founded the C.T.M. (*Confederación de Trabajadores de México*) in 1936. Roughly it resembles the C.I.O. in the United States, and with its close-knit organization and 450,000 dues-paying members it is by far the most powerful labor federation in Latin America. Technically it is affiliated with the Second Socialist International of Amsterdam. But many communists have filtered into it—as they have filtered into the C.I.O.— though they do not dominate it by any means. Lombardo himself is not a communist, but for years he stood for the Popular Front, and sometimes he runs parallel to the party line.

When war broke out in Europe in 1939, Lombardo, the C.T.M., and the socialist newspaper *El Popular* (edited by an American-educated socialist, Alejandro Carrillo) termed it an "imperialist" struggle and called for Mexican neutrality. But Lombardo said also that the working classes must aim to defeat Fascism, and that if the United States entered the war, Mexico would have to do likewise, in order to help check the Nazi threat to the American continent. Later the C.T.M., which swallowed the Nazi-Soviet pact and had customarily been anti-British and at times anti-American, became friendlier to the democracies. Communist influence began to wane. In March 1941 came an important seven-page statement of policy. The C.T.M. condemned the Axis, warned Mexico against Fifth Columnism, and approved whole-hearted co-operation with the United States.

Lombardo finished his term as secretary general of the C.T.M. early in 1941, and, following the Mexican one-term-at-a-time tradition, promptly retired. He remains, however, head of another organization, the Confederation of Latin American Workers, which has international aims. So far it has accomplished little, because trade unionism is so backward in the other hemisphere states. Lombardo also retains directorship of the project closest to his heart, the Workers' University in Mexico City. Here between four and five hundred students learn history, economics, and so on, for a fee of one peso (20 cents) a year.

Lombardo was succeeded as boss of the C.T.M. by Fidel Velázquez, who is more moderate. Velázquez is a veteran labor organizer, a tough *hombre*, and a middle-of-the-roader. He rose from the ranks.

Another trade union exists in Mexico, the C.R.O.M. (*Confederación Regional Obrera Mexicana*), which claims 125,000 members but probably does not have nearly so many. This is the Rightist union; it corresponds roughly to the A.F. of L., and is led by Luis Morones, once a father of the Mexican labor movement, now become rich and conservative.[1] The C.R.O.M. supported Almazán, and is nowadays without real power. The C.T.M. controls 99 per cent of the sugar workers, 95 per cent of railway and petroleum workers; probably 90 per cent of folk in the *ejidos* sympathize with it. The C.R.O.M., on its side, holds little aside from a few textile mills in Veracruz and Puebla, and the leadership is split.

The communist party is legal in Mexico—one of the few states in Latin America where this is true. But only one important union leader is a communist, the secretary general of the railway workers' union, which incidentally—paradox!—is probably the most conservative union in the country. There are no communists on the national executive of the C.T.M. Two events helped to shatter the Mexican communist party: the Russo-German pact and the Soviet invasion of Finland. The communist leader is Dionisio Encina, a hard-boiled workers' man, who was a peasant from the Laguna district and has had many years in the party.

The question, "How Left is Mexico?" is not easy to answer

---

[1] A popular joke is that C.R.O.M. really stands for *"COMO ROBA ORO MORONES"* ("How Morones Steals Gold!").

categorically. Certainly "socialism" in Mexico, in so far as it exists, does not remotely resemble the Marxism of the textbooks. No official socialist party exists, and Mexican "socialism" is largely a program of agrarian reform—cutting up the big estates into collectively worked *ejidos*—plus the oil expropriation, plus a certain amount of government control of other industries, plus very advanced labor legislation. One might list manifestations of collectivism as follows:

1. About 30 per cent of sugar production is controlled by labor, including the great mill at Zacatepec, which, one of the most modern in the Americas, was built as a government project and then turned over to the workers.

2. Big agrarian collectives like those in the Imperial Valley of Lower California (cotton and wheat), the Yaqui Valley in Sonora (wheat and rice), Lombardía and Nueva Italia in Michoacán (rice and fruit), Yucatán (henequen), and especially Laguna.

3. Workers' participation in—but not control of—the oil industry. Ditto railways, which are a complicated story. The National Railways (not the privately owned line which is controlled by British capital) were nationalized, however, by Díaz, not by the revolution. The railways are, as we know, virtually bankrupt.

4. Government control of such institutions as the Central Bank of Mexico, the telegraphs (but not the telephones), and the ubiquitous and charity-supporting lotteries.

No Mexican government has yet come to grips with the problem of the mines, which represent an enormous share of the country's wealth, and which are mostly American-owned. The socialist attitude to mining is that it is much wiser to tax production than to nationalize the industry, since Mexico—"a semi-colonial nation"—does not control the markets. Why expropriate copper, if you can't sell it? The socialists deny hotly that they believe in expropriation.

Mexican living standards are very low, but higher than in several other Latin American states. A rural schoolteacher gets anywhere from 1 peso (roughly 20 cents) to 4 pesos a day. A street-car conductor gets 4 pesos, and a senior official in the telegraph office about 20. A saleswoman in a shop is lucky with 75 pesos a month. The general average for industrial workers is 3 to 3.50 pesos a day; for peasants on the land, 50 centavos or about 10 cents. No wonder Mexicans are poor!

The Avila Camacho Cabinet

The most powerful minister in President Avila Camacho's administration is probably Miguel Alemán, the Minister of *Gobernación* (roughly, Interior). Alemán is the Ed Flynn of contemporary Mexican politics, the party fixer, the boss of the government machine. Alert, smooth, friendly, he had more to do with engineering Camacho's election than any other man.

He was born—probably in 1902—in Sayula near Veracruz. I say "probably," because, as is common elsewhere in Latin America, he is not sure of his own birth date, and secretaries in his ministry give several different dates. His father was a distinguished general, who was one of the first provincial officers to join the revolt against Díaz. The father was killed, and young Miguel was brought up by a man named Cándido Aguilar, a son-in-law of Carranza who incidentally once saved Cárdenas from death. Miguel studied law at the National University, became interested in labor cases, was named a judge, and entered politics. He became governor of the important state of Veracruz when he was only 35. People called him "Miguelito," and voted for him as the son of his famous father.

Alemán's record as governor was exceptionally good. He pushed road building and, his friends say, spent 49 per cent of the state budget on education. Cárdenas liked him, and it was on Alemán's initiative that the governors of all Mexican states met in the capital shortly after the oil expropriation, to declare their solidarity with the President. Alemán became chairman of a so-called "union of governors." Then, energetic and efficient, he began to back Avila Camacho's candidacy, and got 22 governors out of 33 to join him. Later he pulled strings with the C.T.M., since he was known as a friend of labor.

As Minister of the Interior, Alemán is directly responsible for all anti-Fifth Column work in Mexico. His relations with the American embassy are close and cordial, and he is generally ticketed as a strong friend of the United States. He understands and reads English, but hates to speak it. He knows a good deal about American history, and says that both Jefferson and Hamilton are his heroes. One of his favorite books, incidentally, is *Contre l'Un*, by the Frenchman Etienne de la Boetie, which was an answer to Machiavelli's *Prince*.

Avila Camacho's Foreign Minister, Dr. Ezequiel Padilla, is a lawyer with an old revolutionary record. No one would think, to look at him now—suave, carefully groomed, quiet-voiced, handsome—that he fought with both Zapata and Villa, the two fiercest rebels in Mexican history.

Padilla, with Guerrero blood in his veins, was born in 1890; his scholastic record was so good that he won a scholarship to the Sorbonne; then he studied international law at Columbia. He has been much influenced by his associations in the United States, where he spent some years in exile. On his return to Mexico in 1922 he became a professor of law and entered politics. He has been a deputy, a senator, Attorney General, Secretary of Education, and minister to Italy. He found time to write several books, to learn to play golf, to become a friend of Portes Gil, to raise a family, to follow world politics closely, and to admire Beethoven. He campaigned vigorously for Avila Camacho, and then became his Foreign Secretary. Like so many Mexicans, he began his career on the revolutionary side and has gradually become more and more conservative, though he is not a reactionary.

The Foreign Minister, who is tall and with a powerful physique, works a good hard day. He is in his office by nine, as a rule, which is early for Mexico; he returns home for luncheon, the main meal of the day, with his family, as is typical of the country; he is back at the office late in the afternoon, and works into the evening. He relaxes with movies—which he likes to show at home—and with his handsome collection of phonograph records. The American he admires most is John Marshall. He speaks correct but rather stiff English in a slow, measured voice.

On January 14, 1941, Padilla told a press conference that Mexico would consider any act of aggression against any country in the Americas as an act of aggression against Mexico itself. He followed this on March 7 by a speech confirming his complete willingness to co-operate with the United States in matters of defense. He even hinted that a military alliance between Mexico and the United States was possible.

Dr. Padilla's predecessor as Foreign Minister was that fine old gentleman, General Eduardo Hay. General Hay, who was a civil engineer until he became chief of staff to Madero in 1911, has been wounded fourteen times; he is of Scottish descent and looks like a British sportsman; he learned to speak Japanese when he was Mexican consul general in Tokyo; he is one of the most engaging personalities in Mexico. Once he said to me, "What we worry about here is the sixth column, not the fifth. The sixth column is the one that thinks the fifth really exists."

A very important cabinet minister is Eduardo Suárez, the Secretary of *Hacienda* (Treasury), who held the same job under Cárdenas. Suárez smokes innumerable cigarettes from a long black holder, likes an occasional drink of cognac, walks on tiptoe as a rule, plays billiards brilliantly, works at night, and looks like Groucho Marx. He is of Jewish descent.

Suárez, who was born in Texcoco about 45 years ago, has had a lively and industrious career in politics. He was a professor of law for a time—the number of Latin American politicians who have been professors of law is inexhaustible—and then a magistrate, the legal counselor to the Treasury and the Foreign Office, a delegate to various conferences abroad, a member of the United States-Mexican Claims Commission, head of the Mexican delegation to the Havana conference, a director of the National Bank, chairman both of the Petroleum and Railways administrations, and finally Minister of Finance. He was very close to Cárdenas, and was so good at his job—in fact indispensable—that Avila Camacho kept him on.

Suárez speaks English well, and is emphatically pro-American.

General Heriberto Jara (pronounced "Hara"), who was the head of the P.R.M. under Cárdenas and is now Minister of Marine, is the oldest man in the cabinet—he was born in Veracruz about 1876—and is arch-typical of the old revolutionary tradition. Of Indian origin, he started life as a bookkeeper; then he joined the Madero revolution and fought with Carranza. He was successively a deputy, minister to Cuba, governor of the unruly state Tabasco, senator from Veracruz, and director of military education.

His nickname is *El Volcán*, the volcano. This is partly because he has a good sound temper, partly because his dazzlingly white hair crowning a leathery brown face looks like snow on a mountain. Also, his enemies say, he spouts hot air. General Jara is on good terms with the military and naval officials of the American Embassy. His attitude to the United States, so far as is known, has always been very friendly.

Another outstanding cabinet officer is Marte R. Gómez, the 50-year-old Secretary of Agriculture. Gómez, a native of the northern state, Tamaulipas, is an agricultural engineer by profession; he became close to Portes Gil, and served under him as Secretary of the Treasury; a stocky man with short cropped hair and heavy glasses, he is active, intelligent, ambitious. When Vice-President Wallace came to Mexico, he probably saw more of him than any other Mexican; they had a common absorbing interest in agricultural problems, and Gómez escorted him on various trips. Gómez, who is high in Avila Camacho's favor, is a right-winger on the whole.

Dr. Gustavo Baz, the Minister of Public Assistance, is one of

Mexico's foremost surgeons. It was he who operated on Trotsky in a vain attempt to save his life. Dr. Baz, who was rector of the National University under Cárdenas, began his career as a guerilla fighter with Zapata. Then he turned to medicine, and though like all Mexican intellectuals he was deeply interested in politics, for many years his career was occupied with medicine and surgery. He is a fellow of various American medical societies, and is well known in the United States. He is 45, slight of build, serious-minded. His influence on the President—on the conservative side—is very strong.

Another Rightist is Dr. Víctor Fernández Manero, the chief of the Federal Department of Health. He is also a doctor of medicine, and was not only one of Avila Camacho's personal physicians but also treasurer of his campaign. Dr. Fernández professes to be friendly to the United States, but Leftists accuse him of pro-Fascist sympathies. One incident particularly annoyed the Left. A notorious agitator and anti-Semite, Adolfo Leon Ossorio, was recently arrested for having thrown stink bombs in theaters showing anti-Nazi films. Ossorio, from several points of view, had a thoroughly unsavory record. But it was Dr. Manero who helped get him out of jail.

In contrast, Ignacio García Téllez, the Minister of Labor, is very much on the Left. He is a holdover from the Cárdenas administration, in which he was a leading spirit; many Camachistas resented the inclusion of so distinct a Leftist—he has been called a "communist" and all that—in the new government. García Téllez was one of Cárdenas' ablest assistants, though he looks like a dreamer, with his wild unruly hair, his slim delicate hands. He is about 42. He has been Secretary of Education, secretary general of the P.R.M., Attorney General, and rector of the university. It seems that practically every leading Mexican politician has at one time or other been rector of that university.

Another Leftist in the cabinet is Dr. Luis Sánchez Pontón, the Minister of Education. A quiet, well-educated, nonassertive individual, he has been governor of Puebla, but until 1940 he never held an important federal post. Sánchez Pontón has been sharply criticized by the Right for his socialist sympathies. His chief interest is—as it should be—education. He is—unlike some Leftists—intensely pro-United States.

Francisco Xavier Gaxiola, the Minister of National Economy, is a protégé of former President Abelardo Rodríguez. He is handsome, scholarly, silver-gray-haired man in his middle forties, with a good record in law and business and wide popularity with Rightists in the American colony. He has written several books on economics, and knows French and English well.

Beteta and Villaseñor

No gallery of Mexican political personalities would be complete without inclusion of these two men, who are among the most intelligent and attractive in the country, though neither has a cabinet post.

Shrewd, subtle, with an infinitely refined and complex intelligence, Ramón Beteta, who was the brains of the Foreign Office under Cárdenas, has been shunted off to the less conspicuous post of Undersecretary of the Treasury. Frequently Beteta is called anti-American. My impression is that, if this is true, it is a matter of mood and emotion, not of policy. Beteta may dislike some things American—for instance, he may still harbor resentments from student days at the University of Texas, where Mexican boys of the highest breeding were often barbarously snubbed—but he is far too intelligent to pursue a willful anti-American course in political affairs.

Once an automobile siren shrieked through the window while I was talking to him in the Foreign Ministry. It drowned out the conversation. Beteta smiled with pleasant irony: "Let us pause till this example of the Americanization of Mexico disappears."

Of Basque descent, Ramón Beteta was born in Mexico City in 1901. He went to the National University, then to Texas. His wife is a Texan girl. He became a civil servant, and was Director

General of the Department of Statistics. He worshipped Cárdenas, and was largely responsible for carrying out the Cárdenas policies when he was Undersecretary of Foreign Affairs. Beteta has traveled a good deal, and has several times lectured in the United States; he is the author of several works on the revolution and of an amusing book, *La Tierra de Chicle,* an account of a pursuit through Yucatán and Central America of—chewing gum! He is a student above all, deliberate, discerning, and with moments of great eloquence. He would like to be a teacher.

Eduardo Villaseñor, a vigorous liberal with a bubbling sense of humor—he is never saturnine as the complex Beteta sometimes is—has been for some months the head of the Bank of Mexico. Before that he was Undersecretary of the Treasury. Villaseñor, born in Cárdenas' home state of Michoacán, is self-made. A poor boy, he managed to get to the London School of Economics and then became Mexican consul general in New York City. He is a brilliant financier and economist, and inflexibly pro-United States and anti-Axis in policy. His wife is an authoress and playwright.

Mexican Generals—Who and Why

The Minister of War, who as such is the dominating figure in the army, is a quiet 49-year-old officer, General Pablo E. Macías Valenzuela, who was virtually unknown to the public until his appointment late in 1940. General Macías is not demonstrative. He avoids diplomatic parties, and if he must attend one, he goes in mufti. He is tall and powerfully built, with closely cropped black hair. He looks as if he were foreman of a ranch, with his plain dark clothes, soft shirt with soft collar attached, and carelessly tied loose necktie.

General Macías is a man from the north. No one knows much about his origins. He fought with Obregón in 1912, and against Villa later. A professional soldier, he became a brigadier general in 1924, and a general of division—the highest rank in the Mexican army—in 1937. He has commanded about a dozen different military zones in various parts of the country. When chosen

Minister of War he was chief of military operations in the important state of Sonora, where his brother is governor.

Macías has one great qualification. He is poor. There are very few Mexican generals of division who are poor. This means that Macías is honest. And this is the chief reason that Avila Camacho chose him.

His views on politics are unknown, but it is believed that he is friendly to the United States. Recently he gave a dinner to the foreign military attachés in Mexico. Colonel Gordon McCoy, the American representative, was not the ranking guest from the point of view of diplomatic protocol, but Macías insisted that he take the place of honor at his side.

The most picturesque officer in the Mexican army is probably General Joaquín Amaro, who was Minister of War under four different Presidents, and whom competent observers call the ablest War Minister in Mexican history.

A pure-blooded Indian, who wore rings in his ears during the revolutionary days, a wonderful horseman, an athlete with wiry, steel-hard grace, a conversationalist who is reserved at first and then flashes into animation, General Amaro is a type who could scarcely exist outside Mexico. When I visited him, the first thing I thought of was his exceeding toughness. Then I felt that his character had other elements. . . . I saw the photographs of his children on the mantelpiece. I saw the books with which he was surrounded, recent works on political theory, an encyclopedia of law, an English dictionary. . . .

Amaro is generally conceded to be the hardest-boiled Mexican in Mexico, which is no mean distinction. In the old days he would order officers who displeased him to be whipped. He has often been called pro-Fascist, partly because he had a ferocious hatred of the C.T.M. He has also been ferociously anticlerical—a familiar Mexican phenomenon. At one time he was the presidential candidate of the *Partido Revolucionario Anti-Comunista*.

A Mexican friend told me: "Amaro could have been anything.

He has a unique quality of ruthlessness plus intelligence. He could have been a first-class lawyer, a first-class doctor; he was a man born to command." Another friend said: "Amaro is a real character. Imagine it! When he became Minister of War the first thing he did was to take lessons in writing, French, and deportment!"

General Amaro was born in a mining camp in Durango somewhere around 1891. He joined Zapata in 1911, and became colonel of cavalry under Villa. But later—such were the pressures of those agitated days—he joined Obregón against Villa, and was one of Obregón's best officers against Carranza in 1920. He was chief of military operations in various states, and has been a general of division for 20 years. Calles made him Secretary of War, a post he held intermittently until the '30's. He once lost an eye playing polo.

Amaro is often spoken of as a Fascist dark horse. Certainly there are few men in Mexico whose potentialities are more respected—and feared.

Another general of great quality—who is very definitely on the other side of the fence—is General Francisco José Múgica (pronounced Moo'-heeca), a "romantic Leftist" who has been called Cárdenas' political godfather. Múgica, now being talked about as a presidential candidate in 1946, was one of the early revolutionist administrators; when he got control of a province, he went ahead to distribute land to the peasants without bothering to wait for government authority.

General Múgica was born in Michoacán in 1884. He was one of the earliest of contemporarily conspicuous politicians to join the revolution; Madero commissioned him as a lieutenant in November 1910. He was chief of staff to Carranza, and president of the Supreme Tribunal in 1915. He was variously governor of Tabasco and Michoacán, quartermaster general of the army, commander in Yucatán, and Minister of National Economy. He was very close to Cárdenas, under whom he served as Minister of Communications.

Of the old provincial warlords, like General Cedillo, very few survive. They were generals such as Feng Yu-Hsiang in China, anachronistic survivors in an age quickly passing by. But perhaps the doughty General Román Yocupicio should have a word. Like Cedillo, he was the prototype of those peasant revolutionists who first made revolution in order to give their own peons land, and then became greedy for themselves. A pure Yaqui Indian, Yocupicio was boss of the northern state of Sonora for a turbulent decade. He entered the army as a private in 1910, and had the familiar revolutionary career. His trouble-making days are probably over.

One question often asked is why so many Mexican politicians are generals, though the army—which numbers about 52,000 officers and men—does not by any means dominate the nation politically. One answer is that the army considers itself the *trustee* of the revolution. Every politician went into the army in the old days, because it was his duty to fight; he had no other means of expressing himself. *In Mexico the politicians became generals,* not vice versa, as in most other countries.

Then, also, promotions were rapid in those early days, and guerilla bands were often more important than regular troops. Any officer with 100 men became a captain, anyone with a thousand called himself a general. The title "General" in Mexico has the same connotation as "Colonel" in Kentucky in many cases.

One novel point deserves notice. When an authentic general turns to politics these days—to do so he must resign his commission—he usually adopts a civilian point of view at once. This is in considerable contrast to the tradition in other Latin American states, where (as in Japan) a general who takes political office customarily *represents* the army. But in Mexico it is apt to work the other way. Generals in politics usually tend to drop their army affiliations, and the army often dislikes them.

Late in 1940 Mexico introduced conscription for the first time in its history. As the European war progressed, it became clear that Mexico might find its territory some day threatened, and it was obvious that the country would be defenseless without aid from the United States. The Mexican army, though its cavalry is well equipped for guerrilla activity, is in no position to withstand the *blitz* of a modern mechanized attack. There are only about 50 planes fit to fly, hardly any antiaircraft or antitank guns, very little mechanized equipment, and only four small tanks.

What the Avila Camacho administration hoped to do was transform the present ill-equipped army into a well-trained, modern-minded, cohesive force.[2] It was planned to induct 12,000 conscripts a year until a standing army of 200,000 was built up. But the conscription program has been postponed until 1942 because of lack of plant and lack of funds.

Two Former Presidents

Plutarco Elías Calles, the strong man of Mexico from 1924 to 1934—in other words the bridge between the revolutionary period and Cárdenas—was born in Guaymas, Sonora, in 1877. He was a schoolteacher by profession. Bulky, swarthy, competent, ambitious, with big business interests, his career followed the line of most—but not all—Mexican Presidents; that is, he began his term as a liberal,[3] gradually became more and more conservative, and ended up as a fierce reactionary. When Calles was exiled by Cárdenas, the story is that he stepped off the plane with a copy of *Mein Kampf* in his pocket. He lived in exile for some years, ostensibly removed from politics. He carefully did not support Almazán in the 1940 elections, and so, in May 1941, Avila Camacho let him return.

Emilio Portes Gil, a man of Tamaulipas with a strong Indian strain, was provisional President of the republic from 1928 to 1930, during the Calles period. But, an independent-minded and intelligent man, he was not nearly so much under the Calles thumb

[2] And to terminate such anachronistic helter-skelter traditions as that of wives accompanying the troops to do the cooking.
[3] For instance, it was Calles who initiated Mexico's collectivist Six-Year Plan.

as the puppet who succeeded him, Ortiz Rubio. Portes Gil has been called the best lawyer in Mexico, and I heard of him that he was the only man in the country who could wriggle himself through a keyhole.

Portes Gil has strong Indian feelings and a lively sense of humor. Once, when he was visiting New York, one of his hosts thought to flatter him by asking him to meet a minor Hapsburg archduke. The host said, "You must come to meet the descendant of your last emperor." He had Maximilian in mind, of course, but Portes Gil smiled and replied, "Do you mean Montezuma or Cuauhtémoc?"

Almazán, Would-Be President

About General Juan Andreu Almazán little remains to be said, except that he gave up his claims to the presidency late in 1940—charging that he had been "double-crossed" by the United States—and has retired from politics. When Henry Wallace dined at the American embassy on his arrival in Mexico City, crowds of Almazanistas stoned the building. At about the same time Mexican officials brought forward documents which they said afforded "conclusive proof" that the Almazanistas were working hand in hand with Nazi Fifth Columnists. This the Almazán adherents hotly deny, though their relations with the Falange, the Spanish Fascist organization, have been close.

Almazán was born in Guerrero, of Spanish stock, in about 1891. He joined the Madero forces early, but at one period he was a Huertista, viz., a counterrevolutionary. He became a typical enough ambitious officer—a *negociante*, someone interested in business—and amassed a large fortune. He was the head of at least one big construction company, and he became the darling of the landowners, the reactionaries, the *anti-imposicionistas*, and the clergy. Personally he is a man of dignity and charm. But many of his supporters fiercely dislike him nowadays, because they think he bungled his chances so badly after the election, by leaving Mexico.

Many More Mexicans

Mexico is richer by far in political personalities than any Latin American country except possibly Brazil, and it is painful to have to omit or give scant space to many about whom pages could be written.

There is the fire-eating Colonel Adalberto Tejeda, very much on the Left, a former governor of Veracruz who is proud that he was content to remain a colonel and never accepted a general's commission. There is Luis Cabrera, a distinguished lawyer and scholar, a former finance minister, and a discriminating spokesman for the Right. There is Graciano Sánchez, the head of the C.N.C. or peasants' union, with his walrus mustaches and close faith in the soil. There are rich conservative bankers like Montes de Oca, and devoted civil servants like Professor Jesús Silva Herzog.

Among diplomats at least three should be mentioned. One is General Francisco Aguilar, a dashing cavalry officer who has been military attaché in the United States and in Europe, and minister to Japan and France. Another is Dr. Francisco Castillo Nájera, ambassador to Washington, whom I have often mentioned in these pages. Dr. Nájera is a doctor of medicine, a general, and a writer of distinction as well as a diplomat. Third is the ambassador to Peru, Professor Moisés Sáenz, who was educated at Columbia; he is a great specialist on Indian problems, a staunch liberal, and one of the most stimulating hosts in the Americas.

A special case is that of José Vasconcelos, one of the best-known and most complex-minded intellectuals in Mexico. He was born in Oaxaca in 1882, and was the confidential agent of the Madero revolution in Washington; later he was Obregón's flaming Minister of Education, and as such initiated far-reaching reforms. In fact he created modern educational methods in Mexico, and it seemed that Vasconcelos, with his literary talent, the force of his ideas, and his bursting sense of social justice, would be one of the supreme figures of the revolution. He was defeated for the presidency in 1929, and since then his career has sharply declined. He is bitterly anti-American, and his enemies—of whom there are many—call him a Fascist now. He is the author of several remarkable books, including one called *Bolivarismo y Monroísmo.*

Narciso Bassols was another dynamic and powerful Minister of Education, who held this post during part of one administration. I have heard people I trust call Bassols—who was born in Toluca in 1887—the finest intellect in Mexico; I have heard it said that for years he was the only politician in Mexico who would resign a cabinet post on principle. Bassols, an extreme radical, was pushed out of Mexico—he became minister to London and Paris— because of his so-called "program of sexual education," which meant little more than that he ordered the teaching of physiology in the schools! This created such a furore from Church and gentry that he was forced to retire. Bassols' wife was the first woman lawyer in Mexico. He is very close to the communists now.

Art in Politics and Vice Versa

Finally, no word about Mexican politics can be complete without mention of the great Mexican artists, Diego Rivera, José Clemente Orozco, and David Alfaro Siqueiros—though Diego and Orozco deny that they are politicians.

Diego Rivera, who is a painter of literally Michelangelan exuberance and power, has known a mixed—a very mixed!— series of political allegiances. All the time, of course, he remained himself: an artist of towering genius. But for some years he was an official communist and then a Trotskyist. He helped bring Trotsky to Mexico, and later quarreled with him. Then—veering to the opposite extreme—Diego turned to, of all people, Almazán, though the Almazán ranks were larded with Fascists. He romantically "fled" Mexico City for San Francisco, asserting that government agents were pursuing him. Then Diego broke with Almazán (ostensibly because he did not purge Fascist sympathizers from his followers) and after a time returned to Mexico, where he established good relations with Avila Camacho. He is violently anti-Hitler and anti-Stalin, and he fears that Fifth Columnism in

Mexico is on the increase and may conceivably bring civil war. And he now calls himself—a democrat!

Diego swears that he never "participates" in Mexican politics, and that the fact that he is "interested" in politics has nothing to do with the case. "As a painter," he says, "I am interested in my mother or a bunch of fruit and politics too." Why not?

His shifts and aberrations may have perplexed his devoted followers. But the pure burning line of his work has never wavered from a passionate sympathy with the Mexican people, the underpossessed, the crushed, the helpless, their stubborn hopes and frustrations and aspirations.

The one-armed José Clemente Orozco, a less picturesque personality than Diego, belongs to no political party; he considers himself purely an observer, and has never taken part in political affairs of any kind. But it would be silly to minimize the tremendous social message implicit—and explicit—in Orozco's work. All the grinding pain and tragedy of feudal Mexico shine somberly from the great Orozco frescoes. They are more pointedly savage in their political commentary than all but the most outspoken works of Diego. In June 1941, four new Orozco murals were unveiled in the new building of the Supreme Court in Mexico City. They are striking in themselves, but their appearance in the halls of the highest law tribunal in the land was sensational, to say the least. Orozco covered yard after yard of wall space with figures depicting corrupt justice, the greed of the rich, and the scandalous behavior of shyster lawyers.[4]

A third artist, David Alfaro Siqueiros, original, explosive, and spectacular, is a communist who fought with the loyalists in the Spanish civil war. He and his friends conducted violent polemics against Trotsky, and the police charged him with participation in a machine-gun attack on Trotsky's house in May 1940, and the murder of Robert S. Harte, one of Trotsky's guards. Siqueiros

[4] One mural shows the nationalization of Mexico's resources, land and oil and the like; another symbolizes the bloody struggle for workers' rights as embodied in the Mexican labor law.

fled, and was captured in a cave in western Mexico some months later. Meantime a second attack on Trotsky was successful, but Siqueiros was not implicated in his actual death. He was held in jail until April 1941, when the accusation of complicity in the first attack was dropped; he was released on bail pending investigation of minor charges. Siqueiros technically jumped bail, grabbed an airplane, and fled to Havana. Later he went to Chile, the last refuge of the extreme Left in Latin America.

One thing can hardly be gainsaid about the work of Diego and Orozco at least. The visitor to Mexico can learn more about the Mexican Revolution by spending five minutes with their frescoes at the Preparatory School or in the Ministry of Education or at Chapingo than in any five hours of talk with politicians.

Chapter VII
Foreign Policy and Axis Influence in Mexico

~~~~~~

RELATIONS between Mexico and the United States are at the time of writing—the late summer of 1941—probably closer and more cordial than ever before in history.

This marks a profound change. Think back to the years of the last great war, when General Pershing crossed into Mexican territory in vain pursuit of Pancho Villa, when President Carranza was definitely pro-German, when the United States bombarded Veracruz. Or think all the way back to 1846, when the United States invaded Mexico, captured the capital, and took away a huge amount of its territory, including California and what are now our southwestern states.

It was not till 1937—a minor but interesting point—that the United States voluntarily canceled Article 8 of the Mexican-American treaty of 1853, which gave the American government the right to send troops and supplies across Mexican territory at the Isthmus of Tehuantepec.[1]

The American attitude to Mexico began to improve in the middle 1920's, and relations have become steadily better ever since, in spite of the oil expropriation. Washington came to realize that a stable, friendly, prosperous neighbor—which would buy our goods in increasing quantities—was infinitely preferable to a Mexico that was sullen and hostile. Ambassador Dwight Morrow arrived in Mexico City, and made the remarkable discovery that Mexicans were—after all—human beings. He may have influenced Calles to push the Mexican revolution backward domestically, but his work in removing suspicion and promoting cordial relations between the governments was beneficent and profound.

[1] See "Mexico Shifts Her Foreign Policy," by Maurice Halperin, *Foreign Affairs,* October, 1940.

Later came Roosevelt, the New Deal, and the Good Neighbor policy, which carried on the Morrow spirit.

It takes two to make friends—especially in Latin America. On the Mexican side several factors came into interesting play.

1. Mexican foreign policy since Cárdenas has been extremely liberal, and therefore sympathetic to the aims of Washington under Roosevelt.

2. The growing "Americanization" of Mexico played some role in breaking down the old antipathy to the "gringos."[2] Mexicans saw more American movies, heard more American radio programs, bought more American automobiles and manufactured goods.

3. Realization that the world was moving into unpredictably dangerous times and that Mexico, with two long and exposed ocean frontiers, needed American help and political support.

4. Growth of the hemisphere solidarity principle throughout the rest of Latin America—to which Mexico listens closely—as evidenced finally by the decisions of the Havana conference.

5. Realization that the United States needed Mexico, as well as vice versa, which greatly flattered the Mexicans.

6. The mounting importance of the United States in Mexican trade, as the European war and blockade cut off other markets. The United States took 67 per cent of Mexico's exports in 1938—a considerable percentage. This rose to 74 per cent in 1939 and 84 per cent in January 1940.

7. Finally, and above all, the growing conviction in Mexico that the United States Good Neighbor policy was sincere. Washington did *not* send marines to save petroleum for Standard Oil; as I have pointed out, this clinched the Good Neighbor case. General Hay, the former Foreign Minister, said to me, "What really impeded good relations not merely between the United States and Mexico but throughout the hemisphere was apprehen-

[2] The origin of this word is obscure. One theory is that it arose in the Argentine when British visitors sang "Green Grow the Rushes Round."

sion that the United States would revert to interference in domestic Latin American affairs." This fear is now largely banished.

Fifth Column in Mexico

The German colony in Mexico has been compactly and efficiently organized since 1933, and potentially it is probably the most effective Fifth Column agency in all Latin America, though the Mexican government manages to keep its activities under control.

It is worth going into the technique of the German organization in some detail, since the pattern is the same—though not so highly developed—in most other Latin American states. Two skillful Germans were largely responsible for creating the Mexican Fifth Column. The first, Dr. Heinrich Northe—who had a private airplane at his disposal—came to Mexico in 1935, and had official diplomatic status as a secretary in the German embassy. He is now in Shanghai. The second was Arthur Dietrich, who established a "press office" in Mexico City "independent" of the embassy. The Cárdenas government expelled Dietrich for subversive activities in 1940.[3]

The nucleus of the German organization is what is called the "German Popular Community in Mexico," or "German Center" for short. This includes all German social clubs, libraries, schools, and the like; and all German nationals in Mexico—except Jews and anti-Nazi refugees—not only belong to it but are expected to contribute financial support. Also, all "racial" Germans are expected to belong, that is, those who have become naturalized Mexican citizens; such folk, by German law, retain their *German* citizenship. Germans in Mexico are in fact encouraged to become naturalized, because a Mexican law restricts the number of foreigners in any organization to 10 per cent of the total membership.

[3] The Germans send some of their best agents to Mexico. Among them at present are Baron von Wakerbacker, who arrived from Tokyo, where he was head of the local Gestapo; Otto Engling, a Von Papen man; Baron von Falkenheim, who came after work in Portugal; Hans Hellerman, formerly the chief of the Nazi party in Spain; and Baron Karl Frederick von Schleebrugge, who has sought to sell airplanes to the Mexican government. See a story by Jack O'Brine in the New York *Herald Tribune*, March 30, 1941.

Largely, the German Fifth Column in Mexico supports itself. This is the procedure laid down by Hitler in Berlin. Each German colony abroad is expected to prove its own viability, though it may receive help from home under special circumstances. Individual contributions by local members make up part of the budget, and a large share comes from German business houses, banks, importing firms, and so on. Forced assessments are common, and punishment is swift to any German who disobeys. Discipline is enforced almost as if the German Center existed in Leipzig or Hamburg instead of Mexico, and laggards may be brought into line by reprisals against relatives in Germany.

The next instrument of the Fifth Column is the actual Nazi party—the *N.S.D.A.P. Landesgruppe Mexico* as it is officially called—and the Hitler Jugend which derives from it. Party membership is strictly limited to pure Aryan Germans resident in Mexico; sons of German-Mexican marriages are not accepted, though such marriages are not discouraged. The party organization corresponds to that in Germany, with a *Landesgruppen Führer* at the top. Until recently the Mexican Führer was a man named Wilhelm Wirts, who however left Mexico recently because of "internal difficulties." The headquarters of Nazi party and Hitler Jugend is usually the German school in the community; there are dozens of German schools throughout Mexico, and they have turned out about 2,000 militant Nazis since 1935. The youngsters, even if Mexican by birth, take an oath of fidelity to Hitler, and are taught a fanatic German nationalism. One detail is that—in Mexico—they are told that "Nordic" Aryans are superior to "Mediterranean" Aryans.

Party members and the youth speak German when on duty, cling together closely, take Sunday picnics, and listen to propaganda in the evenings. They are not armed on a serious scale, but almost everyone in Mexico has access to hand arms, and surreptitious military drill may take place, disguised as "gymnastics."

Finally every German unit has its Gestapo agent, or agents, who are spies and muscle-men usually sent from Berlin. They do not stay in one group long, but rotate among the communities.

The aims of the Fifth Column are in general to maintain absolute control of the German colony, to promote Axis propaganda among German-sympathizing Mexicans, and to influence opinion against Great Britain and the United States. One factor in German favor is the Anglophobia of many Mexicans; if the British would renounce their claims in the oil dispute and resume diplomatic relations, this would do more to squash Fifth Columnism than anything Mexico itself could do. Another factor is that many Mexicans say that Germany, alone among the great powers, has never taken any hostile action against their country. Many Mexicans thought that the Nazis were "saving them" when in 1938 they took $17,000,000 worth of Mexican oil in a famous barter deal. (But the war came and Germany could not deliver much of the material it promised in exchange.)

The Fifth Column sets out to achieve its aims by several methods, which one may list as follows:

First, propaganda. The Germans subsidize or control several Spanish-language newspapers, notably the *Diario de la Guerra*, which has a considerable circulation and is as anti-American and anti-British as anything in Germany. Other publications—but less important—are the *Deutsche Zeitung von Mexico*, the *National Socialist Herald*, and the *Mitteilungen der Deutschen Volksgemeinschaft*. The German news agency Transocean distributes news to many Mexican newspapers, and Transocean correspondents—there are no fewer than 33 scattered throughout Mexico—live in provincial towns and make excellent propaganda agents. Mexican editors and journalists are entertained widely by the Germans, and before the war, several were given free trips to Berlin. A journal called *Timón*, edited by José Vasconcelos, had wide influence until the Cárdenas government suppressed it. Finally German businessmen are in a position to exert some pressure on local journalism, since their advertisements—of cameras, drug supplies, machinery and the like—are an important source of revenue.

Second, powerful efforts are made to reach Mexicans by other means. The German Center finances night schools for adults where German is taught. Lectures before the German-Mexican Society emphasize that Germany must have *Lebensraum*, and that Hitler saved Germany from communism. Books are distributed, especially to army officers. These are often effective because they carefully omit any overt propaganda; they are "impartial" manuals on physical culture, military science, and similar subjects in which Germany excels.

Third, espionage. German and Mexican agents, especially businessmen and Transocean correspondents in the provinces, compile confidential dossiers on every Mexican official of importance, particularly army officers. The work is systematically done, and the Nazis in Berlin probably know everything worth knowing about the ideological sympathies and personal habits of thousands of leading Mexicans. Additionally, the Germans do their utmost to encourage "amateur photography" throughout the country; the Hitler Jugend take long "hikes" which as often as not are in strategic territory; every interesting inch of Mexican terrain has been explored.

Fourth, the Germans try to put their sympathizers in key industries or government departments, like the petroleum administration and the radio stations.

Fifth, they attempt to corrupt Mexican generals or politicians, and to assist any potentially subversive forces. German agents are believed to have visited Cedillo and other northern warlords, and the Cedillo rebellion was probably assisted by German money, as well as by the oil companies.

Sixth, they maintain close contact with other foreign groups, particularly the Japanese and members of the Falange. The Falange has been suppressed as a party, but it still has considerable influence. The Spanish colony in Mexico probably numbers 150,000, and many Spaniards are pro-Axis. The Falange newspaper, *Boletín de Unidad,* is violently anti-United States.

As to Nazi co-operation with communists, both Nazis and communists deny that it took place, but for a time their policies were identical. Of course, what happens in Mexico, as elsewhere, depends absolutely on the development of relations between Berlin and Moscow. Until the Russo-German pact of 1939, hostility between Mexican Nazis and communists was violent and genuine. Then both groups began to merge their differences; the communists opposed the "imperialist war," and both attacked Great Britain and the United States. But as the war progressed in Europe, and Russo-German relations began to deteriorate, they tended again to fall apart. Then came Hitler's invasion of Russia. And the local communists and Nazis of course split.

Finally, the Fifth Column watches with paternal interest the growth of purely *Mexican* Nazi groups. Everything in this section so far refers to activity by *Germans* or *German*-Mexicans. But I must also include a word about the native Fascist organizations, though none has much power or influence at the moment.

1. The *Partido Nacional Socialista Mexicano,* commonly called by its initials, P.N.S.M., is of course German-dominated. The swastika appears on its official stationery, and its 15,000 members are organized on the German model. It is supposed to contain bodies of "shock troops" who drill secretly; it especially seeks engineers, scientists, doctors, and so on, as members, in order to build up a cadre of experienced technicians. Officers are called "Chiefs of Circle" and the rank and file are "Workers of Enlightenment." The party claims to have affiliations with similar groups in other Latin American states, especially Colombia, through an organization with the unwieldy name of *Liga Latina Americana pro Defensa Continental.* It is ferociously anti-American, saying that the United States defense program is merely a mask for imperialist ambitions; it tells its members that

Japan will attack the United States successfully, and (!) that Mexico will regain Texas and California in due time.

2. The Sinarquista organization. This is an offshoot of the old Cristero movement, which, violently Catholic, rebelled against the Calles anticlerical decrees and fought a guerrilla civil war in western Mexico some years ago. The Sinarquistas are also said to include members of a former semi-Fascist organization, the Gold Shirts, and of the Falange. Sinarquismo is strongest among the backward, poverty-racked, priest-ridden peasants in Jalisco and Michoacán, and is dominated by reactionary elements in the clergy.

3. Smaller groups, all very anti-American, like the National Party of Public Salvation led by the anti-Semitic agitator León Ossorio. Others are the *Acción Nacional*, which is more respectable, and the *Acción Católica*, an extremist Catholic organization.

Between the Indian states of Oaxaca and Chiapas lies the 80-mile-wide Isthmus of Tehuantepec, which is of great strategic importance to the United States. A railway crosses it, the only good rail link between the Atlantic and Pacific in Latin America except Panama. Our authorities have wanted a base at Salina Cruz, on the Pacific side of the Isthmus, since the early 1900's. It happens that Chiapas and Tehuantepec are strongly settled by German coffee planters, who dominate the economy of the region, and that the Mexican Francisco Sarabia airline has a monopoly of local flights in the area. The United States is more apprehensive about Fifth Columnism in the Tehuantepec region than anywhere else in Mexico, except the capital.

A last word. Many reports of Fifth Column activity in Mexico are wildly, absurdly exaggerated. Fifth Columnism is a genuine enough potential threat, and it could become a serious menace if Germany should win the war or if the Avila Camacho government should be overthrown; but as things stood in the summer of 1941 it was thoroughly under control, and incapable of any but surreptitious activity. Any talk that the Germans have large secret forces in Mexico ready for "invasion" of the United States is total nonsense. So are rumors of big German air fields with "thousands" of planes. Mexicans love Mexico: the country will not be a pushover for anybody.

How Things Are Going Now

The United States is, of course, in an overpoweringly good position to express itself in Mexico if need should arise. Our frontier is contiguous, and our bombers are near by. Mexican dependence on our trade is almost absolute. Also, in any emergency we could refuse to buy Mexican silver, or reduce the price of silver drastically, which would be a paralyzing blow. But no one in Washington need think in terms of political pressure or threats of force. Any such development is virtually excluded, since the political relations between the United States and Mexico are so friendly. Mexico is playing ball. Let us inspect the recent record.

In October 1940, the Mexican government canceled a 247,000-acre oil concession that had been granted to Japanese interests, refused a lucrative Japanese offer for Mexican scrap iron, and embargoed shipments of mercury to Japan.

In December 1940, just after Avila Camacho's inauguration, informal negotiations began for a far-reaching defense agreement between Mexico and the United States. It was indicated that naval bases might be built on the Pacific coast, with the United States lending Mexico $50,000,000.

On December 26, 1940, the Mexican senate passed a bill allowing United States army planes the use of several Mexican airfields (Tejería, Minatitlán, and Veracruz) en route to the Panama Canal.

In February 1941, it was reported that a joint United States-Mexican defense commission, similar to the existing Canadian-American defense board, would be set up.

On March 4, identical statements were issued in Washington and Mexico City announcing that formal negotiations for "the consolidation of hemisphere defense" were under way, and that the two countries had agreed in principle on mutual assistance.

On March 7, Foreign Minister Padilla stated that "if any foreign force should attack *any* American nation, Mexico would assist in the defense of the American continent." Far cry from the Villa-Carranza days!

On March 9, Mexico expropriated twelve Axis ships, German and Italian merchantmen, which had been in harbor at Tampico and Veracruz. This came after similar seizure of Axis shipping by the United States; Mexico was the first Latin American country to follow.

On April 3, a convention was signed—and promptly ratified—permitting each country to use air bases of the other.

On May 5, Foreign Minister Padilla stated that "it was the destiny of America to fight . . . The people of Mexico, with full consciousness of the cause they are embracing, are firmly resolved to share that destiny."

Late in summer, Mexico followed the United States in closing all Axis consulates in the country, and rejected vigorously a German protest at the American blacklist of Nazi firms.

What the United States wants most from Mexico is the use of naval and air bases on the Pacific coast, as well as increased facilities at Tampico. Our experts do not think that the Caribbean coastline of Mexico needs additional protection, since the British bases we have acquired in the Antilles are supposed to lock off this approach. But the Pacific side is exposed for 2,450 miles from California to the Panama Canal, without a single defense installation. Points at which the United States particularly hopes for the use of bases are at Acapulco, Manzanillo, and Magdalena Bay.

Note the phrase "the use of." Mexicans, like all peoples, want to keep full rights over their national territory. We may pay for the bases, design them, occupy them, fortify them—if the negotiations to this end are successful—but they will remain Mexican "possessions" according to the current formula, with Mexican title and sovereignty assured. They will be instruments of a Pan-American conception, part of a defense system in which the whole hemisphere has responsibility. The Pacific bases are vital to American defense needs. And Mexico needs them too.

So much, then, for the people and problems of our nearest neighbor. We proceed now to the new world of Central America.

Chapter VIII
Two Dictators on Top

~~~~~~

ONE of the most remarkable characters in the Americas—and one of the least known—is 63-year-old General Jorge Ubico, the "Constitutional President" of Guatemala. This is what General Ubico calls himself, but in reality he is an utterly complete dictator. For the first time in this book (but not the last) we encounter a country 100 per cent dominated by a single man.

Also we enter new realms of the picturesque, with overtones of ruthlessness. Consider this legend of one of Ubico's predecessors, a Guatemalan President who died some years ago. One of his ministers came to him, whispering that twelve men planned to kill him. The informant admitted freely that he was one of them, but pleaded for leniency on the ground that he was exposing the conspiracy. The President ordered him shot at once. Why? Because he was the twelfth and last man of the twelve who had come to reveal the story!—and therefore should be punished first.

General Ubico's uncanny omniscience, his pervasive hold on things—and the way he mesmerizes everything in the country to his hand—are probably just as marked as the similar attributes of his predecessor. And Ubico knows how to be ruthless too. One story, possibly apocryphal, describes an abortive conspiracy against him in 1934. Ubico had fifteen plotters executed in the normal way, but three others were shot in the back, because they had been his friends. In December 1940, twelve seditionists were accused of attempted rebellion, and were promptly put before the firing squad. Guatemala has virtually no crime. It is orderly as an empty billiard table. This is because even thieves and such minor criminals may be shot if caught.

When cabinet ministers are summoned by the unbelievably hard-edged General Ubico, they remain standing. When the General goes out into the countryside—which is often—district officials are numb with terror till he passes. He uses a motorcycle, driving hard and fast, in his inspection tours. When he finds a lazy governor relaxing in an automobile, he takes the automobile away and gives him a motorcycle instead. "Try this for a year and see how it shakes your kidneys up," he likes to say.

Once, driving through Guatemala City, I was told that the President must be on the point of leaving his palace, because the traffic police—there is a policeman at each corner—had removed their platforms and umbrellas, in order to give free passage to the impending furious cavalcade. I learned something else about Guatemala on this occasion. My companion, after lighting a cigarette, would carefully put the used match back in his pocket, instead of tossing it into the street. Guatemala City is the cleanest I have ever seen. Ubico keeps it clean.

General Jorge Ubico y Castañeda was born on November 10, 1878, of European stock. One legend is that his forebears came not merely from Spain but from Dorsetshire in England, and that the original family name was Wycoff or Wykam. He had many years as an officer and *jefe político* in various provinces; he was Chief of Staff and Minister of War before he became President in 1931. In theory he belonged to the Liberal Progressive or anticlerical party (but he has re-established relations with the Vatican and allowed Jesuit teachers, previously expelled, to return to the country). The constitution contains the usual one-term-at-a-time proviso, and Ubico was scheduled to go out in 1937; he contrived easily enough to have it changed, and his term was thus extended till 1943. Government in Guatemala is, of course, by Ubico's decree. Congress meets occasionally to "confirm" his legislation. If you ask what the opposition is, people look at you utterly bewildered.

General Ubico reached the presidency in somewhat confused circumstances, which indirectly helped to cause an important shift in United States foreign policy. Back in 1907 the five Central American republics, under our stimulus, signed a treaty providing that none would recognize any new administration in any other, if it came to power by violence or revolutionary means. This was confirmed by a further treaty in 1923. This "doctrine of nonrecognition" had great significance, because it served to freeze in power what government happened to be holding power. By withholding recognition from a revolutionary government, the United States could cut off its credit and ruin its prestige. Nevertheless we recognized the Ubico regime in 1931, and the nonrecognition doctrine was thus reversed. The 1923 treaty is still in force theoretically, but in practice nowadays the United States recognizes any government that proves that it can maintain effective rule.

President Ubico, a dictator in every sense of the word, has a startling facial resemblance to Napoleon, and wears his hair with a Napoleonic forelock. He works like an impatient beaver, and answers every telegram and letter that he receives within an hour or two. The story is that he does everything by fives: he is up at five, and out of the office by five. He has very few friends—an American business man, Alfred Denby, is one—and no intimate advisers. The great seal of Guatemala adorns one side of his presidential chair, the word *Democracia* the other. He has spies and agents everywhere, and knows everyone's private business to an amazing degree. Not a pin drops in Guatemala without his knowing it.

The general's sources of power are manifest. One is his intense sense of discipline and order, plus his accurate knowledge of the country. Another is his absolute uprightness and integrity. The story is that his father, a wealthy lawyer, threatened to shoot him if he ever took one cent of graft; the father added that he knew he could not live on his salary as a junior government official, and so would pay him a small allowance to supplement it. Ubico hates graft above all things. He pores over books everywhere in the country, and anyone found guilty of corruption is instantly punished. One of his first reforms was a law making it obligatory for every public servant to declare his financial status before taking office—and on leaving it.

Ubico has, however, a healthy regard for money. His salary

is enormous, something in the neighborhood of $150,000 a year. Some years ago he had Congress vote him an additional grant of $200,000 for his services to the country. He maintains several houses, including a *finca* (coffee plantation) in San Agustín, near Lake Amatitlán; his wife—the Ubicos have no children—keeps a mountain chalet on the road to Antigua. Ubico loves radios, cameras, fishing (he classifies carefully his dozens of rods), motor boats (of which he has six or seven), and motorcycles. He is a violent radio enthusiast, and has given the country the best radio system in Central America. He issues orders to his provincial governors by this means—often in highly Rabelaisian language. Sometimes these broadcasts are picked up by amateurs in Panama and elsewhere, who either grin or blanch.

Twice Ubico has been infuriated by American news stories about him. One alleged that the strong German colony in Guatemala wanted to unseat him. He roared in protest that every German in the country was shivering under his thumb—which indeed is true. Once he was quoted as saying that he could invade and "take" Mexico more or less at his pleasure. Maybe the general did say this, but it was embarrassing to have it printed. *Time* used the story, whereupon Ubico barred *Time* from the country.

Guatemala fears and dislikes Mexico (and on the other side of the fence Mexico genuinely fears the tough Guatemalans), but nowadays relations between the two countries are quite good. For years Ubico thought that Mexico was bolshevik, and feared subversive activities by Mexican exiles on his territory. The story is that he allowed a Papal Nuncio to be appointed to his government largely to prevent the Mexican ambassador of the day from being doyen of the diplomatic corps.

Whether you like Ubico or not, you must admit that his accomplishments have been considerable. He cut the public debt in half, balanced the budget, established complete political order, cleaned up the country physically, and started a public works program, as exemplified by the impressive new customs house in Guatemala City. He abolished imprisonment for debt—though peons may be forced to work on the roads in lieu of paying taxes—and built roads. He is no lover of the Indians like Cárdenas, but his work in public hygiene and education has helped them. What he seeks is to bring Guatemala into the modern world, whip it into shape, and make it work. There is no doubt that he is the biggest man in Central America. Given local conditions, he has done a lot.

This Is Guatemala

Guatemala, the most powerful of the Central American republics, with its violent landscape peppered with volcanoes, its primitive agrarian economy based on coffee and bananas, is overwhelmingly Indian. Its population is about 3,000,000, its area roughly that of Mississippi. Very backward, very heterogeneous, the Indians differ in language and costumes hilltop by hilltop; some are too primitive to know what money is, some are isolated in their remote villages all their lives.

Guatemala City, by contrast, is almost embarrassingly rectilinear, regimented, up-to-date—and, as I have said, clean as the cleanest whistle you ever saw. It has undertones of grimness, especially at night. The policemen stand at *every* corner, all night long, under arc lights. There is virtually no traffic (the speed limit is about 10 miles per hour), and everyone has gone to bed, but the police remain on duty hour after hour, watching the sinister and glistening streets. It is forbidden, incidentally, to stand in front of one's door and chat with a neighbor—even by day! Jaywalking is forbidden; so are all forms of gambling; one may not even shake for drinks in a private club.

Guatemala considers itself the first of the countries between Mexico and Colombia, and the stout Ubico's fondest dream is of a Central American federation with himself as leader. The five Central American states were, in fact, once united as a single organism—from 1823 to 1839, after liberation from Spain—and unity today might be wholesome. Yet there are massive obstacles.

1. In four of the five countries the local dictator wants, nat-

urally enough, to remain king in his own bailiwick. (This does
not apply so much to Costa Rica, which is a democracy.)

2. Local nationalisms (and also Indian characteristics) are
sharply divergent, especially between the Guatemaltecos and the
Salvadoreños. The countries with the closest natural links are Honduras and Nicaragua, which have a similar mestizo background;
they talked federation for some years, despite a frontier quarrel.
But, again, Costa Rica is a case apart.

3. Bad communications. At this point the mind rocks. From
Guatemala City to the capital of El Salvador a road exists, but
it takes about eight hours to traverse 110 miles. Between El Salvador and Honduras there are no communications whatever, except by air. The journey *could* be made—by boat and burro—but
it would be a real adventure. Likewise no communications exist
between the capitals of Honduras and Nicaragua (air excepted);
they are 65 minutes apart by Pan American Airways, but a letter
not sent by air must be routed by boat, and takes *two weeks* to
deliver. Nor is there any direct land route between the capitals
of Nicaragua and Costa Rica.

4. The influence of the United Fruit Company, which is enormous in the region. And this potent company prefers to deal with
its republics separately, not together.

On the whole one might say that each country likes to play
with the country just beyond its immediate neighbor. There is a
strong idealistic trend toward unification, coupled with a strong
practical tendency against it. Yet all five countries co-operate
amicably. Recently the five sent a joint appeal to General Franco
not to enter the European war; all five make a common front on
the Belize dispute; the five—acting in unison—endorsed Mr.
Roosevelt's May 27 speech.

Belize is the Guatemalan name for British Honduras, and the
controversy about its frontier ranges far back. When Guatemala
became independent in 1821, the British already had "usufruct
rights" (but not sovereignty) in Belize; then they expanded into
what the Guatemaltecos claim as Guatemala proper. The details are

too complicated for treatment here. But in 1859 Guatemala signed a treaty with Great Britain recognizing the present frontiers of Belize, provided that the British would co-operate in building a road from Guatemala City to the Caribbean. The British haggled, and the upshot was that Guatemala, though surrendering claims on Belize, got in return neither the road nor a projected financial settlement. In 1938, after years of squabbling, the British called the issue closed, and said that they would hold Guatemala responsible for any incidents; the Guatemalans retaliated in effect by voiding the 1859 treaty. No final frontier has ever been drawn, and an attempt at mediation by President Roosevelt was unsuccessful. The issue may seem small, but it is burningly acute to every Guatemalan. Yet, after the fall of France in 1940, Ubico said that he would drop the matter for the time being. He did not want to embarrass the British in their hour of stress!

I stood in Guatemala City—at the corner of Fifth Avenue and Fourteenth Street (streets are numbered *à la* New York)—looked at shop signs. I had been told that Germans were strong in the uplands, that, in fact, 50 per cent of the best coffee *fincas* were German-owned. But I did not expect quite such manifest signs of Germanism in the capital itself. I saw:

Hardware—Topke, Koeningsberger
Photo Supplies—Biener
Haberdashery—Danziger
Films—Roberto Eichenberger
Coffee Importer—Máximo Stahl
Hats—Brachmann
Tobacconist—Schacher
The Germania Tea Shop

In the leading bookstore it seemed that the authorities were encouraging strict neutrality. Both Hitler's *Mein Kampf* and Rauschning's *Voice of Destruction* are banned; oddly enough, my own *Inside Europe* is prohibited, but *Inside Asia* may be sold.

There are 2,200 registered German nationals in Guatemala, and they form a solidly knit community. They became entrenched

—partly through marriage with Guatemalans—many years ago; they are wealthy, efficient, and influential. In two provinces, San Marcos and Mazatenango, they completely dominate the coffee industry; in another, Alta Verapaz, they own the railway which is the only outlet to the sea. Fifth Column agents are very active among them. Germany pays great attention to Guatemala; a reliable estimate is that it spends not less than fifteen *million* dollars per year on propaganda in Central America as a whole. The United States spends scarcely anything.

Dr. Otto Reinebeck, the German minister to the five Central American states and Panama, lives in Guatemala, and is director of Axis activity for the region. For a time the information sheet distributed by his legation, called *Servicio Informativo*, had a wide circulation all over Central America. (It is now forbidden the mails by Guatemala, and can only be distributed by courier.) Just before the Havana Conference, Reinebeck circularized the six governments to which he was accredited, warning them not "to prejudice their neutrality" by any acts against German interests; the governments paid little attention.

The Germans are important in Guatemala—yes—but Ubico is more important. One joke is that the Germans may have a Fifth Column, but that the stiff-sided General certainly has the other four. In May 1939 came a decree outlawing the Nazi party, the Hitler Jugend, and so on. Until that time the Germans had openly marched in brown shirts, carrying swastika insignia. The law additionally forbade any political activity by foreigners, and demanded that diplomatic officials abstain from participation in domestic affairs. In June 1940, a new decree restricted propaganda by naturalized or native Guatemalan citizens.

Three of Ubico's cabinet ministers are, however, commonly regarded as pro-German. They are González Campo, the Minister of *Hacienda*, Ruderico Anzueto (Agriculture), and Sáenz de Tejada (Interior). But the Ministers of War, General José Reyes, and of Foreign Affairs, Dr. Carlos Salazar—both are in their late seventies—are pro-American. In June 1940, sixty

United States army planes flew from Panama to Guatemala City to assist in celebration of the national holiday. Ubico asked them to route their trip so that they would fly over Cobán, a coffee district which is a German stronghold, in order to awe the Nazis.

Relations between the United States and Guatemala are in every way excellent, better than they have ever been before. General Ubico has promised us any kind of facility in case of need, and his associates say frankly that they will be delighted to toss every German in the country into a concentration camp if the United States declares war on Germany. Such an event would, indeed, give Ubico a wonderful opportunity to enrich the nation by confiscation of German property.

General Martínez of El Salvador

The Presidents of Guatemala and El Salvador differ almost as much as their countries do, though both are dictators. For instance, Ubico is of European stock, ruling a country at least 90 per cent Indian. General Maximiliano Martínez, the President of El Salvador, is of Indian origin, but he runs a state where practically no pure Indians are left.

General Martínez (pronounced Mar-*teen*-us), who has given his tiny country a good administration for the past ten years, is full of quirks and oddities. For one thing he is a theosophist. He likes to put bottles of colored water out in the sun; once the sun's rays penetrate them, he thinks the water has therapeutic use, and he gives samples of different colors to his friends. He often rises at dawn, and for years trained himself to look at the sun without blinking. He would stare at it for one minute at the beginning, then two minutes, and so on. His idea was that this would cure shortsightedness.

Martínez stands straight as a ramrod. He is wiry and athletic, with curly graying hair. He plays classical music when he awakes each morning. He is a vegetarian and a teetotaler, something very rare in Latin America. He is able, cunning, patriotic, and ambitious.

The General dominates El Salvador completely and personally, but his government is much milder than Ubico's in Guatemala. The press is moderately free; there are no political prisoners. Martínez thinks of himself as an "evolutionist," a "democratic idealist," and almost everything is done via parliamentary forms. He told me—quite sincerely, I am sure—that he considered democracy the ideal form of government, and that people must be trained to understand it, cherish it, and fight for it. He pointed out that different peoples reach varying stages of development at different times; not everyone can understand the responsibilities that democracy entails. One of his favorite sayings is, "Democracy imposes obligations on citizens as well as giving them privileges."

President Martínez was born in 1882, and spent most of his life as a professional soldier. He was a classmate of Ubico's at the Military Polytechnic School in Guatemala. He became President by coup d'état in December 1931; the United States did not recognize him till January 1934. Like the other Central American Presidents, he has tinkered with his constitution so that he may "legally" stay in office; he began a new six-year term in 1939 . . . The worst blot on his record was suppression of a revolution in 1932, in which between 8,000 and 11,000 people were killed. The official story is that this was a "communist" revolt, inspired by Mexican agents; in actuality the poverty-blighted peasants, no more communists than Martínez is an Eskimo, agitated for a land reform, and were shot for their pains by the landowners. Then the government stepped in. Martínez was not responsible directly for the ghastly bloodshed that occurred, but it took him a long time to live it down.

Martínez, like Ubico, has put his country in shipshape financial order; he has mercilessly attacked graft; his record in road building and other public works is the best in Central America; technically his administration is one that any American state could be proud of. He rigorously keeps government expenditure 10 per cent below revenue, and until recently he had a budget surplus every year, something unique for the region. Among other things he hates influence by outsiders. He takes no loans or gifts from the United States. In the chamber of deputies he set up a plaque reading, "I recommend as a basic principle that this nation never again contract any foreign debt large or small for any reason."

General Martínez has great capacity to relax easily. He is an excellent listener, but no one knows whether he agrees with what you say. He seldom gives himself away; he has no surprise reactions. His personal life is happy, and he has five children. His salary is $12,000 per year. He is modest, and hates pomp and ceremony.

Glimpsing El Salvador

After the grimness of Guatemala, El Salvador[1] seems soft, mild, sunny; to go from one country to the other is like an old-time trip from hard-boiled Latvia, say, to smiling Estonia. El Salvador is the smallest country in the Americas—it covers 13,173 square miles, about the size of Maryland—and one of the most sophisticated. Its population of roughly 1,700,000 crowds its small territory, and every inch is cultivated. It lives 90 per cent on coffee, and the United States is by far its best customer.

Most Salvadorans are *ladinos* (the Central American term for mestizos), with a close-knit homogeneity. White blood predominates in the upper classes, Indian in the lower. But even those with most Indian blood are startlingly unlike the Guatemalan Indians. In Guatemala the Indian lives an almost completely isolated life; he weaves his own straw mats and gets wool from his own sheep; he speaks his own mountain dialect, and lives most of the year on his own small plot of land, growing beans and chickens, earning perhaps 12 cents a day when he works at all. But the Salvadoran Indian is conscious of being a Salvadoran. He has been assimilated into the nation, poor as he may be; the Indian dialects have died out, and he speaks Spanish. He goes into the towns and learns to be a plumber or a blacksmith

[1] Salvadorans want their country to be named properly, *El* Salvador (The Savior). The capital is *San* Salvador.

if he can. If he does stay on the land, his lot is hard, because there has been no substantial land reform in El Salvador. The peons are penniless agrarian workers, a landless proletariat, working a few miserable months a year.

The Salvadoran upper classes are traveled, cosmopolitan, polyglot, and do not suffer the tremendous social taboos of Guatemala; they are amiable folk, with literate and progressive instincts.

There are not so many Germans in El Salvador as in Guatemala, and Fifth Columnism is not so serious a problem. The Martínez government has had, however, to watch Axis penetration carefully; in June 1940, it passed a law forbidding all propaganda against democratic principles. Then it expelled the German consul, Baron von Hundelhausen, though he had been in the country eleven years, and had married a Salvadoran. As the story is told, he wept on being expelled, and the Salvadoran Foreign Minister, Dr. Miguel Araujo, "severely rebuked him for showing self-pity."

Dr. Araujo is seventy-nine years old, and one of the stoutest characters in the hemisphere, as a remarkable incident demonstrates. The German chargé d'affaires, Richard von Heynitz, and the Italian chargé, Baron Filippo Muzi Falcone, called on him to protest against application of the anti-propaganda law. The scene was violent. They told him that he was acting as a catspaw of the United States; the aged Araujo replied, "Do you gentlemen know the Spanish language well enough to realize what you are saying, and that you are attacking the honor of my country?" Von Heynitz lost his temper and shouted, "Wait till we win the war; we'll teach you Salvadorans a lesson." Araujo replied, "Why not now?" and threw them out. He refused thereupon to receive either again, which ended their diplomatic usefulness. The Axis governments had to withdraw them; Muzi Falcone left the country temporarily, and—believe it or not—Heynitz shot himself, though not directly as a result of this incident. Thus did tiny El Salvador defy the Axis!

In June 1941, the Salvadorans shut down a secret Nazi radio

station that was keeping touch with German agents throughout Central America. Later it was reported that Germans were flooding the country with counterfeit coins. In late summer it became known that forty-three United States firms were represented in the country by Axis agents; this will be changed. An American officer is shortly to replace a German general who was in command of the local military school. The German, Colonel von Bohnstadt (he held the rank of general in the Salvadoran army), was expelled from the country.

El Salvador under Martínez is thoroughly pro-United States. On the other hand, one should note that it was the first country in the world (after Japan) to recognize Manchukuo, and the first country in Latin America to recognize the Franco government in Spain. The recognition of Manchukuo was a mistake. A foreign office clerk answered a telegram from the Manchukuoan "government" by accident, and the Japanese instantly seized on this as "recognition."

Chapter IX
The Banana Republics

A YEAR ago if anyone had told me that Costa Rica was one of
the most delightful countries in the world and one of the
purest democracies on earth I would have gaped. Now that I
have been there I know it to be true. Costa Rica is unique. It is a
country of white people, with very little mixed blood; a nation
without an army, where the President is paid $268 a month;
a sober little country, industrious and honest, with all its politics
aboveboard—"a country without secrets."

Costa Rica—"rich coast"—is the southernmost Central American republic above Panama; its 600,000 people live in an area
smaller than West Virginia. It is sharply, picturesquely mountainous, and both coasts lift steeply to the central plateau, where
the capital, San José, perches at 3,800 feet. At the airport, where
the shining Pan American plane glides to an easy stop, three
spectacular plants greet you like sentinels—a banana tree, a great
sprout of sugar cane, and a coffee bush—the three products on
which the country lives.

Central America as a whole suffered turbulently from bloodshed, dictatorship, treachery, civil war, filibustering—an American citizen, Walker by name, was once President of Nicaragua—
in the century between deliverance from Spain and the beginning of the Good Neighbor policy. But Costa Rica, miraculously,
has always been an oasis of propriety and tranquillity. It has
had few revolutions, and most were bloodless. The story is that
the Costarricenses fight their revolutions in the newspapers!

Free and orderly elections occur every four years. The law is
that every citizen must vote. The President may not succeed
himself. He is responsible to a Congress, which may—and frequently does—override his authority. There are two political
parties, which do not differ much except that one is Out and the
other In, and they generally take turns in power. The press is

free—and vigorous. Civil liberties are respected. Political prisoners are unknown.

The first thing I asked in San José was how this condition of affairs—amazing for Central America—had come about. I heard several pertinent answers.

The Spaniards who occupied Costa Rica, coming mostly from Galicia in northern Spain, were not so much *conquistadores* as farmers, settlers, family men. The Indians were killed off quickly. Today there are hardly 500 pure Indians left, and these—the Talamancas—are kept on reservations much as we keep Indians in the United States. In the banana belt along the coast there are many Negroes, imported from Jamaica, but they play little role in the life of the uplands. Hence Costa Rica has almost no racial problem.

Furthermore, the country is not army-ridden. There is no Minister of War. Generals do not become politicians, because there are no important generals. The standing army consists of eighty-two officers, 242 enlisted men, and 220 musicians—members of the band! Officers are appointed by the President and usually surrender their commissions when the administration changes. Everything in the country is on a modest scale. An army captain gets $31 a month, a provincial governor $73, a Supreme Court justice $165, and a Congressman $82.50, plus a little more when Congress is in session.

Costa Rica is poor; nevertheless it is honest. The story is that two Presidents of the republic went bankrupt *after* leaving office! . . . According to the *Hemisphere* (July 11, 1941), ex-President León Cortez Castro recently sued a public official, by name Manuel Marín Quirós, for having said that he, Castro, had stolen some chickens during his term of office. Marín Quirós was found guilty of slander and fined $10.

A third factor making for order and democracy is the inherent good temper of the Costa Rican people. "Of course," a friend in San José told me, "we did have trouble in 1918. Federico Tinoco was President. Not a good man. The people were discontented. Two thousand school children, with their teachers, marched in protest to the President's house. The President's brother turned the fire hose on them, but some youngsters crawled through the gate and cut the hose with machetes. Everyone laughed. The tension eased. We went home to bed. The next day Tinoco resigned."

Incidentally, President Woodrow Wilson refused to recognize the Tinoco regime. From this fact a curious phenomenon derives, namely, that Costa Rica is still officially at war with Germany! It went to war against the Reich when the United States did, but it did not sign the Treaty of Versailles because of the quarrel between Wilson and Tinoco. Theoretically, "hostilities" between Costa Rica and the Germany of Kaiser Wilhelm have never ceased.

The comparatively high literacy and the attention paid by the government to education are another important factor in Costa Rica's democracy. The country is proud of the fact that it has more schoolmasters than men-at-arms, more schoolhouses than police stations—659 schools, served by 2,654 teachers. Every Costa Rican child must go to school. And the schools are free.

Then, again, the country has the highest percentage of individual landowners of any Latin American state—89,389 persons holding 198,629 pieces of property. There are comparatively few big estates, with their attendant feudalism. This is a valuable political asset. Revolution is not likely where 80 per cent of the land is held by small farmers.

Everyone is of the same middle class, more or less. Marriages between the leading families have produced hundreds of cousins and in-laws who have been acquainted since childhood. If they happen to become politicians in opposing camps, they play according to well-defined rules. Finally, the very climate of Costa Rica, with mild summer days and brisk cool nights the year round, stimulates orderly living. Its citizens are neither exhausted by altitude nor debilitated by moist tropical heat.

President Calderón of Costa Rica

The President of Costa Rica, Dr. Rafael Angel Calderón Guardia is a young man, born in 1900 (all his cabinet ministers but one are under forty, incidentally) ; he is a surgeon who specialized in cancer research. His M.D. came from Brussels, and his wife is Belgian. Recently, though he himself had just recovered from a serious illness, he operated on her for appendicitis, and saved her life. He was a deputy for a time, and then President of Congress. He is a devout Roman Catholic. He was elected President of the Republic in May 1940.

Dr. Calderón Guardia, though a medical man, is to politics born. His grandfather was a President of Costa Rica; his father, Dr. Rafael Calderón Muñoz (also a physician) is Costa Rican consul general in San Francisco and first *designado* (Vice-President) of the Republic. The President's brother, Francisco Calderón Guardia, is Minister of *Gobernación* and Public Security, and is third Vice-President.

When I was in Costa Rica the President was ill, and his brother was carrying on the work of the executive. I visited the simple frame house where they live, saw the President as he lay in bed, and presented a letter of introduction from Sumner Welles. In the house I noted printed signs saying that, as the President was ill, he begged to be excused from granting audiences. This is typical of Costa Rica. What brought Dr. Calderón Guardia down was overwork. The President must see everybody, or almost everybody, personally. His reception rooms are normally choked with peasants, workmen bearing petitions, clerks with grievances, and dozens of other supplicants who demand his attention.

Indeed, it is traditional in Costa Rica that the President of the republic comport himself like any other citizen. The Chief Executive goes about the streets without a bodyguard; he may be seen with his elbows up on his front-yard fence, talking to a neighbor; if he goes to the movies, he buys a ticket like anyone else; if he meets a friend at the railway station, he stands in line at the gate like any other passenger. He is no more, no less, than any of his compatriots.

I met the President's brother, the Minister of the Interior, and asked him how the United States could help Costa Rica. He replied, "Economically. Buy our coffee. Give us loans. Help us to develop our resources. You need manganese. We have manganese. But we need assistance in producing it."

The country lives 60 per cent on coffee. Until the war Great Britain and Germany took the bulk of it; now Costa Rica is suffering gravely. The United States—which, through purchases of gold, bananas, cacao and coffee, has always been its best customer—is buying 200,000 sacks of coffee this year, but this is only half Costa Rica's export crop. Last September the Export-Import Bank lent the country $4,600,000 for extending the Pan-American Highway from San José to the Panama frontier. This will take four years; thousands of Costa Ricans will get work, and they are glad to be getting it.

The United Fruit Company plays an important role in Costa Rican economy, though it is not so preponderant as in Honduras, say. It pays 2 cents per stem on bananas, which helps keep the country going; it virtually owns the Caribbean port of Limón, and operates the San José-Limón railway. In 1941 it faced a serious issue with the Costa Rican government. The banana plantations on the Atlantic side have been damaged by disease, and United Fruit is developing properties on the Pacific to replace them. Some years ago the government forbade movement of Negro workers from the Atlantic seaboard further west than the town of Siquirres. Now the company wants to transfer its colored labor across the Isthmus. The Costa Ricans oppose this, but on the other hand they don't like leaving so many unemployed blacks on the Atlantic side.

There are several interesting Costa Ricans aside from members of the Calderón family. One is the venerable Ricardo Jiminez, the Chief Justice of the Supreme Court, who was born in 1859; he has been President of the republic three times, and both his father and grandfather were Presidents. Another is the Foreign Minister, Alberto Echandi, who—like all the Central American Foreign Ministers—is over seventy; a lawyer by profession, he was on the British black list during the last world war, because he represented German firms. Still another is Dr. Luis Anderson, who is half-Scotch, and one of the best-known international lawyers in the Americas. Still another is Alfredo Volio, Calderón's Minister of Public Works, a young man who was first in his class at the University of California.

Hemisphere Versus Axis in Costa Rica

Costa Rica, like all the Central American republics, is of tremendous strategic importance to the United States because of its proximity to the Panama Canal. Luckily the Calderón government is strongly pro-American. United States military planes based in the Canal Zone occasionally use Costa Rican landing fields in practice flights; American officers visited San José recently to establish a permanent military mission. At some future date we might find naval and air "facilities" useful on Cocos Island, in the Pacific off the Costa Rican coast. Anything so close to the canal—within easy bombing range—is vital territory.

Pro-Germanism in Costa Rica, which centers mostly at the Pacific port of Puntarenas, is based on several factors. Many politicians in previous administrations had important business connections with German firms, and the Reich once took most of the country's coffee crop. German priests in a San José religious school have been influential, and so are German engineers and *finca* owners, who hold about 20 per cent of the best coffee land. For some time the most important German was Max Effinger, a naturalized Costarricense who held the key job of director of public works. He was recently dismissed from this post. One odd point is that some of the buildings housing German companies have Nazi insignia painted on their roofs. This is as if the Axis folk expected German bombing planes almost any day.

Costa Rica, which is always willing to play the United States game, has lately stiffened in anti-Fifth Column matters. For a time it was somewhat lax—Germans with swastikas used to parade openly—partly because of its tradition of extreme political tolerance, partly because German merchants were so powerful. Two Axis ships lay in Puntarenas harbor when the United States seized German shipping in American ports; their captains set them afire, and the Costa Rican government subsequently expelled their 121 officers and sailors. A man named Karl Bayer, who was described as head of the Nazi propaganda organization in the country, was also deported, in line with a recent law providing this punishment for any person "circulating Nazi views."

In the summer of 1940 the German minister presented Señora Calderón, the wife of the President, with a bouquet at a public function. Belgium had just fallen, and Madame Calderón is Belgian; she refused to accept the German flowers.

Somoza and Nicaragua

General Anastasio Somoza, the 45-year-old president of Nicaragua, is smooth, amusing, slick, a wonderful showman, and the cleverest politician between the Rio Grande and the Panama Canal.

The glittering Somoza has other qualities. For instance, courage. He is the only head of a Central American state who has ever dared leave his country during his term of office. He visited all his neighbors a few years ago—including Honduras, with which his government was quarreling[1]—and in the spring of 1939 he came to Washington. President Roosevelt met him at the station, which was one of the great moments of Somoza's life.

He passionately admires Mr. Roosevelt, and hoped eagerly for his victory in the 1940 American elections. I happened to be in Managua, Nicaragua's capital, late in October, and I hazarded the guess to Somoza that Roosevelt was bound to win. He asked

[1] Postage stamps caused this quarrel, when, in August 1937, Nicaragua issued stamps in the form of maps claiming frontier territory that Honduras also claimed.

by how many states. I said, "All but nine or ten." The President replied that if it should turn out that I was right, he would declare a two-day national holiday. Which he subsequently did.

President Somoza is the absolute and undisputed boss of Nicaragua, but he enjoys informality. He is a cheerful host. He seats his guests in rocking chairs, gives them cooling refreshment, and talks—in as good American English as can be imagined—a steady, persuasive, bubbling stream. He likes to call the American minister "Boy." Once Mrs. Meredith Nicholson, the minister's wife, complained mildly that there was no good milk in Managua. The next day she found a first-class cow on her doorstep, the gift of the President.

Somoza has machine guns mounted outside his palace, and he travels in a bullet-proof car preceded by a station wagon jammed with armed guards. He is delighted that the Nicaraguan flag is striped blue, white, and blue, because he says this symbolizes "peace between two oceans." He wants to do what he can for the Indians, and he would like to change some place names; he calls Lake Managua Lake Xolotlán, and Lake Nicaragua Lake Cocibolca. He is a thirty-fourth-degree Mason, and one of the very few Latin American Presidents who is not a Catholic.

The President—and dictator—of Nicaragua was born in 1896 in modest circumstances; his coffee-planting family was of the conservative tradition, but he became a "liberal." He was educated at the Pierce Commercial College in Philadelphia, and his American background has marked him deeply. His three children are being educated in the United States now. For a time he worked for an American automobile company, and then returned to Nicaragua, where he became an interpreter for the United States marines then occupying the country. He was a nephew-in-law of one President (Sacasa), and private secretary to another (Moncada). In 1933 he became commander-in-chief of the National Guard, which had been trained by the marines, and he made it his political machine. He has been President of Nicaragua since January 1937.

Let me interject a word about United States intervention in Nicaragua and the unhappy Sandino episode. Our marines first entered the country in 1912, and stayed, off and on, until 1933. In 1926 the liberals, under Sacasa and Moncada, made a revolution against the conservative regime supported by Washington. Colonel Stimson, now the United States Secretary of War, arrived in Managua in 1927 and patched up a kind of truce. Moncada became President, but one of his best generals, Augusto César Sandino, refused to lay down his arms, and decamped into the jungle. He fought a bitter guerrilla campaign against both the marines and the regular Nicaraguan forces, plundered much of the country, and eluded capture for years. We began withdrawal of the marines in 1932, after supervision of a new election that made Dr. Sacasa President. Sandino agreed to cease fighting as soon as evacuation of the marines was complete, and he and Sacasa came to an agreement. Sandino was to get a commission in the National Guard; his men were to be allowed to keep their arms for a year, within their houses. Sandino then surrendered—and was brutally double-crossed and murdered under a flag of truce. Plenty of people in Nicaragua are willing to assume responsibility for his death, highly unpleasant as the circumstances were. General Somoza was chief of the National Guard at the time. He has written a picturesque book, *El Verdadero Sandino,* describing the whole affair.

In theory Nicaragua has a two-party system, with Somoza as head of the liberals, but the conservatives have no real influence. The leading oppositionist is ex-President Chamorro, an exile in Mexico. As a rule, revolutionary movements begin on the east coast and spread westward, because everything on the east is subordinated to Managua, which is on the Pacific side. But General Somoza is careful to see that fermentation does not get serious . . . There are said to be only two political prisoners in the entire country. One is held because he insulted President Roosevelt.

Somoza has done a good deal for Nicaragua on the whole. He

has sought to develop its gold mines, extend the Pan-American Highway, improve public health, and build schools. His energy (a quality rare in Nicaragua), his enormous plausibility, his good humor, and the complete absence of any competition, give him a clear field for what he wants to do.

The President's closest friend and adviser is Colonel Luis Manuel DeBayle, his brother-in-law. Colonel DeBayle, a doctor of medicine, and one of the most engaging personalities in Central America, was trained in the United States, and is director of health services. Another Somoza brother-in-law, Dr. Henri DeBayle, is a surgeon, the director of the national bank, and a former director of the railways. Another, Dr. León DeBayle, is minister in Washington.

The chief problem of Nicaragua, as in so many countries in Latin America, is poverty. A peon is lucky if he gets 15 cents per day. A policeman gets about $3.00 per month, and a good cook about $4.00. Somoza's salary is gargantuan by these standards. It is in the neighborhood of $100,000 per year.

The Lively Nicaraguans

Nicaragua, with its 1,333,572 people, mostly mestizo, in an area roughly that of Florida or Michigan—it isn't as small a country as is generally assumed—is the liveliest of the states below Mexico, and by far the most Americanized. It is, in fact, probably the most "American" country in the hemisphere, which of course is a result of the prolonged—if intermittent—marine occupation.

Nicaraguans resemble Filipinos strongly. They are gay, Broadwayish, cocky, and emancipated. There are 200 baseball teams in the country. The waiter puts his hand on your shoulder and says, "Do you want dinner, chief?"

Nicaragua is certainly a dictatorship, but plenty of political talk goes on. Most people are violently interested in public affairs. Managua is the only capital I have ever visited where newspaper interviewers start calling on you at 6 A.M. One day I found a remarkable document under my doorstep. It was a bold and lively denunciation of Somoza. It started out, *"Nicaraguans are dynnamic* (sic) *people; their rulers, tiranic* (sic) *crooks."*

By terms of the Bryan-Chamorro treaty of 1916, the United States holds the Corn Islands, islets off the Caribbean coast, under a long-term lease, but they remain technically under Nicaraguan jurisdiction. The Corn Islands may turn out to be important as a seaplane base some day. We also have rights at the Gulf of Fonseca (where Captain Horatio Hornblower made his first famous landfall) on the Pacific side, and a United States naval base is being built there. El Salvador and Honduras, incidentally, deny that Nicaragua had the right to give us concessions at Fonseca, which they also claim.

Economically as well as politically, Nicaragua is closely dependent on the United States. The collector-general of customs is an American, Irving Lindberg; so is General Mullins, the director of the military academy of which Somoza is very proud. The United States takes a full 95 per cent of Nicaraguan exports (chiefly bananas, tropical produce, mahogany, gold), and furnishes 85 per cent of its imports. The Export-Import Bank recently lent the country $2,000,000 for work on a highway from Managua to the east coast, which will assist its lagging internal development. Teaching of English is to be made compulsory in the local schools.

Like Costa Rica, Nicaragua did not take Fifth Columnism very seriously until quite recently. German business men were strongly entrenched; one newspaper, *La Prensa,* took a distinct pro-Axis line; several high officials, including members of the Foreign Office and the Ministry of the Interior, were acknowledged pro-Germans; and a well-known Jesuit school at Granada, the Colegio Centroámerica, was a citadel of Falange extremism. Axis agents worked with clandestine radios to jam London broadcasts; a German merchant ship, the *Stella,* sought refuge in Nicaraguan waters in order to evade the British blockade. Later

Somoza—or the government—bought it from the Germans, over British protest.

The Germans then overplayed their hand, United States influence came into play, and the Nicaraguan government began to get busy. The commander-in-chief of the army, whose son-in-law was German, was dismissed; the British blacklist—and now the American blacklist—crippled German firms. An Axis agent named Paul Ernst Strobelt was expelled from the country, and another, Imro Boehmer, a merchant, was arrested. The Nicaraguans say that Boehmer threatened that the German air force would bomb the country after Hitler "had destroyed San José, Costa Rica" (New York *Times*, May 16, 1941).

The Nicaraguan Canal Project

This is an old story. As early as the 1500's Spanish *conquistadores* talked of a canal across Nicaragua, making use of the wide expanse of its lakes. The San Juan river is navigable part of its length; indeed, Lord Nelson lost an eye when his fleet engaged a Spanish fort near Granada, up the river. Hundreds of American forty-niners used the Nicaraguan route to get from the eastern United States to California quickly, before our transcontinental railway was built. French engineers mapped the canal route, and the Vanderbilts held one early concession. One American company got an actual contract to build the canal, and started dredging, but the work was soon given up.

The United States government made a thorough investigation of the Nicaraguan canal project in 1898, before the Panama Canal was built. Then came a strange incident: Nicaragua issued some postage stamps decorated with volcanoes. This frightened the United States into thinking that the canal would be vulnerable to earthquakes, and—for other reasons too—Panama was selected instead of Nicaragua. In 1929-31 the question came up again, and was again looked into by Congress, which set up a commission of inquiry. The idea was, of course, that a canal in Nicaragua would be of enormous strategic importance if anything should ever happen to Panama. In 1938 came a supplementary analysis, to compare the cost of building a new canal in Nicaragua with that of furnishing Panama with new locks. It was estimated that the Nicaraguan canal would cost $1,442,000,000 (with bomb-proof locks) and would take eight or ten years to build. The canal would be 173 miles long (as against forty for Panama) and it would take the United States fleet two days to traverse it—dangerously long if bombing aircraft were near by.

The idea is in abeyance now, but it may be revived at any time. Meantime, the Nicaraguans want our help to build a more simple barge canal which would open up the eastern section of the country.

Honduras

This, Paraguay possibly excepted, is the poorest and least advanced state in the Americas. It is an amorphous country, about the size of Pennsylvania; its 1,000,000 (estimated) people are for the most part mestizo; its young men—reaching education after long travail—mourn their dour circumstances. I heard one Honduranian say that his was the only country in the world without pride or patriotism. Honduras has no national bank, no foreign exchange; its strange little capital, Tegucigalpa, is one of the few in the world without a railroad.

The President of Honduras is General Tiburcio Carias, a handsome Indian with thick curly hair, a heavy white mustache, lively eyes, and the strongest handshake in Central America. He is sixty-five, but he still looks like a Notre Dame fullback; he is an iron mountain of a man, weighing probably 260 pounds. Carias grew up in humble circumstances, and his wife was the daughter of an innkeeper. He has been President since 1933, and his term—by the usual constitutional juggling—has been recently extended to 1949. One of his sons is Honduranian consul general in New York, and another holds the same post in

Liverpool. Carias has given his country respite from incessant political disorder; this is his service. There has been no revolution since 1932.

Like Ubico and Martínez, General Carias lives frugally, and is a teetotaler. Like Somoza, he is well protected. When he attends mass, machine guns are mounted *inside the church*. They are dispensed with only when he visits the American Legation on July Fourth.

Honduras is the banana republic par excellence, and it is little more or less than a preserve of the United Fruit Company. About 30 per cent of all the company's banana lands—valued at about $45,000,000—are in Honduras. The company controls ports, harbors, newspapers, plantations. There are no taxes in Honduras; revenue comes from customs and United Fruit. The government budget (only about $6,000,000) is usually out of balance, and the company helps to make up the deficit. Recently it advanced $300,000 to meet government pay rolls. Honduras is perpetually in debt.

There are 443 Germans in Honduras (of whom 177 live in the capital, Tegucigalpa), 199 Italians, and 2 Japanese. The German chargé d'affaires was, for a time, the well-known Christian Zinsser, who had worked in Austria and Poland, but Honduras declared him persona non grata and expelled him in April 1941.[2] A recent decree prohibits "all foreign residents from engaging in political activity," and in June the Honduranian government ordered the four German and Italian consulates in the country closed, following similar action by the United States. German activity was so active for a time that the local authorities had to suspend the Tegucigalpa postal service in order to keep Axis propaganda out of the mails.

President Carias has said that he will follow the United States completely in hemisphere policy. If we break off relations with Germany, he will too.

[2] Nor would any of the other Central American States take him in.

Airways in Central America

I have mentioned the extreme primitiveness of communications throughout Central America, except by air. The shining clippers of Pan American Airways transform days into minutes. Pan American links all the Central American capitals, and in addition operates a local subsidiary in Guatemala. You can fly from Guatemala City to Panama in an easy day, stopping at all four intervening capitals. A similar journey overland would literally take weeks, if it could be made at all.

One should also mention the remarkable TACA (*Transportes Aéreos Centroamericanos*) service, which was founded by a romantic New Zealander, Lowell Yerex, and which is now owned by American Export Lines. Whereas Pan American concentrates on an international passenger and mail service, Taca's specialty is development within each country, particularly Honduras. Taca has no fewer than 135 regular and 100 flag stops throughout Central America, served by fifty-two airplanes and thirty American pilots. Last year it carried more freight than any other airline in the world, something over 20,000,000 pounds.

Its contribution to opening up otherwise remote and isolated regions has been profound. It carries everything from bridge culverts to live horses to chicle for chewing gum. Rivalry between Pan American and Taca is acute.   ·

Pan-American Highway

It is an astonishing fact, but nevertheless true—and preposterous from the point of view of hemisphere defense—that no overland route exists between the United States and the Panama Canal. The Pan-American Highway, one of the most ambitious projects of our day, will—if and when it is completed—provide this essential link.

Until 1930, only two of the states north of the canal had any international connection at all, Mexico and Guatemala, which were joined by rail. There were no road connections whatever, and indeed, even today, only three countries are directly linked by road—Mexico, Guatemala, and El Salvador. This was partly because the road systems, primitive anyway, tended only to radiate from each capital. Also, for political reasons, no country wanted to be too close to its next-door neighbor. Each liked its isolation.

The idea of a Pan-American Highway was conceived in 1923, and the project has been intermittently pushed ever since, against great obstacles. There are still large gaps; in fact, the road only covers about half of the 3,250 miles between the Rio Grande and Panama. The biggest gap is in Mexico south of Mexico City. Both Guatemala and El Salvador have completed their small but important links; they did so, moreover, without financial help from the United States. The work is about one-third done in Honduras, and there are 150 miles still to go in Nicaragua, a job that will take three years. The Export-Import Bank is helping Costa Rica to push on with its share, which is in difficult mountainous terrain. In Panama itself sixty-five miles remain to be built to the Costa Rican frontier; southward from the canal the road exists for about thirty miles, then disappears into the jungle.

The Pan-American Highway should, it goes without saying, be a vital link for the Americas; work should go on uninterruptedly until it is possible to drive a car from New York to Buenos Aires.

Chapter X
Panama: Country, Zone, and Defense

~~~~~~

THE President of Panama, Dr. Arnulfo Arias, is one of the most difficult and complex characters in the Americas. It is striking that Arias, whose key position is obvious—his government straddles that most vital instrument of defense, the Panama Canal—should be the only Latin American head of state who has avowed emotional sympathies with totalitarianism.

Dr. Arias is suave, confident, vivid, and ambitious. He is certainly the handsomest President in the hemisphere. His conversation is animated; his mannerisms are informal; his instincts are violently nationalist. Born in Panama in 1901, he went to Harwick College in New York, and then to the University of Chicago and Harvard, where he took his M.D. He spent several years on the staff of the Boston City Hospital, and then returned to Panama to practice medicine. But politics were in his blood. He became Director of Public Health, which gave him control of the lotteries and consequent political power; in both 1932 and 1936 he played an important behind-the-scenes role in the local elections. For a time he served abroad as Panamanian minister to Rome. He became President himself in 1940.

His best friend and inseparable companion is Dr. Antonio Isaza, who was Panamanian consul in Hamburg, Germany, for some years, and who strongly influenced him toward totalitarian ideas. I heard it said in Panama that Arias was "mesmerized" by Isaza. When Arias became leader of the *Partido Nacional Revolucionario*, the local wits called him the Nazi-onal leader. Another nickname was the "Führer Criollo."

For a time Arias had close associations with his brother, the distinguished lawyer Dr. Harmodio Arias, who was President of Panama from 1932 to 1936. Then, when Arnulfo became

President (Harmodio pointedly did not attend the inauguration), the brothers quarreled. Harmodio's newspaper, the *Panama American*, bitterly opposed the new President's "reforms," and its foreign editor, Edward W. Scott, was expelled from the country. Mr. Scott, arriving in New York, said that Arias was supported by a "vicious minority," and that the United States "has a large Trojan horse growing on the banks of the Panama Canal."

President Arias' inaugural speech and other early pronouncements gave good indication of his leanings toward a form of Fascism. Listen:

The words democracy, liberty, liberalism, are so bandied about nowadays that they have no meaning. . . .

The "demagogic concept" that all men are free and equal is biologically without foundation.

Panama should give "opportunity to every citizen in accordance with his merits, his patriotism, his moral and physical worth, and his capacity for work."

The concept of liberty as an inalienable and unlimited right of the individual must give way to the more modern concept of liberty conditioned by the social exigencies of the community.

The concept of individual property must likewise yield to the more modern and advanced concept which assigns to property a social function.

The family must likewise be subject to regulation in order that it may co-operate efficiently with the state in the education of the child.

Soon after his inauguration Dr. Arias gave the country a new constitution on strongly corporative lines. It increases the presidential term from four to six years; it gives the nation the right of "eminent domain" over all territory, including air and subsoil rights; it prohibits the immigration of Negroes, Chinese, and Japanese, and removes citizenship from all Negroes who cannot speak Spanish; it gives the government (that is, Dr. Arias) the right to establish government monopolies and expropriate private property.

What Arias stands for above all is the doctrine of *pana-meñismo*, which means Panama for the Panamanians. He denies that he is anti-foreign or anti-United States; he says merely that Panama should "assimilate" its foreign residents. But the virus of nationalism on a racial basis has bitten him deeply. He fiercely detests the Negroes, large numbers of whom have lived in Panama since they were imported to work on the canal. He wants to make Panama white, or at least to keep it from getting blacker.

The President's fanatic nationalism has found several outlets. "We have passed the stage of foreign tutelage," he said soon after he assumed office. He ordered the exclusive use of Spanish in street signs and the like. During his electoral campaign (his enemies charge that all government employees were forced to pay 5 per cent of their salaries to support him) he organized a Guardia Cívica, which has not yet been disbanded. This is in effect his private army, particularly valuable because no regular army exists. In January 1941, Panamanian boys and girls were organized into the Clubs of Urraca, modeled closely on the Hitler Jugend. Urraca was a Panamanian Indian hero who fought the Spaniards.

In a radio speech to the United States, in October 1940, President Arias came as near to public defiance of the American government as he well could. As translated from the Spanish text in the *Panama American*, this speech said in part:

The United States knows definitely that on the basis of good will and frank understanding it can receive from Panama the best possible co-operation for the protection of vital American interests in the Canal Zone. Similarly the United States knows . . . that the Republic of Panama, though small, weak, and lacking material resources for the defense of its rights . . . could, in case of reprisal, affect the high interests of the United States *by granting concessions in its territory to other powerful countries which would have the material force to defend it.* (Italics mine.)

When actually delivering his address, Arias eliminated the ominous second sentence above. Nor did it appear in the English section of the *Panama American*[1] or in other English-language newspapers. It did, however, appear in the official Spanish text. The supposition is that Arias decided to suppress it at the last moment, but overlooked correction of the Spanish text already given to the newspapers.

Then came a policy of minor pinpricks *vis-à-vis* the United States. When distinguished American officers took part in public ceremonies, they were apt to find themselves in the worst seats. When an American admiral, say, called on the Panamanian Foreign Minister—who knows English perfectly—the minister insisted on speaking Spanish, though the Admiral knew none. For a time, the Arias government annoyingly haggled, bickered, and delayed in negotiations with the United States army over airfield sites in Panama territory and the like.

This was all petty enough, and if it had happened in Siam or Bulgaria no one would have paid much attention. But in Panama, the central ganglion of hemisphere defense, it was a nuisance. It was awkward that Dr. Arias should set out to be totalitarian in domestic policy; to have him pursue an anti-United States course in foreign affairs was intolerable. When the new Panamanian ambassador arrived in Washington, President Roosevelt gravely reminded him of the "responsibilities" that defense of the canal entails. Meantime Arias, receding somewhat, said that his government "was ready to lend its co-operation" in the matter of defense facilities. Then, in March 1941, he backwatered a long way, and announced that we could, after all, build air bases in his territory. The United States is to acquire sites for airfields, searchlight posts, and aircraft detectors; this was our first outright acquisition of bases in any Latin American country in recent times. We promise to give "adequate compensation" for them, and to return them to Panama when the war in Europe ends. But— final negotiations have not gone smoothly.

Of course the United States could, if it wished, exert instan-

[1] This newspaper is printed in both Spanish and English, with half the type upside down so that neither language takes precedence.

taneous pressure on Panama at any time—for instance by the simple expedient of barring its territory to our troops in the Canal Zone. This would mean that Panama, which is totally dependent on the Zone, would starve in a month. But we hesitate to take any such drastic steps, because of the Good Neighbor policy. Nor are they likely to be necessary.

When I saw President Arias he insisted that the Zone is Panamanian territory, belonging to Panama, even though Washington holds it under perpetual grant. He said that the United States and Panama should be twins—a big twin and a little twin —co-operating to defend the canal against anybody. But he was adamant that his country's rights be maintained, and its prestige safeguarded. As to the European war, he said that Panama was— and would continue to be—"strictly neutral." Which is, of course, an indirect slap at the United States.

But, pinpricks aside, this does not matter much. The real boss of Panama is the United States army.

The Republic of Panama

This unique little country, bisected by the canal, looks like an elephant's trunk extending out of Colombia, from which it was separated in 1903. Its population outside the Zone is 467,459, which is roughly that of Minneapolis; there are about 80,000 whites, 70,000 Negroes, 42,000 Indians, and 4,100 Orientals; the rest are mixed.

The most interesting thing about Panama, the country, is that here, for the first time in this book, we touch real jungle. Not merely political or racial jungle. In Panama the explosive force of a tropical climate becomes a major phenomenon. Here man fights primitive nature. When I arrived in Balboa I blinked to discover that such animals as the tapir exist within a thousand yards of the canal, that in army camps a few miles from Colón or Cristóbal you may run into twenty-five different kinds of snakes, some as deadly as the bushmaster; that on the Atlantic side there are no roads whatever except for the twenty-five-mile

stretch between Colón and Portobelo; that the Cuña Indians
in Darien have never been subdued and are still definitely hostile.
All this—within a few miles of one of the greatest engineering
feats known to man! The Panamanian Indians are the most
primitive of any on the American continent, except possibly those
near the headwaters of the Amazon. The government makes
hardly any effort to maintain effective rule among, say, either
the San Blas Indians or those near the Colombian frontier. After
the Pan-American Highway stops at Chepo, some thirty miles
below Balboa, everything becomes trackless jungle. Engineers
concede that it will take many years of work—with United States
army help—to push it further, and that it may turn out to be too
expensive ever to be completed. In that case, a barge ferry service
would link the Highway between Cristóbal and a port in Colombia
like Barranquilla.

The Canal Zone is the ten-mile-wide strip that the canal traverses, and it is as much a part of the United States as Omaha,
Nebraska, no matter what Arias says. The country lives on the
Zone. Direct and indirect revenues from the canal, plus the lotteries, make up the budget; there are no taxes. We pay Panama
$430,000 per year as rental for the Zone, but this is only a small
fraction of what it contributes to the country. For instance,
the annual canal pay roll is roughly $28,000,000, and that of the
army and navy units stationed there about as much; perhaps
half this is spent in Panama shops and business houses.

Relations between the United States and Panama are controlled by a treaty signed in 1936, but only ratified by our Senate
in 1939. This treaty—ratification of which the American army
vigorously opposed—commits us to consult Panama whenever we
wish to use *Panamanian* territory, as apart from Zone territory,
for defense purposes. Before the 1936 treaty we could send troops
or build installations anywhere in Panama we wished. Now,
legally, we cannot do so. This was the situation which the Arias
government sought to exploit. Suppose, in order to provide a
proper apron for antiaircraft batteries, we want a plot of land

a few miles beyond the Zone frontier. Obviously antiaircraft precautions cannot be complete or foolproof if they are restricted to a ten-mile strip. Yet we are bound to consult with Panama before acquiring what we need.

In his somewhat sinister October broadcast President Arias accused the United States of occupying certain areas, like Río Hato on the mainland, and the islands of Taboga and Taboguilla, without permission. These were sites that we procured long before the 1936 treaty, by lease from private owners; what the United States wants now are additional leases under the new treaty. Again, it is essential that the United States import labor into Panama for work on the new locks. Arias opposes this, because it means an influx of colored workers. We contend that we have absolute rights in this matter, since the 1936 treaty gives us not merely the right to maintain and operate the canal, but to defend it. Panama contends otherwise. But such disputes are being gradually ironed out since March 1941, when the agreement on bases was arranged.

How Is the Canal Defended? ˙

Defense of the Panama Canal—imperative to United States strategy since it is the only means whereby the American fleet can go quickly from ocean to ocean—has four aspects.

First, political. This means that the United States should maintain close and cordial relations with the governments of those countries near by—particularly Colombia, Venezuela, Ecuador, and the Central American republics.

Second, defense against attack by naval forces, i.e. by the Japanese fleet if we should go to war with Japan. (Attack by hostile land forces is almost out of the question, since the jungle terrain is so impenetrable. General Goethals, one of the builders of the canal, deliberately discouraged roadbuilding in its environs, so as not to interfere with defenses provided naturally by the jungle.)

Third, defense against aerial attack, either from planes based on carriers or from near-by airports that might be utilized by a hostile power.

Fourth, and probably most important, defense against internal trouble or sabotage.

There are geographical categories to consider also; that is, defense on both the Atlantic and Pacific sides. The Atlantic approaches to the canal are screened by the islands of the Caribbean; I will discuss this area and the strategy involved in Chapter XXVII. At present I confine myself to general matters and to the Pacific side.

Our defense against forthright naval attack is based on cooperation between the United States navy and army. The navy's Special Service squadron, comprising destroyer and submarine units, has been greatly strengthened; it maintains a patrol in what is known as the "Defensive Sea Area." An offshore force watches all incoming ships—within a radius of some 900 miles— and passes them over to army control when they get close. The army assumes responsibility for everything within thirty miles of the canal. The army in turn "feeds" any such ships to the civilian authorities of the Panama Canal Administration, which sees them through the canal itself.

Belonging to the army are some of the most powerful coast-defense batteries in the world. I saw these enormous guns— some are 16-inch, some 14-inch—hidden along the fringes of the jungle; I watched a sergeant, with a whip of his wrist, elevate the monstrous gun barrels as easily as he might lift a toy. To fire a gun costs $1,200, so they are not fired often . . . Near the eastern orifice of the canal,[2] watching some defense mechanisms other than artillery, I dipped my hand into a bucket of what seemed to be pale maple sugar. It was moist, faintly sticky; it left silver specks on my fingers. I asked what it was. "T.N.T."

The navy maintains its fanlike patrol largely by use of air-

[2] As everyone knows, the canal cuts crosswise through the peculiar configuration of the isthmus, and the eastern end is on the Pacific, not the Atlantic.

craft. The essential strategy—not merely against naval but against air attack also—is ceaseless vigilance to screen off any approach by a hostile or doubtful ship. Bases are necessary to make this screen really effective, to form an apron over which the planes may fly; otherwise patrol bombers can do little but fly out from Panama and back, which is not enough. What the navy wants are key points above and below the canal, whence planes may fly in a wide arc, meet in the Pacific, and return. The ideal northern base would be Salina Cruz on the Isthmus of Tehuantepec. It has a fair harbor protected by a breakwater, and is a railhead. Supplies might come from New Orleans to Puerto México, on the other side of Tehuantepec, and reach Salina Cruz easily. The next best base to the north is Moneypenny Anchorage in the Gulf of Fonseca, Nicaragua, on which work is beginning. The chief disadvantage here is that the water is apt to be too rough for seaplanes.

The southerly base the navy wants is the Galápagos group of islands held by Ecuador. If we had facilities in Galápagos, the Pacific "apron" protecting the canal would be complete. I deal briefly with the Galápagos question in the chapter on Ecuador below.

The key problem in defense of the canal is the danger of *surprise* attack. The navy patrol renders alert and watchful service. But it is by no means enough. So we turn to what the army is doing on Panamanian territory and in the Zone itself.

I spent a crammed and vivid day driving through the jungle and along the banks of the canal inspecting the army installations. My guides were General Sanderford Jarman, the chief of anti-aircraft defense, and William Dawson, the United States ambassador. We brushed through humid thickets, and found anti-aircraft guns camouflaged carefully in remote clearings. We pushed up roads recently hacked out of the boiling jungle, and came across spick-and-span army units clustering around the searchlight batteries. We watched the lights—some of them are of 800,000,000 candle power—catch planes overhead, and we saw army bombers punch targets with effortless precision.

The army concentrates on three devices, the aerial detectors, which can locate planes several hundred miles before they are seen; the formidable net of searchlights; and the antiaircraft guns themselves. Each army post, apparently isolated in the bush, can be in instant contact with the others. The officers and men live well, work hard, take scrupulous care of their health (malaria has been virtually stamped out), kill snakes for fun, and loaf after hours under the palms. Oil is poured on every spot of water; every bed rests in a pool of insecticide; lime is spread around the kitchen tables to check disease.

You go forward, up a hot, tawny, newly surfaced road, which slices through sienna-colored cliffs. Beyond is the heavy green stillness of the jungle barrier. You come up a hill, and see boys in khaki. You do not see the guns at first. You dive through the underbrush, descend a carefully built channel, brush the sweat from your eyes, look—and still don't see them. But there they are, painted a dull green, thickly oiled, covered with logs and thatch, and ready for instant action. The detectors, lights, and guns are mounted twenty-four hours a day.

The army has several hundred installations—I mustn't say exactly how many—in the Zone, and to visit them all would mean a trip of about 1,500 miles. The work involved has been prodigious. Airfields exist in what were swamps yesterday; whole new towns, like Cocali, are bursting out of the jungle. The chief technical problem, only surmounted by tremendous effort, has been road building. There is very little level ground in Panama (which serves to make airfields, too, difficult to build), and work on roads is practicable only for three months a year, when the rains cease. A plain road costs $30,000 a mile.

Finally there is defense against sabotage. Suppose a Japanese ship should blow itself up while traversing one of the locks. Suppose some "neutral" ship should get out of control and jam itself sideways in the narrow channel. Suppose Panamanian

Quislings should wreck the spillway at Gatun Dam, which might
—a catastrophe—empty the canal.

The Canal Administration has accurate records of every ship
afloat in the world, and any ship approaching is investigated.
First it stops in an area scrupulously laned off, and waits to be
passed. United States officers board it, and take complete command. An independent telephone is set up connecting the bridge
and engine room, and Americans watch at both ends, to obviate
the possibility of false commands. If there is any cause for suspicion, the whole ship is netted, so that no bomb could be dropped.
No ships are allowed to make the transit at night, and their
speed is slow because only one set of locks is used. The other is
being bombproofed.

One possibility of danger is that lighters might approach a
ship waiting for transit, and remove secret cargoes of explosives
under cover of night. It is forbidden to land or handle explosives
in the Zone, but not in Panamanian territory. And in Panama
City and Colón there are German and Japanese warehouses belonging to local business men. We do not know what is in them.
But the precautions we take are extreme, especially at the locks
and spillways. . . . There are about 2,000 German nationals in
Panama, 760 Italians, and 420 Japanese. Everyone is taped.[3]

The United States army has increased its garrison from about
18,000 men to a number much greater. The exact number may
not be revealed, but it is considerable. The navy is at top efficiency,
and both army and navy planes maintain their timeless watch.
Civil authorities are on guard every minute. Nobody attacking
the canal will have an easy job. No amateur is going to blow it
up with a stick of dynamite in his pocket.

New Locks and New Road

To provide additional safeguards, work began in the spring of
1941 on a third set of locks, which will in effect make an alterna-

[3] In June 1940, just after the fall of France, the Vichy government appointed
a *military* attaché to Panama, though Panama has no army. This made American eyebrows lift.

tive passage through the canal if anything happens to the present locks. Today the canal is like a two-way highway; twin locks are side by side. The third set will be built at distances varying from 2,200 feet (at Pedro Miguel) to a mile and a half from the existing locks, thus creating a second channel. The new locks will, of course, be bombproofed.

Congress authorized the new locks in 1939, and the first appropriation came in the summer of 1940. The amount of work is monumental, and it will probably take five years. The main excavations will amount to over 50,000,000 cubic yards; new towns to house workers must be built; Miraflores Lake must be widened; the fruitful spillways must be strengthened. Whereas the original canal cost $375,000,000 as a whole, the new locks alone will cost $227,000,000, according to present estimates.

Engineers have been delighted to find that the old canal, after twenty-five years of hard work, is still in excellent order, and that very few improvements will be necessary. There may be some changes in design—for instance, the new Gatun locks will have intermediate gates so that small ships may pass through without using the whole chamber—but in spite of the tremendous mechanical advances made in the past quarter of a century, the basic methods used in the old canal—the way "mules" haul the ships through, for example—cannot be bettered.

Note one highly important point: the old locks are only 110 feet wide. This has perforce limited the beam of United States warships to this size. The new locks will be 1,200 feet long and 140 feet wide. Which means that we can now build bigger, broader aircraft carriers and battleships.

One astonishing fact is that no *road* exists parallel to the canal across the Isthmus. Indeed, at first thought, this seems inconceivable; it shocked me more than anything else on my whole trip. But the technical difficulties were arduous, and the Panama Railway (which is owned and operated by the United States) had, by charter, the right to veto any proposal for a highway that would cut into its lucrative business.

Defense considerations overrode this awkward detail, and the army insisted that a road be built, since the railway might be bombed. Mr. Roosevelt instructed the railway company to waive its embargo rights, and work on the road has begun, with funds provided by the United States Public Roads Administration. There are still twenty-three miles to be built in the complex terrain near Madden Dam. Tropical rains—which make grading impossible—have held up the project, but it will probably be finished some time this year.

One proposal is that the United States should build a *sea-level* canal at Panama, which would dispense with locks, and thus be less vulnerable to air attack. But a sea-level canal would require such a fantastic amount of excavation that it might take twenty years to build and cost perhaps $1,500,000,000.

Chapter XI

Hail Colombia

~~~~~~

So NOW we reach South America proper. It is fitting that the first country we tackle on the continent itself should be Colombia, because in many ways it is the most "typical" South American state. Consider for instance its preoccupation with Culture. Capital C, please.

In Bogotá, Colombia's isolated mountain capital, there are more bookshops than cafés or restaurants. In Bogotá deputies read their poems aloud to one another, and talk about the quantum theory, the philosophy of Bertrand Russell, the influence of Rimbaud on Gide, and the works of Waldo Frank. Conversation is staggeringly intellectual-literary. I sat down at my first dinner party hoping to hear about the Fifth Column and the Panama Canal. But no one would talk about anything except Marcel Proust. Incidentally, Bogotá is the only capital I have ever visited where you wear white tie to a *stag* dinner.

The first Colombian I met was an interviewer in the charming town of Medellín. The first question he asked was, "Do you think that intellectual fermentations, as represented by the left-wing element of the first phase of the first New Deal, are on the whole more beneficial to democracy than otherwise?"

The last Colombian I met was an interviewer on the airport at Cali. He asked, all in a rush, "Where were you born?—What is your favorite city?—Have you ever been in Russia?—What is your opinion of Dostoevsky?"

In between I met many Colombians, especially young journalists and politicians. They asked questions like these: "Is H. L. Mencken still a force? What do North Americans think of the relative merits of Hemingway and Steinbeck? Who is the leading American graphic artist? What intellectual movements still reach New York from Europe? Is Bernard Shaw considered *démodé*? What Latin American writers are most translated abroad? Does

any modern dancer compare with Nijinsky or Isadora Duncan?
Why do American women read so many books?"

Colombia, with 448,794 square miles, is about four times bigger
than Arizona; it is split asunder by three giant fingers of the
Andes, and holds almost 9,000,000 people. These are about 20
per cent pure white (concentrated mostly in Bogotá and Medellín), 5 per cent pure Indian, 5 per cent pure black (mostly living
on the tropical coast), and the rest mestizo or mulatto, with the
white strain predominating. The country is one of the most democratic and progressive in the Americas. It has strong local patri-
otisms, an advanced economy, a healthy mountaineer tradition,
and great pride in its universities, its free press, its free institutions.

Colombia is the country where small men in black clothes plod
eternally through rainy streets, where news of the day is chalked
on blackboards outside the newspaper offices, where tattered but
respectful ragamuffins shine your shoes with—orange peel! It is
the country which produces more varieties of orchids alone than
all the flowers on the Atlantic seaboard of the United States,
where fantastic quantities of Scotch whisky are consumed at a
price of $7.00 a bottle, and where people are so polite that they call
North Americans *misteres* (from "Mister") instead of *gringos*.
It is the country where everyone always carries an umbrella,
where the principal jail is on the main street (as is common all
over South America), where the taxis give you printed receipts,
and where an automobile honks once to indicate straight ahead,
twice for a left turn, and three times for turning right.

A dominant problem is that of communications, as is true in
most of the Andean states. Bogotá, the lonely "Gray City," is
perched 8,660 feet high in the Andes; the altitude, combined
with the incessant dampness, makes most visitors ill. Nowadays
you can fly from Panama to Bogotá in about 3½ hours. But until
the airplane came, Bogotá was by far the most inaccessible capital
in the Americas. You could reach it from Cartagena or Barranquilla, on the Caribbean coast, only by laborious travel up the

Magdalena river, plus uncertain intervals by rail or road; the
trip customarily took sixteen *days*! Even today, a trip across
Colombia from west to east—over the three tremendous Andes
ranges—will take several weeks at least unless you fly—and you
can't always fly.

Some Generalizations About South America

(1) An extreme preoccupation with "culture" as noted above.
Most South Americans consider their culture to be much superior to ours. It derives largely from Europe, especially Paris.

(2) An excessive sensitiveness about modes of behavior, particularly social. For instance, you can win almost any South
American by leaving cards properly. You can win him for life
if, on your cards, you print your address as "Nueva" York
instead of "New" York.

(3) Segregation of women, the family system, chaperonage,
and the like. This is most extreme in the Andean states and
Argentina. In Bogotá one practically never sees upper-class women
in cafés—heaven forbid!—or even on streets.

(4) The profound influence of the Roman Catholic church,
which in most countries dominates if it does not actually control
education.

(5) Insufferable communications—now being improved by increased use of the airplane—are an obstacle to national development in almost every country.

(6) Three heads of state (in Venezuela, Bolivia, and Paraguay) are army generals; all the others are intellectuals—lawyers,
professors, economists, journalists, or architects.

(7) Lack of industrialization. This is due partly to the fact
that few South American business men are content with modest
profits. They want a 25 per cent return, not 5 per cent or 6 per
cent, before they will invest in an enterprise.

(8) The yawning gap between rich and poor in all countries
except Uruguay.

(9) Nepotism and graft are taken for granted almost every-

where. Politics is a *business*. You go into politics for what you get out of it (exactly as you would, say, if you worked for Tammany in New York). Politics, too, is fiercely *personal* as a rule. The line of demarcation between parties is more often based on the personalities of leaders than on the issues involved, though in some countries this is changing.

(10) Most South Americans think that the United States is soft as a well-done peach, too rich, disunited, and "materialistic."

This latter point has great international importance, and it is closely associated with Point No. 1. The Nelson Rockefeller committee on cultural and commercial relations with Latin America has done much admirable work. But its basic line is apt to produce unfortunate results when it seeks to "uplift" the South Americans, when it seeks to export *our* "culture" southward. The emphasis should be the other way. South Americans (like North Americans) loathe uplift; they cannot endure to be objects of solicitude or improvement. Mr. Rockefeller and his minions should attempt unceasingly to let South America know how much "superior" it is to *us*.

Whenever the United States acts firmly and strongly—whenever it gets really tough, in other words—South Americans like it. So long as they think that we are shilly-shallying, especially in relation to the war, they are distrustful. They doubt that we really mean to fight; therefore they doubt that we can really help the British to win; therefore they themselves sit on the fence. Why should they worry, if we don't? But when we *do* take drastic steps, South America watches us with attentive eyes. As soon as we prove beyond doubt that *we* mean business, they follow us.

In the summer of 1941 the United States government, following investigations by the Rockefeller committee and the State Department, blacklisted 1,800 firms throughout Latin America that did business with the Axis. 17,000 American exporting companies were consulted. At about the same time the United States occupied Iceland. These two events have done more to improve hemisphere solidarity than anything in years.

Why Is Colombia a Democracy?

Colombia is emphatically a democratic country, like Costa Rica and Uruguay. In Chapter IX, I outlined the reasons why Costa Rica is a democracy. Let me do likewise for Colombia; the reasons are not quite the same.

First, sectionalism. In each valley, each hilltop community, utterly isolated by the Andes, the people developed their own special characteristics over generations; even today, such an important and upstanding province as Medellín talks occasionally of secession. Each district zealously sought to preserve its own local freedom; it refused to trust any strong central government; it resented giving up authority. As a result the Bogotá government tended to develop democratically; it never dared to impose itself dictatorially on the people.

Second, the Chibcha Indians were primitive and feeble; they did not even know the use of the wheel until the Spaniards came. Hence the imposition of a unified Spanish culture was easy. Colombia has very little tradition of political violence. There has been no revolution since 1903.

Third, Colombian intellectualism, which made for appreciation of the democratic process. Colombia was sending out scientific expeditions as early as 1795.

Fourth, the liberator of the country, after Bolívar, was Francisco Santander (1792-1840); he was not a general, but a lawyer. He was Vice-President of the country when it was called Gran Colombia; he was President when it was New Granada; he hated militarism, despotism, violence. There have been no conspicuous military men in Colombian history. The country has always been dominated by civilians.

Fifth, climate. Colombia has no seasons; the climate is, as they say, "vertical." One joke is that it is the land of eternal spring—because summer never comes! The fact that the weather always stays the same, at each altitude, with no winter or summer, has had great emotional effect in tranquillizing the country, keeping it reasonably calm and steady.

Politics and Personalities in Colombia

The President of Colombia, Dr. Eduardo Santos, is one of the splendid men of the Americas. Slim, handsome, of medium height, with curly iron-gray hair, he has been a newspaper man all his life, and is the owner of one of the best papers in the hemisphere, *El Tiempo* of Bogotá. He still takes time off from the presidency to write occasional editorials, and it is quite possible that his influence in the country comes as much from *El Tiempo* as from his job. It is as if Arthur Sulzberger, the publisher of the New York *Times*, were President of the United States.

Dr. Santos and his brother Enrique purchased *El Tiempo* about forty years ago. In those days the government of the country was conservative, and the Santos brothers were pronounced liberals; nevertheless, the paper did well from the beginning. Dr. Santos told me that in the early days he set type and sold advertising himself, and that the paper never showed a loss. His profit the first month was 16 pesos, then about $4.00. (Nowadays the President earns $25,000 a year.)

President Santos was born in Bogotá in 1888, of Spanish-Colombian descent. He studied in Paris, and speaks French perfectly. He has had a long political as well as journalistic career, but he has never been ambitious politically; the presidency was thrust upon him. He is an absolutely honest man, without pretensions; he has no bodyguard, no outward appurtenances of power. There is no humbug about him, no swank, no pride. He has been called "an apostle of moderation"; one Colombian writer refers to him as "too good, too generous, too lacking in decision" for political life. He believes in the *convivencia*, the "living together," of parties; his career is archetypically liberal-intellectual.

Dr. Santos received me in the workroom of his offices, which are decorated in the modern functional manner. His huge desk is semicircular, and three shining windows open to a magnificent Andean view. We talked as dusk fell sharply. The President pointed outside, looked at the mountains, and smiled ironically. "Hitler must have a view like this. It's the only thing in which I resemble him."

The story in Colombia is that "every President elects his own successor." But it doesn't always work out that way. Another story is that each *new* campaign—a President serves four years— begins on the day the President takes office. Still another is that in Colombia a man begins to be President the year before his election; he works for two years; during the third year nobody is in power; in the fourth year power is held by his successor.

Dr. Santos' term expires in 1942, and by the summer of 1941 the campaign to succeed him was progressing earnestly. The main cleavage in Colombian politics is between liberals and conservatives; the hallmark of their difference is the church. The liberals, who have held power since 1930, are vigorously anti-clerical; in 1936 they amended the constitution and divorced church from state. The conservatives are, on their side, fervently pro-Catholic. They kept office from 1886 to 1930; their contemporary leader is Dr. Laureano Gómez. Until 1930 it was commonly said that the Archbishop of Bogotá "named" every new President, and it was an indiscretion on his part that helped the liberals to reach power that year.

One must pay close attention to Dr. Gómez. He is a typical politician of the extreme Right, and we shall find one of him— with identical stigmata—in almost every South American country. He is strongly religious, strongly clerical, strongly Spanish, and even if he is not actively pro-Axis, he behaves so that he is of use to Germany. His ideas, his instincts, his sympathies, are all bitterly anti-United States. Dr. Gómez is the first example of this type that we have met in this book. We shall meet several others.

Dr. Gómez is an engineer by profession. He was born in 1883

in the strongly German town of Bucaramanga, in Santander province. He was a senator for years, and then president of the senate; he was for a time Colombian minister to both Argentina and Germany; in 1936 he founded a newspaper, *El Siglo,* which violently expresses his Catholic ideas. Gómez talks like a fanatic. He has big shoulders, liquid brown eyes, and a reddish skin. He is aggressive and magnetic. But do not expect logic from him.

In 1935 Gómez had a stroke, following a furious debate in Parliament. He has openly called President Santos a murderer—totally without reason, it goes without saying—who "sits in pools of conservative blood." He has threatened to make civil war if Santos attacks the church, or if Santos is succeeded by the leftist liberal, Dr. Alfonso López. One of his deputies talked about revolution in a stormy parliamentary session last October. The liberals laughed. The conservative replied, "Laugh all you like. Don't think we have no arms. We can get them just where Franco Spain got them!"

In private conversation Gómez denies that he is pro-Axis. I asked him if he would prefer Hitler to Roosevelt at the Panama Canal—an indelicate question perhaps—and he answered No. What he wants is full recognition of Colombian "rights"; he thinks that North Americans treat Colombians as "second-class" citizens, and that we "swindled" Colombia out of the Panama Canal—which is perhaps true. Lately Gómez has tempered his antipathies somewhat. Partly this is because he is a politician after all—with a presidential campaign going on—and obviously the general temper of the country is against him. Partly it is because continued opposition to the United States puts him too deeply in Axis hands.

So much for Santos and Gómez. A third personage of consequence is Alfonso López, who was President from 1934 to 1938, and who is the leading liberal candidate to succeed Santos now, though the liberals are split. López was born in 1885 of a family of merchants, and was educated partly in the United States. He has one of the best minds in South America.

For a time he worked in the coffee business; he was a bank manager and newspaper owner; he represented investment houses and utility concerns; he entered politics, and went abroad as minister to London. When he was a comparatively young man his family's bank, the Banco López, collapsed. The liquidation was perfectly honorable, and stockholders got all their money back; but López has always blamed "big business" for the failure, and from this—partially at least—derives his so-called radicalism, his friendliness to labor.

The great point to make about Alfonso López is that he is a pronounced Leftist and reformer. This is why the Gómez conservatives hate and fear him so deeply. In his first term as President he wrote a new labor law, revised the constitution, and did more for education than any Colombian for a generation. He put through workers' compensation, collective bargaining, the eight-hour day, and paid holidays; he saw to it that children in school got a free hot lunch every day. López was partly responsible for "University City" and its splendid new buildings on the outskirts of Bogotá. Here—something almost unheard of in South America—classes are co-educational, young women study science, and boys live a campus life much like that of the United States. I spent one of the pleasantest mornings of my trip at this university, under the guidance of its rector, Dr. Nieto Caballero.

The López regime was, in a way, a counterpart of the North American New Deal. Conservatives feel about him—as he is running for office again—exactly as Hoover Republicans feel about Roosevelt. And López is too radical for many of his own liberals, just as Roosevelt is too radical for Al Smith Democrats. The Santos folk are none too happy about the López campaign. They fear his intense energy and activity as well as his ideas.

There are a good many other Colombian politicians of note, but let us limit ourselves to three. One is Miguel López, the brother of Alfonso, and ex-Minister of National Economy. He lived in Worcester, Massachusetts, as a boy; he is blond, astute, deliberate; he looks, thinks, and talks exactly like a Yankee. Miguel López is the author of a Plan of National Development for reforming Colombian economy. He does not fix either his objectives or a time-limit rigidly; what he does seek is "disciplined economic development" to replace haphazard growth. He advocates a zoning system for agriculture; he hopes to develop local industries; he wants Colombia to diversify its products further.

The Colombian Foreign Minister, Dr. Luis López de Mesa, is a unique character. He is a 55-year-old bachelor, a distinguished brain specialist whose early researches led him to sociology, and then to politics. He has written several novels based on psychiatry; he is so profoundly learned that most of his compatriots—even though they are Colombian intellectuals—can scarcely follow him. People talk of his "stratospheric dissertations"; they nickname him "Professor Piccard."

But I shall remember a talk I had with Dr. López de Mesa as long as I remember anything about South America. I thought it was on the whole as brilliant a spontaneous discourse as any I ever heard. His first idea was that Europe was disintegrating, and that in compensation the Americas were growing up; as Europe collapsed further, he concluded, the Americas were bound to become more closely tied together. His second idea was that the cardinal trouble with the world today is that it has lost faith. People no longer have comfortable recourse to God, conscience, morality, science, or ethics; instead they have developed a substitute faith in politics, *in the state*. The state, he feels, has replaced the Almighty. Dictators, he says, are substitute divine agents. Planned economy is God.

Dr. Gabriel Turbay, a dark-horse possibility for the 1942 presidency, is Colombian ambassador to Washington. He is of partially Syrian origin, and has a brilliant intellectual record. He was trained as a doctor of medicine, and became the leader of the liberal party; he was for a time very close to Alfonso López; he has held almost every position the government can offer except the presidency, though he is only forty. He has been Colombian minister to Peru, and Belgium. In the summer of 1941 it seemed that the Santos liberals might back Turbay for President to beat López.[1]

Coffee, Petroleum, Economics

The basic industry of Colombia is coffee, and the United States is by far its best customer. A few years ago coffee cost roughly 13 cents a pound on the New York commodity exchange; then it fell to 8-9 cents, which meant a 35 per cent loss to Colombia of the purchasing power that coffee represented. No wonder hard times hit the country. But following the recent coffee quota agreement in the United States, the price rose sharply, and prosperity has come again.

For a time Germany grew rapidly in Colombia's trade. Coffee exports to Germany rose from about 90,000 sacks in 1932 to 300,000 sacks in 1939. Now, of course, this trade has stopped. The United States took 78.8 per cent of Colombian coffee exports in 1938, and 82.8 per cent in 1939. In 1940-41 the percentage will come near to 100 per cent.

Colombia, more than any other South American state, has built up a diversified export trade. Coffee is basic, yes; but the country exports valuable amounts of petroleum, platinum (of which it is the world's greatest producer), bananas (a monopoly of United Fruit), cotton, cocoa, gold, emeralds, and tropical woods. The United States controls the oil industry. The biggest producer is the Tropical Oil Company, a subsidiary of International Petroleum of Canada, which is in turn a subsidiary of Standard of New Jersey. The celebrated Barco Concession—it is a pity to have to omit, for want of space, consideration of this

[1] Another liberal dark horse is the Minister of Education, Dr. Jorge Gaitán. His origins were humble; he worked himself up to become a professor of law; he is moderately Leftist, and was the best mayor Bogotá ever had. . . . On the right wing of the liberal party is Dr. Alfonso Araujo, the Minister of Public Works. He was one of the protégés of the great liberal President, Olaya Herrera. . . . Dr. Carlos Lozano y Lozano, a former Minister of Interior and at present the ambassador to Brazil, is a criminologist by profession; he is influential, and on the anti-López side.

most daring of modern oil enterprises—is owned jointly by
Socony-Vacuum and the Texas Company, and is now beginning
to produce.

Colombia, like Mexico, has flirted with the winds of expropriation. The Barranquilla municipality recently passed a resolution
to expropriate the American company that operates its public
utilities; Bogotá, sick of the miserable telephone service it was
getting, threatened to do likewise. But in each case a compromise
was worked out. United Fruit has had political trouble along
the coast (and also trouble because the sigatoka disease was damaging its crops); one of its managers spent some uncomfortable
days in jail. In October 1940, the Colombian Supreme Court
announced a judgment whereby four-fifths of the privately owned
oil land in the country "should be returned to the nation." But the
end of this episode is not yet.

What Colombians resent—with some reason—is what they
call the "hole-in-the-ground" policy of United States investors.
We dig out gold, they say, we suck out oil, and leave nothing
for Colombia. But this is not entirely just. . . . The direct
American investment in Colombia is a fairly important sum,
$228,000,000. Most of it is in oil, utilities, and mining.

That Column Again

There are 2,977 Germans in Colombia, 1,148 Italians, and 206
Japanese. The Germans are, of course, the most active in propaganda and subversive activity, and they are closely associated
with Colombian members of the Spanish Falange.

The German methods follow the pattern which by this time
we know only too well. Their most conspicuous leaders are, it
seems, Gottfried Schmitt, who married a socially prominent Colombian and who is—or was—press attaché of the German legation; a business man named Jurgen Schlubach, who was called the
Gruppenführer for Colombia, but who recently returned to Germany, and Emil Preufert, the most important of the lot. The en-

tire colony is, of course, *gleichgeschaltet* ("co-ordinated"); German schools, clubs, gymnasia, and so on, play their familiar role.

German propaganda is powerful in several local newspapers. The *Karibischer Beobachter* is published at Barranquilla. *El Diario de la Costa* (of Cartagena) receives a German news service, and so do two papers in Bucaramanga, the *Vanguardia Liberal* and *El Deber*, which is said to be edited by the local German consul, Gustavo Lubinus. In Cúcuta, another German center, the Nazi paper is *El Norte*. The German Legation maintains a full-fledged press section, and sends out a *Boletín Alemán* to all takers. Copies of *Der Adler* are seen sometimes; this sheet, written in both German and Spanish, is printed in Irún, Spain, but it reaches Colombia just the same.

El Siglo, the newspaper of Dr. Laureano Gómez, is the happy possessor of a new plant. Reputedly it cost 100,000 pesos ($57,000 at present exchange); yet its circulation is only about 20,000. Two of Dr. Gómez' editorial associates are violently anti-American, José de la Vega and Guillermo Camacho Montoya, who uses the pseudonym "Américo-Latino." *El Siglo* is the only newspaper in Bogotá that conspicuously prints the German Transocean service. One thing it likes to say is that the United States contemplates the "military conquest" of Latin America.

The Catholic Falange is of great importance also; its spearhead is another publication controlled by Gómez, de la Vega, and Camacho Montoya. The line it generally takes is that Latin America is still ethnically and spiritually part of Spain. Listen to excerpts from a recent article:

We were born Spanish. . . . We speak the tongue of Castile because we can speak no other. . . . The twenty cowardly governments [of Latin America] have put themselves into the hands of foreign nations, dedicated to false liberalism and to masonic, atheistic democracy. . . . The panorama is desolate. . . . We are still conquered territory . . .

Hispanoamérica, the land of vassalage . . . Each day the yoke of Saxo-Americana [*sic*] is drawn tighter around our throats. Sometimes the yoke is of steel, sometimes of silk, soft and perfidious . . .

But—all is not lost. There is still heard the voice of Laureano Gómez to tell the truth about the future, to direct us to the road of tomorrow, the Catholic Hispanic Empire.

And we will go back to Spain. The five arrows of Ferdinand and Isabella, the symbol of Catholic unity, will be our symbol also. It is written in the future of America by the inscrutable hand of providence.

Other Fifth Column points are these. For a time the Colombian army was German-trained; this influenced some older officers to pro-Germanism. For a time the Germans gave scholarships to Colombian students admitting them to universities in Berlin, where their instruction would be *in Spanish.* The Germans stress their intention to "give Panama back to Colombia." (In Panama, on the other hand, their general line is to promise the Panamanians "internationalization of the canal.")

In January 1941, Colombian newspapers said that counterfeit five- and ten-peso notes (also U.S. $10 bills), made in Germany, were circulating in the country. In June Bucaramanga had a serious Fifth Column scare. In July the deputy Arturo Regueros Peralta, who was to testify in Washington about Transocean activities in Colombia, was found shot to death a few days before his departure for the United States. At about the same time the United States embassy in Bogotá—also the offices of Dr. Santos' newspaper *El Tiempo*—were daubed with swastikas. In August the army squelched an alleged Fifth Column plot within its ranks. And so it goes.

For a time the Santos government—which liked to be optimistic—denied that Fifth Columnism was important, and in fact refused to admit that it existed. Russell B. Porter's admirable series of articles in the New York *Times* exposing the German danger was denounced in *El Tiempo*; like most Latin American states, Colombia is very touchy on the Fifth Column subject. Its efforts to investigate and suppress the activities of German agents were lackadaisical for some time, to say the least. Now, however, this is changing. The government is waking up.

The oldest and best-entrenched German airline on the continent, Scadta, functioned in Colombia from about 1919 till 1939; it was in fact the first commercial airline in the hemisphere. Scadta, under the aegis of a remarkable Austrian engineer, Paul von Bauer, performed miracles in opening up domestic communications. But it was pressingly awkward for the United States that an efficient German airline, with good planes and pilots of great experience, should fly so close to the Panama Canal. Negotiations began to squeeze Scadta out; they were long and arduous—chiefly because Pan American Airways was the biggest Scadta stockholder—and they might not have succeeded but for the shrewdness and stubborn grit of the American ambassador, Spruille Braden. While Scadta was still flying, he arranged that a Colombian officer should accompany each plane; American authorities co-operated with pressure on Pan American, which finally agreed to a new arrangement. The German pilots have now been dismissed, and the old line broken up. A company called Avianca has taken its place, owned partly by Pan American, partly by the Colombian government. In July 1941, Bauer finally left Colombia.

One German air service still exists in the country, however. It is called the Arco line; it has two German pilots, Hans D. Hoffman and Fritz Hertzhauser, and four outmoded planes. Arco has no regular schedule, but flies from Bogotá to the southeast, picking up cargo where it can in the Llanos area—the empty plains toward the headwaters of the Orinoco and the Venezuelan frontier. Arco is not considered to have much strategic importance, but Avianca hopes presently to buy it out.[2]

Defense of the canal is, of course, the prime object of United States countermeasures to German infiltration in Colombia. But also we watch carefully the two pipe lines that carry Colombian oil from the hinterland jungles to the Atlantic coast; they might

[2] As this book goes to press it is announced that Arco has in fact been absorbed by Avianca.

be easy targets for sabotage . . . This is as good a place as any, incidentally, to mention something about which very little may be written in detail—the work of the American F.B.I. in counter-espionage in Latin America. Mr. Hoover's young men are watchful in several countries.

Colombia is, it goes without saying, of crucial importance to the United States because of its proximity to the canal. If Colombia should go Nazi, the shock everywhere in Latin America would be tremendous. People would ask what the United States could possibly do to protect itself or its neighbors further south, if it were unable to protect the country closest to Panama. But Colombia is in no great danger of going Nazi, even though the Fifth Column makes trouble. The United States is in an enormously powerful position, and under Santos the country is on the whole as good a friend as we have in the Americas.

Chapter XII

The High Cost of Venezuela

~~~~~~

THE first thing I encountered in Venezuela was a large sign-board reading CURE YOURSELF OF SYPHILIS. The second was a small hotel bedroom, without any windows, that cost $8.00 per day. Not that the two phenomena are related.

Venezuela, where Simón Bolívar was born, is a country that had fifty-two revolutions in less than a century; then for twenty-seven years it lived under the fierce businesslike tyranny of Gómez. It is a country almost one and a half times bigger than Texas; half of it is empty, with illimitable possibilities for development. Of its 3,491,139 people, about 80 per cent are mestizos, and almost 90 per cent are illiterate; when army conscripts are called up, 95 out of 100 are diseased. Venezuela is a nation that has been cruelly exploited, and where exploitation leaves an ugly mark. It lives on oil, and until recently it was the only country in the world without one cent of debt. Its chief problem is evolution to constitutional democracy after the long Gómez dictatorship; its chief struggle for power is between the tough Andinos of the uplands and the poorer folk who live on the steaming coast.

But the most interesting thing about Venezuela is none of these things. What really impresses—and stupefies—the visitor is its high cost of living.

Prices Up and Up

A dozen eggs costs 95 cents in Caracas (pronounced Car-*ack*-as), the country's capital; bread is 32 cents per pound, bacon $1.28 per pound, milk 24 cents per quart, and a can of soup 40 cents. A Hershey chocolate bar costs 31 cents; a dozen bananas 32 cents, a cake of soap that costs 10 cents in New York is 80 cents; a bottle of domestic beer is 32 cents. Butter is $1.22 per pound, and tea $2.24; a domestic chicken will cost you $1.90, an imported chicken above $3.00. An Arrow shirt that costs $1.50 in the

United States is $7.25 in Caracas; a package of American ciga-
rettes sets you back 48 cents; a 20-cent bottle of peanuts costs
$1.24. A pair of American shoes will cost about $20.00; an
American automobile (price $1,180 in the United States) is
$4,200. I shall never forget the face of an American official,
who, moving his family back home, had to buy some excelsior.
It cost him $1.00 per pound.

Official calculations as of February 1941 are that retail prices
in Caracas are higher than those in New York City by the following percentages:

Milk	209	per cent
Sugar	320	" "
Salt	310	" "
Apples, pears, peaches	575	" "
Canned goods, such as marmalade	483	" "
Ham	340	" "
Beans	270	" "
Eggs	313	" "

If an American of modest circumstances—say a junior executive in the oil business—is sent to Venezuela, his typical monthly
budget will be the following,[1] not including clothes, medicine, insurance, savings, or entertainment:

Rent	500	bolívares	$140.00
Food	600	"	168.00
Servants	270	"	75.00
Electricity	60	"	16.80
Fuel	40	"	11.20
Telephone	22	"	6.16
Automobile	75	"	21.00
Miscellaneous	120	"	33.60
	1,687	bolívares	$471.76

Venezuelan wages and salaries are easily the highest in South

[1] Calculating the *bolívar* at 28 cents U. S.

America, but they do not measure up to the inordinate cost of living. An agricultural worker gets 50 cents U.S. per day; a bricklayer gets 12 *bolívares* a day or $3.36; an electrician gets $4.76, and an expert tool maker $6.16. A good stenographer gets 300-600 *bolívares* or $84-$168 per month, and an experienced clerk anything between $200 and $300. A secretary who knows both English and Spanish will make from $2,650 to $3,350 a year, an expert accountant about $4,500, and an executive anything from $5,000 up.

There are several reasons for the astounding price levels of Venezuela. One is the very high tariff barrier, one of the highest in the world; it averages 60 per cent ad valorem. The country has practically no industry; most manufactured goods have to be imported, and stiff duties boost prices out of sight. Moreover, most *foodstuffs* must be imported. Everything in Venezuela has been sacrificed to petroleum; the country has neglected agriculture to the extent that it must buy such essential commodities as rice and flour abroad, and these are highly taxed too. For instance, eggs pay an import duty of 32 cents U. S. per pound, and corn 18 cents. Finally, transportation is primitive, and freight and marketing costs are enormous.

But the chief reason for Venezuelan high prices is something else—petroleum. Oil is sold abroad for dollars—the country's trade balance is heavily favorable—and so dollars flood the land. Thus dollars are cheap, and the local currency fantastically high.

One may properly ask how ordinary people manage to live. The answer could almost be that they don't. Venezuela, the country, is rich; the rank and file of the people are as poor as any I have ever seen.

Oil on Venezuelan Waters

It really does lie on the waters. Touch Venezuela on its soft crust, dent it anywhere near the sea; oil juts out. In the Maracaibo basin, the richest oil deposit known to man, the derricks rise from the yellow waters of the lake; here oil and water do mix.

Venezuela is the third greatest oil producer in the world (after the United States and the Soviet Union), and the world's first exporter. Its 1939 exports amounted to 20,830,000 tons; those of 1940—figures are not yet ready—will probably be higher, which will make a record year. Oil accounts for about 85 per cent of the country's exports, and for two-thirds of the government's revenue, if you count indirect as well as direct contributions. There are no income taxes, no real estate taxes, no excise taxes, no corporation taxes, in Venezuela. Oil is master. Oil pays all.

The oil industry in Venezuela is just reaching its twenty-first birthday; preliminary exploration began many years ago, but the big boom did not start till 1920. Exploration is still going on; no one knows how or where it will end. Three companies control the bulk of production, Standard of New Jersey, Gulf Oil, and Royal Dutch Shell, which is technically a Delaware corporation but which is controlled by British and Netherlands interests. Standard and Shell ship their crude oil from Maracaibo to the Dutch West Indian islands of Aruba and Curaçao, where it is refined and then re-exported; Gulf ships direct to the United States.

Relations between the oil companies and the Venezuelan government are "normal," but not as good as they might be by any means. The companies pay a complicated royalty based partly on location of the wells; royalties and taxes combined amount to about 20 per cent of the value of the oil. Venezuela considers this as good a bargain as it can get at present, and comparatively few people talk about expropriation. One recent minister of *fomento* (development) did have a certain reputation as an expropriationist, but he was in the minority. Most Venezuelans say, "Why kill the golden calf?" They are content to sit back, take their 20 per cent, and let the future go hang.

Venezuela was unique for a generation: it was the only country on earth with neither an external nor an internal debt. But early in 1941 the government borrowed $10,000,000 from the

National City Bank of New York; incidentally this was the first commercial loan from the United States to any Latin American country since the riotous 1920's. This loan sounds a somewhat ominous note; it came because Venezuelan oil exports, following war and blockade, began to shrink.

Meantime the decline of agriculture proceeds. The country must import such staples as beans, potatoes, and even rice. The Andinos, who depend mostly on coffee, need subsidies to live; the *Llaneros* (the plainsmen) have neglected what should be their prime industry, cattle. Oil has greased the chute. Yet the bulk of the people suffer definitely from malnutrition; some are almost literally starving. There is oil, yes. But you can't eat oil, or even drink it.

Venezuela's future may be brilliant, even if the country cannot feed itself. Who can tell? What will happen if oil should give out some day?

Bolívar and the Andes

Two giant phenomena need brief mention now, because they are important not merely to Venezuela, but to all the countries of the west coast to which we presently turn. One is human—the fabulous career of Simón Bolívar. The other is natural—the *cordillera* of the Andes.

Bolívar, the *Libertador*, was born in 1783, in Caracas, of a wealthy Creole family, and educated mostly in Madrid, Paris, and Rome. His life, like those of most great men, was utterly dominated by one idea; moreover, the idea must have solidified itself in his conscience when he was very young. For he was only twenty-two when he took his famous vow, "I will not give rest to my arm or my soul till I have broken the chains that bind my fatherland to Spain." Later this idea expanded into the principle of Pan-American unity. Bolívar is the essential fountain head of our contemporary conceptions of hemisphere solidarity, good neighborliness, and joint defense. More than a century after his death, his seminal ideas still bear fruit.

In 1810 Bolívar made his first tentative revolution; three years later his men took Caracas. There followed periods of exile and vicissitude. He had formidable energy, and formidable recuperative powers. In 1819, helped by his great general, Antonio José de Sucre, he marched 1,000 miles and crossed the Andes with his small army—the feat is one of the most remarkable in military history—and defeated the Spaniards at Boyacá. This battle freed Venezuela and Colombia, and in effect signaled the end of Spanish power on the continent. Bolívar then added Ecuador to his domains, and in 1824, in co-operation with the Argentine patriot San Martín, smashed the Spaniards in Peru. He went on to install Sucre as President of Bolivia (and also took advice from Great Britain in writing the Bolivian constitution). Altogether Bolívar liberated five countries—Venezuela, Colombia, Ecuador, Peru, Bolivia—six, if you include Panama. The record is unique.

Bolívar was one of the most brilliantly tempestuous characters of modern times. He marched, talked, fought, wrote, and made love prodigiously. He left ten trunks solid with his papers; he had an unending variety of mistresses. He could never endure to be alone; he was always a creature of violently unquenched emotions. According to Beals[2] "his poetry and eloquence always soared highest when he was kneeling at the foot of a volcano or a woman." He hated racial prejudice; he made his sister marry one of his Negro generals. He died at forty-seven, a lonely exile, worn out.

The Liberator was a genuine idealist; of that there is no doubt. But he was one of those misbegotten creatures who live before their time, and apparently he lacked basic political sense. Also he had hard material to work with. His campaigns were of considerable indirect benefit to the United States, and particularly to Great Britain. The British were delighted in those days by anything that weakened Spain. I have even heard Latin Americans call Bolívar a "British stooge," which is hardly fair.

[2] Carleton Beals, *America South*, p. 201.

The Andes are the most stupendous mountains in the world. In the Himalayas some single peaks are higher, but nothing on earth can match the uninterrupted Andean flow from the Caribbean to the Straits of Magellan, some 4,600 miles; nothing can rival their solid, continual, and epochal immensity through seven different countries. Not that the Andes aren't high. There are more than forty peaks over 18,000 feet. Their complex *cordillera* is the spinal column, the backbone, the essential matrix of the continent. And the Andean configuration plays a pertinent role in political, economic, and social affairs. Much of the mineral wealth of South America is in the Andes—for instance silver in Peru, and tin and tungsten in Bolivia—much of its Indian heritage, much of its historical basis, much of its backwardness and poverty.

But no one can appreciate the primitive might of the Andes without flying over them. Try it once or twice.

The Catfish Dictatorship

For twenty-seven years, from 1908 to his death in 1935, Venezuela was ruled by a semi-literate *cholo* (half-breed) named Juan Vicente Gómez. He was called *El Brujo* (the sorcerer), or "The Catfish"; he was a tidy little man, very mild in appearance, with a good business head. He ran Venezuela, usually behind a screen of puppet Presidents, as his private estate; it was *his* country for more than a quarter of a century in almost the way that Pocantico Hills, say, is the property of the Rockefellers, or Cliveden that of Lord and Lady Astor. When he died his fortune was estimated at $200,000,000.

Gómez owned cattle ranches, coffee haciendas (though he wasn't much interested in coffee), sugar plantations, industrial plants, roads and palaces, and an estate at Maracay that is still a wonder to behold. He was not passionately concerned with politics *per se*; all that interested him was that Venezuela should be orderly, prosperous, and lucrative, so that gold might pour into his pockets. Of course, the petroleum boom enriched him and his friends inordinately. . . . Gómez did not drink or smoke. But he *was* interested in women. He never married. But he had between eighty and ninety illegitimate children, a record of which he was not unnaturally proud. On his deathbed—aged seventy-seven—he was still looking for a woman to be a "perfect mother" for a legitimate son, who might be his lawful heir.

The Catfish was—let us not gloss over the fact—a murderous blackguard. He made use of tortures of inconceivable brutality; political prisoners, of which there were thousands, dragged out their lives bearing leg irons (*grillos*) that made them permanent cripples, if they were not hung upside down—by the testicles— till they died. Others became human slime, literally. Suppose some students rioted against the government. Gómez was quite capable of choosing one out of every ten by lot, and hanging them—*by meathooks through their throats!*

Gómez finally died in 1935—people thought wearily that he would never die—which means in effect that Venezuela, as a modern country, is only six years old. Which explains much. All his property was confiscated and nationalized on his death, and most of his children exiled. The government that followed him wisely let the people run wild happily for a day or two; the prisons were emptied, and all the *grillos* dumped into the sea. Venezuela's chief political problem since 1935 has been an attempt to build a modern state on the strange ground that Gómez laid.

Political Situation Nowadays

Gómez was succeeded by General Eleázar López Contreras who for some years was his Minister of War. López Contreras had a reputation for stiffness—one story is that he once ordered his own son to be arrested and beaten[3]—and at first people thought that he might continue the old Gómez tyranny. But quite the opposite happened. With the kind of genuine statesmanship that is not often seen in Latin America—or on other continents—

[3] Cf. *Gómez*, by Thomas Rourke, p. 297.

López Contreras realized that Venezuela's only hope was installation of a constitutional regime and transition to liberal-democratic rule.

López Contreras, a curious character, is an Andino (as was Gómez); he was born in the mountain state of Táchira in about 1882. He is "Greek-minded," people in Caracas say; that is, he is rational, intelligent, moderate, with a poet's ascetic face. He is tall and thin as a match, and has been married three times. What he did for the country was outline a Three-Year Plan for economic uplift, establish some decency and order in political affairs, and above all give the people hope. López Contreras ranks high among the characters in this book. He deserves well of Venezuelan history.

Not only did López Contreras insist on governing with democratic ideology and routine; he deliberately shortened his own term as President from 1943 to 1941. Many people wanted him to continue longer in office, but he thought that it would be a good example—here his attitude is somewhat analogous to that of Cárdenas in Mexico—if he stepped out. On retiring he more or less dictated the appointment of his successor, General Medina, who had once been his private secretary.

General Isaías Medina Angarita, who thus became President of Venezuela early in 1941, was also Minister of War. He is forty-three years old, a competent professional soldier, and an Andino by origin, with an Italian mother. Remotely, like many mountain folk, he is said to have Jewish blood; the Andean highlands were settled partly by Spanish Jews. General Medina spent several months in the United States in 1940; he is called "moderately" pro-American. He is stoutly built, and very affable in character. He married a few days before taking office as President. His salary is healthy, 84,000 *bolívares* per year ($23,520) with 60,000 ($16,800) more for representation.

The party system hardly functions as such in Venezuela, but the government "party" calls itself the *Agrupación Cívico Boli-*

variano. The opposition consists mostly of those who are not in office, plus a socialist party that has growing influence in the towns. Communists are illegal. The press is moderately free, and criticism of the government is permitted. In fact, it is often lively.

After López Contreras and General Medina the most important politician in the country is the venerable ex-Foreign Minister, Dr. Esteban Gil Borges. He was a teacher for many years, then a lawyer, then a judge. He is not an Andino, and Gómez exiled him. He is a tall man, gracious and very lean; he looks remarkably like Sir John Simon. For thirteen years he was an assistant director of the Pan-American Union; he knows the United States well, and is strongly pro-American.

Dr. Diógenes Escalante, a Venezuelan of the old school, was a professional diplomat and the editor of a government newspaper under Gómez. He is called *El inglés;* he is now ambassador to Washington. . . . Dr. Luis Gerónimo Pietri, of Corsican descent, was López Contreras' Minister of the Interior, and is one of the abler young men in the country.

In the old days, at least, the crucial jobs were not cabinet posts so much as those which might turn out to be lucrative on the side. Practically every Venezuelan had romantic hopes of being collector of customs at Maracaibo some day, or consul-general in Curaçao.

Venezuela and Defense

The Fifth Column is not conspicuous in Venezuela; so far it is not a serious problem, if only because American and British oil interests dominate the country. Venezuela was one of the nations that promptly seized Axis shipping when the United States did; a United States naval mission is taking up the work previously done by Italian officers. Politically Venezuela is very friendly.

The United States does not need defense facilities or bases in Venezuela—at least not yet—since its coast is largely controlled by our new installations in the Caribbean. But the country is of cardinal importance because of its proximity to the canal and its essential reservoirs of oil. Do not be surprised if it is announced presently that Pan American Airways is enlarging its Venezuelan airfields. Such enlargement practically constitutes a base, and it is the accepted euphemism for "base" these days.

Chapter XIII

Ecuador on Edge

~~~~~~

IN THE summer of 1941 trouble that had long been simmering between Peru and Ecuador bubbled over the pot and caused the only real hostilities that Latin America has seen since the Chaco war.

Tension began to rise in May, and on July 5 shooting started on the disputed border near the town of Chacras. The Peruvians bombed it without provocation, the Ecuadorians say; Peru put 8,000 troops into the region, and Ecuador mobilized its meager forces. An attempt at joint mediation was promptly made by Brazil, Argentina, and the United States, and it was proposed that each side should retire fifteen kilometers from the frontier. Fighting stopped after a few days, but then burst out again. On July 18 a battle was raging on the Zarumilla river; on July 26 a truce was signed. This, however, was not very conclusive. Early in August more outbreaks occurred, and 12,000 Ecuadorian refugees had to flee from El Oro province.

Straightway the affair became international, and Ecuador claimed that 3,000 *Japanese* troops were fighting for Peru. This can be explained—if any explanation meets the case—only by the fact that a large Japanese colony exists in Peru, and presumably Japanese—if they are Peruvian citizens—could be called up for military service. Peru called the charges of Japanese participation preposterous, and the Tokyo government demanded apologies from Ecuador.

The roots of this frontier dispute—the only serious one remaining in the Americas—go far back. Behind the Andes and between the Napo and Marañón rivers are 50,000 square miles of largely unexplored jungle, leading to the Amazon. Both Ecuador and Peru have claimed this vast and potentially rich tract since 1829; Ecuador says its boundaries follow those of the old Presidency of Quito. Peru, on its side, seeks to reduce Ecuador to a narrow strip along the coast. Negotiations to draw a final border have begun many times, but no settlement has ever been reached. As time goes on, Peruvian claims become stronger, since Peru is in a better position to assert itself; the whole region has gradually filled with Peruvians, and Ecuador has lost effective control of much of it. Thus Peru steadfastly opposes a settlement; the longer the question hangs fire, the stronger Peru is. Ecuador wants the dispute settled. Peru doesn't. This is the gist of it all.

The issue is—and will continue to be—a prickly and invidious one for the United States. In 1936 negotiations opened on what was called "an agreement to try to reach an agreement," but they broke down. It was hoped that Mr. Roosevelt might be able to arbitrate, but Peru didn't want arbitration. The United States meantime is reluctant to put pressure on either party. But so long as we do not take the lead in trying to effect a permanent settlement, we are in effect playing Peru's hand, since Peru stands to gain by delay, and Ecuador to lose.

How Ecuador Differs from Peru

Peru and Ecuador are slices off the same great Andean Spanish-Inca block, and basically the countries resemble one another closely. Yet there are interesting differences.

First, Ecuador is smaller, less developed, and much poorer than Peru. Its capital, Quito—one of the most charming and colorful cities in the hemisphere—is hidden in a mountain valley, 9,500 feet above the sea; it has little of the sophistication and cosmopolitan quality of Lima. Quito, with its church bells and barefoot Indians, still lives in the seventeenth century.

Second, Ecuador's political development has been much more erratic than that of Peru; Ecuador has never had a strong dictator like Leguía. (There are some who say that it is just as well.)

Third, Ecuador is not so heavily overborrowed as Peru, and not so dependent on foreign commercial interests.

Fourth, the Indians in Ecuador are miserably, wretchedly poor,

but on the whole they are better off than Peruvian Indians. They
are freer men, sometimes owning their own land; Peruvian Indians are slaves by contrast, trying to scrape a living out of rock.

Fifth, though Ecuador was once named the Republic of the
Sacred Heart, it is nowadays less dominated by the church than
Peru. Its golden churches are famous, yes; one church agglomera-
tion covers eight square blocks, and three-quarters of Quito is
church-owned. But church and state are separated in Ecuador;
divorce is permitted on easy grounds, and civil marriage is legal;
the colonial taboos are breaking down. In Quito a young married
woman can sit alone in a café, which would be almost unthinkable
in Lima.

Sixth, the Incas never thoroughly conquered Ecuador, and
much Indian influence is *pre*-Inca. The Spaniards, when they
came, killed off the Indians, who were very primitive, mercilessly;
they were much harsher in Ecuador than in Peru, where they
were harsh enough. In Lima today there are people proud of their
Inca blood. But not in Quito.

Looking at Ecuador

No one knows how big Ecuador is, nor how many people the
country holds. This is because of the frontier quarrel with Peru.
If we take official figures—Ecuador claims territory all the way
to the important port of Iquitos on the Amazon—the area is
about 275,000 square miles (the size of Texas roughly), and the
population 3,200,000. But the fiat of Ecuadorian law does not
extend nearly so widely.

The country has had thirteen constitutions; there have been
twelve Presidents in the last ten years. Since 1895, when a hard-
boiled general named Alfaro captured Quito, every government has
been professedly liberal, i.e., anticlerical. Ostensibly the church has
been out of politics for forty-six years. Yet its economic power is
enormous; the country is in effect owned by the church and half a
dozen large *hacendados*. And it is a tradition that though the Presi-

dent is always a liberal, the Foreign Minister must be conservative, that is, a church man.

The chief struggle for power in Ecuador is between Guayaquil, the seaport on the Pacific coast, and Quito, the mountain capital. Guayaquil is the home of merchants and traders, and Quito that of descendants of Spanish *conquistadores*. Guayaquil is middle-class and reasonably progressive; Quito is patrician and archaic. The rivalry between the two cities (like that, say, between Rio de Janeiro and São Paulo in Brazil) is considerable; it is rare, for instance, for a Guayaquil family to intermarry with one from Quito. Guayaquil, finally, controls the country's cocoa crop.[1]

Ecuador lives largely on cocoa. Whatever wealth the country has derives from cocoa. And cocoa is in a very bad way . . . In the old days the landowners sold their cocoa, and then like as not moved to Paris. They were largely absentees; they seldom plowed their profits back into the country. In 1924 came catastrophe in the form of the witchbroom disease. It destroyed the entire cocoa crop, and is still not completely under control; to check the witchbroom blight you have to cut down the jungle where cocoa grows, which is impossible. Ecuadorian economy collapsed. The *sucre* (the unit of currency) fell from about 50 cents to an all-time low of 1 cent in 1940; it has now risen to about 6 cents. The emigré landowners saw their incomes disappear; they returned to Guayaquil and Quito, and tried to find work. . . . Ecuadorian cocoa remains the best in the Americas, and it still finds a market. But it brings nothing like the return of older days. The United States is by far the country's best customer, with Germany second.

In Ecuador a university professor gets about $25.00 per month. A cook gets $1.50, a policeman from $6.00 to $8.00, a minor civil servant $12.00, a captain in the army $27.00, a cabinet minister $120, and the President of the republic $300. Luckily prices

[1] Also many descendants of British officers who fought with Bolívar and Sucre live there; the town is full of Illingworths, Staggs, Wrights, and Stacys, most of whom know no word of English.

are very low. Ecuador is probably the cheapest country in the world to live in. A dozen oranges cost 8 cents, and a liter of milk 2 cents. You can rent a pleasant house for $25.00 a month, and your telephone service will be 15 cents per week. Beef costs 12 cents a pound, and a pair of shoes is $2.00. You can take a taxi for an hour for 60 cents, and buy a spray of orchids for a nickel. Street-car fare is ⅔ of 1 cent. Compare these prices with those of Venezuela!

The headwaters of the Amazon—in Ecuadorian or Peruvian territory as you choose—are largely unexplored, and here live the most refractory Indians in the Americas, the Jíbaros. They speak no Spanish; their language is an intricate tongue resembling Korean; they have no intercourse with white men, and they still hunt heads, which you can buy, nicely shriveled, in west-coast shops. Ecuador is still a paradise for the anthropologist. And romantic adventurers continue to search for the Inca city greater than Cuzco, for the mines the Indians first worked, for El Dorado where the Spaniards hid their gold.

Ecuador means, as everyone knows, "Equator." And it is an interesting experience to drive nine miles out of Quito and stand directly on the Equator while bundling yourself up with scarves and sweaters. The altitude makes it cold.

"Seducers in Ecuador"

The heart of the German Fifth Column in Ecuador is the Sedta air line, which links various local towns. Sedta has about twenty-six officials and pilots, and three planes; it is small, but active and efficient. Early in 1941 attempts began to squeeze it out, as the analogous Scadta line was squeezed out of Colombia. First Pan American-Grace Airways (the west-coast affiliate of Pan American) set up a rival domestic service. Then it was reported that International Petroleum of Peru, the only company from which Sedta can get gasoline, would refuse it fuel. This would seem to be a normal development, since International Petroleum is a Canadian corporation.

Though under attack, Sedta is firmly entrenched in Ecuador. It has shrewdly done favors for many politicians; for instance, it rides deputies back to their homes free of charge, and arranges free junkets for its numerous sympathizers. An ex-President of the republic wanted an air service to his native town. Panagra (Pan American-Grace) could not oblige, but Sedta did. The trip once took eight days, and now is done in 1½ hours. . . . Sedta loses about $60,000 per year, which Berlin presumably pays.

American business men have not been as wise as the Germans in Ecuador. Before the war, at least, German traders offered two-to-four-year credit on easy terms; United States merchants wanted cash. One newspaper man told me that he needed a new plant, but rather than meet American conditions he would "wait till the war was over" and then buy from Germany. A former Minister of War hoped to develop Oriente province, on the Amazon frontier; he wanted material for roads, sugar mills, barges, and the like. He told me that in the United States he could get no satisfactory action at all; in Berlin someone pushed a button, and the deal went through at once.

Quito has an efficient German school, with 200 children in attendance. There are sixteen teachers, mostly German, paid from Berlin. They have the best modern equipment, right up to the pictures of Hitler on the walls. American children had to go to this school, because there was no other; they didn't like it. But it took months of unbelievable difficulty before a rival American school could be set up. Its promoters sought desperately for financial help from the United States. They had a hard time getting it.

The head of the Fifth Column in Ecuador is reputedly Alfredo E. Cuhne, a Viennese army captain whose real name is Irving Hoffmann. If all the stories I heard about him in Quito are true —or even half true—he is certainly one of the most bizarrely remarkable characters in the Americas. One detail is that he contrives to get named in law suits, because no person involved in litigation may be expelled from Ecuador, and this keeps him from being thrown out of the country.

Cuhne arrived in Ecuador a good many years ago; he claimed to be a doctor, a specialist in tropical diseases, but his first job was as a hog-breeding expert on a Guayaquil estate. He spent two years in the Oriente jungle, and then returned to Quito to become the intimate political advisor of the President then running the country, General Páez. Under Páez the enigmatic Cuhne was practically the dictator of Ecuador. He organized a secret service (Ecuador had never previously had one), and drew up a plan of military operations that stunned the general staff. He attended cabinet meetings incognito; he organized a dossier on every man of interest in the country.

Cuhne, the story goes, maintained his influence on Páez by inventing stories that he was about to be overthrown; then he, Cuhne, would single-handed squash the "plot" that he had devised, and thus "save" the President. But after a time his imagination began to run out. His stories grew wilder and wilder. Came revolution; Páez was kicked out of the country. His successor, General Enríquez, clapped Cuhne into jail. Within a month Cuhne was running the penitentiary . . . He was released after a time, and then started serious work for the Nazis, to whom he is invaluable. People say that Cuhne has a wonderful quality of "invisibility." He has lived in and out of Quito for years, but not half a dozen people know his face.

The most sensible thing I heard about Fifth Columnism in Ecuador was this. Raise the standard of living. Pay army officers better. So long as a general gets only $50.00 a month, the Nazis will be able to bribe him. Ensure him a decent livelihood, and he will be less vulnerable.

One of my Quito friends was despondent at the lack of coöperation Ecuador was getting from the United States. But this was in November 1940, and since then things have much improved. He said, "Even America's best friends in this country wonder if your democracy—and ours—are worth all that we are sacrificing for it."

The Ecuadorian government professes complete solidarity with the United States in hemisphere policy and defense, and it has co-operated with us happily. Two prominent Germans have been expelled from the country, Arno Holusa, who was a secretary in the Reichs legation, and who was declared *persona non grata*, and Henry Graf von Matushka, who came to Quito from Peru. Late in 1940 the Italian military mission that had worked in Quito for some years was withdrawn; in 1941 two United States missions, naval and military, arrived to take its place.

The United States navy would like Ecuador to give us naval and air facilities in the Galápagos Islands, which lie 620 miles off the coast, and which would provide a perfect southerly anchor for our Panama patrol. But no negotiations for actual bases have taken place so far, all reports to the contrary notwithstanding. In May 1941 it was announced that two American Coast Guard cutters, to be followed by other ships, would be transferred to Ecuadorian sovereignty and utilized for coastal patrol in the waters between Galápagos, the Ecuadorian coast, and the canal. Which is something.

The Galápagos group is one of the most unusual in the world. No Indians ever got there. One island, Albemarle, has 600 inhabitants; Chatham has 300 and Indefatigable about 100; on Floriana lives one American family named Conway, and one German family. Mail reaches the Galápagos about once a month; there are no shops on the islands, no newspapers, no hotel, no money, no radio; the people live on fruit that grows wild, game, and fish. Naturalists from Darwin to Beebe have found it a paradise. Volcanic craters make perfect natural harbors.

Finally Personalities

The President of Ecuador, Dr. Carlos Alberto Arroyo del Río, is a heavily built man, partly bald, with a big hooked nose and mustaches. His career as a lawyer and public servant has been impeccable; he is polite, dignified, and rather aloof in character. He is in his middle forties. He has one son, who is being educated in the United States.

Dr. Arroyo, who wages a stiff battle against the forces of poverty, lack of education, and political disintegration, was born in Guayaquil of Colombian origin. He was a brilliant law student, and a former President of the republic, Dr. Tamayo, offered him a cabinet post at twenty-five. Dr. Arroyo refused, whereupon Tamayo, deeply fond of this promising young man, gave him his private law practice. Arroyo has been a lawyer for several big American corporations, a rector of the university, and a politician most of his life. He reached the presidency of the country in 1940; his term expires in 1944, and if he lasts it out he will be the first President since 1924 to finish his full four years of office.

President Arroyo, a good Catholic, is a definite liberal in church affairs. In his inaugural address he said, "I refuse to admit that the Catholic church has any right to mingle in politics, and I will suppress any attempt it may make to do so." Most people wish Arroyo well; they are so tired of constant changes in government that they want him to have a real chance. But in August 1941 he found it necessary to begin government by decree.

Dr. Julio Tobar Donoso is Ecuador's Foreign Minister. He is an intellectual, a scholar of the old school, Jesuit-trained, and a strong conservative. His face is chubby, his cheeks pink. He is the author of several recondite works on constitutional law; his character is called "resilient." When I saw him I asked whether Ecuador would declare war on Germany if the United States did. He thought a moment and then answered, "That's a question you'd better ask the President."

The conservative leader—whose ideas correspond somewhat to those of Laureano Gómez in Colombia—is a historian and archaeologist, Jacinto Jijón y Caamaño. He inherited a large fortune from his father; he is a member of the old Quito aristocracy; his library (which was given him by a famous scholar-archbishop) is one of the best in South America. Jijón y Caamaño hates crowds, and dislikes politics; his manner is polished and distinguished; the church would like to see him President. He has never taken sides openly for or against the United States, but the advertisements of his textile mills help support a pro-Nazi newspaper.[2] His son is being educated in a Jesuit college in California.

A quite different type is a young progressive named Carlos Andrade Marín, a doctor of medicine, who is Minister of Social Prevision. He is only thirty-six, the best physician in Quito, strong-minded, slow in speech, and sure of himself. He has great interest in social reform, and is Leftist. While still in his twenties he was rector of the Colegio Mejía, the government school. Ecuadorians who do not want their children to have a Jesuit education send them there.

The most attractive personality I met in Quito—and one of the most attractive folk in the hemisphere—is Galo Plaza. He is about thirty-five, handsome, soft-voiced, vigorous; he is the son of a former President, and he was Minister of War for four years, though not an officer. Galo Plaza is thoroughly pro-American; he went to Georgetown University, and then to the University of California where he played good football; for a time he amused himself by amateur bullfighting. It was Galo Plaza who took the initiative in founding the American school in Quito. He was also the man who kept the army from revolting against President Arroyo; he told the officers that they must learn to respect civilian authority, and stop making useless revolutions. Galo Plaza is almost certain to be President of Ecuador some day.

[2] Harold Callender, the New York *Times*, May 4, 1941.

Chapter XIV
What Peru Is and Isn't

~~~~~~

FIRST you must try to visualize the country. There are three Perus, seen left to right: the narrow strip along the coast, the stupendous *cordillera* of the Andes, and the burning Amazon lowlands beyond. The coastal strip is mostly ochre-colored desert, but it contains Lima, the City of Kings, and other towns that sprout hardily in the transverse valleys—valleys made green by water desperately seeking to trickle down the Andes, and push its way through the parched desert to the sea.

The flight down the Peruvian coastline and then into Chile is like nothing I have ever known. For hundreds of miles you do not see a single road, house, or human being. The pattern is of limitless and desolate emptiness. It is like flying over some monstrous rusty moon.

The automobile trip from Lima up the Andes—"up the hill" as the Peruvians put it—is the most hair-raisingly dramatic I ever took. You climb the blue-gray ribbon of asphalt through tunnels and chasms of savage aggressive rock colored everything from amber to magenta. It is the only road in the world whereon you rise from sea level to 15,948 feet in 85 miles. You crawl from your car at Ticlio, the crest of the pass, and try to walk a step, and then collapse with a crimson roaring in your eyes and an exploding blackness in your ears from the suddenly realized assault of that incredible tropical altitude.

The dimensions of Peru are acute and sharp. From sea level to 16,000 feet in 2½ hours. But from Lima to Iquitos on the Amazon, roughly 650 miles, it will take two weeks unless you fly.[1] In Lima you may see the Torre Tagle Palace, a filigree-fine survival

---

[1] According to Katherine Carr (*South American Primer,* p. 106), Peru found it easier to reinforce its Iquitos garrison from Lima—during the Leticia dispute with Colombia—via the Pacific Coast, the Panama Canal, and Brazil, than direct, a journey of at least 7,500 miles!

of the purest seventeenth-century Spanish architecture; in Cerro de Pasco you will find copper-extracting machinery as contemporary as an electric icebox. There are staggering contrasts in Peru. Consider the San Marcos University, which was founded in 1551 —85 years before Harvard—and which is the cloistered heart of South American intellectual refinement. Up the hill you will see Indians who have not changed much in four hundred years. Their blanched and isolated primitiveness, three days from New York by air, makes Darkest Africa look like Radio City by comparison.

In the gaunt yellowish cathedral on the Plaza de Armas in Lima, the bones and part of the very flesh of Pizarro are still visible under glass. It seldom rains in this part of the world, and the remains of this cruelest and most treacherous of the great Captains-General are as well preserved as those of most Egyptian mummies. Across from Pizarro's tomb is a massive gilt inscription to the thirteen *conquistadores*, the thirteen faithful lieutenants, who were loyal to him to the end. One name among them has particular contemporary interest—De la Torre. For one of his lineal descendants, Víctor Raúl Haya de la Torre, is Peru's leading revolutionary—and leading statesman if you look at it that way—today. More of Haya soon.

Peru is about twice as big as pre-war Germany, but, because of the frontier quarrel with Ecuador, no one knows its exact area. The population is given as about 6,500,000, but this is scarcely more than a guess, since—incredibly—there has been no census since 1876. Political power is concentrated in the coastal strip, where cotton—the chief crop—and sugar grow. The mines are "up the hill." The people are overwhelmingly Indian and *mestizo*. Many Indians have never learned Spanish, and still speak native tongues like Aymará and Quechua. There is almost no middle class, and the country seems to lack *vitality*. A reporter feels almost like an archeologist. The three fixed points of Peru, I heard it said, are God, land, master.

"Lo, the Poor Indian"

Francisco Pizarro, an illegitimate peasant boy, conquered Peru in 1533, and for almost three centuries thereafter Lima was the dominant Spanish city in South America. Pizarro, as everyone knows, liquidated the mountain empire of the Incas; he took Peru with 183 men and 37 horses in a campaign much easier and less spectacular than that of Cortés in Mexico. The climax was the capture of the Inca king Atahualpa. The Spaniards promised him freedom if he would fill a room twenty feet square with gold; he did so, whereupon they brutally murdered him.

As anyone may see who visits the massive ruins of Cuzco, the Indian capital, or the museums of Lima today, the Incas had a considerable civilization before Pizarro came. They built roads, bridges, dams; they "achieved the most thorough and successful social organization in the New World."[2] One-third of the crops went to God, one-third to the state, one-third to the local clan. Messengers followed footpaths all over the empire; a case can be made that communications in parts of Peru were better in the sixteenth century than they are now. The supreme ruler was called "the" Inca, who was supposed—like the Emperor of Japan today—to be descended from the sun; authority then ramified down through priests and clan leaders to the *ayllu*, or agrarian community. The Incas were not so bloodthirsty as the Aztecs, and human sacrifice was rare. They were skillful builders and engineers, beautiful craftsmen in pottery and textiles and gold, and in general peace-loving men—accustomed to bow submissively to authority—whom the Spaniards murdered and enslaved. Their economic system was paternalistic; until Pizarro, poverty was rare, and destitution unknown.

In 1500 or thereabouts the Indians numbered at least 10,000,000; today hardly 5,000,000 survive. The Spaniards had little interest in agriculture; all they cared about were the fabulous gold and silver mines, and they made the Indians work them. Those Indians

[2] *The Republics of South America,* p. 83.

who remained on the soil were bought and sold with the land, like slaves. . . . Today the lot of the Peruvian Indian is grim indeed. About two-thirds of the land is owned by the church or the *gamonales* (big landowners); the Indians, peons still, work as a rule three to five days per week for the master, the rest for themselves; often they get no wages. On the *puna* (the uplands) they are perpetually numbed by altitude, stupefied by the cocaine leaf they chew, and sodden with cheap alcohol.

If you ask what the solution may be for the Indian "problem," folk in Peru shake their heads. But obviously the problem is important, since at least two-thirds of the population *is* Indian; I have heard aristocrats in Lima say that sooner or later the Indians—whom they despise as worse than animals—will "engulf" them. There is no easy political solution, since nine-tenths of the Indians are illiterate; a "social" solution, that is, their incorporation into the community of the nation as a whole, is surely impossible for years to come; as has been nicely said, the Indians form "an extra-social class." There remains economics. If you could raise the standard of living of the Indian, teach him scientific agriculture, give him urban development, in a word put some money in his pocket, then a "solution" might be in sight.

The Peruvian government is sharply aware how easily the underpossessed Indians could become a political force. Just one example. Not many Indians manage to get to the movies; yet the authorities were so alarmed at the implications of *The Grapes of Wrath* that they withdrew the picture after a day or two. Peru doesn't like criticism; even such a fair-minded book as Duncan Aikman's *All American Front* was forbidden.

Political Background in Peru

From 1908 to 1912 and again from 1919 to 1930 the ruler of Peru was President Augusto B. Leguía. He was a small man physically, tactful and adroit with visitors, with a great flair for finance and a genuine enough patriotism. During his second administration some $95,000,000 in American and British loans poured into the country, which was of course far too much. Some startling testimony was heard in the United States Senate about these loans. For instance, officers of one New York banking house paid $415,000 to Juan Leguía, the son of the President, for helping to "arrange" three bond issues. In those days bonds were nicely buttered.

Leguía ruled Peru as it has always been ruled, by the support of the army, the church, and some of the landowners. There has never been a liberal party in Peru like those in Colombia or Ecuador. . . . But in 1930 came revolution, and Leguía was forced out; he fled, was captured, and died a miserable death in prison. His successor was a soldier of humble origin and mixed blood, Sánchez Cerro, who believed in force. In 1933 Sánchez Cerro was assassinated, and most Peruvians were delighted to see him gone. He was succeeded by General Oscar Benavides, who ruled till 1939.

But at this point we must go back to tell something of the story of Haya de la Torre and his Apristas. During the Leguía period, Haya, one of the most remarkable men in the Americas, was a student. He became a revolutionary leader almost overnight. Leguía, to demonstrate his debt to the church, proposed to dedicate Peru to the Sacred Heart of Jesus in a formal ceremony. This was in 1923. Haya was only about twenty-five, but with extraordinary powers of leadership he organized what became a national demonstration against the government. He and his followers felt that Leguía's proposal meant imposition of religious as well as political tyranny in Peru, and their demonstration led to a general strike. After three days of martial law the Archbishop of Lima stepped in and suggested moderation. Leguía then withdrew his idea. But Haya was arrested, and then expelled from the country.

While he was in exile Haya worked out the creed and organization of his *Alianza Popular Revolucionaria Americana,* which is usually called Apra for short; the movement and its doctrine are "Aprismo." In 1930 Leguía fell. At the time Haya was in Berlin. He was nominated for the Peruvian presidency by the Apristas, and on his return he was greeted in the Lima bull ring by the biggest crowd in the country's history. He spoke— the first political speech in his career. Haya meant liberation to Peru. He meant modernity. He meant progress, emancipation, *hope*.

Elections came in 1931, and Haya and the Apristas won them hands down. Even their opponents concede this now. Haya de la Torre should have been President of Peru in October 1931. But strong-arm work and fraud kept him out of office; Sánchez Cerro, supported by church and army, grabbed the presidency. In February 1932 Haya was arrested again. He spent fourteen months in jail without trial. For four months he never saw day- light, and was not allowed to read, bathe, or receive visitors. In 1933 he was released.

In 1936 came new elections. They are a tangled microcosm of South American politics at their most depraved and complex. President Benavides, who legally could not succeed himself, chose a puppet, Jorge Prado, to run instead. (Prado, a banker, is a brother of the present President, and is now ambassador to Brazil.) But many conservatives of the extreme clerical wing thought that Jorge Prado was too "liberal," and they split off from Benavides to run a candidate of their own. . . . The Aprista party, meantime, had been outlawed. That is, a clause was inserted in the constitution making any party illegal that had international affiliations; this of course was aimed at Apra, which prided itself on being an All-Latin America movement. So Apra could not legally enter a candidate in the 1936 elections. Haya obviously could not run himself. But he did some clever thinking. He kept out of the picture until a month before the elections, and then persuaded a small legal party, led by a Dr. Luis Eguiguren, to run for him. This made the race three- cornered; it dumfounded Benavides. As the votes were counted it was seen that Eguiguren (representing Haya and the Apristas) was running far ahead. Thereupon the National Election Board declared that there were "loopholes" in the electoral law, and Congress voided the elections! So—again—Haya was squeezed out. Then the Congress committed suicide, turned itself into a constituent assembly, and voted that President Benavides should remain in office for three years more. Which Benavides did.

In 1939 he retired, after arranging a plebiscite that gave the executive greatly increased powers. Came elections (October 1939) which the Benavides candidate, Dr. Manuel Prado y Ugarteche, could not help winning. Again, the extreme conservatives did not support the Benavides ticket. Haya and his party were not allowed to run in 1939. Haya was living a curious hit-and-run existence as a semi-fugitive.

President Prado and Other Personalities

The President of Peru, Dr. Manuel Prado, an engineer by profession, is a mild-mannered, soft-spoken man of about fifty-five; he is of a distinguished family (his father was a President of the country) purely Spanish in origin. He taught in the science faculty at San Marcos, and spent some years as president of the Central Reserve Bank of Peru. This is typical of Latin American intellectuals, who are almost always versatile; they manage to practice not one but several professions, and then become politicians too.

Dr. Prado, a shy man who wants to do his best for Peru, is white-haired, studious, cautious. When he attends army maneuvers he wears the uniform of a lieutenant of reserve, to show his modesty. He has considerable political courage; he takes long trips throughout the country. When I was in Lima he had just returned from a visit to Cuzco—the first President of the country who ever bothered to visit the Inca capital. His son is a Harvard student.

Like President Roosevelt, Dr. Prado is a spender. He is forced to inflate the budget in order (1) to pay the army, in the good graces of which he must remain, and (2) to create jobs, jobs, jobs, for the bureaucracy, so that the civil service can keep func-

tioning. Prado is a fairly definite liberal, and he faces more danger
from right than left. He has sought to implement and increase
such paternalistic reforms as Benavides[3] gave the country (and
which Benavides stole from the Apristas in an effort to broaden
his basis of popular support). Peru has a well-advanced social
security system; Lima maintains an admirable—but not very
extensive—system of workers' restaurants where anyone can get
a decent meal for about five cents. The three-course menus are
prominently printed in the papers every day.

Dr. Prado would probably like to lift the ban on the Apristas,
but he doesn't dare, because he knows that Haya de la Torre
would sweep him out of office in any forthcoming election. Meantime he seeks to be moderate and conciliatory, and to get representatives of all political groups except extreme left and extreme right in his government. But the result is often confusion
and delay; no one gets work done properly, because too many
folk of widely varying opinions have too much to say. Above all,
the army must be kept satisfied.

Dr. Prado's basic problem is roughly that of the inheritors of
Gómez in Venezuela, to make a satisfactory transition from years
of military dictatorship to liberal constitutionalism. Peru is trying
hard to be a democracy; Congress functions, and the laws are
mostly good—on paper. But, as happens elsewhere in South
America (and on other continents), there is a great disposition
among politicians to think that *passing* a law is enough. Dr.
Prado's intentions are admirable. But his job is not an easy one.

Dr. Prado's Foreign Minister is the strongly Catholic Dr.
Alfredo Solf y Muro, who was professor of law and then rector
of San Marcos University. He is a gentleman of the old school,
Spanish in descent; his personality is self-effacing. His policies

---

[3] Ex-President Benavides, who was born in 1876, is still a considerable political force. For a time Dr. Prado was little more than his puppet, ruling with
Benavides men. Then Prado managed to get Benavides out of the country by
naming him ambassador to Spain. Benavides once spent five years in the French
army. He is now in Buenos Aires.

have to date been vigorously pro-American, though he has never visited the United States. He told me that if the United States declares war on Germany, Peru would follow at once by breaking off relations with the Reich. But he added that if the United States and Japan became engaged in war, the situation for Peru would be delicate, since the local Japanese colony is so prominent.

One of the ablest and most attractive personalities in Peru is David Dasso, the Finance Minister. He is a graduate of the University of Illinois and of the M.I.T.; he spent many years in Europe and the United States as an engineer. He has steel-blue eyes framed in steel-gray spectacles; his hair and mustache are gray, clipped, neat; he looks and talks like a prosperous New England business man. Dasso has never been in politics before. He happened to be visiting Lima on a holiday last year. President Prado, an old friend, asked him what he had done for his country in the past ten years. Dasso had to admit, "Nothing much." Prado suggested that it was about time for him to begin, and offered him the *hacienda* ministry. Dasso took it, and has been hard at work ever since.

Dasso, admittedly a man of the Right, wants to give Peru two cardinal things, work and peace. The people are sick of army generals and crooked politicians, he says; they *want* things on a progressive, orderly basis; what they need is courage, pride in themselves, patriotism. Dasso hopes to fight the national indifference, the inertia and complacency of the old Peru. His first big job, late in 1940, was to raise a 100,000,000 *soles* (roughly $16,000,000) internal loan; ostensibly it was for public works, especially sanitation and roads. Indirectly, of course, it will make employment, maintain the social services, and keep the people quiet politically.

The heart of extreme conservatism in Peru—of Fascism, one might fairly say—is the Miró Quesada family that owns the great Lima newspaper *El Comercio*. Carlos Miró Quesada Laos, its chief proprietor, once went to Italy on the invitation of Mussolini, and wrote a book about him in Italian; he is ardently pro-clerical and pro-Fascist; people in Lima call him a Fascist dark horse. The *Comercio* prints daily a complete list of Berlin radio programs, and gives it prominent place. The paper is almost as important in Lima as the Chicago *Tribune* is, say, in Illinois.

In May 1935, Antonio Miró Quesada, then the owner of *El Comercio* and head of the family, was assassinated together with his wife by a young Aprista, Carlos Steer. The Benavides government refused to execute Steer, because he was a minor; instead he was sentenced to twenty-five years. This caused the break between the Miró Quesada-*Comercio* clique and the Benavides-Prado administrations that has persisted bitterly to this day. It is on account of this killing that the extreme conservatives, both in 1936 and 1939, put up candidates against Benavides and Prado; it is also a reason why the Apristas may never come to power, because the conservatives would almost certainly make a counter-revolution to forestall them.[4]

The stanchest pro-United States politician in Peru is probably Rafael Larco Herrera, the first Vice-President of the country, and editor of the newspaper *Crónica*. He owns a marvelous collection of Inca ornaments; he has big sugar interests near Trujillo, and calls himself a farmer.

Who Owns Peru?

Peru is the classic example in South America of what has come to be called "colonial economy." Native Peruvian capital controls a certain amount of the country's sugar, wool, and cotton, but almost everything else is owned by foreigners. Which gives nationalist Peruvians much cause for heartache. I take the following facts and figures from the article on Peru in *Fortune* of January 1938. Let us classify foreign interests, country by country.

---

[4] Another leader of the extreme Right is Luis Flores, an exile in Chile. He derives from a group originally known as the Civilistas, who were antagonists of Dictator Leguía and who had the support of *El Comercio* and the Miró Quesadas. Flores reorganized this group under Sánchez Cerro, whose right-hand man he was; he wore a black shirt, ran Fascist marches, and the like. But Benavides kicked him out of the country.

The *United States* controls 80 per cent of Peruvian oil production, through the International Petroleum Corporation, which
is a subsidiary of Imperial Oil of Canada, which is in turn a
subsidiary of Standard Oil of New Jersey. Also United States
interests control close to 100 per cent of the mineral output; the
Cerro de Pasco Corporation exports 95 per cent of Peru's copper,
75 per cent of its silver, 50 per cent of its gold. Other American
producers account for the rest, the Guggenheims in copper and
the Vanadium Corporation in vanadium, of which Peru produces
80 per cent of the world's supply. An American concern, W. R.
Grace and Company, grows 24 per cent of the country's sugar;
it has big textile interests and does a dominant shipping business;
it is half-owner of Pan American-Grace Airways. Finally, I. T.
& T. controls Lima's telephones.

The *British* are represented chiefly by the Peruvian Corporation, capitalized at $109,000,000, which owns the spectacular
Central Railway; this railway, climbing the steep and stubborn
Andes to Cerro de Pasco, is one of the most remarkable engineering achievements in the world. The British also control
the Southern Railway and shipping on Lake Titicaca, which links
Peru to the barren uplands of Bolivia. Other British investments
account for 33 per cent of Peruvian cotton, 18 per cent of its oil,
and its biggest brewery and flour mill.

The *Italians* are very important in Peru. An Italian company,
capitalized at $19,000,000, gives Lima and its port, Callao, elec-
tricity, light, and power. The most important bank in the country
is the Banco Italiano Lima (balance sheet roughly $73,600,000),
which does about half of Peru's total banking business. Its director, Gino Salocchi, is a powerful political personage; he was a
close friend of Miró Quesadas, and has helped finance more
than one Peruvian government; at present he is in Italy, unable
to return to Lima. Italians also control the Peruvian postal
service.

German interests are represented by the great Gildemeister
family that owns Casa Grande, one of the biggest sugar properties

in the world. The Gildemeisters own 43 per cent of total Peruvian sugar production; they are Peruvian citizens. The head of the house has built up a certain reputation for himself as an *anti-Nazi* (the Gildemeister director-general in Lima is a Jew), but his brother is Peruvian ambassador to Berlin. . . . Finally, the *Japanese* own much sugar and cotton land. One Japanese company, Nikumatzu Okada, is the biggest single cotton producer in the country.

One thing the Peruvians have got for themselves—it is a curious detail—is guano, the bird droppings that are valuable as fertilizer. Valuable? According to *Fortune*, these deposits, mounting on islets off the coast for centuries, have brought Peru $375,000,000, which is "more treasure than came from all the mines of the Incas." Since 1936 guano collection has been a national monopoly, strictly administered so that the crop may not be wasted. Guano exists in Peru for a variety of peculiar meteorological reasons. A frigid antarctic stream known as the Humboldt Current flows northward, and millions upon millions of fish follow it; gulls and other sea birds hover over the parched islets, and eat the fish.

Haya de la Torre

I saw Haya three times, and each time I felt that I was meeting one of the great personages of America. The interviews were easy enough to arrange, through the courtesy of friends, though technically Haya is in hiding. He is a refugee, with the police just around the corner; the police certainly know where he is, but they do not arrest him. The reason is, of course, that the government cannot risk the scandal that his overt arrest would cause. It pretends meanwhile to have no knowledge of his whereabouts; it is not officially disclosed whether or not any indictment against him is still in force. But whenever Haya goes to a secret Aprista meeting, his friends may be arrested after he leaves; the organization has no legal right to exist, and any acknowledged Aprista may be clapped in jail at any time.

Haya looks exactly like what he is, a lineal descendant of the *conquistadores*. He is tallow-skinned, of medium height, with broad heavy shoulders. His jet-black hair sweeps into a flying wedge over each ear. His nose is powerfully aquiline; his ears are shaped like stirrups. He has bright olive-brown eyes and a lively sense both of political realities and of humor. He speaks English as well as you or I.

Víctor Raúl Haya de la Torre was born on February 22, 1896, at Trujillo, in northern Peru, one of the very few Peruvian towns with a Spanish rather than an Indian name. His birthday is that of George Washington, which pleases him; it also pleases him that his mother's name was Cárdenas, since he has great admiration for ex-President Cárdenas of Mexico. His father was a journalist, and one of his uncles was a priest. He grew up in a thoroughly respectable, Catholic, bourgeois atmosphere.

As a boy Haya read Unamuno and Nietzsche, learned French and German, studied the piano, climbed mountains for sport, and noted that of the forty-odd *haciendas* producing sugar in the Trujillo neighborhood when he was a child, only two remained when he was twenty. It was his first lesson in the penetrative power of big business. Then, in his early twenties, three things happened to him; he has never recovered from the three.

First, he visited Cuzco, the ancient capital of the Incas. Young Haya was transfixed—but not just by the ruins. He saw what the old Indians had left, but he also saw their descendants crushed, whipped, and beaten. When he returned to Lima, he wanted to build some kind of monument to Manco Capac, the first Inca, the founder—as he would put it—of Peruvian nationality. (Haya never erected his statue. Many years later, the Japanese colony in Lima did.)

Second, Haya went to the University of Córdoba in the Argentine, and witnessed the social and political fermentation, the "spiritual revolution" as he calls it, going on among the students there. Most of the old universities, like San Marcos in Lima, were cathedrals of reaction, or, in one of Haya's phrases, "viceroyalties of the spirit." Córdoba was different. The young men were emancipating themselves from the Catholic European tradition; they sought to think in terms of Buenos Aires instead of Paris. "In Córdoba, back in 1919, I felt the death of Europe," Haya says. Presently the nationalist "revolt" in Córdoba spread upwards and outwards, to Chile and Peru. Haya brought it to Lima, and became president of the Students' Federation at San Marcos.

Third, Haya was tremendously influenced by the Mexican revolution, then working its turbulent way forward. Mexico showed him something positive: a social revolution attempting to bring freedom to the peasant. Also study of Mexico convinced him that all the Latin American states should be a single unity. "Argentina and Mexico are no more different than Vermont and Arizona," he says; he felt that all might become united if the various peoples were released from feudalism. Haya looked to the politicians—and found them wanting. "All the old men were too old," he puts it.

"I was sure of only two things in those days," he told me. "First, that Córdoba was my mother, and Mexico my father. Second, that the Americans must stand together, and that all of us must be different from Europe."

At that time—about 1919-20—Haya had no intention of becoming a politician. He was against all politicians. He wanted merely to observe, to study. But he was impelled by events to a life of action. In 1921 he founded the "Popular Universities" in Lima, where students gave free instruction at night to others too poor to attend regular classes. They shouted *"¡Viva cultura!"* and "Long Live Education!" In a year Haya had 30,000 followers; in two years he could put 60,000 youngsters in the streets. At this time he was only about twenty-five.

Then, as we know—see above—Haya came into conflict with Leguía and was exiled. There followed eight years of travel, during which Aprismo was born. First Haya went to Panama, and then to Cuba and Mexico. He was delighted to find his theories confirmed, in that conditions in both countries resembled those in Peru closely. In Mexico he came strongly under the influence of the radical Minister of Education, José Vasconcelos, whose secretary he became, and of Professor Moisés Sáenz, who was then head of the Mexican department of Indian affairs, and who now, by an odd turn of the wheel, is Mexican ambassador in Lima. Haya went on to New York, and then—like all radical intellectuals in those days—to Moscow. He spent four months in Russia, and met Lunacharsky, Trotsky, and Stalin. He did not become a communist; indeed, he told Trotsky that communism could never flourish in Latin America. His health broke down, and he spent some months in Switzerland; later he visited Italy and finally England, where he studied at the London School of Economics and Ruskin College, Oxford.

This was the happiest time of his life, he says. He made a living as a journalist, worked in economics and anthropology, and developed the Apra program. He returned to the United States in 1927, lectured at Harvard and Williamstown, and went on to Mexico. He was getting closer home. He proceeded to Guatemala, and was promptly deported (as he had been deported once from Switzerland); on arrival in Panama he was arrested by Canal Zone police and packed aboard the first boat out. It happened to be bound for Bremen, so Haya, with only tropical clothing, found himself in Germany, penniless, in the middle of winter. He got a job teaching Spanish in Berlin, and stayed there for three years. Then came the 1930 revolution against Leguía in Peru, and Haya reached home at last.

Haya stood for an emancipated Peru in a modern world, as against the hard-bitten conservatism of the old regime. He was a radical; he was called a "communist" (which he isn't); against him the forces of reaction brought every pressure they could bear. Haya had no practical political experience, and his long absence from Peru was a handicap. He was a dreamer and an idealist; he abhorred bloodshed and violence; he might have seized power by force of arms, but he would not do so. There is a touch of Gandhi in Haya, and also a touch of Jawaharlal Nehru, that other friend of other Indians.

The government of that fierce little *cholo* Sánchez Cerro did not mind bloodshed, however. After Haya was arrested in 1932— the twenty-seven Aprista deputies were arrested too, some of them on the floor of Congress—the Apristas in Trujillo, Haya's home city, revolted in protest. The army, navy, and police proceeded to clean up Trujillo, and some *six thousand* Apristas, mostly young men, were rounded up and executed. Thousands more were jailed. Even today, under the much milder Prado government, several thousand political prisoners, mostly Apristas, are still in jail, and perhaps a thousand others are in exile. One Aprista exile—the Prado government did not like it much—won a $2,500 Latin-American prize novel contest in the United States in 1941.

Practically everyone in Peru, at one time or other, has sought to buy Haya de la Torre, but without success. In 1930, on his way back to Peru, when it seemed certain that he would become President, representatives of big American business offered to bribe him to be "reasonable." In the 1936 election Benavides twice offered Haya "guarantees," if he would drop his opposition to the government candidate, Jorge Prado. Haya demanded freedom for Aprismo first. In 1939 he sent an open letter to all the candidates, suggesting creation of a National Union party under some compromise leader. But the government would pay no attention.

The Aprista program is difficult to sum up, to define. Haya is an idealist, with a long-range view, and though his idealism has remained constant, his views have altered with the years. In general, it may be said that he stands today for three things: First, liberation and education of the Indians, and their incorporation into the life of the state. Second, intra-American unity, close friendship with the United States, and eventual coalescence of Latin America into one country. Third, social progress. Haya is not a Marxist or even a socialist—the communists detest him and attack him fiercely—but he believes in land reform and restrictions on foreign and local capital.

Haya has always disliked imperialism, and for a long time he was outspokenly anti-American. He felt no bitterness against the American people, but he feared and distrusted North American policy *vis-à-vis* Latin America. He talked the familiar dreary subject of "Yankee imperialism" and a major tenet in his program was "internationalization of the Panama Canal." Until the canal was made the common property of all the Americas, he felt, the hemisphere states could never be more than puppets of the North American "colossus."

Today—note well—Haya's attitude toward the United States has completely changed. He is no longer anti-American. He explains that it is not he who has altered his convictions but the United States that has transformed its policy. He is an ardent admirer of President Roosevelt, the "Good Neighbor."[5] But whatever is responsible for the shift, it has occurred. Haya and the Aprista movement have undergone conversion. They are no longer anti-United States, but vigorously pro-United States.

One factor in this conversion is of course Adolf Hitler and the Nazi menace to Latin America. Haya may not like Yankee imperialism very much, but he has enough political sense to realize that it is far better for Peru than Nazi imperialism would be. The Nazi-Fascist success in Europe opened Aprista eyes. The specter of Hitlerism over Europe, of Hitlerism marching toward South America, frightened the Apristas into common sense. Haya de la Torre is violently anti-Nazi. Therefore, a realist, he is pro-American.

If Haya should ever happen to read this book, he will be annoyed with me because I use the term "Latin America." He prefers a locution that he invented—"Indo-America." This derives from his preoccupation with the Indians, his fondness for the submerged Indian mass. "We should not be ashamed to be called Indo-Americans," he says. He thinks that "Latin America" is a misnomer, and that "Hispano-America" is impossible. Similarly

[5] Haya sent messages of congratulation to Mr. Roosevelt on his re-election; the American embassy in Lima stupidly and tactlessly refused to receive them.

he dislikes the term "Pan-Americanism," which has an imperialist touch that worries him. He prefers "Intra-Americanism."

Haya's philosophy of history derives partly from a belief in continental groups. In the middle ages we had small feudal states, he says; then came the emergence and growth of powerful competitive nationalisms; in the future we shall see a *continental* conception of politics, he hopes. Thus comes his vision of a United South America co-operating with the United States to the north. He hates frontiers. He hates limited nationalism. He believes that most frontiers are meaningless, and he points out that almost everywhere in Latin America, frontiers are drawn through uninhabited regions, on empty or nearly empty soil; they exist only as lines on maps, with no human or political reality. He says, "No country is an island." He says, "We must learn to think in *continental* terms."

As to other elements in his program, Haya believes that the Americas must work together for economic betterment. "I am not against capital as such," he told me. "I simply believe that we should control it, instead of letting it control us. I am not even against foreign capital. We must simply make it more useful to us." He thinks that continuation of the Good Neighbor policy is essential, but that no permanent good neighborliness is possible between someone very rich and someone very poor. Therefore we should make every effort, he feels to build a new and better economic basis between North and South America.

Every time I saw Haya he was at pains to talk about the German, the Italian, and the Japanese menace to the hemisphere, especially to Peru and its close neighbors. He adduced figures and produced maps. He even drew maps. I have one before me as I write, scrawled with his pencil, showing how Iquitos on the Amazon—where Peru, Ecuador, Colombia, and Brazil meet—might become the focus of German penetration. So much for Haya, who is incomparably the most interesting living Peruvian. It is a pity his life is being so largely wasted.

Quinta Columna in Peru

Peru has, on the whole, taken as drastic steps against Fifth Columnism as any Latin American state. Climax came in April 1941. Crews of five German merchantmen sought to escape from Callao and then burned their ships when it became clear that Peru would follow the United States in seizing them. The Peruvians were annoyed, and in retaliation did three things: (1) forbade operations in the country by Transocean, the German news service; (2) withdrew diplomatic immunity from Axis mail pouches; and (3) canceled the German Lufthansa concession, and confiscated its planes. Thus Peru became the first country in the Americas (including the United States) to outlaw Transocean, and the first country that overtly kicked a German airline out.

Another development had to do with the factory built some years ago near Lima and operated by the Caproni company of Italy, with an exclusive contract to build planes for the Peruvian air force. Peru had been dissatisfied for some time with what Caproni did—the company succeeded in building only twelve slow training planes in five years—and early in 1941 the Caproni plant was nationalized. Meantime, the Italian aviation mission that had been in Peru for some years was squeezed out. It was succeeded by a United States Marine Corps Mission, headed by Colonel James T. Moore. Colonel Moore was appointed chief of the Peruvian Air Corps, with Peruvian rank and complete authority.

The Peruvian army has been trained by a French military mission since 1896. But when France collapsed in 1940, the status of the mission became uncertain, and most of the officers left; some, however, are remaining in Lima in a private capacity. The Peruvian police force of some 10,000 men, well equipped and built up by various dictators as a counterpoise to the army, was trained by an Italian officer. His contract has been canceled. The Peruvian navy has been trained by a United States mission since 1922, and recently a United States officer, Captain William M. Quigley, was appointed chief of staff of the Peruvian navy. So both Peru's air force and navy are commanded by Americans.

There are about 3,000 Germans in Peru, and perhaps 7,000 Italians; obviously both colonies have great potential strength through their entrenchment in local finance and industry, through the Gildemeisters and the Banco Italiano Lima of Gino Salocchi. Oddly enough, neither the Gildemeisters nor Salocchi are on the British black list, for one thing because Britain needs Gildemeister sugar, for another because pressure on the Banco Italiano might hurt Peru, the country, too gravely. One story is that, if Salocchi promises not to return to Peru, the British will continue to do business with his bank. The Germans are, of course, more consequential than the Italians in Fifth Column matters. As is true everywhere in Latin America, the Italians assimilate quickly, and many of them are anti-Fascist. One reason that they assimilate is the Catholicism of the continent; Italians feel that they may adopt a new nationality without the religious conflict that non-Catholic Germans are apt to feel.

An important element in the Fifth Column problem in Peru is the Japanese colony, which is strongly established and probably numbers 32,000. Anybody born in Peru is a Peruvian citizen, and thus first-generation Japanese can, in theory at least, reach any position in Peruvian national life. The mayor of at least one town—Ayacucho—is Japanese. By contrast a native Peruvian who belongs, say, to an illegal party like Aprista, cannot reach public office. . . . Most of the Japanese are small farmers or shopkeepers. In towns like Arequipa they have captured a good share of the local trade, as the street signs colorfully testify.

The Japanese have a tendency to cluster in seaports, for instance at Chimbote, a good natural harbor that might some day make a naval base. Another district they like is Tingo María, of considerable latent importance strategically, since it is a kind of bridge between the *sierra* and the Amazon. Japanese farmers have properties—oddly enough!—near airports in several parts of Peru, particularly Lima. And Japanese are frequently servants in officers' clubs and barracks.

Economic bonds are close between Peru and Japan—normally Japan buys about a third of the cotton crop and all the strategic minerals it can lay hands on—and Japanese immigration has proceeded during most of this century. The Japanese are closely organized under their ambassador and consuls; one story is that the colony once told General Benavides that it could furnish him 5,000 armed men on short notice, to help put down any "communist" rebellion. During the Leticia dispute with Colombia, Peru got arms from Japan; later a Japanese mission surveyed the Peruvian coast. The Peruvian politicians whom the Japanese seem to admire most are General César de la Fuente, the Minister of War, and Dr. Lino Cornejo, the Minister of Justice. General Fuente is reported to have said on one occasion, "What this country needs is 100,000 more Japanese."

But the rank and file of Peruvians hardly agree with him. In May 1940, serious anti-Japanese riots broke out in Lima; the government—which at the time was quietly studying alleged espionage by Japanese—apparently kept the police out of action until the damage (calculated at $1,600,000) was done. It was then announced that further Japanese immigration to Peru would cease. Later, however, after bitter protests from Tokyo, a compromise was worked out; 200 Japanese immigrants may enter Peru each year, provided that 200 others are deported. So the Japanese withdraw their old men and women, and send youngsters in.

The United States has great interest in Peru, and for an obvious reason: the great Talara oilfields and the town of Iquitos, 2,300 miles up the Amazon, are both within a 1,000-mile radius of the Canal Zone. So is the Paíta region in the extreme north of Peru, where there are six airfields, three of them good. Our haunting fear is, of course, that enemy bombers might somehow take off from some such field, and make a surprise attack on Panama. Iquitos is interesting on another count: it is the natural link for any future northerly air route across the continent, via the

Marañón and Amazon. Seaplanes could land on either river in Peruvian territory, but so far the route does not exist. German airlines have tried for years to get into Iquitos, but to date it is served only by a small American company. The Iquitos landing field is soft, muddy, and inadequate; it has no real facilities for gasoline storage or equipment.

One shrewd maneuver by the United States has been promotion of a series of bomber flights between the Canal Zone and Peru. During the last year American Flying Fortresses, the most impressive military airplanes in the world, have been quietly "circulating" along the west coast; they dip into Lima, fly up and down the country, and take Peruvian officers for "unofficial" visits to Panama and back. This is a procedure that we might well extend to other Latin American states. Power—American air power—is impressive.

Sixth Column

Peruvians like to call the cultural and literary missions that the United States sends to South America the "Sixth Column." They do not mind military or naval advice, but they are inclined to think that we overdo the "good will" business. So, not unnaturally, do many other South Americans.

Chapter XV

Tin and Tintypes in Bolivia

THE long and short of Bolivia is that it is a kind of "company town" of the tin merchants, dominated by the army also, and slowly trying to achieve a freer political and economic life. Perhaps this generalization is too broad, but it fits most of the facts of the case.

To visit Bolivia, the third largest country in South America, is a vivid and exhilarating experience. Your Panagra plane lands on the *altiplano*, the enormous central plateau, at an altitude of 13,300 feet, which is much higher than most transport planes in the United States ever fly at all; the airport is three miles long, to give the planes room to take off in the rarefied air; the "crash wagon" goes out and chases cattle and llamas off the field as the planes prepare to land. Then, by motor car, you *descend* to the capital,[1] La Paz, which is built in a terraced canyon; even so, it lies at 12,000 feet, and is the highest capital in the world.

"The lofty intermontane plateau of Bolivia," says *The Republics of South America* (p. 9), "is an area unique in the world, for nowhere else does a state with modern industries, railways, and cities exist at such an altitude." Most Bolivians vary in character-pattern from extreme apathy, apathy almost to the point of physical numbness, to an intense nervous irritability that may burst out very suddenly, on account of the altitude. Nothing is so unpredictable as a Bolivian.

There are about 3½ million people in landlocked Bolivia, about 90 per cent of them pure Indian; Bolivia is the Indian republic *par excellence*. Most Bolivians are illiterate, and most are grindingly, intolerably poor. I have seen some bitter poverty in Latin

---

[1] Technically the "capital" is another city, Sucre, where the Supreme Court sits. But La Paz is the center of government and administration. The cities are about 350 miles apart, but the rail journey between them takes twenty-two hours.

America, as in Ecuador, say, but Ecuadoreans at least grow crops—they don't starve. But on the Bolivian *altiplano*, people do starve. There are virtually no crops. Bolivia, like Venezuela, must import food to live.

I heard it said in La Paz that Bolivia was "not a country, but a problem." The nation is still a frontier; "it has not yet conquered its own physical medium." It is very heterogeneous, with four distinct areas, each with its own character: the *altiplano* centering on La Paz, where the Aymará Indians live, plus many *cholos* (half-breeds); the Cochabamba district dominated by Quechua Indians; the region near Sucre (the nominal capital) which is the center of old Spanish culture; and finally the remote, primitive, and largely unexplored jungle beyond Santa Cruz.

For a time—so the story goes—Bolivia did not exist (like the island of Malta) on official British maps. This was because a nineteenth-century dictator named Melgarejo, a somewhat flamboyant character, insulted the British minister after a quarrel, sat him naked on a donkey, and drove him out of town. When this unhappy episode was brought to Queen Victoria's attention, she ordered Bolivia erased from the maps and charts. Anyway, this is the legend.

Bolivia, a perfect example of the buffer state, keeps Peru, Chile, Brazil, and Argentina from having a common frontier; if it didn't exist, it would be necessary to invent it, like the old Habsburg Empire. But its exposed position among its powerful neighbors has led to much domestic grief. Bolivia was rich, with immense untapped resources in minerals and petroleum, which its neighbors coveted. The first important instance of commercial imperialism in South America was Chilean; enterprising Santiago businessmen first opened up Bolivia, and even fifty years ago Chile's investment in Bolivian mines was something like $85,000,000, an unheard-of figure for the day. Argentina has very little petroleum, and Brazil none; Bolivia has plenty, which has made for considerable political and diplomatic pressure. A struggle over railways is going on in Bolivia today much like that in Persia, say, twenty or thirty years ago. Chilean capital built the first railway in Bolivia, the line that dips down from La Paz to Antofagasta for 283 unbelievable miles. Then the Argentines penetrated part of the Chaco with a line of their own. Now Brazil wants to build a railway to Santa Cruz, which would mean that the continent would be spanned, if Bolivia could push a line through from Cochabamba to meet it. The Argentines also want to reach Santa Cruz. This region is sparsely inhabited, and the Indians are not in fact really subjugated; the whole story reminds one of development in the American West in the last century.

During colonial days Bolivia was part of the Vice-royalty of Peru at first, and then of La Plata under Buenos Aires. Both Argentina and Peru quarreled over its frontiers, and so did Chile, which sliced off the nitrate coast in 1883. Ever since there have been intermittent border disputes, which Bolivia usually loses; because it never conquered itself (as I heard it expressed in La Paz), it could not keep from being conquered. The last disaster was the Chaco War with Paraguay in the early 1930's; since then Bolivia has been suffering the traditional ills of a defeated country.

Bolivia needs two things above all: more and better communications, and more population. As things stand now, it is underdeveloped and vulnerable. So long as United States influence is strong, via the Good Neighbor policy throughout Latin America, Bolivia is safe from attack by any neighbor. But if Germany should win the war, and North American prestige should suffer a serious setback, then intra-hemisphere (especially Argentine) imperialism may develop, with Bolivia an obvious victim.

The Emperor of Tin

The most important character in Bolivia has not set foot in the country for nineteen years. He is Simón I. Patiño, the greatest tin merchant in the world, and one of its wealthiest men. No one knows exactly when or where Patiño was born; he is three-quarters Indian, and is in his middle seventies. At first he was a small

merchant somewhere in southeastern Bolivia; he ran mule and
llama trains up into the hills, and expanded nicely. Another businessman couldn't pay a debt. He gave Patiño an interest in a tin
mine instead.

Then began the fabulous Patiño career. He worked his tin
mine himself, night and day; gradually he accumulated other mining properties, and soon, at Catavi, he was owner of the largest
tin deposits in the world. This was about 1903, but all the dates—
and many facts—are shadowy. Within the next ten or fifteen
years, as use of the ubiquitous tin can spread over the earth,
Patiño got richer and richer; presently he controlled 60-70 per
cent of Bolivia's tin production, and by 1925 his fortune was estimated at $500,000,000. He was then supposed to be the seventh
richest man alive. Patiño was inordinately clever. He knew that
Bolivian tin is of poorer quality than that of Malaya, and that
production and freight costs were too high because Bolivia was
so inaccessible to world markets. So he capitalized his companies
abroad, bought into the Liverpool tin smelters, and then invested
heavily in the business of his chief competitors, the producers of
Malaya. In return, he sold some of his Bolivian properties to British capital. So eventually Patiño became the dominant factor not
only in Bolivian but in Malayan tin as well. He was tin king of the
world.

Patiño went abroad in 1922, and has never returned to Bolivia
since. The story is that the altitude hurts his health. He has never
given anything to the country whose riches so stupendously re-
warded him; there is no "Patiño Foundation" *à la* Rockefeller. . . . Patiño was Bolivian minister to Spain from 1922 to
1927, and then to France until 1940, whence he came to New
York. The *cholo* from the remote Bolivian highlands became very
"social." His son Antenor, the "Crown Prince," married a Bour-
bon princess, a niece of King Alfonso of Spain, and is now Bolivian minister to Great Britain; both his daughters married high
into the European aristocracy. One, who became the wife of a

Spanish grandee, the Marqués del Mérito, got a reputed dowry of 40,000,000 francs.

But the Patiño interests are not the only tin producers in Bolivia. Nowadays Patiño accounts for roughly 50 per cent of Bolivian production. Another great company is that organized by Mauricio Hochschild, a German Jew of Argentine nationality, and a brilliant promoter and speculator; he dominates about a quarter of the country's yield. The rest is mostly controlled by the *Compagnie Aramayo des Mines en Bolivie*, a Swiss corporation owned by the Aramayo family. Its head, Carlos Víctor Aramayo, is a Bolivian who—unlike Patiño—retains close affiliations with his country; he has held many public jobs—for instance, as Minister of Finance and Bolivian delegate to the League of Nations; *Who's Who in Latin America* calls him "confidential agent of the Bolivian government to the United States." The Aramayo company is more diversified than Patiño; it has large gold mines, and is the country's biggest producer of antimony and tungsten.

Production and prices of tin all over the world are controlled by an international cartel in London. Each country has a basic quota; without this, Bolivia could never compete successfully. If the cartel should break up—as it might if Germany should win the war—the country would starve. The tin companies turn over 42 per cent of their foreign exchange to the Bolivian government, with which it buys food (mostly from Argentina) and thus keeps alive. Bolivia lives at least 95 per cent on its exports of minerals, which are about 65 per cent tin. At present, as a result of the war, the price of tin is high, and Bolivia prospers—in a manner of speaking. What will happen to the country if tin collapses some day? The thought—for Bolivians—is almost too gruesome to be borne.

Late in 1940 came a highly important agreement between Bolivia and the United States; more accurately, between the Hochschild and Aramayo groups and the Metals Reserves Corporation, a subsidiary of the R.F.C. The United States is to take 18,000 tons of Bolivian tin per year, which is just half the total produc-

tion, for five years. Before this the United States had bought its
tin from Liverpool (where Patiño ore is smelted) or Malaya.
Technical arrangements are not yet complete whereby the United
States will smelt the Bolivian tin it buys; a plant is to be built in
Texas, with the help of a Netherlands firm. The Patiño interests
did not take part in the Metals Corporation deal, though they wish
now that they had. Patiño tin continues to go to England.

In May 1941 came another agreement between the United
States and Bolivia; we agree to buy the country's total output of
tungsten for the next three years, worth about $25,000,000.
Tungsten is indispensable to the manufacture of high-grade steel
urgently needed for munitions; this tungsten agreement plugs a
yawning gap in the American defense program. The Japanese did
their utmost to outbid the United States for Bolivian tungsten—
in fact they offered a better price—but they were unsuccessful.
They could not promise to maintain delivery for three years, and
Bolivia knows well that if the United States and Japan went to
war, its tungsten would never leave the country.

Army and Políticos

The political situation in Bolivia is that Patiño and the army
dominate it. No single party is strong enough as a rule to make a
cabinet, and therefore the army easily controls the coalitions that
strive to govern. Most of the officers are *cholos*, and they consider
civilians an inferior class. The army—well trained by such Germans as General Hans Kundt and the late Captain Ernst Roehm—
gets about 40 per cent of the national budget; it includes two fac-
tions, one led by the chief of staff, General Antenor Ichazo, the
other by an ex-President of the republic, Colonel David Toro. The
saying is, "Whatever the army wants, the country wants."

The President of Bolivia today is General Enrique Peñaranda
de Castillo, an honest forty-nine-year-old Indian whose career has
been honorable but hardly distinguished. He has been in the army
all his life, and has never been outside Bolivia. For a time, during
the Chaco War, he was commander-in-chief. He works hard,

means well, and does his best. President Peñaranda came to power by the first free elections held in Bolivia in years, and his government is the nearest to a constitutional regime that the country has seen in a long, long time. Well-meaning and patriotic Bolivians, tired of dirty politics and military coups d'état, hope he lasts.

General Peñaranda received 70,000 out of 85,000 votes cast in the 1940 elections, the largest vote in the country's history. A left-wing candidate named José Antonio Arze got the rest. There are six or seven different leftist, socialist, and semi-socialist parties in Bolivia, but none have much solidity. The Germans try to flirt with them.

The Foreign Minister, Dr. Alberto Ostria Gutiérrez, is a career diplomat who has also been a professor of law and editor of *El Diario* of La Paz; he has been Bolivian minister to Peru and Brazil, and a foreign correspondent for *El Sol* of Madrid. An able poker-faced young man, he knows his job thoroughly. He is pro-American in tastes and instincts. He told me that 80 per cent of the people of Bolivia are pro-United States, but that 80 per cent of the propaganda that floods the country is German.

Colonel José David Toro, whom some people call the real boss of the army, is a youngish officer of a kind familiar in the less-developed states of Latin America; he is heart and soul an army man, but his social point of view is leftist; he is an officer, but a radical. We shall see others of this type soon in Paraguay. Toro was born in 1898, the son of a doctor; he spent some years in exile, which broadened him. He was President when Standard Oil was expropriated in Bolivia; he was deposed by General Busch.

Who Killed Germán Busch?

This remarkable young man—his first name was Germán and his father was a German doctor who came to Bolivia many years ago—was President of Bolivia from July 1937 to August 1939. Had he lived he might have become one of the cardinal men of the Americas. More than anyone in a generation, he had the good of his country at heart; if he had had ten or twelve years of rule, he might have whipped it into real coherence, brought it into the light of modern times, made it work.

Germán Busch was born in a jungle region that is still mostly a savage wilderness. His mother was Spanish, and he was nicknamed "Camba," meaning that he came of mixed blood. As a boy he loved to roam the jungle, alone; his sensitiveness to nature and folklore were extraordinary. In the Chaco War, utilizing his knowledge of the country, he organized guerrilla bands that made spectacular raids on Paraguayan forces. By the end of the war he was a lieutenant colonel and an almost legendary hero.

Colonel Toro made a coup d'état against the civilian government in 1936, and Busch—then a youngster in his early thirties—became his chief of staff. The next year, though he loved Toro like a father, he kicked him out as a result of personal differences. Busch knew that he did not have education enough to be President. His tragedy was largely that he wanted to do too much too soon. On July 13, 1937, he suddenly abolished Congress, and set up the first avowedly totalitarian dictatorship in the Americas. He was not, however, pro-German. His instincts were purely Bolivia-for-the-Bolivians. He hated foreigners. Particularly he hated Standard Oil. Also he hated some Bolivians, like Patiño.

Busch was very athletic and good looking (except for some bright gold teeth), with glittering blue eyes and pale brown hair. He was neurotic, ambitious, brutal, and naïve; he had never seen a city until, late in boyhood, he came to Santa Cruz, and he thought that La Paz was the greatest metropolis in the world. Busch was, the doctors say, a manic-depressive; sometimes his too-bright eyes would almost jut from their sockets. He had enormous energy, deep frustrations, and an almost maniacal temper. He drank like a fish.

Busch killed himself in August 1939, after a night of drinking.

Màny people think that he was murdered. But the circumstances of the case refute any explanation but suicide. Busch was undergoing a period of terrible despondency, caused by discovery that most of the people around him, whom he had trusted, were crooks and grafters. The country's cash was almost gone. Everywhere he turned he found disloyalty, pernicious intrigue, and corruption. He took a few more drinks, talked all night, and then shot himself. There was no "plot" against him; no military or other conspirators had made any plans to take over the government or name a successor. Moreover, the medical evidence of suicide is conclusive.

Bolivia, Standard Oil, and the United States

For many years United States influence in Bolivia was slight— in 1938 we took only 4.6 per cent of the country's total exports— but with the signature of the new tin and tungsten agreements our importance rose. American loans to Bolivia amount to about $60,000,000—in a country where the budget only averages about $12,000,000!—and have been in default since 1928. La Paz is the only capital in the hemisphere without an American bank.

Next to mining, the most important business in Bolivia is local commerce and trade. Of the eighteen big wholesalers and retailers, twelve are German and three Bolivian; the United States, Great Britain, and Italy have one each. Most American exports to Bolivia are handled by German firms. If you bought a United States radio or automobile, like as not part of the proceeds went to the Fifth Column.[2] This is now changing, since the American black-list of Axis agents in the summer of 1941.

Standard Oil of New Jersey had a $17,000,000 investment in Bolivia, which the Toro government confiscated in 1937. The story is tangled and lugubrious, with much to be said on either side. Standard spent some years in drilling, and then was disap-

[2] For instance, a German-Bolivian named C. F. Gundlach was agent for General Motors, United Aircraft, Pilot Radio, Wonder Bicycles, and many other U. S. firms.

pointed in production. It did not find as much oil as it had hoped
for, and marketing was difficult. The obvious market was Argentina, but the Argentines, cultivating their own oil industry, increased their duties, and transportation costs were very high.
Standard began to think of giving up its investment, and capped
some of its Bolivian wells.

Concurrently came the Chaco War. Bolivia desperately needed
oil, especially gasoline for airplanes. Standard, the Bolivians say,
refused to build the refining plants necessary. There were other
pinpricks and irritations, and on a minor technical point the Bolivians, out of temper, shut Standard down. This is the only case
outside Mexico of Latin American expropriation of United States
property. Intrigue from Buenos Aires may have helped cause the
break—the Argentines wanted Standard out of Bolivia—and also
the oil company, an international organization, hesitated to offend
Paraguay. Bolivians accused Standard of prejudicing their chances
in the Chaco War, and at the same time Paraguay formally charged
the company with *helping* Bolivia. Standard, of course, claimed
that it was strictly neutral.

The situation today is that Standard, though it apparently has
no intention of re-entering Bolivia, wants some kind of settlement, at least a token settlement. The question is not so much of
cash as of prestige. Meantime Bolivia discovered that it had
neither the capital nor the technical experience to run its own oil
business; nowadays it must actually import oil from Peru—and
from a Standard subsidiary!—and sell it to domestic consumers
at a lost, in fact for less than cost, in order to disguise its failure
to operate efficiently.

The issue is still noisy. In April 1941 some Standard officials
(of Bolivian nationality) were indicted in La Paz for "offenses
committed against the security of the state during the Chaco
War." This may, however, be window dressing, for prestige's
sake, because at about the same time the Bolivian Congress approved in principle that Standard should get some recompense
for its expropriation. The company, it is believed, will be satis-

fied with a comparatively small sum, say $1,000,000. The reason Bolivia is willing to pay is that it wants a sizeable loan from the American Export-Import Bank, which apparently will not be forthcoming until the Standard matter is cleared up.

"Vain to Trust the Faithless Column"

Almost 8,000 Germans live in Bolivia—including, however, a good many anti-Nazi refugees who are not Fifth Columnists— and they form a powerful and tightly knit community, with great commercial influence and tenacious roots in the army, which was for years German-trained. Several leading politicians, like Colonel Toro and ex-President Carlos Quintanilla, have a pro-German reputation, and at least half a dozen newspapers are pro-Axis, partly because they depend so closely on the advertisements of local German firms. Bolivia's military mission is Italian. And until recently the local air force, the Lloyd Aereo Boliviano, was in German hands.

But no more. Lloyd Aereo Boliviano was squeezed out of Nazi control in May 1941. The Bolivian government expropriated the company, and a United States government mission—among its members was the New York lawyer Allen W. Dulles—arrived in La Paz to set up a new organization. The nonvoting stock was made voting, and the company, under the same name, was turned inside out. The Bolivians had been dissatisfied with the German service for some time; there were several accidents (and it was hard to collect insurance from Berlin), technical standards were not maintained, and the Germans refused to train Bolivian pilots. The Americans in La Paz discovered, among other things, that whereas the German Junker planes were old and shabby, forty-eight brand-new American engines were hidden away as a reserve; the company had bought them before the United States instituted its export control. Agreement between the United States and Bolivia was reached partly as a result of splendid collaboration by Joaquín Espada, the Bolivian Finance Minister. He had to take time out during the negotiations, however, to fight a duel with a pro-Axis editor.

The United States proposals were, of course, all but impossible for Bolivia to refuse. We offered fast modern planes, easy access to gasoline, capital, management, and service. The agreement gives Panagra (Pan American-Grace Airways) a five-year management contract to operate as far as Corumbá on the Brazilian frontier, where Panair do Brasil takes over. This means that the German airline *crossing* the continent (through contact with Peruvian Lufthansa and Condor in Brazil) has been broken, and that an American line now takes its place. Bolivia promises not to give any concessions to Europeans during the life of the Panagra contract, to use only equipment made in the Americas, and to employ none but American pilots and technicians. The United States —through the Defense Supplies Corporation of the Federal Loan Administration, which is owned by the R.F.C.—lends Bolivia $660,000 to pay for new planes, and the country promises to give the line $192,000 per year as subsidy.

Aviation, as is obvious, is of the most extreme and dramatic importance to Bolivia. The country cannot, with its impossibly difficult terrain, afford to build many roads; so it leaps in one jump from burro and llama to the airplane. . . . And aviation in Bolivia is—or should be—of tremendous importance to the United States. A few dozen bombers at Corumbá, say, or Puerto Suárez near by, can come close to dominating the entire continent. Corumbá has become a vital link connecting Panagra and Pan American in their new transcontinental route, and its air facilities will be much enlarged.

In July 1941 came news that the Germans were planning a coup d'état in Bolivia. A letter was intercepted from Major Elías Belmonte, the Bolivian military attaché to Berlin (who had been sent there to get him out of the country), allegedly to the German minister in La Paz, Ernst Wendler, sketching plans. Part of it reads as follows:

I have the pleasure of acknowledging your interesting letter in which you inform me of the work which you, your Legation staff, and our Bolivian civil and military friends are carrying on in my country with so much success. I am informed by Wilhelmstrasse friends that, according to information received from you, the moment is approaching to strike our blow to free my poor country from a weak government with completely capitalistic inclinations.

I will go farther than that: the coup should be fixed for the middle of July, for I consider that the right time, because, according to information received in the Foreign Ministry in Berlin, I am pleased to see that all the consuls and friends throughout the whole republic of Bolivia have prepared the ground and organized our forces with cleverness and energy.

No one knows—or will say—exactly how this remarkable letter was intercepted and made public. The Germans denounced it as a forgery, but the Bolivian government rose in wrath, declared a state of siege, expelled the German minister, struck Belmonte off the military register, arrested one German consul, and imprisoned several local politicians—including a former Minister of Finance —whom it accused of being Axis agents. In Washington Sumner Welles announced promptly that the Bolivian government would get "full assistance" from the United States if the affair should result in "any international incident." American diplomacy works fast—and shrewdly—these agitated days.

The Chaco War

This stupid, bloody, and useless war lasted for three years, from 1932 to 1935, and killed about 135,000 young Bolivians and Paraguayans. Its origins were slipshod statesmanship and even more slipshod draughtsmanship by Spaniards in the sixteenth century, who never properly defined the boundaries of the *audiencias* that later became Bolivia and Paraguay. The disputed territory, called the Chaco Boreal—and colloquially known as the "Green Hell"—stretched between the Pilcomaya and the Paraguay rivers above Asunción. It is largely uninhabited swamp and torrid desert, though it may hold potential wealth; it is one of the least known regions in the world. . . . Let nobody think that Europe holds any monopoly on carnage. The Chaco War was one of the bitterest and most sanguinary ever fought anywhere. At one point, the peace negotiators flew over a battlefield, and saw there *ten thousand* skeletons shining under them. The Paraguayans, who at the beginning had practically no arms, made desperate forays with machetes, killed Bolivian sentries, and armed themselves with the rifles of their enemies. Bolivian troops, who had spent all their lives on the *altiplano,* descended into the merciless lowlands of the Chaco and died like insects; they could not survive the sudden change in altitude.

Officially the war was a draw, with no victor, but in reality Paraguay won. (But the Paraguayans like to say that though they won the war, they lost the peace—which sounds a disconcertingly European note—because in the final settlement they accepted a line somewhat behind their farthest advance.) Bolivia surrendered about 90,000 square miles to Paraguay; in compensation Bolivia got a narrow corridor to the Paraguay river, and thus an indirect—a very indirect—outlet to the sea.

The peace conference, one of the most strikingly difficult experiments in negotiation ever held in the hemisphere—or elsewhere —lasted longer than the war, three full years. The negotiators represented the good offices of six American republics, the United States, Argentina, Uruguay, Brazil, Chile, and Peru. Every conceivable difficulty, and some that were nearly inconceivable, dogged the weary plenipotentiaries in Buenos Aires. For one thing, both Paraguay and Bolivia had two revolutions each while the conference was going on. Literally months were consumed in argument over one letter in one word: Paraguay claimed that the preliminary truce referred to a "line" of demarcation; Bolivia said that the word was "line*s*." On this hinged vital questions of the distances between opposing troops, control of neutral roads, and so on. Eighteen different attempts to arbitrate the dispute were made, and *sixty-five* different formulae for settlement were presented to the conference as a whole. The Argentines, who like to think of the La Plata basin as their own private preserve, were maddeningly obstructionist during most of the conference; their chief delegate for most of the time, the Nobel Prize winner Saavedra Lamas, was stubborn, vain, suspicious, and afflicted with caprice. But a peace treaty was, despite every obstacle, finally drawn up. Most credit for the settlement should go to the American ambassador to the conference, Spruille Braden, whose indefatigable patience wore out everybody else. Mr. Braden was willing to take twenty years for the job. Saavedra's tactics were to stall, hoping thus that the conference would break up, whereupon Argentina could pick up the pieces. But Braden outstalled him. His Brazilian friends called him a *garrapata*, leech.

Chapter XVI
Popular Front in Chile

THE President of Chile, Pedro Aguirre Cerda, the head of the only Popular Front government in the Americas, is an affable, optimistic, and highly confident and astute politician in his early sixties. With his vigorous posture, shining black hair, and bristling mustachios, he looks much younger. Though he has written several weighty books on economics, and is a thorough and conscientious student, he is not what you would call an "intellectual" in the usual South American meaning of that term. He is not much given to abstractions or theory. By profession he is a farmer. When I saw him first, in the presidential offices, he was wearing rough riding boots, and he looked exactly like what, in a sense, he is—the owner-manager of a prosperous *fundo* (estate). His nickname is, in fact, "Don Tinto," from the red wine growing in his vineyards at Conchali.

President Aguirre's consuming interests are the land, public health, the enormously difficult social problem of Chile, and above all, education. I met him a second time at tea with Dr. John S. Long of the American Public Health Service; he discussed tuberculosis with the avidity of a specialist. Even his small talk was about diseases. . . . Not that he has no sense of humor. His manner is jovial. He likes to laugh and make mild jokes. He said that I should call my next book "Inside Moneda," since this was the name of his palace, and I was inside it.

Aguirre Cerda, who has one of the most ticklish jobs in the Americas, was born in 1879 in San Felipe, a small town near Santiago. He was one of eleven children. His father was a farmer of modest means. He went to school with other neighborhood children, the sons of *rotos* (literally "ragged ones") and the very poor. All his life he has felt close to the soil, close to the poor. From the beginning, too, he had a strong sense of uplift. His first job was teaching school in his native village. Then he went to Santiago to study law. At that time, about 1903-4, Chile passed through a series of strikes and labor troubles that sharply pointed to a disturbed social future, and Aguirre Cerda watched these events carefully. In 1910 he went to Europe to study law and education, and later visited the United States to inspect industrial schools. Meantime he had entered politics, and in 1915 became a deputy; by 1918 he was Minister of Education, and he initiated legislation for compulsory private schooling; also he saw to it that poor children were given free meals. After 1920 he was in and out of office, as Chilean politics pursued their complicated way; he became a Senator, a treasury adviser, a professor of economics, and president of the Chilean Wine Growers' Association, a powerful agrarian group. In 1934 he was chosen chairman of the Radical party, which, like that of Pre-Vichy France, was not particularly "radical." Four years later, in October 1938, the Radicals became the dominant group in the Popular Front, and Aguirre was elected President of the Republic. Two of his first cabinet ministers were big landowners.

President Aguirre married his first cousin in 1914, and she has been a sustained and powerful influence on his career. Señora Aguirre Cerda was rich, of the *fundo* or land-owning class, but she believes in social reform as much as her husband. In fact, people in Santiago say generally that she has stimulated his leftist convictions, rather than the contrary. The Right hates her, much as rightists in the United States hate Mrs. Roosevelt.

The President is very friendly, very accessible, very popular. His salary is only about $3,300 a year. He is unassuming, and goes almost everywhere alone; crowds cheer and follow him. He is no great orator, no magnetic personality, but his political acumen, his shrewdness and adroitness in negotiation, are considerable. He is strongly pro-United States, and one of his best friends is the American ambassador, Claude G. Bowers. He admires Mr. Roosevelt warmly.

President Aguirre told me that, to improve hemisphere relations, he would like to see an essay contest held in every country.

The winner would be the student who described his own country best. Then these essays should be exchanged, printed cheaply, and distributed as a pamphlet for workers and students everywhere. Once he said, "If I had the power, I would strew Chile with schools as a farmer sows wheat on rich land."

The extreme Left calls Aguirre Cerda a "bourgeois" and a "catspaw of the Right"; the Right calls him a Bolshevik. Nowhere else in Latin America, except possibly in Mexico, did I hear any President so bitterly, so *personally* attacked. The Right foams at the mouth at mention of his name. They call him "that man" (shades of Washington!), *El Negro* (because his skin is swarthy), and other names which I cannot print, as the phrase is, in a family newspaper. I have heard that rightists, meeting him at a diplomatic dinner, have refused to shake his hand.

But before going into Aguirre Cerda's Popular Front and what it has and has not done, we must survey the background of Chile as a whole, and study briefly what is probably the most complex political situation in the world.

Chile, Its Charm and Character

Chile is the pleasantest country in Latin America, bar none. Let me say this at once. Mexico may be more dramatic, Argentina more powerful, Brazil more brilliant, Uruguay more progressive; but Chile is the pleasantest, by all odds. Never have I met more charming people—even if they don't eat dinner till 10 P.M.

Chile looks like a bellrope frayed at its southern end. Superimpose it on a map of the United States, and put Arica, at its northern frontier, on San Francisco; the extreme southern tip, Cape Horn, will just touch Boston. Or put Arica on Seattle; Cape Horn will lie in the Atlantic beyond Norfolk. The Chilean snake, bellrope, or spinal column, as you prefer, is 2,900 miles long; its width averages a hundred miles. The population of the country is 4,634,839, much less than that of New York City. But it has a political importance far beyond its size.

The Spaniards, led by one of the most extraordinary of all the

conquistadores, Pedro de Valdivia, never conquered the Araucanian Indians who inhabited Chile. In this Chile (with the
possible exception of Paraguay) is unique in Latin America. The
Araucanians had their own sturdy administration—for a time
they were ruled by a French "king"—and they refused to admit
Chilean sovereignty till late in the nineteenth century. Those
Araucanians who survive today are isolated and poverty-blighted
(as is almost everyone else in Chile), but with completely equal
rights as citizens. Chile, the modern nation, is almost purely the
product of healthy white immigration (Scotch-Irish, French,
Basque, German); there is no Indian problem, and scarcely any
mestizo problem. It does not remotely resemble countries like
Ecuador or Bolivia.

The deliverer of Chile from Spain was a fighting Chilean-
Irishman whose father came from county Sligo, by name Bernardo O'Higgins. The name O'Higgins is today seen everywhere;
countless plazas, streets, and hotels bear it proudly. The Chileans
were for long years the toughest, most aggressive, and most
progressive folk on the continent. They are the only people in
Latin America who ever fought Spain twice; in 1866 came a
Chileno-Spanish war that Chile won. Indeed, the country boasts
that it never lost a war. It beat Peru early in the nineteenth century, and in 1879-84 beat Peru and Bolivia together in the "War
of the Pacific." (But I have heard astute Chileans say that this
victory was a tragedy for the country, which gained its great
nitrate fields as a result. Nitrate gave Chileans too much wealth
too easily; it led to profligate borrowing and spending, and then
to a harsh awakening.)

There are three Chiles, seen from top to bottom; the sun-baked,
windy, and absolutely arid Atacama desert to the north, near
Antofagasta, where the copper and nitrates come from; the central
valleys, comparatively green and lush, which are the agricultural
and industrial heart of the country; and the southerly regions
below Valdivia and Puerto Montt, where it rains all the time, an
untouched wilderness of fjords, Andean promontories, steel-like

glaciers, celebrated lakes, virgin forest, and rough, wild pasture land like that near Magallanes, the most southerly town in the world.

According to McBride,[1] not one-tenth of 1 per cent of the land is arable in the north, and only 8 per cent in the center. "Southern Chile has little more weight in national affairs than has Alaska in the United States." Most good land is owned by a handful of large *hacendados*. For instance in the fourteen central provinces 375 big landowners, less than half of 1 per cent of the population, own 52 per cent of the land. In one province (Curicó), 437 owners hold 83 per cent. One *fundo* near Santiago is half as big as Rhode Island. Thus arose the power—now beginning to be broken—of the landed oligarchy, which utterly dominated Chile for many years.

Chileans live on the flank of the great Andes *cordillera* and its exposed and attenuated valleys. They live hard. From the beginning the *chilenos* fought nature. They did not have, like Argentina, a luscious fat plain to loll in. They had to build bridges over foaming precipitous streams to get from town to town; they had to wrest foodstuffs out of impossibly barren soil. So they grew close-minded, hard-fibered, enterprising. Also they were further from Europe than Brazilians or Argentines. The trip around Cape Horn or through the Straits of Magellan (in the neolithic years before the Panama Canal) was no picnic. The country grew up isolated, because only the hardiest folk got there. It learned to live by itself.

Late in the nineteenth century Chile began to develop a middle class, something excessively rare in Latin America, and an industrial proletariat. Both derived in part from the nitrate and copper industries. Chile found itself with a bourgeoisie and its attendant social-urban problems. Radicalism grew fast, and the country's labor legislation became the most advanced on the continent, that of Uruguay possibly excepted. It had a middle class, and so it turned into a democracy.

[1] *Chile, Land and Society,* by George McC. McBride, pp. 16-25 and 124-25.

Chile is the country with the most dilapidated taxis I ever saw, and the most lusciously beautiful fruit; it contains three first-class universities, and has periodic shortages of meat and bread. It brought the first railways to Latin America, and has the most reliable statistics. It is an upstanding nation, adult and sturdy, but its infant mortality is enormous, and its beggars are the most pitiable I have ever seen. For more than a hundred years its domestic politics were comparatively unclouded; it is the only country in the hemisphere, except Brazil, that had no serious revolution for a century.

Then, as if in reaction, it exploded. For instance, in 1924-25 it had six Presidents; between July 1931 and December 1932, it had eight more. And it is still exploding.

Politics and Popular Front

The basic political struggle in Chile is much like that of Argentina, which we shall inspect presently. It is a struggle between Right and Left, between the landed oligarchs and the rising radical underpossessed. But in Chile the radicals are much stronger than in Argentina—they run the government—and they are much more complexly split up and intermingled. Nor is the church so much a factor of Right support as it is in Argentina. In Chile the church is disestablished—it takes a liberal line on the whole— and church and state are separated.

The story of contemporary Chilean politics is awry and tangled, but we must get at least the main details straight. Begin with 1920. In that year a bizarre and flamboyant character named Alessandri—more about him soon—was elected President. He inaugurated far-reaching social reforms, and subsequently swung heavily to the Right. But in 1920-24 he was a radical; for instance, he established the first income tax in Chilean history. He ended ninety years of exclusive domination by the Right. But Alessandri had severe difficulties to cope with. There were no less than sixteen cabinet changes in his first four years of office. The nitrate industry virtually collapsed, and the peso dropped from 27 cents

(U.S.) to 9 cents. Army pay fell into arrears, and in September 1924 army and navy conspirators threw Alessandri out. He took refuge in the United States embassy, and then fled the country. He came back for a brief period of power in 1925.

Early in 1927 the Minister of War, General Carlos Ibáñez del Campo, seized the presidency. Ibáñez is now an exile in Buenos Aires; for a time Chilean politicians shuttled across the Andes like corks popping from a bottle. Ibáñez was Fascist-inclined; he reorganized the nitrate industry, nominated his own Congress, brought in fantastic quantities of foreign money (like Legúia in Peru), declared himself dictator, and squelched the Left. Presently the Left revolted, and Ibáñez was overthrown; what helped beat him was an extraordinary "general strike of intellectuals," in which doctors, engineers, lawyers, participated. This was in 1931. Then came chaos. For twelve days a leftist *Junta* ruled as the República Socialista de Chile, with Marmeduque Grove as leader. Then Don Carlos Dávila, who had been a brilliant Chilean ambassador to Washington, exiled Grove to Easter Island, an islet far out in the Pacific, and became provisional President. But he lasted only three months—"the hundred days." The great Alessandri came back to assume the presidency for a third time, supported by a national coalition. People were sick of disorder, intrigue, and corruption.

Alessandri, the Lion of Tarapacá, served out his full term, from 1932 to 1938. But during this time came his Rightward swing, caused partly by the influence of his Finance Minister, the formidable Gustavo Ross. His government harassed and oppressed the Left; strikes were put down harshly. So, capitalizing on the radical discontent growing in the country, the Left formed a *Frente Popular* (Popular Front) to fight the 1938 elections. The socialists and communists joined hands first, and then the powerful Radical party entered; a Popular Front convention nominated Aguirre Cerda for the presidency. The rightist candidate was Ross, Alessandri's Finance Minister. Everyone thought that Ross would win hands down. But he didn't. On

October 25, 1938, Aguirre Cerda was elected President by the close margin of 4,111 votes out of 443,525. On December 24, 1938, he formed a Popular Front government, and assumed the presidency.

The rightists—Ross especially, who is now an exile in Argentina—have been bewildered ever since that they lost this election. They still talk of it like an unreal nightmare; they can't get over it. Moreover, they admit candidly why they did lose. They lost because they were ignorant of the temper of the country, egotistical, superconfident, and greedy. As I heard it said in Santiago, "they talked cynically of the failure of democracy at the same time that they bought votes wholesale." They thought that spending 40,000,000 pesos would "fix" the elections; later they said that they "should have spent" 100,000,000. What they had not understood—Ross particularly, who loathed the masses—was that Chile was growing up. Ignorant *rotos* had for years voted the way their *patrón* (boss) said to vote; urban riffraff voted according to what group bribed them most. But times were changing. The Left was getting organized. It was teaching people. The days of "fixed" elections disappeared.

But Aguirre Cerda and his Popular Front might not have won —they might easily have been beaten—but for an extraordinary episode on September 5, 1938, when the so-called Nacistas of Jorge González Von Marées attempted to make a coup d'état, and were beaten down in blood. This event may turn out to be a seminal fact in Chilean history, like—say—the defeat of Hitler's Munich Putsch in 1923. Let us explore.

González Von Marées—about whom more presently—is the leader of the indigenous Chilean Nazis, then called the Nacistas. Closely associated with him was General Ibáñez, the Fascist-minded President who had been deposed in 1931. In the 1938 elections Ibáñez was running again—it was a three-cornered race —against Aguirre Cerda and Gustavo Ross. González Von Marées and Ibáñez must have sensed that they were losing—full details of this story have never come out—and they made a

demonstration against the government on September 5, six weeks
before the elections were to be held, that might easily have overthrown it. Remember, Alessandri (with Ross as his Finance
Minister) was still in power. The Nacistas shot a policeman
outside the Moneda, the presidential palace, as their forces gathered. Alessandri, whom no one has ever accused of lack of
courage, happened to see the shooting from his office window.
He rushed out into the street and—alone!—dragged the dying
policeman into a doorway.[2] He ordered out the troops and *carabineros*, and the Nacista demonstrators fled into a modern sky-
scraper next door. It is in the heart of the city, and is the headquarters of the great Chilean social security organization. Someone in the Alessandri government—no one knows just who—
gave the order to storm the building. What happened then was
a massacre. Not one of the sixty-one Nacistas came out alive.

Ibáñez and González Von Marées were jailed. From behind
bars, they declared bitter political war on the Alessandri-Ross
government—with the elections still six weeks away. They threw
their support to Aguirre Cerda and the Popular Front against
Ross; this shifted the balance of power and made the Popular
Front victory possible. *Aguirre Cerda reached office by means of
Nazi votes.* He did not like the Nazis personally or politically,
but he duly paid his debt. He visited Ibáñez in prison, and immediately after his election pardoned González Von Marées. It was
his first official act in office. *The Popular Front President let the
Nazi leader out of jail.* Don't say politics in Chile aren't complicated.

The history of the Popular Front since Aguirre Cerda's inauguration in 1938 is largely that of inner squabbles and tussling
for power between socialists, communists, and radicals. The
inordinately warped details hardly matter. Aguirre offered the
communists places in his administration; they refused (as they
had refused Léon Blum in Paris), preferring to remain behind
the scenes. The Right accused Aguirre of being a "Bolshevik";

[2] See Walter Kerr, New York *Herald Tribune*, Nov. 27, 1940.

	AREA (Sq. miles)	POPULATION	CAPITAL	RACIAL COMPOSITION	ILLITERACY	PRESIDENT	CHARACTER OF GOVERNMENT	CHIEF PROBLE
ARGENTINA	1,078,278	13,129,723	Buenos Aires	Largely white	21%	Dr. Roberto M. Ortiz	Democracy	Export of pluses; pol lobsidedn
BOLIVIA	537,792	3,426,296	La Paz	90% Indian	75%	General Enrique Peñaranda	Dominated by army	Political instabilit poverty
BRAZIL	3,275,510	44,115,825	Rio de Janeiro	50% white 22% mulatto 14% negro 13% mestizo	60–70%	Getulio Vargas	Dictatorship	National i gration; co nications; c
CHILE	296,717	4,634,839	Santiago	Largely white	About 50%	Pedro Aguirre Cerda	Democracy	Evolution Popular F
COLOMBIA	448,794	8,701,816	Bogota	About 20% white	55%	Dr. Eduardo Santos	Democracy	Liberals versus conservati
COSTA RICA	23,000	616,000	San José	Predominantly white	20%	Dr. Rafael Angel Calderón Guardia	Democracy	Lucky cou hardly has
CUBA	44,164	4,228,000	Havana	Much negro & mulatto influence	35%	Colonel Fulgencio Batista	Dominated by Batista	Sale of sugar
DOMINICAN REPUBLIC	19,332	1,581,248	Ciudad Trujillo	Mostly negro & mulatto; no Indians	Very high	Dr. M.I. Troncoso de la Concha	Complete dictatorship	Export o surpluse
ECUADOR	275,936	3,200,000	Quito	51% mestizo 38% Indian 10% white	75%	Dr. Arroyo del Río	In transition toward Democracy	Dispute w Peru; pove
GUATEMALA	45,452	3,044,490	Guatemala	Overwhemlingly Indian	Roughly 75%	General Jorge Ubico	Complete dictatorship	Internal developme
HAITI	10,204	3,000,000	Port-au-Prince	Negro & mulatto	Very high	Élie Lescot	Dictatorship more or less	Export o surplus coffee
HONDURAS	44,275	1,000,000	Tegucigalpa	Mestizo & Indian	Very high	Dr. Tiburcio Carias Andino	Dictatorship	Banana poverty
MEXICO	763,944	19,478,791	Mexico, D.F.	30% Indian 60% mestizo 10% white	About 60%	General Avila Camacho	Democracy more or less	Land refo & Indian
NICARAGUA	60,000	1,172,324	Managua	Indian & mestizo	60%	General Anastasio Somoza	Dominated by Somoza	Internal reforms
PANAMA	33,667	467,459	Panama	Highly conglomerate	High except in Canal Zone	Dr. Arnulfo Arias	Democracy in theory	Relation with U.S
PARAGUAY	174,854	1,000,000	Asuncion	Predominantly Indian & mestizo	80%	General Higinio Morínigo	Dominated by army	Political instabilit
PERU	482,258	6,672,881	Lima	50% Indian 35% mestizo 15% white	75%	Dr. Manuel Prado	In transition toward Democracy	Internal consolidati
EL SALVADOR	13,173	1,704,497	San Salvador	Mestizo & Indian	50%	General Maximiliano Martínez	Dictatorship	Sale of surpluses
URUGUAY	72,153	2,093,331	Montevideo	White	Very low	General Alfredo Baldomir	Democracy	Domestic tussles betw Left & Rig
VENEZUELA	352,170	3,491,159	Caracas	Largely mestizo	90%	General Isaís Medina Angarita	In transition toward Democracy	High cost of living

he was probably tempted more than once to get rid of the communists, and form a center coalition, but he could not afford politically to do so. For one thing, the communists are the best organized party in the country, and the most spectacular. When Aguirre Cerda needs a thumping good political demonstration, it is the communists who can give it to him. They are his most effective *cadre*.

The Nacistas—now known as the Popular Socialist Vanguard —nowadays hate the Popular Front government more than they hated Alessandri-Ross. This is of course because they are bitterly anti-communist. But between the Russo-German pact of 1939 and the Nazi invasion of Russia in 1941, they had sympathies in common . . . Aguirre Cerda has nothing to do with the Nacistas any more. But the Right—which plays with the Nacistas—says that Aguirre Cerda has been tempted to use them on occasion against the communists, when the communists get *too* strong. Don't try to make sense out of it.

The socialists alternate between hating the communists with fierce passion and co-operating with them grudgingly. In December 1940 they demanded communist expulsion from the Popular Front, and they fought the congressional elections of March 1941 as an independent party, which in theory—but only in theory— meant the breakup of the *Frente Popular*. When Germany attacked Russia, the socialists and communists tended to pull more closely together. (Previously the socialists had accused the communists of working with the Nazis, which may quite possibly have been true.) Now, as it is said in Santiago, "the socialists declare that they support Russia but lament the betrayal of 'Marxist' ideals by Stalin, while the communists call the socialists 'fascists and anti-democratic.' " Meantime, Aguirre Cerda vetoed a bill for suppressing the communists altogether.

The trouble with the Popular Front at the beginning was not merely its lack of cohesion and the ideological feud roaring inside it, but the fact that it did not control Congress. In the Senate, the Rightist bloc and the Popular Front were tied 22 to 22; in the Chamber of Deputies, the Rightists had 71 seats, the Popular Front 62. This anomaly came about much as similar anomalies have occurred in the United States; presidential and congressional elections take place in different years, and often a President must try to govern with a Congress that can outvote him. But on March 21, 1941, came a new—and highly important—general election. At first the Right, knowing that it would be beaten, refused to vote. But President Aguirre made absolute guarantees that the voting would be fairly held, under strict military supervision; probably it was the most orderly and honest election in Chilean history. Not even a fist fight occurred. The opposition, when the returns were in, sent telegrams of congratulation to the government—even though it was beaten—for the manner in which the voting was conducted. The Popular Front not only won this election; it gained direct control of both houses of Congress. The radicals rose from 31 to 44 seats in the Chamber, the socialists from 10 to 15, and the communists from 7 to 14. In the Senate the radicals gained two votes, the communists three, and the socialists one.

But Aguirre Cerda's troubles were by no means over. In April, a month after the elections, his own radical party seceded from his coalition. What happened was that Arturo Olavarría, the Minister of the Interior, shut down two newspapers, the rightist *Imparcial* and the communist *Siglo*. The papers resumed publication in a day or two, but the radical party congress said that Olavarría must quit, since his action (equally against communist allies of his own government and the rightist opposition!) was undemocratic and unworthy of the Chilean tradition. But President Aguirre refused to let Olavarría resign. Whereupon the radicals withdrew their five other cabinet ministers from the government. Aguirre Cerda replaced them with one radical socialist and four nonparty men.

It is too early to write a balance sheet of the Chilean Popular Front, which has now—in effect—become the personal government of Aguirre Cerda. On the whole its "radicalism" is very mild. In its first phase it had no majority in Congress, and it faced the staggering problems caused by the European war, which cut off a large share of Chile's export trade, and the disastrous earthquake of January 1939, when fifty towns were totally destroyed and some 25,000 people killed. Its second phase has lasted only since the spring of 1941, and is unpredictable. What clinches it together is hatred of the old oligarchy, hatred of the Right. Its greatest accomplishment, as I heard it put in Santiago, is that "it tenaciously adhered to constitutional procedure in the face of persistent and aggravating opposition." It gave the people new hope and spirit, and it maintained complete political order against stormy obstacles. Chile will never have a tyrant like Ibáñez again, its people say. Civilians would throw him out with their bare hands.

The Briand of South America

Arturo Alessandri Palma, who was born of partly Italian origin in 1868, dominated Chilean politics for nearly twenty years, and is one of the great men of the continent, whether you like his contemporary views or not. When I saw him I was staggered by his remarkable resemblance to Aristide Briand, the late French Foreign Minister. Alessandri has an enormous leonine head, as had Briand, sunk deep in hulking shoulders; he has the swelling chest, the heavy mobile lips, of the demagogue, the orator. Like Briand, he was—and is—one of the most passionately effective public speakers of his time. He liked to lean over the balcony of his palace and address the crowds spontaneously. They would listen, hour after hour.

Alessandri's strength of character is legendary. I have mentioned his feat—when he was President of the republic!—in dragging a wounded policeman out of a mob single-handed. In May 1938 he was addressing Congress with his annual message. It was a solemn occasion; the diplomatic corps was present in full uniform. Suddenly a thin voice sounded from the floor, "You are wrong." No one had ever interrupted the President of Chile before. He paid no attention. The voice came again, "I disagree with you." It was the voice of Jorge González Von Marées, the Nacista leader. Still Alessandri paid no attention. Then González took out a revolver, and fired two shots at the President, which missed him by a foot or two. González was dragged from the chamber. Alessandri went right on speaking.

When he was President Alessandri walked every day, alone except for his dog, along the Alameda. His posture never changed; he walked slowly, with head bent (again like Briand), and holding a stick firmly behind his back. In the early days his dog was a small fox terrier, called Toni. Now it is Ulk, a great Dane. . . . On one walk Alessandri, while President, met by chance a deputy who had insulted him. Without hesitation Alessandri beat him over the head with his stick, and tossed him into a fence.

Alessandri is rough-tongued; when I saw him my interpreter was a young lady; once or twice it seemed that she would have to leave the room. On his walls stand autographed portraits of political celebrities from all over the world, including Hindenburg, the Prince of Wales, and Hitler. I do not dare repeat what Alessandri said when he picked up the photograph of Hitler, and rapped it with his huge knuckles. Nor do I dare repeat the message—about the Chilean Popular Front—that he asked me to transmit to Sumner Welles. Alessandri does not like the *Frente Popular*.

The Lion of Tarapacá is seventy-three, but his vigor is that of a healthy—a very healthy—man of fifty-five. He began life as a lawyer, but his ambition and eloquence soon brought him into politics. He is the essential father of Chile's paternalism, its social security system, its leftist reforms. There have been few people on the continent so fanatically worshiped. When he returned from exile in 1925, a crowd of 100,000 met him; several persons were trampled to death in the confusion, and his house was almost torn apart, as people grabbed bricks for souvenirs. Today, they might throw the same bricks in his face. But Alessandri would heave them back. He has never admitted that there has ever been another President of Chile.

Ross, Ibáñez, Dávila

About Alessandri people sometimes said, as his career turned more and more rightward, "Everybody loves him, and no one trusts him." About Gustavo Ross Santa María, they were apt to say, "Everybody hates his guts, and trusts him absolutely."

Ross was born in Valparaiso, Santiago's seaport, in 1879. He was a promoter, speculator, and business man most of his life; he has an enormous fortune, most of which he keeps outside of South America. He lives in Argentina nowadays. His great defect as a leader was that he had no confidence in the people; he thought it was a kind of bad joke that they should be allowed to vote. The Popular Front today fears him more than any living Chilean, because of his economic power, and the story is that police agents watch him closely in Buenos Aires.

Technically Ross was a superb Finance Minister. He believed basically in control of national economy by the state; he was only incidentally a friend of big business. What he wanted, arrogantly, was to run everything himself. It is Ross who, more than any other person, is responsible for the financial rehabilitation of Chile since the collapse ten years ago. But he was a shockingly ineffective politician.

Ross pushed Chile strongly toward economic nationalism; he never threatened to expropriate foreign interests, but he whittled them down. In 1933 he reorganized the nitrate industry, and ended its control by a bloated Guggenheim corporation called COSACH; a year later he squeezed the copper industry (95 per cent dominated by the United States) for steeper taxes, and organized distribution of petroleum into a kind of government monopoly; in 1935 he forced the American and Foreign Power Corporation, which owns light, power, and local transportation in Santiago and Valparaiso, into a reorganization under Chilean control. One-third of the profits of the new company, the Compañia Chilena de Electricidad, goes to the Chilean government, one-third to cutting the cost of its services, after its fixed charges are met.

General Ibáñez del Campo, who was President and then dictator from 1927 to 1931, and who like Ross is now an exile in Argentina, was a professional soldier. In extreme contrast to Alessandri, whom he bitterly hated, he was (and is) one of the most taciturn of men. He was born in Linares in 1877, and was graduated from the military academy in 1903. His first wife was a Salvadoran, his second a Chilean lady named De Koch. He was not, as they say, a "breast-beater"; he was slow, methodical, and he believed in discipline; he hated all the political parties (except the one that vaguely became his own), and he wanted to "take politics out of government."

Under Ibáñez Chile borrowed the staggering sum of $208,600,000 from the United States. His loans were among the most famous of the "sucker loans" that drained cash out of small investors in North America during the late lamented 1920's; he built roads, bridges, and public works with considerable efficiency, and American holders of Chilean portfolios paid the bills. Ibáñez was often blamed for borrowing "too much," and Gustavo Ross performed technical miracles in trying to reduce the huge debt he accumulated. But Ibáñez's answer to critics was that American bankers, with charming optimism, tossed the money at him, and that he would have been a blockhead not to take it.

Though he has some adherents in the army, ex-President Ibáñez is hardly reckoned to be a political force any longer. He remains nominal chairman of the Alianza Popular Libertadora, an organization composed mainly of his friends.

Ex-President Carlos Dávila, who held power briefly in the turbulent year 1932, is a lawyer, journalist and diplomat; he was for many years editor of La Nación. He was born in 1885, and was a popular ambassador to Washington. In the early days people thought that Dávila, with his restless energy and penetrating intelligence, might become Chile's great radical leader, but he slipped off into the byways of journalism instead. Late in 1940 the United States army flew his wife, who was critically ill, from New York to Santiago in a Flying Fortress, the first time an army bomber was ever used on such a mission. Dávila lives in New York nowadays.

Any list of the most prominent living Chileans would have included, up to a few months ago, the name of Agustín Edwards MacClure, the owner of Santiago's most important newspaper, *El Mercurio,* who was for many years ambassador to Great Britain. He was immensely rich, and personified the entrenched privileges of the old regime. He was of Jewish origin,[3] descended from one of the oldest families in Chile. He wrote several standard histories of his country, and also a children's book called *The Boy Who Was Almost a Vegetable.* Edwards died in June 1941.

The Leader of the Chilean Nazis

I thought that Jorge González Von Marées, the leader of the Popular Socialist Vanguard, was one of the most remarkable personalities I met in the American republics. There is distorted and perverse brilliance to this man. Also—witness his attack on Alessandri—he is capable of homicidal mania.

A *chileno* friend took me to the Vanguard headquarters, a big barracks-like building. A smart young adjutant watched the door, uniformed in a gray shirt, blue trousers, a peaked cap, and a swagger stick; in theory uniforms of private "armies" are forbidden in Chile, but the authorities seemingly wink at them if they are not too conspicuous. Everywhere I saw the insignia of the movement, a crooked bolt of lightning. In the hall was a memorial to the sixty-one Nacistas killed in September 1938;

[3] Many of the earliest immigrants to Chile from Spain were Jews. Some became converted to Catholicism to avoid being sold to the Moors by Philip II, and then set sail for Chile.

it reads: No Importa Camaradas, Nuestra Sangre Salvara a Chile (Don't worry, comrades; our blood will save Chile).

González Von Marées is in his late thirties; he is lean and of medium height; he has deepset dark brown eyes, heavy lashes, a mole near his lip, and a high sloping forehead. This is a very German face, I thought. He talks vividly and with great animation, clasping and unclasping his hands and tapping with his feet. His voice is harsh and metallic. Once or twice in the hour I had with him he exploded into violent temper. I kept watching his eyes. These are a fanatic's eyes, I thought. Sleep-walker's eyes.

González is supposed to know German perfectly, but he preferred to talk in Spanish. His mother was German, and he visited the Reich as a child. But he has not been there since about the age of six, he told me. He has six children. He said that his chief intellectual influences had been, first, the works of Spengler, second, the fact that Chile "had nine Presidents (*sic*) in one year." Hitler, he thinks, has "lived out" the Spengler theories, though Spengler wrote before "the age of Caesarism" and Hitler himself discredits him.

This leader of the Chilean Nazis founded his party, which he called originally the *Movimiento Nacional Socialista*, late in 1932, because, he told me, parliamentary democracy no longer met the situation: Chile needed something more dynamic, more creative. "The fundamental weakness of democracy is that it solves its problems—on paper," he snapped. He admitted freely that he had supported the Popular Front for a time, but that he knew while doing so that it was bound to fail. Now, he said, his movement was gathering in all the *discontented* folk of Chile. He averred that only his Vanguardistas and the communists had any essential vitality, and that the political situation in Chile would "be polarized between the two." I asked him why he did not collaborate with the communists now, if only to gather in all the forces of the street. He said that the "fundamental differences in doctrine" were too great.

González was overt, cynical, and completely Machiavellian. He called the communists "woolly hypocrites." He admitted candidly that he was co-operating with the extreme Right, though representatives of the Right had killed his sixty-one men in the September putsch. "It is the essence of leadership to try all routes," he shrugged. I asked him—holding my breath—if he were a prisoner of the Right, or vice versa. He didn't like the question, but he answered, "Time will tell."

He denies absolutely that he has any contact with the German embassy; he calls his movement purely native. In fact—an odd turn of the wheel—he told me that he had *attacked* the big German colonies in the Valdivia region because they were more German than Chilean. As to the United States, he says frankly that he doesn't trust us, and that the Good Neighbor policy is bad for Latin America because "friendliness between the strong and the weak is always disadvantageous to the weak." He thinks that Pan-Americanism under Roosevelt is an attempt to *divide* Latin America against itself, so that it can never deal as an entity with the United States. "Your friendship means our servitude." Then —with engaging cynicism—he concluded that although a German victory would be "more convenient" for Chile than the opposite, it didn't really matter, because the United States was bound to have to protect Chile no matter what happened eventually. I asked him whom he liked better, Hitler or Roosevelt. He answered "Neither," and then said that he thought the United States and Germany would compose their differences some day.

González Von Marées and his Vanguardistas were thoroughly beaten in the elections of March 1941. They polled only 10,311 votes, and elected only two deputies. Formerly the movement had boasted at least 60,000 followers. In disgust, González decreed the dissolution of the party; formally, he declared it to be disbanded. Yet it has maintained plenty of activity, In May its armed street fighters attacked the Radical convention being held in Santiago; one Radical was killed, and two others wounded. The government acted promptly, accused the Vanguard of attempting a coup d'état, and arrested thirty-two of its leaders.

When the police came to take González, he opened fire on them, and was captured only after tear-gas bombs were hurled into his headquarters. He was then brought to an insane asylum and placed under medical observation. A few days later he was released, because of his immunity as a deputy.

Another local Nazi party is known as the National Socialist Movement of Chile; another is the blue-shirted Fascist "Army" of General Ariosto Herrera, an exile in Mexico. In the summer of 1941 these groups were reported to be drawing together under González's unified leadership. González Von Marées has not given up the Nazi fight.

The Chilean Falange

The leader of what is called the *Falange Conservadora* is thirty-two-year-old Bernardo Leighton, who was a cabinet minister under Alessandri at the spectacular age of twenty-five. Leighton is one of the most unusual men in Chile; boyish, earnest, precise, and intelligent. He is slight of build, and has been an amateur jockey.

The Chilean Falange has no connection with the Spanish Falange, and the correspondence in names is an accident, Leighton says; in fact he has used it since 1935, long before Franco and Serrano Suñer did. Leighton resigned from Alessandri's government—he was Minister of Labor—in protest at the suppression of a satirical newspaper, *Topaze*; then he founded his movement to wean the conservative youth away from the extreme Right. He wanted to give new leadership, new blood, to the *conservadores*.

He is hotly anti-communist and anti-Nazi; he refuses to take the Nazis seriously, however, and says, "If we wipe out the communists, we wipe out the Nazis too." He closely follows recent Papal Encyclicals in social policy, and hopes for a "Christian solution" of political ills; he denies that he is pro-totalitarian, and says that his movement seeks to harmonize "liberty and authority." Even so, most people call him Fascist-minded. He has five deputies, and one senator.

Socialists Schnake and Grove

The most interesting and potentially the most important socialist in Chile is Oscar Schnake Vergara, the Minister of *Fomento* (development). He is about forty-two; he came of a good German-Chilean-Jewish family; he studied medicine for some years, and then became a journalist; a political exile, he visited Argentina and Uruguay; he was one of the founders of the socialist party in 1932. Schnake is a handsome powerfully built man with bright black hair *en brosse*; he is direct, competent, and reasonable, with great power of logic and a sense of humor.

I talked to him in his modest house in a Santiago suburb. I noticed an ashtray, mounting a toy anti-aircraft gun. He said that Chilean members of the International Brigade in Spain had given it to him. "It's the only anti-aircraft gun in Chile," he laughed somewhat ruefully.

His wife, Señora Graciela Contreras de Schnake, was for a time the socialist mayor of Santiago, Chile's capital. This was an unheard-of development for Latin America. She has been active in socialist organization among women, and is the president of MEMCH, or *Movimiento de Emancipación de las Mujeres Chilenas*, which aims to liberate Chilean women from the bondage of church and social custom. But the women of the country are, in any case, by far the most emancipated in South America.

Schnake told me that he had been profoundly influenced by Bakunin and Kropotkin as a boy, and had anarchist leanings until he was twenty. Anarcho-syndicalism was very strong in Chile in those days, as it was in Uruguay. But during the troubled 1920's Schnake came to the conclusion that the old-style syndicates were not strong or modern-minded enough to defend labor satisfactorily, and he turned toward socialism. He loathes and despises the communists. What he hoped to create was a democratic socialist party to represent the middle class, and to replace communism among the workers. His political ideas are somewhat like those of Haya de la Torre of Peru, whom he met in exile.

Schnake had a certain reputation for anti-Americanism for a time; then he went to the Havana conference as a Chilean plenipotentiary, and proceeded to make a five-month visit to the United States. This influenced him profoundly. He was deeply impressed by North American standards of living and political behavior; he became pro-American almost overnight. Moreover he returned with something tangible, a promise by the United States to buy 300,000 tons of Chilean nitrate and 75,000 tons of copper. Schnake is an ardent believer in economic collaboration by the whole hemisphere.

Colonel Marmaduque Grove Vallejo, the president of the Popular Front and in theory the No. 1 socialist in the country, is one of the most melodramatically picturesque characters in the Americas. He is big, bald, beak-nosed. His father was an Irish doctor; he is in his early sixties. Grove represents what is often called *Grovismo* rather than any orthodox brand of socialism. He is a soldier of fortune, an adventurer, an opportunist. He likes to call himself "a victim of the oligarchy." Probably he has never read a line of Karl Marx in his life.

Colonel Grove—who led the junta that made the short-lived "socialist republic" in 1932—was trained as a youth in both army and navy. In 1906 he went to Germany, and had four years in the German army. He was an able and enterprising officer, with great boldness, and he rose quickly on his return to Chile. His energetic vicissitudes thereafter would fill a romantic chapter. . . . He took part in the Ibáñez coup against Alessandri in 1925, and later joined Alessandri *against* Ibáñez. He became chief of the Chilean air force; then he was shipped abroad as military attaché to London to get him out of the country. Presently, "for political reasons," he was dismissed from the army; he refused to stay dismissed, went to Buenos Aires, and managed to get an airplane from the newspaper *Cronica*, which was always looking for a sensation; he flew back to Chile and attempted to make a revolution. The Ibáñez government thereupon sentenced him to ten years of exile in Easter Island, which is 2,400 miles out in the Pacific, and where a boat calls—maybe—once every six months.

This did not daunt Marmaduque Grove. Some of his good and distinguished friends chartered a schooner, and promptly rescued him. In 1931 he returned to Chile, after Ibáñez had fallen, and became Minister of National Defense. The next year, with Carlos Dávila, he overthrew the government and proclaimed a socialist state. By this time Grove had become a fanatical "workers' man." In one unbelievably bizarre week Grove threw Dávila out, and then Dávila threw Grove out. *Again* he was arrested and exiled to Easter Island. The experience is roughly comparable to that of being hit twice by the same autobus. But Grove contrived to return from Easter Island in 1932, laden with honors and a candidate for the presidency of the republic![4]

The most statesmanlike achievement in Grove's career was his voluntary withdrawal as a presidential candidate on another occasion five years later. The Popular Front had recently been organized, and its nominating convention was deadlocked. Most people thought that Pedro Aguirre Cerda would make a more substantial candidate than Grove, and after two days of argument the colorful Marmaduque patriotically withdrew his claims. Grove was given a consolation prize as head of the Popular Front, and Aguirre Cerda, as we know, became President.

The socialists have about 50,000 registered members, and they more or less dominate the CTCH, the confederation of Chilean trade unions, though communist influence is steeply rising. By and large the socialists represent the artisans, the workers with trades; the communists have the unskilled workers, the peasants on the fringes of the towns. The socialist vote rose from 46,000 in 1937 to 65,000 in the elections of March 1941, and the party holds the

[4] The government of the day claimed that it did not know where Grove was. One story was that he had been incarcerated on Navarino Island in the Straits of Magellan. Grove's supporters found him, and took up a public collection for a boat to go to Easter Island and bring him back. To this the government contributed 9,000,000 pesos. But the boat could only do eight knots an hour and Grove got back to Chile too late to make a satisfactory campaign.

balance of power in both Senate and House. The socialists have
—or had—their own militia, called the "steel shirts." Communist shirts are red. Chile is—or was—as full of shirts as a textile factory.

Two other socialists aside from Schnake and Grove need brief
mention. One is Dr. Salvador Allende, a thirty-four-year-old doctor of medicine who is Minister of Health, and obviously a man
marked to rise; the other is the Minister of Lands and Colonization (his job is one of the most difficult in the republic), Rolando
Merino Reyes.

Contreras Labarca and the Communists

The general secretary of the communist party, which is daily
growing more powerful in Chile, is the forty-one-year-old lawyer
Carlos Contreras Labarca. He works at *El Siglo*, the party organ,
which has an excellently equipped new plant; he was a deputy for
eight years, and became senator for Santiago in the 1941 elections. In these elections the communist vote rose from 17,162
four years ago (when the communists ran disguised as the "National Democratic Party") to about 55,000. In Santiago province
Contreras outpolled all other candidates. He is stocky, rather nervous in manner, and bespectacled. As far as I could gather, he has
never been in Moscow.

The communists are the best-organized party in the country,
and they claim 72,000 members. They say that they hope to become a truly *national* party (it was founded in 1921), and that
meantime the Popular Front is the hope of Chile. "The communist party is stronger than any laws passed against it," Contreras told me proudly. Twice President Aguirre Cerda has offered him a cabinet post, but he declined it each time. He hopes
by staying outside to make it easier for the government to give
real application to the Popular Front program.

Until the German invasion of Russia the communists were
abusively anti-American. Their relations with the Nazis—during
the era of the Russo-German pact—were obscure; people said

that the Nazis used them as the "Fifth Column inside the Fifth Column." The sudden alignment of Soviet Russia with Great Britain and the United States made communist heads in Santiago buzz and whirl, but Santiago is not unique in this respect. Nor were the Chilean communists less spectacularly agile than their comrades in other lands in looking for their feet again.

Another prominent communist is Pedro Pacheco, who was for some years mayor of Valparaiso. Back in 1931 he had been leader of a naval mutiny, and the naval forces stationed in the harbor hated him violently. He gave the city a good administration, but he lost his job when he let municipal employees who were members of the Popular Front take time off to attend political meetings. So anyway the story goes. Another leader is Elías Lafferte. After the fall of France, he was the only communist senator in the world, and he was a candidate for President in 1932.

Others in Chile

So many more Chilean politicians need mention that one scarcely knows how to begin—or end. But we cannot linger. It must be sufficient merely to list the names of such folk as Benjamin Cohen, a journalist and career diplomat who is known all over the Americas; Dr. Eduardo Cruz-Coke, a surgeon-professor who is the country's best expert on public health; and Guillermo Labarca Hubertson, one of the ablest men in Chile, who was impeached from his job as Minister of the Interior because the Right hated him.

Nor have we space for many recondite complexities in the Chilean political scene. For instance, one center party is called the Partido Democratica; another is the Partido Democratico. Another party (*Alianza Popular Libertadora*) is known as the Aplista, not to be confused with the Apristas of Peru; however, Apristas exist in Chile too. But definition of such refinements is beyond the scope of this book.

The conservative party has no single dominant leader—which is one of the reasons it has declined; its grand old man is Miguel

Cruchaga Tocornal, its nominal head is Senator Horacio Walker Larraín. Cruchaga, seventy-two years old, immensely dignified and very rich, is a kind of patriarch of the oligarchs. He is Elihu Root plus Nicholas Murray Butler, plus high church influence. He has twice been ambassador to Washington, and once to Berlin; he is honorary president of the local Friends of Germany society. . . . Senator Walker, president of the conservative party since 1931, is a professor, financier, and corporation lawyer.

In Chile the Liberal party is conservative. Both Alessandri and Ross were officially "liberals." The Liberal leader today is Eduardo Moore Montero, a forty-five-year-old professor of history and law. He was born in Germany, and spent his youth in Berlin. . . . Another important personage on the conservative side is Jaime Larraín García Moreno, who for ten years has been president of the National Agricultural Society, the chief landowners organization; he is only forty-five, violently ambitious, and a bitter enemy of the government. People call him the "Duke." Once President Aguirre Cerda wondered mildly whether Larraín would sit down to dinner with him. Larraín did.

The Radicals are the largest single party in the nation. They are not very radical. One of its leaders is Juan Antonio Rios, the president of the government mortgage bank. He is on the right wing of the party, and was once expelled from its ranks as an Ibáñista. Antonio Rios, born in 1888, is clear-cut, taciturn, energetic; he hates the communists, and is sometimes spoken of as a Rightist dark horse. . . . Marcial Mora Miranda is ex-president of the Central Bank of Chile, and a former Finance Minister and Foreign Minister. He is very close to Aguirre Cerda. . . . Guillermo del Pedrigal, a former head of the Fomento Corporation, a government institution devoted to the development of industry, is one of the most important men in Chile; he is now Minister of Finance.

The Minister of Foreign Affairs is an unknown quantity named Juan B. Rossetti, of Italian middle-class stock. He is only thirty-seven; for some years he has been president of the Radical

Socialist party, which is noisy, aggressive, and more leftist than the orthodox radicals. Rossetti was a minister in the revolutionary Dávila government. He did not join the Aguirre Cerda cabinet until June 1941, and his attitude to foreign affairs is little known. But people expect good things of him.

So to conclude this long litany of contemporary *chilenos* and their political complexities. One dominant fact stands out—that Chile is as democratically minded and governed as any state in the Americas.

Chapter XVII
Chile Getting Hot

~~~~~~

THE case may well be made that Chile, for all its enormous intellectual vitality, was all but murdered by a German chemist named Fritz Haber thirty-odd years ago. Let no one ignore the influence of science on politics.

Chile was, and is, the only producer of natural nitrates in the world, and until the first World War it had a 100 per cent monopoly on this material preciously indispensable for fertilizer and munitions. Then the estimable Dr. Haber came along, and invented a process for the fixation of nitrogen, that is, its withdrawal from air; thus synthetic nitrates could be made. And Germany, the United States, and other countries began to build artificial nitrate plants. For half a century Chile had absolutely controlled the world nitrate market. But, as a result of Haber, its nitrate industry came near collapse.

"For fifty years," wrote Archibald MacLeish in *Fortune* (May 1938), "Chile was a sort of elegant remittance man among the nations of the earth. Year in and year out she received her average royalty of $25,000,000 from nitrate fields largely operated by foreigners. Nitrates paid up to 68 per cent of her costs of government, relieving her ruling-class landowners of the unpleasant necessity of imposing taxes on themselves. Nitrates produced a steady flow of foreign exchange for the purchase of manufactured goods from abroad, making it unnecessary for the republic to create its own manufacturing industries. Nitrates thus permitted the Chilean landowners to retain on their vast estates a medieval economy with practical serfdom for their laborers and European educations for their numerous families of blond and lovely daughters and aristocratic sons."

Nitrates have recovered somewhat from the nadir of the late 1920's and early 30's, and they still play a cardinal role in Chilean economy. The country depends on nitrates—and copper—for 60 per cent of its foreign exchange. (If you want to give any Chilean a severe headache, tell him that someone may invent synthetic *copper* some fine day.) The nitrate industry is, like copper, largely owned by the United States; our investment in Chilean nitrates alone is $93,000,000. But the Chilean government, through an agency known as the Nitrate Sales Corporation, controls its operation and takes 25 per cent of all nitrate profits; these revenues, however, leave the country again, since they are earmarked for servicing the foreign debt.

Copper is dominated by two American companies, Kennecott and Anaconda, with a Chilean investment of about $290,000,000. Anaconda has, at Chuquicamata, the most prodigious copper mine on earth; it holds about 25 per cent of all the copper in the world. The copper companies pay 33 per cent of their net profits to the Chilean government; of this, 18 per cent goes to pay the foreign debt, and 15 per cent to the Fomento Corporation, which closely resembles the American R.F.C.

The war hurt Chilean economy drastically. Normally 60 per cent of nitrates went to Europe, and close to 100 per cent of copper went to Europe and Japan. Now Europe is, as we know, cut off; Central Europe is blockaded, and Great Britain cannot buy in important quantities except in sterling areas. Production of copper dropped from about 32,000 tons a month before the war to 14,000 tons in July 1940. So Chile turns with something like desperation to the United States. The obstacle to American purchases is the 4-cent-per-pound tax that we impose on foreign copper. Nevertheless, United States trade with Chile has increased enormously. We are buying more nitrates, and we need copper for national defense. Chilean exports to the United States (New York *Times*, June 2, 1941), rose from 15 per cent of her total exports in 1938 to not less than 58 per cent in 1940. Imports jumped correspondingly. (In 1936, incidentally, Germany had squeezed out the United States as first exporter to Chile, largely by use of barter and "Aski" marks.) Currently Japanese trade with Chile is increasing also. The Japanese buy important quantities of nitrates and copper, some of which they transmit to Germany.

The United States investment in Chile is our largest in the hemisphere, after Canada and Cuba; it amounts to about $700,000,000, including loans valued at $182,000,000. Bethlehem Steel controls the Bethlehem-Chilean iron mines (Chile is the only country on the continent except Brazil with good workable deposits of iron and coal). The American investment in Chile has by no means been an unmixed blessing. The country has the largest per capita foreign debt in the world; its debt has all but strangled it.

Chile is being industrialized hard and fast, with shoes, textiles, clothing, chemicals, paper, all expanding. But the heart of Chilean economy remains the land. More than 40 per cent of all Chileans live by agriculture, and most of these—workers on the great estates—live in intolerable misery. The *pelucones* (landowners) are probably the most archaic-minded in the Americas; their peasants get wages of 2 to 7 pesos (8 to 28 cents) per day. One estate near Valparaiso employs 4,000 workers, and does not use one single piece of machinery. Most landowners set themselves against even the slightest form of social amelioration. The Popular Front is doing what it can to make a land reform, which is not much. The government does not dare attempt to break up the big estates, but it is buying up land that the *pelucones* want to sell, settling people on public domain, and helping them to fend for themselves.

Under the Popular Front, Chile has set up a kind of embryo machinery of controlled economy, and there are close resemblances between various government departments and New Deal agencies in the United States. The Chilean government dominates credit, partially controls public utilities, runs the nitrate industry, and has developed a tremendous social-security program. Its Junta de Exportación Agrícola almost precisely corresponds to the American A.A.A.; the Caja de Crédito Agrícola to our Farm Credit Administration, and the Caja de Colonización Agrícola to the Federal Farm Mortgage system. The Caja de Habitación Popular closely corresponds to the Federal Housing Administration, the Caja Nacional de Ahorros to the Home Owners Loan Corporation, and the Superintendencia de los Bancos to the S.E.C.

Social welfare and security legislation is probably more advanced in Chile than in any other country in the world. Its heart is the *caja* (roughly, guild) system; it was started by Alessandri, not by the Popular Front, though the Popular Front spends more money on it than previous governments.

Four basic laws provide for compulsory workers' insurance, a central welfare institute that administers the hospitals of the country, compulsory arbitration of labor disputes (though strikes are legal and frequent), and discharge benefits. If you keep an employee for more than a few years—this is true in Argentine also and to a less extent in Uruguay and Peru—the chances are that you will keep him for life, since it is so expensive to get rid of him.

There are about thirty *cajas* in Chile, each for a different class of occupation; the biggest, the Caja de Seguro Obligatorio, has an annual budget of almost $4,500,000, a very large sum for the country, and a membership of several hundred thousand. The employer (in industries employing manual labor) pays 5 per cent of the worker's salary into the *caja*, the worker pays 2 per cent, the state pays 1½ per cent. In white-collar work, the employer pays 16.33 per cent, the employee 8 per cent, the state nothing. The *caja* contributes retirement pensions, lifetime medical and hospital service, co-operative shops, and facilities for buying homes. Vacations are compulsory. So is the eight-hour day.

The Caja de Seguro Obligatorio paid out 48,214,641 pesos ($1,928,585) in medical expenses in 1939, and 14,830,943 pesos ($593,237) in pensions. The Caja Nacional de Empleados Públicos y Periodistas (for government workers, civil servants, journalists), handled 12,743 pharmacy cases in the single month of June 1940, 2,678 dental cases, 1,320 medical cases; it made 2,060 laboratory tests, and took 826 X-rays and 80 electrocardiographs. This service is all paid for by the *caja*. The Caja de Habitación Popular has built 3,299 houses since its foundation, at an average cost of 26,000 pesos ($1,040); the worker can buy a house for 150 pesos ($6.00) per month.

One odd detail on the Chilean economic front is the ferocious warfare going on between wine and beer. The powerful agrarian wine growers compete, as is natural, with the urban brewery interests. The wine growers usually come out on top, though they are steeply taxed. For instance, the government limits beer production to a quota, which works out to twenty liters per consumer per year; the wine growers say that this is good in that it induces temperance. Sometimes the quota is exhausted by November, say; then no more beer flows until the first of the next year. Wine (and good wine it is) is cheaper than milk in Chile. Wine costs 1.60 pesos (about 6½¢) per liter, milk 2.80 (a bit over 11 cents).

Another odd thing: one of the first things the Popular Front did was to let people redeem anything they had in the state pawnshops.

A.B.C.

The well-known A.B.C., which existed from the days of World War I to about 1925, was never an outright alliance, but a kind of informal understanding; the three chief countries of South America—Argentine, Brazil, Chile—agreed tacitly to work together. For years Argentine and Chile had been widely separated. Buenos Aires was much nearer to Europe than to Santiago. Until the Andean Railroad was built in 1904, it took longer to get from Buenos Aires to Valparaiso than to New York.

Argentine, the source of most South American ideas, prompted the A.B.C. agreement, partly in order to offset growing United States influence in the hemisphere. Later, Argentina more or less discouraged its development, partly because the Foreign Minister,

Saavedra Lamas, wanted his country to be stronger on its own. Then came the Chaco war; Chile tended to support Bolivia, while Argentina supported Paraguay. The A.B.C. combination broke up.

Nowadays Chile tends to think in terms of a "Pacific Bloc," including Bolivia, Ecuador (with which it has always been very friendly), and Peru. Also it likes to be close to Brazil, since Brazil is on the other side of Argentina, its most powerful neighbor. This sounds like old-time European politics in microcosm. In the spring of 1941, Chile negotiated nonaggression pacts with both Bolivia and Peru, in the interests of Pacific (and hemisphere) solidarity.

Chilean relations with Argentina are quite good and normal, but with a vague substratum of uneasiness on Chile's part. Argentina is too rich, confident, and aggressive, the Chileans think; they fear that some Argentines have designs on their wheat and mutton country near Magallanes. Chile, though its army is good and its navy the best in Latin America, is poor, and it is somewhat isolated; probably it would like to have A.B.C. back again.

In November 1940 the Chilean government suddenly laid claim to an enormous region in the Antarctic, including the South Shetland Islands and Graham Island, and part of the Weddell Quadrant where Admiral Byrd recently established a base. These frigid wastes have no discernible value now; some day, however, a valuable meteorological station might be built there. Argentina protested at once when the Chileans announced their claims, though it had never made a claim itself. Washington listened closely, and said nothing.[1]

Germans Are Here

The most typical German colony in the Americas is that of Chile. It centers on the town of Valdivia, about 575 miles below

[1] Argentina and Chile have a longstanding minor quarrel over the sovereignty of Beagle Island, in the channel south of the Straits of Magellan, near Tierra del Fuego.

Santiago, and is the prototype of similar German communities in the Misiones region of Argentina and Santa Catharina in Brazil. Here a powerful race-conscious group of native-born and Chilean Germans live like Germans in The Reich; they are a kind of foreign fungus attached to the body politic of the nation.

I had a sharp introduction to Fifth Column influence in Chile when I read in a pro-ally paper, a few days after moving into a seaside hotel, that the hotel was looking for a new hall porter. The manager wrote one applicant for the job that he must remember, if hired, to keep his eyes open, since he would be in a key position to serve the German fatherland.

No one knows exactly how many Germans of the first and second generation live in Chile; a reasonable estimate is 80-90,000, and they are, of course, compactly organized. Their clubs, schools, shops, are German; they read German newspapers, use German radios and cameras, listen to broadcasts from German stations, and are buried under German tombstones. I heard it said that every newspaper in Chile below Valparaiso is German-controlled. At least half the population in the Valdivia region has German blood.

The heart of Fifth Columnism is, as always, the German embassy. The ambassador, an old-school diplomat named Von Schoen, is not so active as some of his subordinates. But his counselor, Wilhelm von Pochhammer, and Walter Boettger, the commercial attaché, are busy. One embassy secretary, Dr. George Leisewitz, who is partly English and who went to Cambridge, is a kind of roving delegate; for instance, he was German "observer" at the Havana and other Pan-American conferences. The Chilean army was German-trained for more than twenty years, and deputies said in the national Congress recently that 95 per cent of its officers were pro-German.

The *carabineros*, a picked semi-militarized police, were also German-trained. But their instructor, Otto von Zipellius, was discharged recently. He remained in Santiago, and has written letters to Berlin signing himself "chief of the district leaders of the German Nazi party in Chile." (New York *Times*, July 13, 1940.)

No apparent contact exists between local *Chilean* Nazis, like those of González Von Marées, and the official Germans; on the other hand, some Rightist circles are glad to accept covert German support, because they hate the Popular Front so much. Perhaps they do not like Nazism, but any stick is good enough to beat Aguirre Cerda with. It is not the Right that uses the Nazis, but the Nazis who use the Right. . . . The Germans, of course, dislike the Popular Front, not merely on ideological grounds but because it is friendly to the United States.

In June 1941, the German government gave a four-masted schooner, described as "one of the best sailing vessels in the world," to the Chilean navy as a gift for training purposes, and Chile accepted it. The German ambassador, presenting it, spoke as follows:

A new link has been forged between the navies of Germany and Chile. In accordance with naval tradition, all vessels are part of national territory, but if this gift is accepted this portion of German territory will be symbolically converted into Chilean territory. We would like to have the German flag deposited in the heart of this vessel so that in the future the flags of both Chile and Germany will be always united as proof of the solid friendship existing between the two countries.
—New York *Times*, June 7, 1941

One thorny problem was that presented by sixty-three sailors from the German battleship *Graf Spee*, who escaped from internment in Argentine and reached Chile. The German consul general in Valparaiso gave four of its officers false passports, so that they could proceed to Japan; the Chileans discovered this, and expelled him from the country; later he returned and was again expelled.

Early in 1941 a hush-hush conference of German ambassadors was held in Santiago. Baron von Thermann, the envoy to Argentina, slipped over the Andes secretly, but newspaper men discovered him; at the same time the German ministers from Peru and Bolivia arrived. One story is that this meeting was also attended by Dr. Kurt Rieth, who, when he arrived subsequently in the United States, was arrested and deported. After Thermann's visit to Santiago the Germans showed their new propaganda picture, *Victory in the West*, to a picked group of Chilean army officers and other guests.

The Chilean government has for some time watched the Fifth Column carefully. In July 1941, it refused to permit the German minister to Bolivia, Ernst Wendler, who had just been expelled, to remain in Chilean territory. In August, the government forbade any radio propaganda that favored any belligerent state. Then five Germans who were members of a Nazi organization in Puerto Montt were arrested, and some arms seized. Pro-ally newspapers announced that the Chilean government had squelched an attempted coup d'état, just in time.

Chile and Hemisphere Defense

The Straits of Magellan cut through Chilean territory, and the country largely dominates the turbulent waters around Cape Horn. This is the gist of Chile's defense problem in relation to the United States. If the Panama Canal were ever bombed out of commission, the American navy could not move from Atlantic to Pacific or vice versa except via Cape Horn or the Straits. Thus a friendly Chile is important in the extreme to United States strategy. Moreover, a war between the United States and Japan would be a Pacific war, and Chile has a longer coastline on the Pacific than the United States itself.

The Straits of Magellan are not fortified, by reason of a long-standing treaty between Chile and Argentina. The passage could not, therefore, be easily closed to transit by American ships, or for that matter to ships of any other power. Coastal batteries might be installed, but not quickly. The Chilean navy is an excellent force—it has one 33,000-ton battleship—and its six submarines are useful. It is to United States advantage to keep the Straits permanently open, and to cultivate close and cordial relations with Chile by every means.

The United States has not asked for bases in Chile, but it is generally understood that the country will, if America goes to war, gladly give us help, and permit full use of its facilities. We also hope that Chile, perhaps with our co-operation, will meantime enlarge its defense facilities, for its own sake as well as ours. The chief strategic points are Valparaiso, the Juan Fernández islands, Talcahuano (the chief Chilean naval station), and Magallanes. Easter Island, Chile's possession far out in the Pacific, might be useful as an outpost, but it has no harbor. Ships can, however, anchor outside; Admiral Von Spee's squadron used it in the last world war, and it might conceivably be a future stepping stone for the Japanese. At present Easter Island is under lease to a British company that grows sheep there.

An American military air mission is stationed in Chile; the former British naval and German army missions departed some years ago. The strongest local defense force is probably that of the Carabineros, who are tough-minded, thoroughly trained, and loyal to themselves; by tradition, they support whatever government is in power. Chile is worried about its defenses, and late in 1940 it passed a billion-peso defense bill (roughly $40,000,000), a staggering sum for the country; it is half the total budget. Chilean relations with the United States are excellent.

What Chile Needs

I asked a dozen or so Chileans what they thought their country needed most. The answers came out this way. (1) Raise the standard of living, especially in the middle class. (2) *Honesty* in politics and business. (3) More and better education. (4)

Break-up of the biggest estates. (5) A firmer program by the Popular Front.

So much for the Andean countries and the long West Coast. We cross the Andes now, turn briefly to Paraguay, and then enter the broad glittering world of Argentina and the east.

Chapter XVIII
Paraguay Is Ruritania

~~~~~~

THIS is Ruritania. Paraguay, the most remote and picturesque state in the Americas, is a kind of forlorn and almost forgotten fairyland, with overtones of brutal contemporary reality. This is the country of flaming red *flamboyant* trees, of streets "paved" with glistening sharp cobbles, of tranquil sunsets over the broad meandering River Paraguay. It is the country where office hours are from 8 to 11 A.M., where appointments are canceled if it rains, where women roll big black cigars on their thighs, and puff them stolidly.

Paraguay is the country where 60 to 70 per cent of the people are illegitimate, where a distinguished general may have eighty children, and where everyone is good-humoredly related to everyone else. No one knows who anybody's grandfather is; Hitler would have a hard time in Asunción. It is the country where people like to laugh and make jokes, where most salaries—pitiably small—are months in arrears, where the newspapers print patriotic homilies between the headlines, where a European woman may be stoned if she wears slacks, and where Rutherford B. Hayes is the best-known American President, because he once settled a frontier dispute. It is the country of political *confusionismo* (a pretty word), Argentine imperialism, and appalling poverty.

The history of Paraguay is like that of no other American republic. Paraguay is unique. During the nineteenth century it was dominated by three extraordinary dictators and by one tragic war. A bizarre creature named Gaspar Rodríguez de Francia ruled from 1814 to 1840; he was called *El Supremo,* and he shut the nation off from the world almost to the degree that Japan, for instance, was shut off before the Meiji restoration. Paraguay was his prison. Then came Carlos Antonio López, the dictator from 1844 to 1862, and his son, Francisco Solano López, who ruled till 1870. The younger López had a fabulous Irish-French mistress, Madame Lynch, who really ran the country. The Paraguayans were—and are—tough-fibered and aggressive folk, with a violently intense nationalism, and between 1865 and 1870 they waged war against Argentina, Brazil, and Uruguay, and almost beat all three. But the struggle decimated the nation. Literally. More than literally. *All but 28,000 of Paraguay's male population perished.* Ever since, women have done most of the country's work. Paraguayans still talk of the catastrophe of 1870 as if it had happened yesterday; it is still an intimate and pressing preoccupation. One cannot understand Paraguay without realizing this. It is as if North Americans still burningly discussed the affairs of General Grant.

Paraguay is unique for another reason, namely that it is the only hemisphere state where the Indians dominated the Spaniards instead of vice versa. The virile Guaranís of Paraguay were exceptional, and still are. Almost every Paraguayan speaks Guaraní as well as Spanish, and conversation often breaks down into the Indian tongue. The Spaniards never conquered the Guaranís, as they never conquered the Araucanians of Chile; when Spanish settlers—of a superior Basque and Catalan type—arrived in Asunción in 1536, the Guaranís asked for their help against other Indians, and the Spaniards happened to agree. Paraguay has been a united and homogeneous country ever since.

Paraguay, which like Bolivia is landlocked, covers about 175,000 square miles, the size of Colorado plus Nebraska. Its population is fewer than a million; illiteracy is so high that Spanish newspapers don't reach more than about 20,000 people. Poverty is formidable. Yet, though the people may be undernourished, they are not, as in the sterile highlands of Bolivia and Peru, actually starving. Nor does their poverty keep them from being *simpáticos* in the extreme.

Totalitarian Rumblings

The President of Paraguay is the little-known General Don Higinio Morínigo, a young army man who has never been outside the country. He is in his late thirties, and is of amiable disposition; his black eyes shine like marbles, his black hair starts an inch above his brows. His origins were humble and obscure; it appears that his father was a merchant in the town of Paraguarí. Under a former President named Franco he was chief of staff; then he became Minister of War as a representative of the young radical officers. He has been President since September 1940. In May 1941 his seven-year-old son, an attractive boy, came to Warm Springs for treatment of infantile paralysis.

President Morínigo has, like Dr. Arnulfo Arias in Panama, pronounced totalitarian sympathies: this is the most important thing about him. When I saw him—in a glittering white uniform, his shoulders crushed by enormous golden epaulettes—he said that he believed in "selective democracy"; but it is clear that his government is trying to build something close to a corporative state.

In his presidential proclamation of November 30, 1940, Morínigo announced that the principles of his rule would be *Disciplina, Jerarquía, Orden*; discipline, hierarchy, order. He said that, under God, he would guarantee "the inalienable human rights" of people, but that anybody who expressed political doctrines against his regime, or spread ideas of a subversive character, would be "subject to confinement." He announced that army and people must act under his Sole Command, and that Congress would not meet again.

On Christmas day the President broadcast a message to the nation. Listen:

In the absence of the House of Representatives, I deem it my duty to explain the general plans of my government and the ideological content of the *Revolución Paraguaya Nacionalista*. . . .

We reject exotic political regimes in Paraguay. We favor authentic democracy. But unless the people are *educated*, elections are controlled by demagogues, and they debase and corrupt the masses. . . .

Government by parties must be replaced by government by and for the *nation*. . . .

We reject liberalism, the product of the nineteenth century. We stand above all for the intervention [of the state] in the economic field and especially in relations between capital and labor. . . . The inertia of the liberal state should give way to the dynamics of the protecting and directing state, in the interests of social justice.

The state should be free of the influence of private capital, particularly foreign capital. . . . We stand for intervention and permanent control by the state in all enterprises associated with concessions or public services. . . . Private property should be respected.

I invoke the protection of Almighty God, Supreme Maker of the Universe, begging that He give new animation to our efforts.

Then Morínigo went on to outline his concrete program. Reform of the electoral law. No exploitation of the proletarian class. Housing. Roads. More roads. Rural electrification. Social security. Old-age pensions. Creation of a career diplomatic service. Redistribution of the real property of the country, so that every home shall have its own productive plot of land. Free and compulsory education. Close relations with the church.

Thus one may see that the enticing winds of modern social doctrine—strangely mixed up with atavistic Catholicism—have reached the orange frangipani trees of Asunción at last.

Politics, Paraguay, and Paradox

Behind Morínigo is a clique or *junta* of young officers and students, a kind of anonymous brain trust. No one knows just who the members are, and rule is almost as if by secret society. These officers inherited a basic political situation that was all but intolerable.

The traditional parties in Paraguay are the *Colorados* (Reds), who are conservative and who represent the landed oligarchy, and the Blues or liberals. The Colorados have been out of office for more than thirty years. The liberal administrations that followed became corrupt, inefficient, and decadent. As I heard it said in Asunción, they had their noses in the trough, and wouldn't budge.

Then came the Chaco War, and thousands of young officers and soldiers returned to the capital—after insufferable hardships—and bitterly resented their exclusion from political and economic life. The army (like the Japanese army) was a Have-Not army, with just grievances; it decided to take things over, and kick the soft and greedy civilians out.

So a young officer, Colonel Rafael Franco, made a revolution in February 1936. This ended the liberal regime. Eighteen months later Franco was in turn overthrown by a military *junta*. We have little space for the tangled interlude that followed. But in August 1939, Marshal José Félix Estigarribia became President. He had been commander-in-chief in the Chaco War, and his record was enlightened; he was very close to the United States, and promised to give Paraguay the best administration it ever had. In theory Estigarribia was a liberal; what he hoped to do was make a bridge between the army and normal constitutional rule. He might have succeeded, but he was killed in a luckless airplane accident in September 1940.[1] Then Morínigo, his Minister of War, took over.

Quickly Morínigo strove to entrench himself in power, though he was only supposed to serve an interim two-month term. But he managed to postpone the projected elections until 1943, and on November 30 he proclaimed himself dictator. Meantime four of his cabinet ministers—Estigarribia men—resigned. Two of them were arrested, the Ministers of Finance and Interior, and are believed to be still in jail. A third, Pablo Max Insfran, who was Minister of Public Works and one of the most competent living Paraguayans, fled into exile.

After November 1940 Morínigo continued to clean house. He dismissed four ranking generals, including the commander-in-chief, General Delgado, who had just returned from an official visit to the United States, and Colonel Ramón Parades, the so-called

---

[1] Pro-Nazi newspapers in Buenos Aires accuse the United States of "responsibility" for this accident, which is total nonsense. Similarly Axis papers said that the United States "murdered" Germán Busch in Bolivia.

"strong man" behind him. All went into exile except Delgado. Later another "strong man," Colonel Dámaso Sosa Valdés, the Minister of Interior and commander of a powerful cavalry regiment, was thrown out.

Morínigo then turned his attention to the old liberals. They wanted to get back to the trough; they were conspiring to oust his government, he said. Several dozen arrests were made in Christmas week, and a minor reign of terror came. Some prisoners—not many—were sent "up the river" to the penal colony at Peña Hermosa, which was bad luck for them. The army radicals continued to seize "suspects." If a man so much as had lunch at the Union Club—the essential rendezvous of Paraguayan politics—or bought a new suit of clothes, he was likely to be called an enemy of the state. I happened to be visiting the American legation in Asunción, chatting with Findley Howard, the United States minister, when one frightened liberal bounced in, and asked for diplomatic protection. But Mr. Howard couldn't give it to him.

The comprehensiveness of Morínigo's activity produced natural reaction. In February 1941 a conspiracy by the garrison at Concepción in the north had to be suppressed. Then rumors were heard that Colonel Franco, who had made the original coup against the liberals, and who is even more radical than Morínigo, was coming back; for some years he has been an exile in Montevideo. But Paraguay prevailed upon Uruguay not to let him out. In April the government put down an attempted revolution apparently incited by navy elements. Another "revolt" came in July, but it was also crushed.

It isn't easy to make a counter-revolution in Paraguay, since the army gets about 50 per cent of the national budget, and no single leader is prominent enough to unite the civilian forces. The only way to throw the army out is by using the army itself, that is, by influencing one army faction—with arms—to act against another. The way to "influence" the army is with money. But the army has it all.

Look at Paraguayans

The Foreign Minister of Paraguay, Dr. Luis A. Argaña, was born in Asunción, and is about forty-five; he was Jesuit-educated. He was Minister of Justice and Public Worship in a previous government, and dean of the faculty of economics at the National University. He is a lawyer by profession, and a fanatically devout Catholic. He goes to church every day; his nickname has to do with his devotions. Dr. Argaña's views on foreign policy seemed, when I saw him, somewhat undefined; he said that if the United States declared war on Germany, Paraguay would be neutral "unless attacked." Dr. Argaña looks like an old-style actor or magician. You expect him to pull a rabbit out of his vest at any moment.

The most picturesque of contemporary Paraguayans is probably the former chief of staff and commander-in-chief, General Nicolás Delgado. He is very pro-United States, and American officers think that he is a first-class soldier. Delgado is of Guaraní origin, like almost everybody else in the country. His nickname is *Puchita puchita*, roughly "Little by Little." He is a beguiling character. Some years ago he went to France to learn French. In three weeks, every Frenchman in the village where he lived was speaking Guaraní.

Colonel Rafael Franco, the ex-President exiled in Uruguay, was the popular hero of the Chaco War. He was a poor boy, and has strongly leftist tendencies. Nowadays he runs a soap and cosmetics factory in Montevideo.

A Word on Economics

Paraguay lives, if you can call it living, mostly on the export of meat products, *yerba mate* (an aromatic tea), and *quebracho* (literally, "ax-breaker"), an exceptionally hard wood from which tannin is derived. . . . In Paraguay economic affairs take weird directions. The country is a cattle producer, but it has to import butter and cheese. Cabbages and potatoes, which are imported, are an extreme luxury; potatoes cost 6 cents per pound. Paraguayan currency is probably the cheapest in the world; for one American dollar you get 280 Paraguayan pesos at the official exchange, and more illegally. . . . To put the country thoroughly on its feet will cost $19,000,000 in loans, American financial advisers in Asunción say.

Much land in Paraguay is still public land, and anybody can buy it who has the money. Some estates reach colossal size; one, owned by an Argentinian *estanciero* named Carlos Casado, is bigger than anything in Argentina, and measures 56 *million* acres. The peons on the land get nothing but their food, and sometimes not too much of that. During the Chaco War a soldier could be kept for 19 *centavos* a day. A Paraguayan cabinet minister gets $125 a month, and a telegraph clerk about $10.

Axis and U. S. Interests

There is a large German colony in Paraguay, about 18,000 German-born and first-generation Germans in all. Many of them, however, are concentrated in Mennonite colonies in the Chaco, and they are not politically active. But the Axis representatives in Asunción—and also the Encarnación region—are very busy. Several local banks, like the Banco Germánico, are influential, and one of the capital's four newspapers, *La Tribuna*, is German-controlled. During 1939, the German legation in Asunción imported 2,936 kilograms (about three *tons*) of propaganda material, enough to go a long way in a country as largely illiterate as Paraguay; this goes to show how important Germany considers it to be. Also, late in 1940, $200,000 in American cash reached the Italian legation—a lot of money for the country.

The government of Marshal Estigarribia was strongly pro-United States, and he and his ministers would have been delighted to give us actual air bases in the country—something that, as we know, most Latin American states are loath to do—in exchange for financial help. The present government, in spite of its domestic totalitarian leanings, is not unfriendly. Staff talks between Paraguay and the United States have proceeded cordially, and Asunción has asked for an American naval mission. (The country's military mission was French, but it broke up after 1940 when several of its officers joined De Gaulle.)

The Morínigo administration has taken fairly strong action against Fifth Columnism. For a time the newspapers were asked not to print any editorial comment on the war, for or against either side, so that local opinion would not become excited. One paper, a flagrantly Fascist sheet called *Tiempo*, has been suppressed. No foreign-language newspapers are permitted, no foreign uniforms or insignia, and no political activity by foreigners. Censorship is strict. Charlie Chaplin's *Great Dictator* was forbidden.

The church is very powerful in Paraguay, but its chief dignitary, Archbishop Sinforiano Bogarín, is said to be pro-American and on the liberal side. The President of the country must be a Roman Catholic—a heritage of Jesuit days—and church and state are of course united. Yet lay Catholics in Asunción told me that on the whole politicians guided the church rather than vice versa. I found no Falange influence. . . . The communist party is illegal in Paraguay, as it is in most of South America, but communists nevertheless dominate the most important union.

Argentine Imperialism in Paraguay

Economically, at least, Paraguay is little more than a colony of Argentina next door, and the Argentines exploit it mercilessly. Politically, the men of Buenos Aires do not interfere much. They do not care a great deal who governs in Asunción provided that the government does not (*a*) interfere with Argentine interests, or (*b*) flirt with Brazil. What they want mostly is that Paraguay shall remain weak and self-divided. Factors in Argentine exploitation of Paraguay are the following:

First and foremost, Paraguayan currency is quoted only in terms of the Argentine peso. To get any foreign exchange at all, the Paraguayans must go to Buenos Aires. Even a recent $500,000 credit from the United States Export-Import Bank had to be paid through the medium of Argentine exchange.

Second, the Argentine government owns 75 per cent of the Paraguayan Central Railroad, which runs from Asunción to the Paraná river, where there is a frontier ferry. The Argentines could stop traffic here on almost any pretext, if they chose, and cut Paraguay from all rail connections outside.

Third, Paraguay depends on Argentina for essential food, particularly bread and wheat. The Argentines have their own mills in Asunción; they send up their own flour, and manufacture and sell bread locally. If Argentina should embargo exports of wheat to Paraguay, it might starve.

Fourth, Argentina largely controls the Paraguayan *quebracho* industry (though one tannin-extracting company is American-owned), and is by far Paraguay's best customer.

Fifth, about 80 per cent of Paraguayan trade is carried by the Mihanovich company, the great Argentine shipping firm. Mihanovich controls all traffic on the River Paraguay, and charges fantastic rates. Its revenue from Paraguay alone is said to be in the neighborhood of $1,500,000 per year, and it costs more to ship some categories of freight from Asunción to Buenos Aires, a distance of 750 miles, than from Buenos Aires to New York, which is 6,000 miles.

The Argentines do not like it at all that American companies are financing Paraguayan road development. One vital road is being built eastward from Asunción to Villarrica; it will tap the undeveloped area near Brazil. Paraguay hopes, with United States help, to push this road eventually to the Brazilian frontier—it also hopes for a railway to Brazil—but Argentina looks on with heavy disapproval.

A final factor is emotional. To most Paraguayans, Buenos

Aires is the heart of the world, just as Paris is the heart of the world to most Argentines. Socially, culturally, intellectually, Buenos Aires is as much the capital of Paraguay as is Asunción. If a Paraguayan has once laid eyes on Buenos Aires, he has fulfilled a major ambition; he is a great traveler, and will die happy.

Chapter XIX
The Argentine Complex

~~~~~~

W E COME now to Argentina, which is the key to everything. Here is the richest state in Latin America, the most powerful, and the most progressive from the material point of view. It is the least "American" country in the hemisphere, because its roots, its instincts, its markets, have been largely European; it sometimes seems almost like a projection of Europe into the Western Hemisphere. It is a country piercingly sensitive to affront, and deeply proud of its nationalism and its acknowledged mission, which is to be the dominant state of Latin America. It is the country where beef is king, and Buenos Aires the resplendent queen.

I know no state more difficult to understand, or more fascinating. A diplomatic anecdote comes to mind. One ambassador to the Argentine Republic says to another: "I have been here six months, and I understand nothing." His colleague replies, "My friend, I congratulate you. Your perceptions are quicker than mine. I have been here three years, and I have now reached the same conclusion."

One very small point to begin with. Buenos Aires is a city of 2,364,263 people, with traffic that churns, roars, grunts, seethes, on shining boulevards as wide as those of Westchester, or on the cobbled outlying streets that so startlingly remind one of the environs of Paris. I have never seen traffic so violently agitated. The ugly aggressive busses are called *matagente* (man-killers) and the drivers are known as *asesinos*. Yet there is not a single traffic light in all of Buenos Aires, not one flicker of red or green or amber from dusk to dusk. Reason: the Argentines experimented with traffic lights, and then gave up the idea, because no one would obey them. They consider themselves superior to such mechanical controls.

(My Argentine friends will sigh when they read this paragraph, and dismiss me as a *Yanqui* savage interested only in materialistic phenomena.)

Argentina today is gripped by profound crisis. Not merely political crisis, though of this I shall have much to report presently. Not merely economic crisis, though that is obviously severe. The country is the greatest producer and exporter of agricultural goods on earth, and as a result it has been savagely hurt by the war and the blockade. But the crisis I mean goes deeper. It is a spiritual crisis roughly like that of a powerful, attractive, and sensitive young man facing the problems of turbulent maturity, after being cut off from the family that protected him when he was younger.

The Argentines have long had four master bonds to Europe. First, historical. The country is essentially white; there is no negro problem, and scarcely any Indian or *mestizo* problem. The Indians had no civilization in the La Plata region; they were nomads—they did not even weave blankets—and were killed off early. Second, economic. European and particularly British capital built up the country—British investments alone are still worth about $2,000,000,000—and about 40 per cent of total exports customarily went to Britain. Third, cultural and intellectual. Practically all intellectual currents came from Europe, and every Argentine of the upper classes thought of Paris as his spiritual home; I have met Argentinians who never read a book in Spanish till they were 20. Everything had to be French. Fourth, religious. The all-powerful Church represented a profound European influence, not merely for historical reasons, but because almost all priests in Argentina were Spanish or Italian.

I owe the foregoing summary to an eminent Argentine economist. During our conversation he said, "Every time I visit the United States I feel that I am abroad." This puzzled me until I realized what he meant, that he was *at home* in Europe.

But now Europe has been cut off. It is lost. Hitler is destroying the old Europe; already it is transformed beyond recognition. The Europe of 1941 is not the Europe that the Argentines knew thirty or twenty or even ten years ago. Physical exports have shrunk, and spiritual imports have dried up. There is no sustenance out of Europe any more. So the Argentines are disturbed and frustrated. Their culture is a recent culture, like that of the United States; it does not lie deep. They do not know what to think in a world of collapsing values. They do not know where to turn.

And so have developed three dominant trends in their contemporary politico-intellectual life: first a vibrantly intense and defensive Argentine nationalism, second a derivative feeling of stewardship for the rest of Latin America, third a highly complex attitude *vis-à-vis* the United States.

One of my Argentine friends, a distinguished lawyer who has often visited North America, goes so far as to think that, with Europe in collapse, his country must become the leader of the Latin race all over the world. He envisages the future civilization of the Western Hemisphere as a combination of Anglo-Saxon and Latin, with Argentina as the inevitable, the predestined, the almighty Latin spokesman.

As to Argentine relations with the United States, that is a thorny topic which I must deal with later.

Country with Two Presidents

In the late summer of 1941 the Argentine Republic had a President, Dr. Ortiz, incapacitated by illness. It was ruled instead by an Acting President, Dr. Castillo. The confusion produced by this anomaly has been considerable, especially since Ortiz and Castillo are pronounced political opponents. Ortiz is a radical, and Castillo a conservative. Moreover, a third figure, a former President named Justo, is almost as powerful behind the scenes as the other two, which makes the confusion worse confounded. The story in Buenos Aires is that Ortiz is the hope of the radicals, that Castillo is the hope of the conservatives, and that Justo is the hope of—Justo.

But before tackling these paradoxes and difficulties it is necessary to go back a little. The story is incomprehensible without its background.

Argentina, with its 13,129,723 people, its area of 1,078,278 square miles (almost five times the size of France), most of it in the temperate zone,[1] was part of the Vice-royalty of Peru until 1776. It was the first state in Latin America to win its independence; its deliverer was a remarkable Creole adventurer, José de San Martín, who had fought in the Spanish army in Europe and who returned to free his country. He campaigned not only in Argentina but on the west coast and the mountain states, where he collaborated closely with Bolívar. The name "Argentina" derives, incidentally, from "silver." So does the name "Plata" which is the country's great river mouth.

The century 1820-1920 was one of terrific development, with three great men, all of whose names begin with R, successively dominating it. Bernardino Rivadavia, the first President, sought to give the country constitutional shape and form during the period of anarchic quarrels and civil wars between provincial chieftains. Juan Manuel de Rosas, who was dictator from 1835 to 1852, the first great radical *caudillo*, was a kind of cowboy Andrew Jackson, with overtones of contemporary dictatorship. For instance, he had his own red-shirted private army, his own Gestapo. He helped establish a federal system. Julio Roca, President from 1880 to 1886 (and also later), pushed the frontier west and south, pacified Patagonia, and killed off most of the Indians that still survived. His career is strikingly like that of frontier builders in the United States. Meantime came tremendous immigration from Europe. Hundreds of thousands of Europeans—Irish, British, Germans, Basques, Spaniards, Italians—journeyed to Argentina just as they came to North America, to settle in its fat cattle lands, its rising industrial towns.

For the last 30 or 40 years Argentine politics have been, in the

[1] But the seasons are inverted as compared to the United States. Our summer is winter in Argentina.

main, split by a single enormous cleavage. The complexities are endless—and the friendly experts of Buenos Aires drive themselves and their listeners to frenzy explaining them—but the main point is clear enough. The struggle is the most simple and natural in the world, that between Right and Left. On one side are the conservatives who represent, by and large, the old creole aristocracy, the great landowners, the surviving feudal relics. On the other side are the radicals who, by and large but not exclusively, represent the townsfolk, the middle class—Argentina is the only country in South America with a well-developed middle class— the sons of immigrants, the shopkeepers, the business men. Mostly the conservatives represent the old colonial tradition of Spain. Mostly the radicals represent the newer tradition of modern Europe, especially Italy. One out of every four Argentines, be it remembered, has Italian blood.

The conservatives (*Conservadores*) have the meaningless name *Partido Demócrata Nacional*. With them are allied a branch of the radicals, known as the *anti-Personalistas*. The coalition is called the *Concordancia*. The opposition radicals, who are the largest *single* party, call themselves the *Unión Cívica Radical*, or U.C.R. for short.

There are not so many landowners, members of the Jockey Club, bull breeders, and other representatives of the oligarchy as there are townsmen, industrialists, shopkeepers, members of the middle class. Naturally. Thus the paramount issue. The conservatives want to hold power and the manifold advantages it brings. Naturally. But the bulk of the people are radical, and the radicals will win any honest election. Therefore the conservatives, to keep from being thrown out, must bend their overwhelming effort to prevent fair elections from taking place. They are able to govern at all "only through coup, coalition, accident, or coercion." (*Time*, May 5, 1941). This is the root problem of Argentine politics.

Turn back briefly to 1916. In that year, before the contemporary stratification became so obvious, Hipólito Irigoyen (pronounced

Eari-*go*-jen) became President.[2] He was in the Rosas tradition, more or less, and a fantastic character. He was called the *peludo* (mole), because he looked like one, and his followers were known either as the *Peludistas* or *Genuflexos* (knee benders). Irigoyen was the first genuine people's man to reach the presidency in any South American republic. In his early years he was as powerful and picturesque a character as, say, Theodore Roosevelt, whom he resembled a good deal. During his decline he was an unbearably uncouth old man, bewildered and befuddled, a prisoner of his secretaries, who charged 1,000 pesos for an interview with him. He did not add to the dignity of the Casa Rosada, the White House of Buenos Aires, but to this day, people love or hate him violently as if he were a living man. He was elected President for a second term in 1928, and then ousted by a conservative coup d'état in September 1930.

Since that date the conservative oligarchy has ruled Argentina. First came a Fascist-minded general named Uriburu. Then came General Don Agustín P. Justo, who served from 1932 to 1938. After Justo, about whom more presently, came something more complicated. Let us explore.

The conservatives, frightened by the rising clamor in the country, did not dare to "make" the elections overtly, as they had made those of 1932, when, in fact, the radicals were not even allowed to vote; they planned to buy off radical discontent by running a coalition ticket. They thought they would get some radical whom they could control as President, with a conservative Vice-President as a further safeguard. The radical they chose was Dr. Roberto W. Ortiz. He was a wealthy lawyer, a member of the *anti-Personalista* group,[3] a Justo man, and an amiable character. The conservative they chose was a venerable judge, Ramón S. Castillo. The Ortiz-Castillo coalition won. But even with Ortiz as bait for

[2] In the first elections ever held under secret ballot. See *South American Primer*, by Katherine Carr, p. 50.

[3] Old followers of Irigoyen were sometimes called *"Personalistas,"* i.e., his personal men; hence those who split from Irigoyen became *anti-Personalistas.*

radical votes, the election had to be violently rigged to make victory sure.

Then an astonishing thing happened. I have mentioned (regretting the oversimplification I indulge in) the conservative landowners and the radical middle class. But there are other folk too in Argentina. There are some ten million peasants, some of them landless peons, on the edge of starvation in remote Chaco swamps and Patagonian mutton pastures. Ortiz went all over the country electioneering. He saw children of families too poor to afford meat—in the greatest meat-producing country in the world. He saw mud hovels, crushed farms, unbearable destitution, villages sunk in squalor and corruption. He found that in some districts 30 per cent of the conscripts called into the army were so diseased and undernourished as to be unfit for service. He came back, and told his supporters that he intended to fulfill his electoral promises, that he intended to insure free elections thereafter, that he intended to work for the good of the people as a whole.

The conservatives were horrified. They said, in effect, "Ortiz is a *Peludista* (follower of Irigoyen) after all." Which was worse than calling him a communist. . . . It happens that Ortiz, a capaciously built man, not in first-class health, was fond of food and drink. One legend is that the outraged *conservadores* decided to get rid of him by banqueting him to death.

Ortiz' health did in fact deteriorate, and in July 1940 he was forced to retire, a victim of diabetes and blindness in one eye. He was granted an indefinite leave of absence, *with the right to return to office if his health improved.* Then came a minor scandal, the so-called Palomar affair; the Ministry of War paid too much for a military airport, and though Ortiz himself was not implicated, he felt that he must resign. He did so; the legislature refused to accept his resignation. But in any case he was too ill to work. Crisis came, the whole cabinet resigned, and Castillo took over as Acting President. He appointed a new government of his own men. But—in law and theory—Ortiz remains President of the republic.

A bitter quarrel then developed between the Ortiz and Castillo camps. As a result came a parliamentary stalemate and a virtual breakdown of government. Castillo's two best ministers (Roca of Foreign Affairs and Pinedo of Finance) resigned in January 1941, since effective work was impossible; the radicals boycotted parliamentary legislation, and the government could not pass a budget or even the most pressing emergency laws. The radicals are the largest party in the chamber, and Castillo was forced finally to govern by decree.

Friends of Ortiz say that though partially blind he is reasonably competent to resume the burdens of office. But the Castillo group will go to almost any length to keep him out. In April 1941 a special committee appointed by the senate made an official investigation of his health. They found that the impairment of "the visual functions of the President is so grave as to impede reading and hence to forestall personal knowledge of documents before signing them."[4] So Argentina has, in effect, two Presidents. Ortiz, the radical, is not allowed to work, and the conservative Castillo carries on. And the immediate future of the country becomes predominantly a medical question.

To summarize: there has been no free or fair election in Argentina since 1928. The bulk of the country is democratic and radical, but the conservative oligarchy manages to retain political power.

Three Musketeers, Assorted

Roberto Marcelino Ortiz, called *El Gordo* (the Stout), was born in Buenos Aires in 1886 of humble origin. His variegated career was self-made. He studied medicine for a time, and then law; he became a highly successful barrister. Almost everyone wanted to retain his services, because his personal connections— he is gregarious, convivial, and fond of people—reached every camp. At various times he was legal adviser to British railway companies, the Argentine subsidiary of I.T. & T., Standard Oil,

[4] New York *Herald Tribune*, April 17, 1941.

and Ernesto Tornquist & Co., the country's leading private bankers.

He entered politics as a young man because that was the thing to do. Also he had genuine social sense; he helped found a Workers' School in the Boca, the Buenos Aires waterfront district. He entered the radical party, and became a deputy for Buenos Aires in the federal legislature. In 1925 he reached cabinet rank as Minister of Public Works in the government of Dr. Marcelo T. de Alvear, the radical leader who was President between the Irigoyen terms. As such he pushed development of the Port of Buenos Aires, worked on drainage projects, and reorganized the state railways (78 per cent of the Argentine railways are British owned, but the rest belong to the state). His thesis at Buenos Aires University, years before, had been on railway legislation.

In 1928 Ortiz retired from politics for seven years in order to resume his law practice; he returned as his friend General Justo's Minister of Finance. He was one of the shrewdest Finance Ministers in Argentine history; for instance, he cut the foreign debt in half by cleverly buying up the country's United States-owned securities as their price fell on the New York exchange, which was exactly what Gustavo Ross had done in Chile. Then came his campaign for the presidency in 1938; his opponent was Alvear, his old friend and chief. The Alvear radicals actually got a majority vote, but the Ortiz-Castillo coalition "won."

Ortiz's tragic illness, and his courage in offering to resign after the Palomar scandal, won the hearts of the nation. I have heard it said that he is the most popular man in Argentina since Irigoyen.

When he was in good health, Ortiz reputedly never went to bed till dawn, consumed enormous amounts of pastry, smoked cigars eleven inches long, and knew—and liked—practically every human being in the country worth knowing. When he went to the races he sat in a chair specially manufactured to hold his bulk.

No one could possibly be a greater contrast to Ortiz than

Ramón S. Castillo,[5] the Acting President, who now does his job. Castillo is called *El Zorro*, the Fox. He is as cautious as Ortiz is exuberant, as dry and frugal as Ortiz is capacious. He gets up at six and still—at the age of 70—studies law for an hour. He takes a ten-minute nap after lunch, has dinner alone in bed so that no one will disturb him, and works till two o'clock every morning. He is, of course, a devout Catholic. By law, the President of the Argentine must be a member of the Roman Catholic Church.

Dr. Castillo was born in the province of Catamarca in 1871. He took his law degree at the University of Buenos Aires, and for some years was a teacher of law; Ortiz was one of his students many years ago. He was an expertly successful judge; he retired from the bench to go into politics—as an arch-conservative—and his rise was distinguished. He was senator from his native state, Catamarca, in 1932, and then Minister of Justice and Interior under Justo.

Castillo is called the Fox, but with his clipped gray hair and mustache, his shy blue eyes, he doesn't look like one. He is one of the most uncommunicative heads of state I ever met. I saw him in the Casa Rosada. He sat in a room paneled solidly in rosewood —one of the most beautiful rooms I've ever seen—with flowers piled about in luxuriant profusion. On the mantel was a portrait of San Martín; under it, a vase holding a small Argentine flag. The doors are open, and stay open. They lead to a wide gallery with glistening floors where secretaries wait and watch. First, Castillo pointed out—as all Argentines invariably point out—that Argentina is a great nation, and will be greater. Second, he said that he had been deeply impressed by his meetings with Roosevelt and Hull. Third, he did not care to comment on what the Argentine point of view would be if (a) the United States entered the war, or if (b) Germany won it.

I have heard Castillo described as "a mountaineer," and this

[5] Pronounced Casti*j*o in the Argentine fashion which makes j's out of double l's.

is a good indication of his caution, his frugality, and his provincialism.

General Agustín P. Justo (pronounced Hoosto), is sterner stuff. He holds substantial power behind the scenes because he controls large sectors of the army, and sometimes he is called the "third President." His father was governor of the province of Entre Ríos, and he entered the army as a boy and has been a professional officer all his life. He was born in 1876. He is called the best director of military education—he was commander of the Argentine equivalent of West Point for some years—that the country ever had. He was Minister of War from 1922 to 1928, and President of the republic from 1932 to 1938.

When President Roosevelt visited Argentina in 1936, great crowds greeted him with the cry, "*¡Viva la democracia!*" The story in Buenos Aires is that this demonstration was genuine enough, but that it was not merely pro-Roosevelt but anti-Justo as well. It was the first opportunity the citizenry had had to shout for democracy for a long, long time.

A favorite story about Justo, possibly apocryphal, emphasizes his imperturbability. He was riding in a military airplane in bumpy mountain weather. The pilot looked back, and was horrified to discover that the general was no longer there. Justo didn't like the bumps, had calmly bailed out, and was found later taking a quiet nap under a tree.

General Justo has a sloping forehead, a bristling aggressive mustache, and a powerful swelling chest. He is a passionate nationalist. He is neither pro-totalitarian nor pro-U.S.A. He likes to eat chocolates rapidly one after another. His nickname is Little Golden Buttons.

Traits and Characteristics

I heard it said in Buenos Aires that "during the colonial period and most of the nineteenth century the Creoles of Argentina were more isolated from the centers of western civilization than any other people of western European stock." Thus developed one of the most closely knit and self-sufficient landed oligarchies that survive in the world. Its sources of revenue were the great *estancias* (ranches) producing almost limitless quantities of beef; its citadel was the Círculo de Armas in Buenos Aires, which is quite probably the most exclusive club in the world; its hallmarks were a "patriarchal family life" and "clannish aloofness"; its culture was an enameled mingling of Marcel Proust, strict Catholicism, the latest novelties from Paris, and holidays in Biarritz. Also it produced (and produces) some of the most *chic*, the most sophisticated, and the most intellectually cultivated folk that exist anywhere. The top-flight Argentines are top-flight indeed.

Several traits distinguish this group of splendidly cosmopolitan aristocrats, as well as the rank and file of Argentines, if one may generalize somewhat broadly. For one thing, their intense nationalism. I have never seen anything like it except in Japan. Even the matchboxes carry patriotic slogans. Nearly every Argentine I met, with justifiable pride in the great qualities of his nation, told me at once just how great it was, and why. Argentina was the only country in the hemisphere where I found people burningly eager to know what I thought of them, what I would write about them. They considered themselves infinitely superior to their neighbors; they dismissed such folk as Venezuelans or Ecuadorians as remote savages. Every Argentine *knows* that his country has a great imperial destiny. Every Argentine *knows* that Buenos Aires is the finest city in the world.

Most Argentines, it seems, dislike thinking of themselves as part of *Latin* America. I heard bitter protests at the projected title of this book: my title should be simply "Inside *America*," everybody said. I was bewildered to find that if you are leaving Buenos Aires for a trip, Argentines say that you are going "to South America." Closely connected with this point is the extreme Argentine sensitiveness to the matter of race. This is odd, since the country is the whitest on the continent. But I heard one politician say, "Everybody in the Irigoyen cabinet was a nigger except my cousin." And a distinguished lady, watching the performance of a peasant dancer in one of the great houses of Buenos Aires, turned to me and said, "The man has Indian blood, but no negro blood."

An Argentine friend told me quite seriously that Argentina was "bigger" than Brazil. But Brazil has more than 40,000,000 people as against Argentina's 13,000,000, and I looked puzzled. My friend then "explained" that Argentina has more *white people* than Brazil, and is therefore "bigger"!

The Argentine superiority complex—which of course is based on an inferiority complex—produces much anguish among the barbarous *norteamericanos* who live in Buenos Aires. One friend of mine found his customarily superb *bife de lomo* (beefsteak) not quite so good as usual at his favorite restaurant. He protested. The waiter replied loftily, "*All* Argentine beef is good." (Indeed, I thought it was the best I ever ate.)

Argentines are, as a rule, like Spaniards and Italians, very chary of receiving foreigners in their homes. One of my good American friends, prosperous, pleasantly mannered, with a charming wife, is director-general of an important company, and is in minute-by-minute contact with Argentines every day, but he has never once seen the inside of a Buenos Aires house. Which perhaps serves to give rise to remarks as cruel as the following, "If you bought an Argentine for what you think he's worth, and sold him for what he thinks he's worth, you'd be a millionaire."

Most Argentines are not afraid to be candid and sharp, which is sometimes refreshing. The White House sent out amiable young Douglas Fairbanks as a good-will missionary. Note the comment of an Argentine lady of society: "It would have been so much more a compliment to us if a scientist, an educator, or a jurist had been named to this post. We admire Mr. Fairbanks as an entertainer, but we have not been educated to him as a diplomat."[6]

Leading Argentine families intermarry a great deal, like the great Unzué clan, and the scarcity of last names is sometimes

[6] New York *Herald Tribune*, June 9, 1941.

embarrassing. Practically everyone in the top flight is related to everyone else, as in Hungary or pre-Hitler Poland, which countries Argentina resembles a good deal. The "common" people know all the names and characteristics of the upper set, much as in England; they follow their careers with vicarious snobbery. Much formality dictates the social behavior of the *estanciero* class, and the nomenclature is bewildering. Take Rodolfo Alzaga Unzué. Alzaga is his father's name, of course, and Unzué his mother's. But how should one describe his wife, and properly include her name in his? The solution in the society columns is to say, if husband and wife are described together, Rudolfo Alzaga Unzué y su señora Agustina Rodríguez Larreta. If she is seen alone, she becomes La señora Agustina Rodríguez Larreta de Rodolfo Alzaga Unzué.

Social taboos are enormously strict—not merely in the upper classes. I have heard Argentine friends argue seriously that theirs was the most "sex-starved" country on earth. President Justo, under church influence, abolished open prostitution; the "Road to Buenos Aires" runs no more. Many young men cannot afford mistresses, and they may have to wait years to marry. It is still unusual to see young men and unchaperoned women together, and young girls are guarded more strictly than in any other Latin American country. Divorce is, of course, absolutely forbidden.[7] But two factors are serving to break down social taboos. First, many young women work for their living nowadays, and this makes for independence. Second, American movies. Not only do the movies themselves show a different kind of life that Argentinians might like to emulate, but the theaters are a convenient rendezvous for young lovers who have no other place to go.

A last minor point: Argentine customs examinations are probably the stiffest in the world, next to the Russian. Even personages with diplomatic passports are subject to inspection. Argentina is

[7] Some emancipated folk run off to Montevideo and get Uruguayan divorces, but these are not recognized in Argentina.

the only country I have ever visited where I was searched. Not that I minded much.

The Camp

The body of Argentina is the land, the pampas, "The Camp," as it is called. I take liberty to quote part of a prose poem by Archibald MacLeish, because his description of the country where the railway stations "come every twenty minutes as though . . . laid out not by geography but by clocks" is incomparable :

Argentina of the pampas, Argentina of the enormous plains, Argentina flowing out into the morning beyond the hills like a sea beyond capes . . . Argentina without towns, with few roads, with fences straight and wide apart as meridians on a map . . . It is a country in which the distances from house to house are too great for the barking of dogs even on the stillest night, a country in which the cocks crow only twice because there is no answer. It is a country so level that even time has no hold upon it and one century is like another; a country so empty that the watchers at night put their eyes along the ground to see the circle of the horizon; a country in which the sky is so huge that men plant islands of eucalyptus over their houses to be covered from the blue; a country in which the space is so great that all the visions end in eternity. It is the country of grass, the country without stones . . . the country in which the green goes on and on like water, and the gulls follow the plows as seagulls follow ships—the country in which the women are always together under the dark trees in the evening, their faces fading into loneliness with the night.[8]

At least 70 per cent of Argentinians live by agriculture— though the production of industrial goods is steadily increasing —and about 95 per cent of the country's total exports are animal or agricultural products. Argentina is overwhelmingly the leading world producer and exporter of beef, and the world's first exporter of corn and linseed; she is the second exporter of wheat (after

[8] *Fortune*, July, 1938. The fourth article in an anonymous series on Latin America. Mr. MacLeish (it is an open secret) wrote those on Argentina and Chile.

Canada), wool (after Australia) and mutton (after New Zealand).

Much of the fattest land is held by individual landowners whose *estancias* reach fabulous size. In Buenos Aires province alone (the "queen province") fifty families have holdings of 75,000 acres or more; the holdings of these fifty comprise 15.2 per cent of the total area of the province. The following families own more than 250,000 acres. The value is the assessed valuation according to the latest Buenos Aires tax returns:

	Acres	Value (dollars)
Alzaga Unzué	1,091,586	$26,624,814
Anchorena	945,194	15,970,121
Luro	573,869	5,096,436
Pereyra Iraola	472,308	11,317,336
Pradere	461,973	5,831,523
Guerrero	450,749	7,578,372
Leloir	447,158	6,383,921
Graciarena	409,446	5,336,622
Santamarina	391,949	9,762,693
Duggan	318,731	9,244,872
Pereda	301,846	7,662,314
Duhau	279,934	3,468,907
Herrera Vegas	270,657	5,959,091
Zuberbühler	261,447	2,320,119
Martínez de Hoz	250,109	5,673,955

Some names of the great landowners sharply underline the varieties of European blood that have made Argentina what it is. Consider Drysdale (194,000 acres), Bosch (190,000 acres), Bunge (186,000 acres), Pourtale (151,800 acres), Stegman (107,100 acres), Perkins (100,680 acres), Maguirre (97,200 acres), Tornquist (91,000 acres), Lyne Stivens (90,000 acres), Van Pannwitz (87,800 acres), Parracivini (79,900 acres), Hale (80,900 acres). But—all are Argentinians.

The *estancieros*, the cattle-breeding aristocracy, have several leading ideas. First, they are on the whole rather anti-United States, partly on nationalist grounds, partly because we exclude their beef. Second, they tend to oppose industrialization, which Argentina needs. The landowners may make money and build textile factories with it, but then they are apt to resink their proceeds in cattle, so that they may continue to show off fabulous prize bulls. They fear that if the country becomes thoroughly industrialized it will no longer import manufactured goods, which would mean drastic reductions in the export of their beef.

The landed class, most observers agree, has lost much of its former power. The growth of an urban middle class has cut into its political preserves; the collapse of European markets has severely cut down its exports; winds of social reform threaten its prerogatives.

For instance in August 1940 a Homestead Law was passed sketching the beginning of a land reform; it aims to divide up unproductive big estates, settle small farmers on the land, and improve housing conditions of the peons. I asked an eminent *estanciero* why his class was, in fact, losing grip. He answered, "Because we have no brains." What he meant was that, in the turbulent modern era, a landowning aristocracy can no longer exist merely as a luxury. It must work, it must pay its keep. Another shrewd observer of Argentine affairs told me that some intelligent and progressive *estanciero* must stand up *against his own class*, if it is to survive the ardors of the next twenty or thirty unpredictable years.

I spent one of the happiest week ends of my life as a guest on one of the greatest of Argentine *estancias*. It covered about 120,000 acres; it held 40,000 sheep, 30,000 cattle, and between 6,000 and 7,000 horses. It had its own railway station, its own telegraph; it had its own churches, hospitals, shops, a dairy, a police post. It was—and is—a kind of self-governing autonomous community, rare and wonderful to behold.

The road, rutted, muddy, tawny, at least 175 feet wide, sweeps up to a castle closely resembling a Loire château. Surrounding it are thousands upon thousands of trees; every one of these trees had to be imported, transported into what was then the wilderness, duly planted, and then tended till they grew up. (But before the trees, a church was planted.) I have never seen such a throbbing variety of animal life: deer, hawks, pheasant, ostriches darting across the yellow linseed fields, owls squatting on fence posts, enormous white horses, rabbits fat as raccoons.

The heavy red earth is so incredibly rich that fertilizer is unknown. Ask the major domo about fertilizer, and he doesn't know what it is. No one even collects the natural manure. You plant wheat, and it grows twice in a season. The cattle live on grass, on natural heather and alfalfa; they get no corn, no seed-cake, no special food at all. Even pedigree bulls (which are as a rule imported from England) are left out in the open all the year around, to forage as they will, and to grow as strong as Samson.

My host, one of the most technically competent farmers I ever met—to say nothing of his delightful qualities as a human being—loved his *estancia* with outright passion. He had ideas far beyond those of many of his fellow *estancieros*. He wanted to buy the very latest North American machinery; he wanted expert advice from specialists on fruit, on special cultivations, on varieties of by-products. He *did* want to make his work productive.

Steers are sold to the great Buenos Aires *frigoríficos* (packing houses) when they are two to two and a half years old. They weigh 500 kilos on the average (about 1,100 pounds); they bring 31 centavos a kilo (about 8 cents) for chilled beef, 20-22 centavos for beef to be frozen. If a steer is heavier than 500 kilos, his price —oddly enough—goes down; the animals get heavy with age, and don't make such good meat. There is an incessant movement of cattle all over the country, as farmers buy and sell herds, and as they are sent to slaughter.

British investment bites deeply into Argentine profits. The British own the railway that takes the steers to Buenos Aires; they own several of the great *frigoríficos*; the beef goes to Britain on British bottoms; it pays duty when it enters England. But the

Argentinians cannot protest or object, since, if the British market were lost, they would perish.

An *estancia* owner must, by law, will four-fifths of his property to his family. One-fifth he may dispose of as he wishes after his death; the rest *must* be divided in equal parts between wife, sons, and daughters. There is no distinction between male and female heirs. If no sons or daughters are living, their share of the property reverts to the *estanciero's* father and/or mother. Brothers and sisters get nothing. The progression ascends or descends. A childless owner bequeaths two-thirds of the estate to his wife, and may freely dispose of the other third.

A *gaucho* (ranch hand) on a prosperous and progressively administered *estancia* like the one I saw gets from 70 to 80 pesos (say $17.50) per month, with all his keep. The peons get an average of 60 pesos (about $13.50) with lodging, a small plot of land to till, and all the beef they want to eat. When an *estanciero* is hard up, he may be forced to sell his cattle, alive. They bring 60-70 pesos a head. Another who has cash enough for the transaction will buy them, fatten them, and sell them next year for roughly 120 pesos each.

So much for beef to begin with. But we are not done with the subject yet.

Chapter XX
Beef, Fifth Column, and Bases

~~~~~~

THE fundamental issue between the United States and Argentina is the hoof-and-mouth disease. Again, let us keep in mind the influence of science—or lack of science—on politics. Essentially the development of hemispheric solidarity depends on relations between the two chief countries, the Argentine Republic and the United States. These, in turn, depend on—believe it or not—an unidentified filterable virus in the marrow of diseased cattle.

A wonderful example of Argentine nationalist pride was provided recently by one of the country's leading statesmen. He said: "We don't have the hoof-and-mouth disease. We only have a mild form of it."

First let us say a word about Argentine beef exports, which exist in four categories. *First,* chilled beef, which is the best. Before the war it went chiefly to England; it was carried on refrigerated ships, and kept at four degrees above freezing, cool enough to keep it for a time, not cold enough to freeze it solid. The fast ships carrying this prime chilled beef were timed to the minute, as if they were carrying first-class mail. Now shipping schedules are so uncertain that export of chilled beef is virtually impossible, and beef goes to England frozen.

Second, frozen beef. This is of slightly inferior quality, and it keeps longer. Normally it went to the Continent, particularly to France and Germany. German imports of Argentine frozen beef rose from 11,000,000 pounds in 1935 to 110,000,000 pounds in 1938. *Third,* canned or corned beef, much of which goes to the United States. *Fourth,* salted beef, dry or in brine, which we take if it has been specially cured for a certain period. We also take Argentine hides and other by-products, provided they are prepared under stringent sanitary supervision.

The great point to make is that the United States, though it is an important customer of canned beef (which has been sterilized by cooking), refuses absolutely to buy Argentine chilled or frozen beef, ostensibly on sanitary grounds. This enrages and humiliates the Argentines. They consider our exclusion of their beef (which is indeed of superlative quality) a national affront, a stigma. The issue is bitterly, personally, wounding to every Argentine, not merely to his pocketbook but to his patriotism and pride.

The virus causing hoof-and-mouth disease, a violently contagious and damaging ailment of cattle, sheep, hogs, has never been identified; it is like infantile paralysis, for which no cure is known. Little is understood about it, partly because it is so contagious that even laboratory work on it is forbidden in the United States. It is, however, known that the virus exists in the bone or marrow of the infected animal, and that it spreads through careless disposal of meat scraps, bones and refuse. Heat kills the virus; freezing does not.

The disease is widespread throughout Europe, and is endemic in mild form in *parts of* Argentina; in the United States there have been half a dozen outbreaks in a hundred years. The last was in California in 1929; relatively minor, it was stamped out with ruthless vigor, but 400,000 animals had to be slaughtered. It is highly important to mention that cattle in Argentina have built up an immunity to the ailment that our cattle do not possess; what is a mild cold on the *pampa* is double pneumonia in the United States.

Human beings almost never get hoof-and-mouth disease. The issue is protection of the enormous United States cattle and livestock industry.[1] And in order to safeguard our 67,000,000 head of cattle—to say nothing of other livestock—we have maintained for some years a strict quarantine against fresh beef, not merely from Argentina, but from fifty other countries where hoof-and-mouth disease occurs. In 1930 this quarantine was formally embodied in a new tariff act; moreover, a 6-cent per pound duty was

[1] An outbreak can cost terrific damage. The disease runs like wildfire. An epidemic in Germany and Switzerland in 1920-21 cost $189,000,000 in destruction of herds.

put on fresh beef, as a further measure to keep it out even if the quarantine should be lifted. Senators and representatives from American cattle-producing states were of course responsible for this. It is the crux of the whole question from the Argentine point of view. The Argentines say, with much reason, that we are making an economic boycott by use of a sanitary pretext. They say that our discrimination is not based on legitimate medical grounds, but as a matter of trade protection. They say, "If you want to exclude our beef, raise the tariff to 20 cents a pound and do so. But do not hide behind the hypocrisy of the hoof-and-mouth disease."

In 1935 a Sanitary Convention was signed by the United States and Argentina. This provided for a *regional* application of the quarantine, since—a most important detail—the great area in southern Argentina known as Patagonia is free of the disease. If the Convention were to be ratified, Patagonian meat could enter the United States, though it would still have to pay the 6-cent duty. The Convention was initialed six years ago, but it has never been ratified by the United States Senate, because of the opposition of the cattle Senators. It happens that Patagonia does not produce much meat; the whole kill is only about 10,000 tons per year. Even so, ratification of the Sanitary Convention by the United States Senate would be a vital stimulus to better relations with Argentina. The Argentinians would consider it a beneficent moral gesture.

When President Roosevelt visited Buenos Aires in 1936 he said that he hoped application of the quarantine on a regional basis (thus freeing Patagonia) would come about. Ever since, Argentines have complained, "Ah, yes, your President said he would do what he could, but nothing has happened." Of course it is beyond the power of the President to ratify a treaty. But other Argentines say, "If Mr. Roosevelt really means so well by us, why can't he influence Congress to buy our beef?" To which the answer is—he can't.

It is also pointed out that Great Britain takes great amounts of Argentine beef, and that the British are a healthy people with a healthy cattle industry. The American reply is that, on the contrary, outbreaks of hoof-and-mouth disease do occur in England—in very mild form—almost every year. But the British have no choice. They must continue to import an adequate meat supply, under strict sanitary control, even at the risk of deterioration of the health of their own cattle. Fifty per cent of the meat Britain eats comes from the Argentine.

In March, 1941, the United States navy proposed to purchase 2,000,000 pounds of canned beef from Argentina, partly because it was so much cheaper than domestic, 19 cents a pound as against 33 cents. The cattle Senators violently fought even this proposal to import *canned* beef, and it was defeated by 33 votes to 32, after Vice-President Wallace, by momentary absence, lost his chance to decide a tie. Later the measure was compromised. At the moment of writing, it has not yet been voted on by the House.

One of the most intelligent Argentines I know put forward—with a certain wistfulness—this idea. He suggested that the United States buy 100,000 tons of chilled Argentine beef per year, which is about 3½ per cent of total American consumption, during January-February-March, the three months when the United States cattle industry does not produce. Moreover, he said that Argentina could *bone* the beef before shipping it, which would remove any chance of infection.

This proposal, what with contemporary political realities in Washington, is probably chimerical. But if the United States would buy even so small an amount as 100,000 tons, it would open the gates of paradise to Argentina.

Why Some Argentinians Dislike the U.S.A.

First and foremost, the crucial question of beef just mentioned, as well as general commercial rivalry.

Second, nationalist jealousy and latent fear of North American imperialism. Argentina considers itself the competitor of the United States for hemisphere leadership.

Third, lack of knowledge, insularity. Few prominent Argentines have ever visited New York or Washington.

Fourth, the tactlessness of many American businessmen in Argentina. The revolting provincialism and vulgarity of many American movies. The inadequacy of American radio programs. The conviction of many Argentinians that most citizens of the United States are savages from the cultural point of view.

Fifth, many of the British who had a profound influence in developing Argentina were colonial-minded Yankee-haters, and the Argentines came to reflect this attitude.

Sixth (it seems incredibly remote), the Spanish-American war. Many Argentines remember this war vividly, or were told about it by their fathers, and most of them took the Spanish side.

Seventh, psychological envy of United States power, wealth, and influence.

Behold the British

The roots of British influence in Argentina go very far back indeed. A British explorer, Sebastian Cabot, visited the Plata estuary and built forts and settlements on its banks as early as 1526. During Napoleonic times the British twice sent expeditions to capture Buenos Aires, each time without success. Early in the nineteenth century the British took the Falkland Islands, which officially at least the Argentines still claim.

Meantime British bankers, traders, railway builders, and a few settlers came into Argentina; they entrenched themselves largely through virtual control of the railways. Stationmasters in provincial Argentine towns were Britons just as they are in India today. The British had, indeed, a distinct colonial mentality. They mixed with the Argentines very little. They had their own clubs, their own polo fields, their own department stores, their own social enclaves.

One odd point is an illustration of Argentine nationalist pride. Some Argentines thought that the tactics of British commercial penetration during the last century should be investigated. But the idea never went through. The country might find that it had been bilked; the Argentines might discover that their own forefathers had been dupes. Such an idea was, of course, unendurable, and the investigation was called off.

Argentina became so important to Great Britain, both as a source of imports and as a field of investment, that it has often been called the "Sixth Dominion." Argentines loathe this. As to British feelings toward Argentina, Hubert Herring (*Yale Review,* Autumn, 1937), tells the little story of an Englishman saying to an American, "You may take Canada from us, but never Argentina."

The Falkland Islands—which the Argentines call the Malvinas —do not make a real point of issue any more, though the Nazis try to drum up Argentine hopes to get them back. The Argentines realize that the Falklands, which are a British naval station and coaling base, are highly useful for their own protection.

Fifth Column in Argentina

The nucleus of Fifth Columnism in Argentina, where it is powerful and dangerous, is of course the local German colony. There has been no census in Argentina since 1914, and therefore accurate statistics are scarce. But reliable estimates have it that 59,415 German-born Germans live in the country, about 135,000 Argentine-born sons of Germans, and about 250,000 with some German blood. Half of the pure Germans (who are technically citizens of the Reich) live in Buenos Aires. Another powerful cluster is in the Misiones region, the narrow Argentine appendix between Paraguay and Brazil; these Germans are closely adjacent to the German colonies in Brazilian states like Santa Catharina. Some towns in Misiones are almost exclusively German, as are those in the Valdiva district of Chile. There are 203 German schools in Argentina, which, the heart of each community, strongly resist "Argentinization"; these schools have 13,500 students.

Nominally the head of the German organizations is the Reich's ambassador, Baron Edmund von Thermann. He flew to Berlin (via the L.A.T.I. airline) early in 1941, and returned to Argentina to announce that, after the war, Germany would become the country's biggest market, and that it had "no future" with the United States or Great Britain. But a man named Gottfried Sandstede was probably more important than the ambassador,[2] since he was reputedly head of the local Gestapo; recently he fled the country to avoid arrest. The German organization in Argentina is the biggest and most widespread in Latin America with the possible exception of that in Mexico. There is a German chamber of commerce, a German hospital, the Hitler Jugend, the "Girl Scouts Alemanas," a sailor's aid society, the *Unión Popular Alemana*, the *Sociedad Protectora de Inmigrantes Germánicos*, an Argentine National Socialist party, and even a *Partido Nacionalsocialista Femenino* for the women.

The Nazi propaganda machine works full-blast in Argentina. Late in 1940 it was sending out about 30,000 leaflets a day; by mid-1941 300,000 copies a week—of various kinds of printed matter—were being distributed. (New York *Post*, April 19, 1941.) These range from pamphlets attacking the British Empire to violent fulminations against Yankee imperialism; recently the Germans have paid more attention to the United States than to Great Britain. Recently it was disclosed that the German Embassy spent $1,562,000 in Argentina last year; the American Embassy spent $120,000.

The principal Nazi vehicle is a daily afternoon paper called *El Pampero*. The British have tried to stop its supply of newsprint (which would normally come from Canada), but so far unsuccessfully. *Pampero* gets its news from Transocean, the official German agency, and from the Italian Stefani service; its circulation (about 80,000 a day) is not great, but its influence is considerable. It pretends to be patriotically Argentine and nationalist; in reality it is a Goebbels megaphone. In July 1940, one of its

---

[2] The German embassy in Buenos Aires has a staff of 44 persons, more than could possibly be necessary for routine business. The Consulate General has a staff of 17. There are fourteen German consulates in the country. The United States has one.

editors, Enrique Oses (who also edits another pro-German sheet, *Crisol*), was arrested for having "referred in obscene terms to the British people." What he had done was print a verse about Mr. Churchill which read innocently but which contained an acrostic, *Hay que ser inglés para ser hijo de puta*. Which means simply, "One must be English to be a son of a bitch." Altogether there are between ten and twelve Argentine newspapers definitely pro-Axis, and others which use much German-supplied material. One German-language paper, the *Deutsche La Plata Zeitung*, was founded in 1863; it has a Spanish-language supplement and a substantial reputation. An *anti*-Nazi German paper is the *Argentinisches Tageblatt*, which is old-established (circulation 28,000) and still manages to survive.

Propaganda is one thing; espionage is another, and incitement to riot still something else. As to espionage, German agents in Buenos Aires were instructed in the winter of 1941 to attempt to make contacts with sailors aboard the U.S. cruiser *Phoenix*, which was calling in the Plata; they were asked particularly to copy details of the ammunition hoists. As to political rioting, crowds of German-influenced Argentine Nazis have been making minor demonstrations day in and day out. One Nazi manifesto, found in a raid in Misiones, read as follows:

Alert! Germans who have their country at heart! Argentines who would see their country as powerful as ours, instead of being weak and crumbling! You have sworn to keep a solemn oath! Hear our song of victory: "Today Germany is ours and tomorrow the whole world will be ours." We expect you to imitate the example of your brothers in Holland and Belgium . . . —*Time*, August 26, 1940.

In this raid were also found the usual Nazi dossiers and organization material, and maps showing South America down through Brazil and including Misiones to be German.

Several important United States companies were for years represented in Argentina by German agents, which served to give the Germans great prestige and profit. American firms had been accustomed to use such agents—which had been long established in the country—as part of a perfectly normal business procedure; then, as we know, 1,800 firms in Latin America were blacklisted by the United States government. So Nazi Fifth Columnism is no longer being financed—inadvertently enough of course—by American exporters.

In February 1941, Argentina authorized the Axis airline, L.A.T.I., to extend its services from Dakar and Natal to Buenos Aires.[3] This annoyed the British, who would like to see the L.A.T.I. service stopped. They could possibly stop it—by blocking shipments of high-octane gasoline at the Cape Verde Islands and Villa Cisneros—but the Argentinians (the Brazilians too) have pleaded with them not do do so, on the ground that L.A.T.I. is the only direct link between South America and Europe. The United States government was recently asked to intervene in this dispute. Recently a L.A.T.I. plane made an experimental flight from Rio de Janeiro to Buenos Aires, with the permission of the Argentine authorities. When it was about to return, 800 kilos of mica, a strategic raw material, were found abroad. The Argentines protested first, and then let the plane go.

Italians in Argentina do not form so serious a problem as the Germans. There are probably some 3,000,000 folk of Italian blood in Argentina, but, as we know, the Italians assimilate very quickly. In ten years they become more Argentine than the Argentines; they are the despair of visiting Fascist officials; they are as a rule more anti-Fascist than pro. Italian influence in the country is profound (as witness the way Argentines pronounce Spanish; *Callao* becomes *Cajow*, and so on), but it is not predominantly a *political* influence.

The Italian ambassador is considerably less active than his German colleague; yet it was his direct intervention that caused the Buenos Aires municipality to forbid showing of Charlie Chaplin's

[3] With the proviso that 80 per cent of the personnel be Argentinian. New York *Herald Tribune*, Feb. 22, 1941. But see below, Chapter XXIV.

"Great Dictator." Another American film recently banned was "Confessions of a Nazi Spy." The "Great Dictator" issue provoked confusion, rage and mirth. Thousands of good *porteños* (residents of Buenos Aires) flocked across the river to see it in Uruguay. Six months after the original ban, in June 1941, the city council decided after all to allow it to be shown. But ten days later the federal government stepped in and forbade it all over Argentina, on the ground that it "wounded the sentiments" of the Fascist countries.

Falange influence is not particularly conspicuous in Argentina, despite the great bond to Spain and the influence of the Church. Most middle-class Argentinians sympathized, it seemed, with the loyalists during the Spanish civil war. But the present Argentine government (apparently under stimulus from Great Britain) has played closely with Franco; Argentina shipped 350,000 tons of corn to Spain early in 1941, and a similar amount of wheat is promised. Spain, on its side, courts Argentina hotly. When the new Argentine ambassador arrived in Madrid late in 1940, he was the recipient, in the words of the New York *Times*, of "unique attentions."

For some time the Argentine government conspicuously avoided any definite or comprehensive measures against Fifth Columnism; it was the most laggard state in the hemisphere in this regard. In the summer of 1941, however, came drastic change. Alarm grew at the vociferousness of Axis propagandists and their rapidly spreading influence. Thirty leading Germans were arrested, including the secretary of the Argentine Nazi party, and a German-controlled radio station was closed down. The chamber demanded that the government make a real investigation of the Fifth Column problem, and a kind of Dies committee was organized with full powers to investigate subversive activities, by a vote of 95 to 1. At once Washington offered to co-operate, and everything that we know about Nazi activities in Latin America will be made available.

In late summer this committee, headed by Deputy Rául Damonte

Taborda, and called the Congressional Committee Investigating Anti-Argentine Activities, issued its first reports, and they exploded over Buenos Aires like firecrackers—noisy firecrackers. It was charged that 500,000 German Storm Troopers are organized throughout South America, 60,000 of them in Argentina alone, and that they are under oath to serve Hitler "to the death." The Fifth Column leaders, it is alleged, "have ordered the establishment of bases in Brazil and in the northern countries of South America," and hope to "obtain political and economic control . . . and by use of enormous sums of money to put Quislings in power through fomenting revolts." (United Press dispatch, September 6, 1941.) According to the committee, Germans in Argentina are taxed between four and 32 percent of their earnings to pay for the Nazi organization. There are said to be 64,319 party members in the country.

Baron von Thermann, the German Ambassador, meantime shook in his shoes. The committee charges that Thermann received 84 packages from Germany, via a Japanese steamship, in July; one package contained a 60-page booklet indexing—and presumably blacklisting—the names of 3000 Argentines known to be unfriendly to the Nazis. The German Embassy likewise got into trouble when, apparently, it attempted to send radio apparatus to other German missions under cover of diplomatic immunity. Thermann's recall was demanded in the Argentine chamber, as the committee's findings were turned over to the attorney-general and the supreme court. It was revealed that in 1940 the German Embassy received 1,300,000 letters, weighing something over 30 tons and carrying more than $25,000 worth of postage. Meantime, the records of various German organizations were seized and scrutinized, and 30 leading Germans were arrested.

There are two basic reasons why Fascism could—conceivably—grow at an alarming rate in Argentina. One is the prevailing dissatisfaction among the youth, especially those of the upper class, at the state of the nation. They have never seen democracy work well; they know it only in theory, and they are aware that something is radically wrong with the present system; they are restless, confused, and dissatisfied. They want to *do* something for their country; they don't know what to do. Second, there is the influence of the army, which was German-trained for a generation. Of this more presently.

Acción Argentina or Sixth Column

An important *anti*-totalitarian movement is the *Acción Argentina*, which was organized in the spring of 1940 and now claims 800,000 members. It is not a party, but a kind of fluid movement comprising adherents of almost all parties. It is strongly pro-British and more or less pro-United States; it stands against all breeds of totalitarianism, whether Nazi, Fascist, or communist; its ideology combines nationalism and democracy, and its avowed aim is "to defend the Argentine way of life."

The trouble with the *Acción Argentina* is that it has no real leader. A set of strange bedfellows are its conspicuous members: Dr. Antonio Santamarina, an extreme rightist; Marcelo T. de Alvear, the venerable radical leader; two prominent socialists, Nicolás Repetto and Alfredo L. Palacios (Palacios' nephew is its secretary general); a former Minister of Finance, Dr. Federico Pinedo, and the leader of the *anti-Personalista* radicals, Carlos A. Pito. Which is as if a similar organization in the United States should include Henry Ford, Senator George W. Norris, Norman Thomas, Sidney Hillman, Secretary of the Treasury Morgenthau, and Bob LaFollette.

Questions of Solidarity and Defense

The Argentine attitude to World War II is that of absolute neutrality. This has been reiterated again and again; Acting President Castillo recently reaffirmed it on opening the legislature. I have heard more than one Argentine say, "Look at Brazil. It was the only country in South America to declare war on Germany in the last world war. What did Brazil get out of it? Nothing."

Most Argentines have, as we know, close associations with

Great Britain, and most hope emotionally that the British will win. But they have no intimate feeling that they themselves are involved (except economically), or that the British fleet is in effect protecting Argentina just as much as the British Isles. And they have no intention of risking anything if they can possibly avoid it.

As most Argentines see it, any one of four things may happen. First, the British will win. Very good. Second, the United States will enter the war and help the British win. Good, but less good. Third, Germany wins. Bad, but bad as it may be, Germany will need to buy some Argentine goods. Fourth, a deadlock will come, with the United States dictating a peace.

When I asked my Argentine acquaintances why they were not willing to co-operate with the British (their friends) *plus* the United States (which is helping their friends) in order that all three countries might stand shoulder to shoulder in the same camp, they were apt to answer (a) that Hitler might win the war anyway, and (b) how could the United States defend Argentina in the event that Germany became annoyed and attacked them?

This is, indeed, the burning apex of the issue. Argentina is so unwilling to risk participation in the war for the simple reason that she fears the United States could not, even if we wished, render her effective protection. Put a string on a globe. From New York to Buenos Aires is almost exactly as far as from New York to the Persian Gulf, or from San Francisco to the China coast. The distance is, to say the least, awkward from a defense point of view. Some United States experts, in fact, do not think we should attempt to defend South America below the bulge. A fleet sailing around Cape Horn would have to travel 12,000 miles —and fight with foul bottoms. And so Argentines say, *Can* North America defend us?

Thus has arisen Argentine obstructionism—usually overcome at the last moment—at various Pan-American conferences. Thus arose Argentine reluctance to commit itself fully to an all-out policy of hemisphere collaboration, though it did finally sign both the Declaration of Lima and the Act of Havana.

The Argentines listened to President Roosevelt's May 27 speech with polite attention, and pro-Anglo-Saxons welcomed it warmly. But even the *Prensa*, somewhat cautious in its approval, wondered why the President had spoken in the name of "all" the American republics. Some time before, the Argentines had *not* followed the example of the United States, Mexico, Venezuela, and Peru in confiscating Axis ships.[4] Some time after, Argentina carefully rejected a proposal by Uruguay that any American country at war with a non-American country should be considered non-belligerent, i.e. should receive friendly sympathy and assistance.

Of course many Argentines take the point of view—and so do many people in the United States for that matter—that the lightning may not strike after all, and that it is foolish to court mishap by any determination of policy in advance. They are, moreover, addicted to such nationalist optimism that they cannot conceive that any disaster *could* befall them. They are apt to say, "If worst comes to worst, the United States will have to try to defend us anyway, so why worry?" Ostrichism is not exclusive to the Argentines by any means. Think of isolationists in the United States. . . . The worst blow Argentina has had, by and large, was the fall of France, because the French tradition meant more to them than any foreign influence.

All of which brings us to the vexed question of hemisphere bases. In the autumn of 1940 the United States government, in circumstances of the utmost secrecy, dispatched a group of officers to Chile, Argentina, and Uruguay to conduct informal exploratory talks about the *possibility* of creating hemisphere defense facilities in the La Plata region. The story leaked out. And such an anguished howl arose from Argentina as had never been heard below the bulge. The howl is only a whisper now. But when I was in Argentina, people were saying, "When the United States talks about bases it is like stamping on every finger of our two hands."

The key to the defense of Buenos Aires is, as anyone may see

[4] But in August 1941 the Argentines *bought* sixteen Italian vessels in their harbors, paying $12,000,000 for them.

by glancing at a map, the Uruguayan capital Montevideo, which commands the entrance to the Plata estuary. Buenos Aires itself would be worthless as a base, since it is 150 miles inland along the river. Montevideo controls the Atlantic approach to Argentina; it dominates Uruguay, the up-river approach to Paraguay, and much of Buenos Aires province. But the Argentinians would think it an insufferable affront to their nationalist prestige if the United States should acquire "facilities" at Montevideo, and thus, on Uruguayan soil—the soil of a small neighbor—be able to dominate Argentina.

On the other hand, the Argentine government, gradually moving into the orbit of hemisphere solidarity, has agreed in principle to bases provided they are not at Montevideo or Punta del Este near by. I quote a recent United Press dispatch: "It was reiterated that the Argentine government is ready to co-operate with the United States in the construction of naval and air bases in the South Atlantic, including points on the Argentine coast. Opposition to the Punta del Este base is that it would be a threat to Argentina's foreign commerce, 90 per cent of which traverses the River Plata in which the new base would be located."

Many Argentines have come to accept the idea of hemisphere bases for the period of the emergency—while Mr. Roosevelt is President. But suppose Mr. Roosevelt goes out of office—what then?

What guarantee have the Argentines that the United States will not utilize its emergency bases as permanent instruments of economic or political imperialism? The answer to this should, of course, be obvious, though many tangled details remain to be worked out. It is that new facilities should be held by the countries concerned in common, under some kind of hemisphere trusteeship that would obviate the possibility of individual exploitation.

In any case the world moves—and so does Argentina. We are much closer to the development of hemisphere facilities in the Plata region than we were a year ago.

"Stern Men with Empires in their Brains"

Argentina for years feared a combination of Chile and Brazil against her. This was a dominant note in its foreign policy before more onerous events pushed it aside. Nowadays relations with Chile—which once had designs on Patagonia—are satisfactorily adjusted, and are symbolized by the statue of Christ on the Andean frontier, with its eloquent inscription that these great mountains will crumble before Argentina and Chile ever make war upon each other. There are no serious outstanding differences between the two countries now.

Argentinian relations with Brazil have vastly improved also. In 1937 the United States proposed to lease six over-age destroyers to the Brazilian navy. The Argentine government, through its then Foreign Minister, Saavedra Lamas, let loose such vibrant cries of legalistic protest that the idea had to be dropped. But now Argentine-Brazilian friendship is close and the two countries work together cordially.

Bolivia is, as we know, a link between Chile and Brazil; hence for years Argentine foreign policy was preoccupied with what it called the "Diagonal," that is the Chile-Bolivia-Brazil combination. Chile dominated Bolivia, and Argentina felt itself out in the cold. But gradually Bolivia, like Paraguay and Uruguay, came under the expanding influence of Argentine imperialism. As to Paraguay, it is, as we have seen, virtually an Argentine protectorate. And most Argentines consider Uruguay a kind of colony also, though it is considerably more than that.

Argentine diplomacy—all this being a rather small-scale imitation of European power politics—has recently been active in Colombia. This is to insure that Argentina shall have a good friend on Brazil's northern frontier, in the event of trouble with Brazil. Argentine relations with Peru are also close, and the Argentinians have attempted to mediate in Peru's dispute with Ecuador. Argentines, in short, act toward the rest of Latin Amer-

ica much as it feels that the United States—in older days at least
—acted toward Argentina.

In December 1940, Dr. Roca and Dr. Guani, the estimable foreign ministers of Argentina and Uruguay respectively, met in a
two-day conference at Colonia, on the Plata, and agreed to co-
operate for "the defense of the estuary with *continental* forces,
without endangering the territorial integrity" of either party.
This, though an alliance between a giant and a pygmy, happily
coincided with United States conceptions of hemisphere policy,
and it was warmly welcomed in Washington. In February 1941,
five countries—Argentina, Brazil, Bolivia, Paraguay, and Uruguay—met in a formal conference at Montevideo to study means
of co-operation in the Río de la Plata area. The work—which it
is hoped will lead to a customs union—was mostly in economic
fields.

La Prensa and La Nación

No discussion of Argentine political affairs can be complete
without a word about these two newspapers, which are among the
finest in the world, and which wield great influence. It may surprise readers in the United States that *La Prensa*, for instance,
prints more foreign news than any other newspaper on earth,
and that its technical and professional standards rival those of the
New York or London *Times*. *La Prensa* is *the* Argentine newspaper: liberal, dignified, paternalistic, and irrefragably itself; no
Prensa man has ever gone into politics. It was founded in 1869 by
José C. Paz; it has remained in the hands of the Paz family ever
since, and is completely independent financially. In foreign policy
it is pro-democrat, pro-British, and moderately pro-United States;
domestically it usually—but not always—supports the government
in power. Dr. Ezequiel P. Paz, its editor in chief, told me that it
opposed any administration that "varied from the principles of
law, order, liberty, justice or constitutionalism."

La Nación, controlled by the Mitre family, is as dignified as
La Prensa, but its circulation is less (about 220,000 as against

255,000) and its influence not quite so universal. It is strongly Catholic and conservative. Its Washington correspondent likes to make fun of the U.S.A.

La Prensa, a United Press client, is the fountainhead of U.P. strength throughout Latin America. The United Press distributes about 20,000 words per day in Argentina; its staff in Buenos Aires alone numbers 138 men. The Associated Press works with *La Nación,* and distributes about the same wordage, but its staff is smaller. The biggest foreign distributors of news are Trans-ocean, with a daily file estimated at about 40,000 words, and Havas-Reuter, with 30,000.

It is highly characteristic of Argentine folkways that one of the chief editors of *La Prensa* has never once in his life been outside Buenos Aires, and that Señora Z. Paz de Anchorena, the daughter of its founder and sister of the proprietor, one of the most influential women in the country, has never once met either Ortiz or Castillo, the two Presidents of the republic.

Chapter XXI

These Are Argentinians

ABOUT one-fifth of the total population of Argentina lives in or near the great capital city Buenos Aires, which is a kind of glittering screen to the rest of the country. Buenos Aires, the city, is an enormous mouth, sucking in and absorbing what the countryside, the "camp," produces, if I may change the metaphor. The disequilibrium between capital and camp has been a major political and economic problem since the foundation of the republic.

The city of Buenos Aires is a federal district, like Washington. But also to be considered is the *province* of Buenos Aires, by far the richest and most powerful in the country. When Buenos Aires the city and Buenos Aires the province were one organism—as was the case until the 1880's—it was practically an independent duchy. For instance, customs revenues from the port of Buenos Aires were reserved exclusively to the province; until these revenues were nationalized, the country was a virtual shambles. Gradually, during the past half century, the *federal* system became integrated. Federalism, as in the United States, was essential and inevitable as the nation came to political maturity.

In order to strengthen itself *vis à vis* the provinces—particularly against Buenos Aires—the federal government developed the *interventor system*, which is the root of much contemporary political difficulty.

If the President of the republic does not like the way things are going in any province—for instance, if there has been fraud in an election—he may step in and appoint a federal interventor to run it, if congress is not sitting. The interventor rules like a proconsul, in the name of the President. In theory the interventor is supposed to call new elections, under federal supervision, as soon as possible; in practice he is apt to take his time. This interventor system obviously serves to give any unscrupulous President an enormous field for power.

Four provinces are at present being ruled by federal inter-ventors: Buenos Aires itself, San Juan, Catamarca, and La Rioja. Take Buenos Aires, the "Queen Province." During the Justo presidency an extreme right-winger, Dr. Manuel A. Fresco, was "elected" governor, though Buenos Aires is the most radical province in the country; he was chosen because Justo needed a strong man to prepare the next *national* elections. And Fresco duly helped make possible Ortiz's subsequent election as President of the republic. Then Ortiz, as we know, drifted left. He decided to get rid of Fresco, and he did so by appointing an interventor, Octavio Amadeo, to take his place. Ortiz's excuse was that the *provincial* elections had been fraudulent (he could not say that the national elections were fraudulent, since they had elected *him*). His motive was, of course, to gain control of the Buenos Aires political machine.

Late in 1940 came provincial elections in Mendoza, one of the frontier provinces, and in the great radical province of Santa Fé. Anti-Personalista radicals, close to Castillo, "won" both of these elections, though cries of fraud rose to the vault of heaven. Then came something topsy-turvy. The regular radicals in the legisla-ture, who as a rule dislike extremely to see the President appoint interventors, wanted Ortiz (still in theory President) to name interventors in Mendoza and Santa Fé, in order to force out the legally "elected" Castillo governors over Castillo's head. If con-gress is in session, the President needs its approval to appoint an interventor. Castillo thereupon contrived to keep congress laboriously in session, in order that his coalition majority could defeat any radical proposal to put Ortiz interventors in. It sounds very complicated. It is.

As 1943 will be a Presidential year, various groups and candi-dates are already jockeying for position. So let us make a brief roll call of prominent Argentine *políticos*, and find out where they stand.

Radicals of Several Breeds

The orthodox radicals, though they have been out of power since 1930, are generally conceded to control 80 per cent of the true voting strength of the country. They are particularly powerful in Buenos Aires and in Santa Fé, the "gringo province" (so called because it was settled mostly by Basques and Swiss), with its growing industrial towns like Rosario. The radicals hold 68 out of 158 seats in the present chamber, and are the largest single party.

Speaking broadly—very broadly—the landowning aristocracy in Argentina are the conservatives, and the middle-class townsmen are the radicals, as I have pointed out above. But this statement needs some qualification. Several very wealthy and socially prominent *estancieros*—like the former ambassador to Washington, Dr. Honorio Pueyrredón—are radicals, not conservatives. And several important industrialists and business men are conservatives, not radicals. The line is almost as difficult to mark as that between Republicans and Democrats in the United States. One rough hallmark is that most radicals are immigrants or sons of immigrants; it was the triumph of the radical party, under Irigoyen, to bring these newcomers into politics, to give the amorphous middle class a means of political expression. One eminent Argentine told me that "no one has ever defined a radical exactly." They are, like the radicals in pre-Vichy France, not so much a party as "a state of mind."

The leader of the radicals, and one of the grand old men of the country, is the former President, Dr. Marcelo T. de Alvear. Born in 1868, a lawyer by profession, he has been in politics since he was 20; he was an early revolutionist, a founder of the U.C.R. (the official name of the party), and one of Irigoyen's first disciples. He stemmed from the old aristocracy, and was President of the republic from 1922 to 1928. He was a very big man indeed for many years; most people think his importance has diminished now. His presumptive successor, and the vice-president of the party, is Dr. José P. Tamborini, a doctor of medicine.

Dr. Alvear is tall, dignified, sober-faced, long-necked. As President he quarreled with the Vatican, something that few Argentine politicians do; he intervened at one time or other in eight provinces; he was responsible for much social legislation, including a strict pension system; he saw to it that salaries and so on were paid in national currency, not in the separate monies of the provinces. He was arrested after the Uriburu coup, and spent some time in exile. He started both Ortiz and Justo on their careers, and in general gave the country a sound, stable, progressive administration.

An example of the social taboos of Argentina is that Dr. Alvear, many years ago, married a Portuguese opera singer, by name Regina Pacini. It was considered a national scandal that a personage of his rank should marry an artist, and for years she was not received by "polite" society.

Of the anti-Personalista radicals (those who seceded from the official radical party and are now part of the ruling conservative coalition), the most interesting is the bald, venerable Dr. Leopoldo Melo, who has led Argentine delegations to many conferences. Dr. Melo committed one unfortunate *gaffe* late in 1940. After the Havana conference he was received at Hyde Park by President Roosevelt; on his return to Buenos Aires, a guest of honor at an American Chamber of Commerce luncheon, he quoted him to the effect that he, Roosevelt, would "settle" the beef question between the United States and Argentina "after" the American elections. This was big news to Buenos Aires—and to the United States! When the story got out, Washington had to repudiate it.

Most radicals, of whatever breed, are cautious and "legalistic." This is partly because they do not want to provoke the army.

Argentine Army and Navy

The army, which is dominated in part by General Agustin P. Justo, is a decisive political influence. It helped make the Uriburu coup in September 1930; one clique of extreme nationalist officers is still called the "Septembrists."

The army is, on the whole, fairly representative of the nation, since the officers are drawn largely from the middle class, and the rank and file are conscripts. It can overthrow any government at any time—so all politicians treat it gently—but it seldom goes in for such adventures. There has been no serious political bloodshed in Argentina for forty years or more. At the present time the army does not want trouble—it would inherit an appalling economic crisis if it made a coup d'état—and hence is fairly benevolent to Castillo and Ortiz both.

From about 1915 to 1940 the army was trained by a German military mission, and this has given the *older* officers a profound pro-German slant; in fact, probably 90 per cent of officers over the rank of major are Germanophile. In July 1940, this German mission was disbanded, because the Argentine high command (some months late) thought the situation "inconvenient" in that Germany was fighting a war in which Argentina was strictly neutral. Then something happened that annoyed the Argentines extremely. The chief of the mission, General Niedenfuhr, was promptly named by Berlin as German military attaché to Brazil, and his first assistant, Colonel Wolf, was similarly sent to Chile. These two officers knew, of course, every detail public or secret of the Argentine general staff. And the Argentines don't like them stationed so strategically in neighbor states, with their inner knowledge of every Argentine military plan.

Four conspicuous generals, all retired and of the old Uriburu group, are generally dubbed the heart of Argentine pro-Germanism. They are General Juan Bautista Molina, General Basilio R. Pertine (a former Minister of War), General Martínez Pita (the interventor in Catamarca), and General Juan Pistarini, who studied in Germany and is in charge of Argentine arms purchases abroad.

General Molina, one of the most important officers in the country, was Argentine military attaché to Berlin for a time; before that he served briefly in the German army itself. He is a patron of the National Youth Alliance, the chief pro-Fascist body in Argentina; he was Uriburu's right-hand man for years. His avowed Axis sympathies got him much publicity in November 1940, when he gave a formal luncheon at the Jockey Club for the German ambassador. Among the guests, aside from Molina's comrades in arms, were Dr. Melo, Senator Sánchez Sorondo, and many other prominent politicians.

General Pertine studied military tactics in Germany, and was military attaché to Berlin—and observer with the German field armies—from 1910 to 1918; he held the rank of quartermaster general in the German army, and he has three German decorations. He retired from active Argentine service in 1936, after having been inspector general of infantry, director of arsenals, and commander of the Fourth Army division. For a time he was Justo's Minister of War, and he is president of the influential Club Militaire.

From time to time come whispers of army trouble. In April 1941, General Carlos D. Márquez (a former War Minister who resigned after the Palomar land scandal), was cleared of charges of complicity in a "revolutionary project," details of which are not known. In June 1941, the commander of the army air force was required to investigate alleged membership by several of his officers in the National Youth Alliance. In July 1941, the Minister of War required General Carlos von der Bocke, commander of the Fourth Army, to check up on allegations that his staff was spreading totalitarian propaganda.

General Juan N. Tonazzi, of partly Italian descent, is the present Minister of War. He has been a sound professional soldier since he was commissioned an artillery lieutenant in 1907; he served as military attaché in Rome for some years, but he is not regarded as pro-totalitarian. One of the youngest generals in the army, he was promoted over the heads of many to reach his present appointment; he had been Justo's aide-de-camp, and was sponsored by Ortiz and Justo both. In Argentina the Minister of

War is always a general on the active list and is thus boss of the army not only in name but in fact. Tonazzi's best-known colleague is probably General Guillermo José Mohr, until recently the inspector-general. Mohr was for a time thought to be protototalitarian, but he was among the Latin American officers invited by General Marshall to visit the United States last year, and he returned to Argentina enthusiastic about his North American experiences.

The Argentine army, which numbers about 50,000 officers and men on active service, with a reserve of some 280,000, is by all odds the best in Latin America. Officers, rank for rank, get higher pay than those in the United States; after 30 years of service they retire on full pay, which should make American officers envious. The country is at present embarking on a $300,000,000 arms program to be devoted mostly to modernization and mechanization of equipment. A campaign to train 5,000 pilots is under way, though Argentina has no more than 400-500 fighting planes.

The Argentine navy is much less political than the army; it is the sixth largest navy in the world, and is highly regarded by neutral experts. For the past few years it has been trained by a United States naval mission. The Minister of Marine, Admiral Mario Fincati, has also been commander of the fleet; he is moderately pro-British in temperament and policy.

Foreign Office and Cabinet

When I was in Buenos Aires the Minister of Foreign Affairs and Public Worship was that delightful old gentleman, Dr. Julio A. Roca, son of the frontier-building Argentine President who conquered Patagonia. He has a delicate small face, a tiny mustache over a tiny mouth, and glistening pink child's cheeks. His courtesy is exquisite; his cleverness is famous; he has great capacity to grasp things quickly. He has never been to the United States, but he likes to speak colloquial English. Once, when I departed after a formal interview, he astonished me by saying, "Well, so long."

Dr. Roca was born in 1873 in Córdoba, that lovely town in the shadow of the Andes. He has had a long and distinguished career as deputy, senator, governor, ambassador, and Vice-President of the republic. In 1933 he negotiated the Roca-Runciman agreement for clearing Anglo-Argentine trade balances. He is strongly pro-British, partly because he is a devoted lover of English poetry: a poet himself, he has expertly translated Shelley and Keats.

Roca, an arch-conservative, made a slip in the Chamber once. He said, "We must steer a little to the Left." This made a great sensation. People have joked about it ever since. In January 1941 Roca resigned. His friends say that he could no longer endure the legislative stalemate and the equivocal position between Ortiz and Castillo. Officially it was given out that he "was irked by parliamentary inactivity."

Roca is a firm believer in hemisphere solidarity; he says that the United States must realize how important Argentina is, that the two countries have a great deal in common, and that in any case—the basis of his policy—"we are all Americans together."

His successor in the Foreign Office, a considerably less well-known man, is Dr. Enrique Ruiz Guiñazú, a lawyer and diplomat, born in 1884. He was appointed after a five-months interregnum, when he was serving as Argentine ambassador to the Holy See. Little is known of his political orientation. He was a professor for a time, then a banker, and later Argentine delegate to the League of Nations and minister to Switzerland.

A former Foreign Minister, José María Cantilo, also needs mention. It was the estimable Cantilo who arrived at the Lima conference on a battleship, and then retreated to the Chilean lakes while it progressed. But the tactful Mr. Hull finally won him around. Cantilo, born in 1877 and educated at the Sorbonne, a poet in both Spanish and French, was a professional career diplomat. He has never visited the United States, and was indifferent rather than hostile to things American. For a time he seemed to be strongly under Italian influence, especially after a term as ambassador to Rome. But his heart was always French, and the collapse of France in 1940 crushed him.

Two cabinet officers of ability and consequence are Dr. Miguel J. Culaciati, the Minister of Interior, of Italian origin, and C. Massini Ezcurra, the Minister of Agriculture. Culaciati, an anti-Personalista radical, one of Justo's men, does his best to combat Fifth Columnism, and so has one of the hardest jobs in the republic. Ezcurra is an agrarian and banking specialist, with no party affiliations. He is very friendly to Great Britain and the United States; his daughter went to Vassar.

Dr. Pinedo and His Plan

As able and attractive as any living Argentine is Dr. Federico Pinedo, who has twice been Minister of Finance. Lithe, wiry, of medium height, he is packed with vitality; his hazel eyes are clever, quizzical, penetrating. He knows what you want to say long before you finish a sentence; he speaks English, French, and German fluently, and keeps an adding machine and other calculating devices by his bedside. Pinedo, of aristocratic family (he and Roca were the only two aristocrats in the Ortiz-Castillo government) was born in Buenos Aires in 1895. He got his Ph.D. at the age of 20; his thesis was a study of the rights of property and "concrete manifestations of socialism."

Dr. Pinedo began political life, in fact, as a red-hot independent socialist. He founded a socialist newspaper, *La Libertad,* and became a deputy when he was only 25. A strong rationalist, he is probably the only Argentine cabinet minister who refused to give the customary oath to God on taking office. He gave up official socialism years ago, but many people still think him too radical, too clever, too "dangerous." They fear him as English tories feared Churchill, though they freely admit his sense of public duty and that he has the best financial brain in the country. He is a stalwart anti-Fascist. The United States has no better friend in Argentina.

During his first term as Finance Minister (under Justo in

1933-35), Pinedo all but turned the country upside down. He worked twelve, fourteen, sixteen hours a day; he held press conferences at 7 A.M. He converted the national debt, set up new taxes (income tax scarcely existed in Argentina), instituted a reciprocal trade policy, and established a Central Bank. In his second term he was author of the short-lived Pinedo plan, a New-Dealish scheme to take over agrarian surpluses, move and store the crops, and get purchasing power back to the farmer. It aimed to establish a rural housing program, expand intra-Latin American markets, and in general checkmate the mounting economic crisis.

But the radicals refused to accept the Pinedo plan, unless—as quid pro quo—the government should declare intervention in Santa Fé and Mendoza. Ortiz might have done this, but he was powerless. Castillo refused to do so, because it would have meant the displacement of his own governors. Came stalemate. Pinedo went to the resort town Mar del Plata to see Alvear, the radical leader, and attempt to arrange a compromise. It fell through, and Pinedo resigned office. Castillo would not accept his resignation, and decreed it invalid. Stubborn, Pinedo resigned again.

Together with his able assistants at the Central Bank, Dr. Paul Prebisch and Edgardo Grumbach, Pinedo was closely identified with a trade policy that for a time was much resented in the United States. He said, in effect, "We will buy only from those who buy from us" (which in a way served America right), and severe discriminations against imports from the United States were put in force. For instance, an exchange surcharge added 20 per cent to the price of dollars; certain American articles were limited by quota (tractors, automobiles, tin plate, barbed wire), and others were prohibited, like shoes and cigarettes. In 1927 the United States had supplied 18 per cent of all Argentine imports of cotton textiles. This fell to 1 per cent in 1938. Similar drops took place in iron and steel products (48 per cent to 16 per cent), leather (22 per cent to 3 per cent), fruit (32 per cent to 9 per cent). For a time—in September 1940—American goods were in effect embargoed altogether.

This situation has now changed completely, as we know. The war and blockade cut off a flat 40 per cent of Argentine exports, and the country was forced by implacable necessity to turn to the United States. We began to buy Argentine goods in unprecedented quantities; our purchases went up 59 per cent in the first months of 1941 as against 1940. Early in 1941 we contributed 23.6 per cent of total Argentine imports, and took 38.7 per cent of its total exports, far surpassing British figures in both categories for the first time in history. Argentina was particularly pleased in that we bought more than we sold, giving the country a heavy favorable balance. Meantime Argentine trade with the rest of Latin America, hitherto unimportant, has almost doubled.

But the British continue to have something of a stranglehold on the country's economy. Argentina sells more to Great Britain than it buys, roughly in a ratio of 10 to 6, so customarily, it has a credit balance in London. Normally this would be transferred to dollars and utilized in the United States, but the British now block it in sterling; Argentina has between £2,500,000 and £3,000,000 thus sterilized. This is cause for considerable worry. Suppose the British should lose the war; suppose sterling should crash. One proposal is that Buenos Aires might ask the British to sell some of their colossal Argentine investments, which, mostly in railways, amount to about £2,000,000,000.[1] But London has not been heard from.

Pinedo hoped to include road development in his famous plan, but it was difficult to do so. Reason: the British have always bitterly opposed road building in the country, in order to prevent competition with their railways. This is one reason why Argentine roads are so indifferent.

No one could reasonably want to be Argentine Finance Minister at this moment. The budget deficit is enormous, amounting to about a quarter of the total budget. Above all there is the question

[1] By contrast the U.S.A. investment is about $500,000,000. Argentine bonds held in the U.S.—on which Argentina has never defaulted—amount to $268,000,000.

of agrarian surpluses. Millions of tons of wheat and corn are, for instance, piled up in storage. But the wheat surplus, critical as it is, does not demand instant emergency measures, since wheat will keep. But corn spoils after twelve or fourteen months, and the government is faced with the problem of disposing of at least six million tons of corn from last year's crop, with a large new crop coming in. It sells some corn—at a staggering loss—to industrial firms for use as fuel. Argentine is burning corn just as Brazil burns coffee, though in a different manner.

In 1940 the United States lent Argentina $110,000,000—no mean sum—of which $60,000,000 came from the Export-Import Bank, the rest as a direct loan from the U. S. Treasury to support the peso. Which goes to show what a vital stake we have in Argentina's financial stability.

Argentina's Leading Fascist

This is probably Dr. Matías Guillermo Sánchez Sorondo, the one man in the senate who voted to accept Ortiz's resignation when he was ill. Sánchez Sorondo, born in 1880, helped make the 1930 coup d'état; he has been Minister of the Interior, Vice-President of the republic, and provisional President. Justo made him chairman of the National Cultural Commission—an interesting post for one of his views—and at present he is the Will Hays of Argentina, as head of the Argentine Cinematographic Institute.

Sánchez Sorondo has vaguely expressed ambitions to be the Führer of Argentina, but most people think that, rather old and isolated, he has missed the boat. Democratically minded Argentines flinch when you mention his name, even if they do not think that he is dangerous any longer. When I saw him he told me he had been received by Hitler, Mussolini, and Franco during a recent trip to Europe, and that in Germany—he mentioned this with naive pride!—his itinerary had been arranged by the German state.

Sánchez, who has great vigor of mind, expresses his views vividly. I asked him point-blank if he really would prefer Hitler to Roosevelt at the Panama Canal. He laughed explosively. He thinks that Germany is bound to win the European war, that the Nazis are no real threat to Argentina, and that if his country has no reason to fear Germany, it has less reason to fear the United States. He asked me—in December 1940—if I thought Britain could hold out another "six months."

Other folk on the extreme Right, though it would not be fair to call them Fascists, are Dr. Robustiano Patrón Costas, the vice-president of the senate, and the immensely wealthy *estanciero* Senator Antonio Santamarina. Both are last-ditch oligarchs. Another eminent leader of the National Democratic Party is Alberto Barceló, who is called the *Caudillo* of Avallaneda, a prosperous Buenos Aires suburb which he controls. He is the party fixer, the political boss, par excellence.

One should also mention the first Archbishop of Buenos Aires, Cardinal Santiago Luis Copello, one of the two cardinals in all Latin America. Catholicism is the exclusive state religion of Argentina, and the Cardinal outranks every political leader except the President. His influence, on the conservative side, is however indirect rather than explicit.

Argentina Has Socialists Too

Numerically the Argentine socialist party is unimportant, with only one senator and five deputies in parliament. Its influence is more considerable among the middle-aged than the youth, which has largely turned to fascism or communism; most of its leaders are venerable intellectuals, closely resembling the old school socialists of Belgium or Scandinavia. But they are experienced and worthy men, and though their party is small it makes itself widely felt.

The lone socialist senator, it happens, is probably the single most vivid personality in Argentine political life—Dr. Alfredo L. Palacios. He has a shock of long hair and picturesque expanding mustaches; he is compared variously to D'Artagnan and Danton; he likes to fence despite his sixty-one hard-working years; he is probably the best orator in the land. It was Palacios who "broke" the Palomar land scandal; it is Palacios who gives the socialist party most of the intellectual vitality it has.

The patriarchal Dr. Mario Bravo, one of the few Argentine political leaders of partly Indian origin, has great moral authority. Like so many Argentine politicians, he talks like a Frenchman, with lucid rationality and a perfect flow of the language; time and time again in Buenos Aires I blinked and thought that I must be in the Chamber of Deputies in Paris. Dr. Bravo, who calls his white Pekingese Pituca his "secretary," says that Argentina should be a happy country; it has no race problem, no unassimilated foreign groups, and a sparse population. But, he says, a terrible despair is afflicting the peasants on the land. Like all socialists he is an optimist, and he hopes that better times will come.

Other leading socialists are Américo Ghioldi, a youthful professor and theoretician, and Nicolás Repetto, one of the party organizers. In conversation with me Repetto was chiefly interested in what kind of people buy books in the United States, what the Soviet Union is doing for education, what attitude North Americans have toward the Catholic Church. The socialist program in Argentina of course includes separation of church and state. Repetto thinks that fascism may be dangerous in his country; he feels that many misguided Argentinians actually hope that Germany will win the war, on the ground that Argentina can then trade with Europe as a whole.

The communist party lives half underground. It is legal in Córdoba, Entre Ríos, and Tucumán, illegal in the province of Buenos Aires and the federal capital. On the whole the communists seem stronger among the intellectuals than among the workers, though they have a certain influence in the C.G.T., the chief Argentine trade union.

The Two Pueyrredóns

Dr. Honorio Pueyrredón, a distinguished lawyer and public servant since he participated in a revolution in the remote days of 1893, has been Minister of Foreign Affairs and ambassador to

Washington. He is a vigorous Alvear radical, and may very well be President of the Republic some day if the radicals ever get a chance to vote. His cousin, on the opposite side of the political fence, is Carlos Alberto Pueyrredón, the Mayor of Buenos Aires who banned the "Great Dictator." He is an enthusiastic bibliophile, and a most charming gentleman. He has 240 different editions of *Don Quixote*, and about 500 books of foreign impressions of Argentina.

Prize Winner in Conclusion

The only Latin American personage ever to win a Nobel prize is the incredibly accomplished Carlos Saavedra Lamas, who is the Nicholas Murray Butler of Argentina, and who was its subtle-minded and sometimes anti-American Foreign Minister from 1932 to 1938. Saavedra's prestige and self-confidence are so enormous that, with a peculiar inversion of vanity, he does not include his Nobel prize in *Who's Who in Latin America*. He received the prize largely because Mr. Hull, with consummate tact and an eye to the future, gently pushed it in his direction.

One of the most learned men of our time, Dr. Saavedra is nicknamed Don Cuello, because he keeps his chin—and collars—high. He was born in 1880, and was variously a professor of finance, political economy, and international law. He was to politics born; his grandfather was General Cornelio Saavedra, his father-in-law the liberal President Sáenz Peña. He represented Argentina at most of the international conferences when it was considered good clean fun to pinprick the United States, and he took some credit for settling the Chaco war. Saavedra retired to private life in 1938.

Good-by to Argentina

We must leave Argentina now. The great world of Brazil is waiting, to say nothing of that of the Caribbean. About Argentina, the most important country in Latin America, one could continue to write almost indefinitely, but we must press on. In conclusion, let me summarize briefly the main conflicts of power we have seen.

First, the conflict between the conservatives, represented by Castillo, and the assorted radicals of Ortiz and Alvear. The conservatives were, in the late summer of 1941, still on top. But no one can know how long they will remain there.

Second, the conflict between indigenous Argentine nationalism, with its fierce chauvinistic character, and such *intra*-national conceptions as hemispheric solidarity promoted by the United States.

Third, the conflict between old-established British commercial interests and the rising importance of the United States in matters of trade.

Fourth, the conflict—as striking in Argentina as in any country in the world—between an old feudal order and the newer vision of the young. The youth of the country are its greatest hope.

Fifth, the conflict between Anglo-American political influence and the dangerous pressure of the Nazi Fifth Column.

Chapter XXII

Uruguay, the Denmark of Latin America

〰〰〰〰〰〰〰〰〰〰〰〰〰〰〰

I MEAN pre-Hitler Denmark of course. Uruguay, like the old Denmark, is a compact and homogeneous small state living on agriculture, highly progressive, orderly, and honest; a country that believes deeply in democratic institutions and honors them in practice as well as theory; a republic with as advanced social legislation as any in the world. Moreover it is probably the best friend the United States has in the Americas.

Often Uruguay, with its 2,000,000 people—in area it is about the size of North Dakota—is called an appendage of Argentina, and indeed Argentine influence is, as we shall see, profound. More accurately, Uruguay is a buffer state between Argentina and Brazil. But it differs from both profoundly. No one in Uruguay is very rich, and few are poor; white European stock predominates; the upper classes have real social vision; church is separated from state, and clerical influence is slight; the people are healthy, upstanding, and adult. Montevideo, the capital, is much like cities in the United States, with broad boulevards, neat suburban homes, and an informal social life. "Emotionally and spiritually," a friend told me, "it is the Left Bank of Buenos Aires."

Officially the name of the country is República Oriental del Uruguay, which derives from the fact that it lies east of the Río de la Plata. In the old days it was called "La Banda Oriental," and even today the people often call themselves the "Orientales." The creator of Uruguay was a great man José Gervasio Artigas, who lived from 1764 to 1850. For a time he ruled at least four Argentine provinces as well as what became Uruguay—the Argentines still call him a "bandit"—and he wanted a federal system throughout all the "Cuenca" or Plata basin. For some years the

United States refused to recognize Argentine independence; we recognized Artigas instead. He defeated invaders from both Buenos Aires and Brazil; he was the George Washington of his native land.

In the twentieth century Uruguay produced another great man, one of the indubitable master statesmen of the modern period, who ranks near the top by the standards of any nation. His name was José Batlle y Ordóñez (pronounced Bajé) and he dominated Uruguay as President or more often behind the scenes from 1903 until 1929. Before Batlle Uruguay had been one of the most turbulent states in the hemisphere; interminable civil wars took place between the leading parties, the Blancos (whites or conservatives), and Colorados (reds or liberals). First Batlle, the leader of the Colorados, restored order. There has been no revolutionary bloodshed in Uruguay since 1904. Then he set out to build a modern state.

Batlle came of a distinguished family, and was the son of a former President. By profession he was a newspaper man, as is his son, who is today the editor of *El Día*, the country's leading newspaper. Batlle spent long years in Europe between his presidential terms, studying, writing, investigating; he was also a passionate admirer of the United States, and is one of the founders of Pan-Americanism. He made reforms that were unheard of for Latin America in his time; for example, compulsory free education and compulsory free suffrage, including votes for women. His dominant idea was that fair and free social development would eliminate the class struggle and diminish poverty; his life objective was to make a paternalistic state whereby everyone would be employed in his productive years, and supported by the state thereafter. His legislation was in advance of anything then known in the world except perhaps Scandinavia and New Zealand. One of his early regulations was the "law of the chair," which obliges employers to provide seats for all working women, for instance in bakeries or textile factories. Much of his work startlingly resembles that of Franklin D. Roosevelt's New Deal—which it preceded by a considerable margin.

Social Reform and Paternalism in Uruguay

Almost everything in contemporary Uruguay derives from the character and attainments of this one man, José Batlle y Ordóñez, including widespread state intervention in private enterprise. Consider the *Entes Autónomos* (roughly, autonomous administrations) that give the country a form of state socialism unique in the Western Hemisphere.

The state controls banking through its ownership and operation of the Bank of the Republic, the State Insurance Bank, and the Mortgage Bank.

All forms of insurance—life, fire, marine, industrial, accident, and so on—are an exclusive government monopoly; Uruguay is the only country in the world where this is true.

The government owns and operates a State Electricity Plant, and controls all light, power, telephones, and hydroelectric development.

The ANCAP (Administración Nacional de Combustibles, Alcohol y Portland) holds a monopoly on cement, alcohol, and fuel. It refines all the country's petroleum. Also it produces and sells *caña*, a cheap kind of rum made of sugar, which is the national drink.

The National Ports Administration controls all port and river traffic in Montevideo and elsewhere.

The railways are largely British-owned, except for one company; but when I visited Uruguay I was told that the government proposes to buy them back as part of a complex trading agreement covering beef exports to Great Britain.

Broadcasting is not a state monopoly, but the government owns and operates the leading station, which is probably the best in South America.

Such enterprises as ballet and symphony orchestra (and even

one night club, located oddly enough next to the town morgue)
are government-run.

An administration known as SOYP controls the state fisheries.
A *frigorífico nacional* (packing plant) has a monopoly on domestic beef, though it competes with American packing houses
in export business.

The chief hotels—especially those along the beaches—and
casinos are owned and operated by the Montevideo municipality.

Finally the government owns important amounts of land—
there are few big private *estancias*—through its control of the
mortgage bank.

In another paternalist category are various kinds of social
legislation that Batlle originated. Uruguay had an eight-hour day
and a minimum wage law long before the United States; minimum wage extends not merely to government employees, industrial workers, household servants and the like, but to *rural* workers.
This law, like so much in Uruguay, is unique in the world. Rural
workers—the landless peons on the ranches and wheatfields—get
a minimum of 30 Uruguayan pesos (about $13.20) per month.
The law applies to everyone in the country, and is rigidly enforced.

An old-age retirement pension system, corresponding to our social security legislation was put in force twenty-two years ago, long
before it was dreamed of in Washington. Free medical attention—
covering doctors, surgeons, dentists, and midwives—is guaranteed
to the poor. Every worker is entitled to get—and gets—vacations
with pay. Government departments work only half a day; in the
mornings during summer (which is opposite to our summer), in
the afternoons in winter. Oddly enough, trade unionism is weak;
there has been little necessity for workers' organizations. Unem-
ployment is unknown.

Something else that Batlle did—he might not be so happy about
it now—was demilitarization of the country. Uruguay, like Denmark, virtually abolished its army. There were no military budgets
(except for police and shore patrol) for roughly thirty years;

hence Uruguay was able to afford what it spent on education and social services. It was the only country in South America without conscription. But as the pressure of world events gripped closer in the past few years, Uruguay began to worry about its defenses. A bill for formal conscription was killed in February 1940, after long argument, but a kind of substitute service bill was passed instead, providing for military *training* but not regular army enlistment. This followed a serious Fifth Column scare. Volunteers began to drill privately to protect their democracy when the government hesitated, and youngsters rushed to join private aviation clubs and the like.

People and Politics

The President of Uruguay, General Alfredo Baldomir, looks like what he is, a competent, successful, and well-esteemed professional man. He is big and heavily built, with iron-gray hair *en brosse*. An architect and engineer by profession—architecture, incidentally, is considered the highest of callings in Uruguay— he entered the army after the 1903-04 civil war; he was professor of engineering at the National Military School, and for a time chief of police in Montevideo. He was active in politics for many years, but kept up his work in architecture; for instance, he built the Carrasco hotel, one of the great modern structures that dominate the Uruguayan beaches.

General Baldomir, who is head of the Colorado party, was born in 1884. His culture, like that of so many of his compatriots, is basically French. He is straightforward, dignified, and friendly. He has never been in Europe or the United States. I met him at the Montevideo races. He seemed to be liking them, but on a somewhat abstract plane.

The Foreign Minister, Dr. Alberto Guani, is of a different type. This immensely learned lawyer-professor-diplomat, who was born in 1878, looks like nothing so much as a Renaissance Pope who has lived both well and wisely. Dr. Guani's stately girth, his enormous bald head, the beaked aristocratic nose, the icy-pale

and penetrating gray eyes, make one wish that Titian were alive
to paint him. He is vain, deliberate, shrewd, and subtle-minded.
He wears formal clothes with immaculate precision, and relaxes
by playing the violin. He was Uruguayan minister to the old
Austria-Hungary as far back as 1911; he was minister to the
Court of St. James's in 1936; he has been president both of the
council and assembly of the League of Nations.[1] Few people
know the art of living better. He loves good books, good music,
good food, good wine.

Like so many pro-French politicians in the hemisphere, Dr.
Guani was stunned by the fall of France. When I talked to him
he asked over and over again *how* such a calamity could have
happened.

The domestic political situation in Uruguay is one of the most
complicated in the world. We must go back to Batlle once again.
The central issue in Uruguay is *constitutional reform*, and it
derives from Batlle's conception of what is called the "collegiate
system" of government. He thought that a strong executive was
dangerous; he wanted checks and balances so that no dictator
could run wild. So some cabinet ministers are constitutionally
responsible directly to the President, others to a permanent Administrative Council. Then, after Batlle, the constitution was
amended to divide power further. For instance, three cabinet seats
go, by law, to the party polling the *second* largest number of
votes, with the result that the opposition is represented actually *in*
the government. This is as if Mr. Roosevelt, on his re-election,
had been obliged to give three portfolios to Mr. Willkie. Moreover, the opposition gets one-half the senate, no matter what the
vote is. The chamber is elected by proportional representation.

Now this might all be splendid—if it worked. It is democracy
at its most extreme development—but it became a *reductio ad
absurdum* of the democratic process. Consider only one detail.
The opposition party (the Blancos) controls about one-sixth of

[1] But—like so many Latin American Foreign Ministers—he has never visited
the United States.

the electorate, not more. But, by this strange constitutional device, it automatically obtains three seats in the cabinet, and one-half the senate. The Blancos are thus able to harass the government Colorados and block legislation almost indefinitely; unless they agreé to a measure, it can scarcely pass. So a party which represents only one-sixth of the nation can nullify the will of the party representing five-sixths of the nation. The situation became intolerable in Baldomir's administration and he urged reform of the constitution as the only solution. The three Blanco ministers then resigned.

General Baldomir became President in 1938 as a compromise candidate pledged to reform. He is a brother-in-law of a former President, Gabriel Terra, now dead, who ruled dictatorially after an anti-Batlle coup d'état in 1933. Baldomir's opponent was a surgeon named Blanco Acevedo, who was Terra's son-in-law. It was a family party, but it was bitterly fought. Baldomir's term expires in 1942.

The constitutional reform issue has split all the parties. In the government camp both the Baldomir and Acevedo groups support reform. Groups outside the government also urge reform, and an assorted lot they are; the Batllistas (who have refused to vote since Terra's 1933 coup), the Independent Blancos, the socialists, the communists (who have one deputy), and the Catholics. Opposing reform are the official Blancos, together with some few Colorados who do not like Baldomir. But—hold your head—the official Blancos, the opposition party, who fight reform, are included in the government, which wants it! Another group of Blancos, called as a rule the Nacionalistas, also oppose reform, but refuse to vote.

The leader of the official Blanco opposition is the venerable and wealthy Dr. Luis Alberto de Herrera. His strength is in the provinces, where the *gauchos* and small ranchowners support him. What counts about Herrera is that he is violently anti-United States and strongly pro-Axis. Several years ago he visited Europe, and Hitler and Mussolini received him cordially. He uses his Axis leanings in playing domestic politics. For instance he bitterly fought acquisition by the United States of defense facilities in Uruguayan territory, which he said meant *yanqui* imperialism all over again. But it seemed that he was willing to bargain with the government. He controls half the senate. He opposes reform of the constitution which would end this control. If the Baldomir government were willing to give up reform, then Herrera might give up his opposition to co-operation with the United States. Thus the issue of hemisphere bases became a whipping boy in domestic Uruguayan politics.[2]

Two other Montevidean leaders deserve mention. One is César Charlone, the Vice-President of the republic, and an outstanding candidate to succeed Baldomir in 1942. He has blazing blue eyes; he is one of the ablest men in the Plata basin; I have heard him— during the same afternoon—called pro-Fascist on the one hand, pro-American on the other. He visited France during the Popular Front days, and hated it violently; at the same time he praised Italy. Yet his newspaper warmly supports the United States. People either like or dislike Charlone intensely.

The other is the Minister of the Interior, Pedro Manini Ríos, who is the strongest personality behind Baldomir, and who will probably be a presidential candidate to succeed him. He is distinguished by his moderation, his common sense, and his parliamentary ability. He represented Uruguay, with great skill and success, at both the Panama and Havana conferences. He is vigorously pro-American, and has led the fight against the Uruguayan Fifth Column.

Colossus of the East

Unquestionably Argentina considers Uruguay its own private preserve, and seeks to control its policy. But the stout Uruguayans

[2] One of the shrewdest observers in Montevideo, sketching this situation to me, said that the political situation had "no logic whatever." For instance, two of the three Herrera ex-cabinet ministers are pronouncedly *pro*-United States and *anti*-Nazi.

resist incessant Argentine pressure by whatever means they can. Their country is not, like Paraguay, a semi-colony.

As we have seen in the preceding chapters, Argentina thinks that defense of Uruguay is *its* job; the Argentines are delighted that the country has virtually no navy, and loathe the idea that the United States might acquire bases at Montevideo. The Argentine line is to say to Uruguay, "But you, yourselves, can do nothing; therefore let us do it for you."

Pressure from Buenos Aires comes chiefly by way of economics and the tourist trade. For years Uruguay has hoped for a trade treaty with Argentina—its balance of trade with its great neighbor is heavily unfavorable—but the men of Buenos Aires try not to listen. Argentina controls all shipping between the two capitals, and charges fantastic rates, as it does *vis-à-vis* Paraguay; it buys gravel and sand—which, having only alluvial soil, it needs—but none of Uruguay's meat, fruit, or dairy products. In a word, Argentina behaves toward Uruguay much as the United States behaves toward Argentina, in regard to beef and so on.

Thousands of Argentines come to the cool beaches and vivid blue waters of the Uruguayan littoral every year. The tourist trade is probably worth 13-14,000,000 Uruguayan pesos (say $6,000,000) per year. If Argentina should cut this traffic off, by charging an exit tax from Buenos Aires, it would disastrously hurt Montevideo. So the Uruguayans must watch their step carefully; even so, they manage to outwit their powerful neighbor occasionally, and in recent international conferences they have more than held their own, partly because of United States support.

If the Nazis should ever attempt a coup d'état in Argentina, a similar coup would probably come in Uruguay. The Uruguayan Fifth Columnists and Blanco nationalists would then count on Argentine help *against* the United States.

Once More That Column

In the summer of 1940 a Nazi plot to seize Uruguay and transform it into an agricultural colony of the Third Reich was discovered and squelched. The conspiracy did not aim merely to install a Nazi-dominated government in Uruguay; its alleged purpose was actual annexation of the country.

Twelve Nazis were arrested originally. Among them were both Uruguayans of German descent (who had German citizenship, of course) and German-born Germans. Among them—I quote a story by John W. White in the New York *Times*—were "Arnulf Fuhrmann, South American director of anti-Semitic operations; Otto Klein, South American director of espionage and of Nazi efforts to convert South Americans to totalitarian economic and industrial principles; Julius Holzer, commander of the Uruguayan storm troops, and Rudolph Paetz, Uruguayan director of Nazi propaganda and penetration in schools, colleges, and universities." An important agent who escaped arrest, because he had diplomatic immunity, was Julius Dalldorff, the press attaché of the German legation; he is called the little "Führer of Uruguay." Also he was manager of a wool-exporting concern. The roots of the Fifth Column were the big German commercial organizations. The arrests took place on June 17.

Came storm and turmoil. The German legation protested violently at the arrests, and threatened to break off diplomatic relations. Concurrently it announced that the Nazi party in Uruguay, as well as the German Labor Front and subsidiary organizations, had been dissolved and membership cards withdrawn. All the property of the party was "surrendered" to the German legation; this, of course, served to protect it. Then the Germans launched a strenuous diplomatic campaign to free the prisoners.

Some months before, Professor Hugo Fernández Artucio, a courageous teacher at the University, had opened a campaign against the Fifth Column. He wrote a book, *Nazis en el Uruguay*, which made such a sensation that it led to the formation of a congressional committee of investigation. Had it not been for this book, the German arrests would probably never have been made. They were forced on the government—which at first refused to take the Nazi threat seriously—by outraged public opinion. One detail that aroused people was the revelation that German colonists in both Argentina and Brazil intended to "invade" Uruguay when the local plotters moved.

Then the United States got interested. It was not a coincidence that, in the third week of June, the American cruiser *Quincy* arrived suddenly in Montevideo, ostensibly on a "good-will mission." It was followed posthaste by another cruiser, the *Wichita.* The American minister, Edwin C. Wilson, made a strong speech on June 23 to the effect that the United States—by avowed policy—would co-operate fully with any other American government that wished help in crushing activities that "arise from non-American sources," i.e., from Axis trouble-makers. This was language about as strong as it well could be.

But—the Germans were released! Pressure from the Nazis did its work. The leader, Fuhrmann—who admitted the conspiracy but dismissed it as a joke—fled to Argentina. There he was subsequently arrested again. Then Professor Fernández Artucio, who had exposed the plot, was sued for criminal libel by a pro-Axis editor. He was cleared after a short trial. The judge moreover praised him for having brought the story into the open.

The Germans were still free, however. But then the hard-boiled Manini Ríos, returning from Havana, became Minister of the Interior. He defied German influences, reopened the case, re-arrested eight of the original twelve, and indicted them. He ordered a census of German citizens throughout the country, and asked for the resignation of the Montevideo chief of police. The Foreign Minister, Dr. Guani, "expressed amazement" to the German legation that Dalldorf, its press attaché, "had been permitted to act as chief of the Nazi organization." This was the first time in Latin America that a government took such action.

The 80-page indictment against the eight prisoners has 29 main points. I summarize some of them: •

The German National Socialist Labor party, N.S.D.A.P., exists in Uruguay. This party is a section of the party which under the same name functions as the only party in Germany. The union between the two is maintained by the foreign organization of the N.S.D.A.P. through the German Ministry of Foreign Affairs. Our country, for the purposes of the party's organization abroad, is considered as a *Gau* (district) . . .

All members of the N.S.D.A.P. are obliged as a duty to the party to spread its ideas among German residents in Uruguay.

No one can be a member of the party except German citizens who have accepted the party's program. No one can be a German citizen except those of German blood who have proved their fidelity to the Reich and to the German people and have received certificates of citizenship.

German residents of our country cannot be legal Uruguayan citizens and at the same time members of the party. They must choose between Uruguayan citizenship and party membership.

The party constitutes a movement—a *Bewegung*—strongly organized from the top downward in such a manner that all members of the party are united in the relationship of absolute obedience to the party Führer.

Members of the party take an oath of fidelity and obedience to the Führer and to the party leaders chosen by the Führer. This oath is administered, even in our country, by the party's district chief.

In the political and territorial organization there exists the District of Uruguay, which forms a part of the overseas *Gau*. Within this district there are the subparty of Montevideo and "support points" (*Stützpunkten*) at Peñarol, Rincón de Bonete and Paysandú. Within these organizations are the minor groups of cells and blocs.

The political leaders—the district Führer, subparty chiefs and support-point leaders—who are considered to possess sovereign power over party members, are appointed by E. W. Bohle, head of the party's foreign organization in Germany.

The party carries out in our country an intense campaign of propaganda by word of mouth, by radio, and in the German and local press, with an office specially charged with watching and influencing local newspapers.

There exists a plan to attack this country, drawn up by an ardent propagandist of the National Socialist movement. Preliminary hearings have produced at least semiconclusive evidence that this plan was discussed and approved.

The plan for the attack against Uruguay contains measures tending to insure the functioning of our country as a German agricultural colony, the plan being similar in this respect to those put into effect by the Germans in their recent conquests.

In our country there are united in one person the duties of Führer for the District of Uruguay and those of attaché of the German Legation.—New York *Times*, Sept. 23, 1940.

The Nazis are making the most strenuous efforts to defend their prisoners. One of the Wilhelmstrasse's best legal experts, Paul Barandon, is the chief defense counsel. He had been German consul general in Chile, and he is assisted by a lawyer sent especially from the Reich. The Chilean government had previously declared Barandon *persona non grata*, on the ground that he helped German sailors from the *Graf Spee* to escape the country, by giving them false passports. The trial—up to midsummer 1941—has not yet taken place. The Germans are still being held.

Uruguay, Hemisphere, and Bases

In June 1940 two United States officers came to Montevideo, and presented a long secret questionnaire to the Uruguayan government. It stated that the United States government was beginning conversations with the other American governments to examine local defense problems, and to outline a basis of cooperation for continental defense in case the hemisphere was attacked. It asked Uruguay what help it might need in case of aggression by a non-American power or combination of powers, what the Uruguayan government could do to defend itself, and what facilities Uruguay would be prepared to put at the disposal of the United States in the event of emergency.

Similar questionnaires were presented—though not by the same officers—to other countries; Uruguay was the first country to be approached, and the first to reply. A special military commission of the government gave its answer to the United States on June 22, 1940, and negotiations of a sort have been going on ever since. The first answer accepted the United States point of view fully, on the understanding that any facilities would not be the exclusive property of any one country, but should be for the use of the hemisphere as a whole. It stated that the defense personnel of new bases should be provided by the country where they are located, and that munitions and so on (to be provided presumably by the United States) should not cost more than the reasonable capacity of the local country to pay. Otherwise, Uruguay pointed out, Fifth Columnists would have a pretext for internal trouble-making.

News of these conversations—but not all the details—leaked out in the autumn, and caused tremendous excitement. As I have mentioned, the Herrerista opposition used the question as a stick to beat the government with; Herrera insisted on airing it in parliament, and got the senate to adopt a strong anti-base resolution. Meantime Argentina rose angrily, fearing that a United States base in Montevideo would cut off the Plata. But on November 27, 1940, the Uruguayan chamber approved the discussions and authorized the government to go ahead, provided that the new bases will remain under Uruguayan sovereignty. After this the opposition dwindled, and then—even among Herreristas—died away. Most Uruguayans approve the base idea, not merely out of friendship for the United States, but because closer cooperation serves to make their country less dependent on the Argentine.

Parenthesis on the Falange: On November 17, 1940, the Madrid newspaper *Arriba* said that if Uruguay ceded bases to the United States, it would be "an act of suicide," as if the country were "throwing itself into an abyss." On November 19, the rector of the University of Madrid sent telegrams to universities all over Latin America, asking "the intellectuals of our America not to consent, either in spirit or body, that any foreign power should install itself in the body of *Hispanidad*." There were many other protests, some in violent and scurrilous language. One accused Uruguay of selling itself to the United States for "30,000 pieces of silver" under intimidation by American airpower.

The present situation is that the United States would like to see the airport of Carrasco, eleven miles from Montevideo, improved so that big bombers may land there easily. We hope also for dock and repair facilities elsewhere, as well as possible installations at Garité, an island three miles off Punta del Este which is not fortified but which has a good natural harbor.

On June 7, 1941, President Baldomir made it clear that cooperation between the United States and Uruguay is well advanced. He said, "The granting of base facilities will not compromise the rights and sovereignty of Uruguay and will not involve the cession of territory. The bases would simply be points in support of our defense. Access to the bases will be granted to friendly countries in the event of aggressions against the continent." (New York *Times*, June 8, 1941.)

Later in 1941, the Uruguayan government took the initiative (which was warmly welcomed in Washington) in a step of the utmost consequence. It suggested that "any American nation engaging in a defensive war against a non-hemisphere power should be treated as a nonbelligerent by the other American republics." This means, in simple language, that each republic would automatically allow all the others complete use of its harbors and facilities, which would go a long way toward solving the base problem.[3] In 1917 Uruguay opened its harbors freely to American warships. With its key position, it is willing to do the same thing again.

[3] At the moment of writing—September 1941—sixteen of the hemisphere states have accepted this proposal. The four which rejected it are Argentina, Colombia, Peru, and Chile.

Chapter XXIII
Getulio Vargas

~~~~~~

S ET against the enormous flamboyance of Brazil, its girth and
depth and proliferating luxuriance, is the small, sensible, smiling figure of Getulio Vargas. If Brazil is a gigantic tapestry, embroidered with every variety of line and mood and blazing color, Vargas is a kind of human spotlight, darting neatly from one edge to the other, inspecting and pondering the fabric. If Brazil is a monstrous combination of desolate plateau and strategic coastline and steaming jungle, with its squalor reeking on the surface, its reservoirs of wealth largely unexplored, Vargas is a kind of human microphone, listening to every whisper.

Brazil is a demi-continent, larger than the continental United States. Vargas is a man. He is not a superman. But for ten years he has not merely watched and listened and inspected but has run Brazil's 3,275,510 square miles and 43,246,931 people as a one-man show. His first ten years, the *Década Getuliana*, have just concluded. Able, friendly, slippery, he means as much to Brazil— in his own Brazilian way—as Hitler means to Germany or Churchill to Great Britain. He is easily the most important political figure in Latin America, and his interest to the United States— which he intends vaguely to visit one of these days—is profound.

Before pinning Getulio Vargas, like some phosphorescent bee, to the Brazilian backdrop, it is perhaps necessary to survey the backdrop itself for a paragraph or two. Historically Brazil is unique in the hemisphere, first because, as we know, its language is Portuguese, not Spanish, second because it was an Empire until as recently as 1889. Brazil has the largest unexplored jungle region in the world, fed by its mighty Amazon; it has the largest undeveloped iron-ore reserves in the world; it was for many years the world's greatest producer of rubber; it is still the world's first exporter of coffee. Of its vast coffee crop it burns about 15 per cent each year. There are at least four Brazils, and one of the great problems of the country is national integration. The Bahia region near the Atlantic bulge, which is largely negro, differs as much from the white cattle country in Rio Grande do Sul as England differs from Egypt. The industrial nexus at São Paulo is as different from remote Amazonas as Chicago is different from Addis Ababa.

Throughout its history Brazil has tended to be more friendly to the United States than any other Latin American state. The reasons are several. For one thing, Brazil subconsciously fears Argentina, and hence looks to us for protection. For another, Portuguese-speaking Brazil likes to associate itself with English-speaking North America *vis-à-vis* the rest of the hemisphere, which (tiny Haiti excepted) speaks Spanish. For another, we are far and away Brazil's best customer, and we have no competitive exports. These things are—and must be—much in Getulio Vargas' agile, clever mind.

The Brazilians are on the whole cultivated and easygoing people; they dislike bloodshed, they admire tolerance, they aspire to the more civilized virtues. Brazil is one of the few countries in Latin America—or on other continents—where people of sharply divergent political views meet amiably at dinner and discuss their differences. A luncheon party at Petrópolis may be startlingly like one in Bloomsbury. People talk about Getulio—he is almost universally called by his first name—much more freely than one would suppose; they even make jokes about him, more or less openly, and he relishes them. One story is that he can be silent in ten languages. Another is that he can take off his socks without removing his shoes.

Life Story of Getulio

Getulio Dornelles Vargas, President and dictator of Brazil (though he dislikes the appellation "dictator"), was born at São Borja, in the southern state of Rio Grande do Sul, on April 10, 1883. This is the heart of the *gaucho* (cowboy) country, where flat plains stretch endlessly to the horizon, where cattle ranches cover thousands of green-tawny miles. In those days Rio Grande do Sul was a veritable frontier, like Arizona. Getulio grew up with a lasso in his hands and a horse between his knees. His *gaucho* background has strongly marked and colored his character and habits of mind, his friendships and his political orientation. The lasso has become a kind of silken glove, and it is Brazil, not a horse, that is between his knees now, but Getulio is still a Rio Grandense, a *gaucho*, a cowboy.

He entered the army at 16, as a private, and then studied for a year at the Rio Pardo Military College, training to be an officer. Then in 1903, aged 20, he gave up military life for law. He enrolled at the University of Porto Alegre, the capital of Rio Grande do Sul, and took his degree four years later. Thus, still, he is sometimes known as "Doctor" Vargas. Inevitably he became interested in politics, and while still a student he founded an opposition newspaper, *O Debate*. The year 1909 was an important one for several reasons; he established a law practice in São Borja and became a deputy in the local legislature; then, taking time out for army matters, he fought in several local revolutions and rose to the rank of lieutenant colonel. But the world of federal politics was beckoning, though it took a long time before he reached national as distinct from provincial stature. In 1923 he was elected federal deputy for Rio Grande, that is, deputy to the national parliament that sat in Rio de Janeiro, the capital of the country. Then his rise was rapid. In 1926 he became federal Minister of Finance; in 1928 he returned to Rio Grande as governor; in 1930 he led the revolution that made him President.

For some years prior to 1930 Brazilian politics had been largely dominated by the Paulistas, that is, the group of politicians, rich industrialists and coffee *fazendeiros* (landowners) centering on São Paulo, the great manufacturing city which is the third largest in Latin America. São Paulo had been accustomed to run Brazil much as Tammany Hall ran New York, along with the near-by iron-producing state of Minas Geraes, with which it alternated in control of the presidency and the federal legislature. The cowboys

and plainsmen of Rio Grande do Sul in the south considered themselves frozen out of political life. So a group of *gauchos* led by
Oswaldo Aranha and João Alberto (at first Vargas was more or
less a secondary figure) began revolutionary work together. They
chose Vargas as a presidential candidate against the Paulista candidate in the 1930 elections, hoping thus to reach power legally.
Vargas and his backers were convinced he won these elections and
was only counted out by Paulista fraud. They decided to fight, and
on October 3, 1930, the revolution began. It lasted only twenty-one
days. The *gauchos* had an excellent military organization, and
rapidly, under Vargas, they built up a genuine popular movement. The Paulista President fled to Portugal and Getulio Vargas
succeeded him in the Cattete Palace. He has been in power ever
since.

Since that time there have been, one might say, five great crises,
five great dates, in Vargas' political career:

1932. São Paulo was restive after the events of 1930, and
threatened counter-revolution. São Paulo felt as Chicago might
feel if Illinois and the Middle West were suddenly withdrawn
from all political influence. The Vargas group decided to cripple
São Paulo, to end its strength; they appointed a succession of
interventors, like João Alberto, to boss the unruly coffee merchants. The Paulistas joined forces with some disaffected army
officers and a revolt began which became a genuine—though
minor—civil war. After three months of fighting (July-Septem-
ber, 1932), the Vargas government won, largely because of better
organization and superior military power. Since the 1932 revolt
the Paulista *political* antagonism to Vargas has largely disinte-
grated, though one group of exiles in Argentina tries to keep the
fires of opposition burning. Vargas was very shrewd in dealing
with São Paulo after the revolt. There were no executions, no
revenge. He declared a general amnesty almost at once, and even
Paulista army officers were forgiven. A good many of them
actually hold high rank in the national army today. Gradually then
Vargas acceded to the principal Paulista demand, that they should

have a civilian government. The Paulistas asked for a new national constitution, and in 1934 Vargas gave it to them.

By this time Vargas' popularity was increasing. He began to show those characteristics which have kept him in power. He refused to play favorites; he set it forth as a principle that there should be no bar between government and people; he declared himself against what the Brazilians call *politicagem*, that is intrigue for unscrupulous ends.

Another thing that helped him was resentment in the powerful state of Minas Geraes at Paulista tactics. Normally a Paulista succeeded a Minero to the presidency and vice versa. But in 1930 the Paulistas had broken the rules by attempting to keep the presidency twice in succession. So Minas Geraes joined Vargas against São Paulo.

1934. In this year Vargas "reconstitutionalized" the country. He called a constituent assembly (of his own men, of course), and, having already had four years of power, had himself elected President together with a new parliament. The assembly proceeded to write a new constitution, on strongly nationalist lines, to replace the outworn federal constitution of 1891. Vargas was now "legal."

1935. A so-called communist revolt occurred, which the Vargas government suppressed with great vigor. Minor street fighting took place, and thousands of communists and leftists were rounded up and arrested. Some of them, like the communist leader Luíz Carlos Prestes, are still in jail. Unfriendly critics of the Vargas regime say that about 1000 political prisoners are behind bars today. The government says this figure is preposterous.[1]

1937. This was a year of considerable political excitement because the 1934 constitution provided for a general election in 1937 to choose a President for 1938-42. By terms of the 1934 constitution, Vargas was forbidden to succeed himself. This is a familiar clause in Latin American constitutions, as we know, and Vargas circumvented it in the usual way. Till the last moment, he

[1] The government claims that no purely "political" prisoners exist; all are imprisoned for actual crime. See Chapter XXVI below.

declared himself out of the race; moreover, he refused to support
any of the other candidates. Nominally the government "candidate" was José Americo de Almeida, a cabinet minister, but Vargas never gave him official approval; the Paulista opposition nominated a distinguished politician, Armando de Salles Oliveira, who
is now an exile in Buenos Aires. While the two candidates were
busy electioneering, Vargas quietly worked behind the scenes, put
the country under martial law, and on November 10, 1937, made
one of the swiftest, neatest coups d'état in history. The elections
were called off. They have never yet been held. And Getulio remained in power.

But with a difference. He became dictator. When the deputies
arrived at the chamber on November 10, they found mounted
police there; they were told that the senate and chamber had been
dissolved (neither has ever met since), and that a new constitution would be promulgated that day. Vargas' men, chiefly the
Minister of Justice, Dr. Campos, had been working secretly on it
for months. There was no trouble, no bloodshed; hardly any troops
appeared on the streets. This constitution—the one now in force—
made Vargas not merely a dictator, but a dictator in perpetuity.
True, it did vaguely provide for a plebiscite to be held at some
future date, but the plebiscite has never been held, and probably
never will be.

1938. In this year Vargas squashed a revolt of the green-shirted
Integralistas, the Fascist party, just as in 1935 he had squashed
the Left. After the November coup he had abolished all political
parties, the Integralistas included—though he had made use of
this powerful Rightist organization in his previous campaigns.
The Integralistas thought with considerable reason that they had
been brutally double-crossed, and on May 10 they attempted to
rise and seize the government. What followed was a wonderful
mélange of Hollywood, Latin American atavisms, bloodshed,
cowardice, confused ineptitude, and farce.

The Integralista leaders—who were in close touch with German
Nazis—bribed guards at the Guanabara Palace and contrived to

get inside wearing bogus uniforms, in circumstances strikingly like those attending the Nazi putsch against Dollfuss in 1934. These Integralistas occupied the palace gardens, but they did not quite dare to storm the inner stairways of the building where Vargas was alone with his family and four guards. The insurrectionists had cut key telephones, which perhaps explains the somewhat puzzling delay with which the army came to the rescue. General Góes Monteiro, the chief of staff, and today the most important man in Brazil after Vargas and Aranha, could not arrive because he was surrounded in his own house. Finally the Minister of War arrived, personally, and with a detachment of troops scattered the insurgents. Meantime the Vargas family had been besieged for hours. About twenty thousand shots were fired by the Integralista mutineers. Vargas and his daughter Alzira hid behind curtains and fired back with rifles. Twelve men were killed.

More than one fabulous detail attaches to this episode. The organization of the plotters was excellent; they planned to burn the gasoline at the Pan American airport; they thought of means to keep the Rio fire department from helping Vargas (for some reason in most Latin American countries the fire brigades are super-loyal to the government). The plot failed, not merely because one of Getulio's aides managed to climb a fence and communicate with the Ministry of War, but because Brazilians are so Brazilian. All the plotters failed to do was *attack* the palace once they were inside. But Brazilians by and large have no instinct to kill or be killed or even to obey orders. One Brazilian legend is that there are two thousand laws in Brazil but no law saying that people should obey the law. Brazilians will take drastic action for love, for instance, or because someone is *simpático*, but not for money or by command.

Thousands of good Rio citizens, attracted by the ferocious noise, turned out to see the fun. Among the bystanders seriously wounded was Dom João de Bragança Orleans, descendant of the last Brazilian Emperor.

Since the failure of this Integralista plot Brazil has been very quiet politically. Getulio has mellowed, and his regime has expanded slowly, like some invisible ether, to fill all the nooks and corners.

Face to Face with Vargas

Vargas lives and works these days in two palaces in Rio de Janeiro, except when he is summering in the mountain capital, Petrópolis. His residence, the Guanabara Palace, is a government-owned building, like our White House. Formerly it was the home of Princess Isabel, daughter of the Emperor, Dom Pedro II; it was modernized in 1922 for King Albert of the Belgians when he visited Brazil. As a rule the President works at Guanabara—in a very small room—till after luncheon, reading his correspondence, going through the newspapers, and seeing his more intimate advisers. He then walks briskly for about ten minutes to a street corner, where his automobile picks him up and takes him to his official seat of business, the Cattete Palace, about 1½ miles from Guanabara. This palace, surrounded by a palm-studded courtyard, heavily decorated in the rococo manner, was formerly the residence of a rich coffee planter, Baron de Novo Friburgo. It is now owned by the Brazilian state. The President ascends in an elevator lined with mirrors and decorated in bright gold and cerulean blue. The reception room is crowded with officers in somewhat sloppy white uniforms. On the wall is an enlarged snapshot of Vargas in careless civilian clothes receiving ex-President Justo of Argentina in full uniform. Vargas is jovial and Justo is very chesty.

Here in the enormous baroque cabinet room Vargas does his formal work. He very seldom holds full cabinet meetings; instead he has invented an ingenious system whereby he sees his subordinates in pairs, two a day. On Mondays come the Ministers of Justice and Education; Tuesday is for Foreign Affairs and Agriculture; Wednesday, Finance and Labor; Thursday, Army, Navy and Propaganda; Friday, Communications. The President listens carefully. He does not talk much. He returns to Guanabara for dinner, which is almost invariably with his family; he rests for 15 minutes, and then works again till midnight or beyond. His working day is usually a full fourteen to sixteen hours. At night he signs papers and gives orders. He reads everything himself, and reputedly will sign nothing without reading it.

Vargas' health is so good that few in Rio can recall the name of his doctor or remember when he has last seen one. Before going to bed, he relaxes by reading, and then sleeps like a stone. He has never had insomnia in his life. For amusement he rides whenever he has the opportunity, and occasionally sees new American movies. Also he plays golf. As a rule he plays every Saturday, usually with his friend Valentim Bouças, the Brazilian representative of International Business Machines. He likes to play nine holes, then have lunch, then play nine holes again. The best score he ever made was 122. When newsreels showing his golf are presented in Rio, the audience rocks with laughter. When his game is finished, he sometimes naps. Vargas has no pretentiousness, and one story is that two members of his club, the Itanhanga, could not get to their lockers because the President, naked except for a towel around his middle, was sound asleep on the metal bench in the locker room.

Vargas' only other hobby is a delight in aviation. He has flown 647 hours, and has visited every state in Brazil except the Territory of Acre, behind Amazonas. His total mileage in the air is somewhere between eighty and ninety thousand. He flew for the first time in 1929, when he was governor of Rio Grande do Sul. At that time he made an agreement with his wife, whom he adores, never to fly unless she was in the same plane. But in 1931 he happened to be visiting a military aviation camp. Most of the planes had been purchased in France. Then an officer pointed out a new type of plane designed by a Brazilian. Vargas asked, "Does it fly?" The officer said, "Perhaps. Why not try it?" Vargas hopped in. The plane was too small to hold his wife too. The plane flew, and Vargas was enchanted. He promoted its designer, and has been flying ever since.

Vargas eats normally and drinks moderately. He never touches hard liquor, but he will sip wine at dinner, especially on Sunday nights when he likes to be with his whole family. These evenings are often hilarious. His favorite beverage is *mate*, a non-alcoholic brew made from a local herb; it tastes like mild gingerbeer, and may be served hot or cold. He smokes cigarettes only rarely; what he likes are long, delicate, Brazilian cigars from Bahia.

His attitude toward money is that he is not particularly interested in it. He owns no property except the ranch at São Borja that was—and is—his family home. His salary is 20 *contos* ($1,000) per month, and he has an allowance for entertainment that is accounted for strictly. In the current budget, the total sum allotted the presidency (not the President) is 1.995:000$000 *milreis* (do not gasp; Brazilian currency is written in a manner all its own), which is just under $100,000. Out of this come salaries for his military aides, secretaries, and servants, as well as travel expenses and the upkeep of both Rio palaces.

Vargas speaks tolerable French and Spanish. His English is rudimentary, but he can read it. His daughter Alzira, the pretty apple of his eye, skims through American books and magazines and gives him what she thinks will most interest him for bedside reading. A recent book that impressed him was Rauschning's *Voice of Destruction*—with some reason, since in it Hitler tells Rauschning of his designs on Brazil! He glances at *Life*, which comes to him airmail, every week. He has never traveled outside Brazil except for brief trips to Argentina and Uruguay, and Paraguay. The chief of state whom he most admires is Franklin D. Roosevelt.

His attitude to religion is complex. Brazil is, of course, an overwhelmingly Roman Catholic country—so much so that, for instance, divorce is still forbidden—and Vargas is too shrewd a politician ever to risk affronting the Church. He admires the Cardinal, who is one of his close friends, but his instinct is to be very tolerant in religious affairs. He seldom goes to mass, and his friends do not think that he is an ardent believer; in fact, he named his first son for Luther, something a good Catholic could hardly do. The story is, moreover, that he wanted to call his second son Calvino, but that his wife persuaded him to choose Getulio instead. In his very early days Vargas reportedly opposed the continuance of subsidies to the Catholic schools; now, however, he would not dream of doing any such thing. His constitution unites Church and State.

Getulio's family life is very happy. His wife was named Darcy Sarmanho, the daughter of a prosperous Rio Grande ranchman and neighbor. They were married when she was 16; she is about 45 now, a handsome woman who looks much younger. She takes no part in public life except to devote herself to charities. Three times a week she goes to the Ministry of Labor, and there sews for the poor. She has founded homes for derelict newsboys and orphan girls, manifestations of a social conscience hitherto little known among Brazilians.

The Vargases have five children. The eldest, Luthero, aged about 27, is a doctor of medicine who studied in Germany and married a German girl, Inga Elizabeth Anita Ten Haeff. Official circles tend to play down this German connection with the Vargas family, and to deny hotly that Dr. Luthero is pro-German. The marriage was a love match, and after a period of mild disapproval Vargas *père* and *mère* accepted it. Young Luthero is a well-mannered studious boy, practicing medicine now, holding an appointment in a hospital, and ambitious to have his own clinic.

The second son, Getulio (nicknamed Getulinho), who went to Johns Hopkins and studied to be a chemical engineer, is an intelligent and attractive youngster, rather Americanized in looks and speech, and very pro-American in attitude. Like all the Vargases he is modest and has been well brought up, so that he finds it embarrassing to ask for a job, since he is afraid people will give it to him only because he is his father's son. Recently he was called up for military service, and is serving as a rookie in Copacabana fort at a wage of 21 *milreis* ($1.05) per month. He made no effort to evade conscription or to ask for favors, as he might easily have done. A third son, Manoel, uninterested in politics, is in charge of his father's ranch at São Borja.

One of the Vargas daughters, named Jandyra—who recently presented her parents with their first grandchild, a seven-pound boy—is married to Commander Ruy da Costa Gama, one of the managers of the L.A.T.I. airline,[2] the Italian service that flies from Rome to Natal, Brazil, via Dakar in Africa. Costa Gama— who seems to link the Vargas family to Italy—is an enthusiastic aviator, and for some years was a leading pilot for Panair do Brasil, the local subsidiary of Pan American Airways. His health failed, and he was forced to give up piloting. He hoped to remain with Pan American in some office job, or else volunteer for work in Brazilian civil aviation, but the Italians began to cultivate him, and L.A.T.I. offered him an important post. Costa Gama had planned to marry Senhorita Vargas only after her father left office; he did not, he reportedly said, want people to think he was courting her merely because she was the President's daughter. Finally the wedding was set for a time after which Vargas *was* to have resigned. But the President did not resign and the marriage took place anyway. Vargas gave his daughter a trip to Italy as a wedding present, and Mussolini presented her with a motor car.

But the most important child of the Vargas family is neither Luthero nor Getulino nor Manoel nor Jandyra. The one who counts most is 24-year-old daughter Alzira (Alzirinha in the diminutive), who is probably closer to the President than any person in Brazil. About Alzirinha one may say much. She is small, dark, freckled, very good-looking, and bursting with efficient vitality. She loves to travel. She loves to dance. Also she loves to work. She was first in her class at Aldridge College, the English-

[2] As this book goes to press it is reported that Costa Gama has resigned his L.A.T.I. post.

speaking girls' school in Rio; she was also first in her class at Law School, where she took a brilliant degree. Her father not only adores her, but trusts her political judgment greatly; she is a full-fledged member of the Vargas secretariat, and works a full day as such. A few years ago she married a naval officer, one of her father's aides, Commander Ernani do Amaral Peixoto, who is now the interventor (governor) of the state of Rio de Janeiro. Alzirinha has been to North America several times, once as a guest of the Oswaldo Aranhas when Aranha was Brazilian ambassador to Washington, and again on her honeymoon. She loves the United States, and is a strong and beneficent influence on the President in regard to things American.

Vargas' father is still alive, over 90. He lives on the family estate at São Borja, and still flies occasionally to Rio to see his son. The President has three brothers. One, Spartacus, is a *fazendeiro*, and takes no part in politics; another, Colonel Benjamin Vargas, has considerable importance. He goes everywhere with the President, likes high life and night clubs (when off duty), and is a member of the official secretariat and also a kind of sublimated bodyguard.

If one should ask who are those closest to Vargas, Alzirinha and Benjamin would be near the top on any list. Others of his entourage who are important are Dr. Luis Vergara, his chief private secretary, who oddly enough is both shortsighted and hard of hearing, and Dr. Andrade Queiroz, who does much research work. The head of the military household, General Francisco Pinto, is also influential. Among Vargas' closest friends are two *gaucho* companions from early years, Oswaldo Aranha, the fabulous foreign minister, and João Alberto, who has been called both the "Schacht" and the "Knudsen" of Brazil, and who is now minister to Canada.

Sources of Power and Qualities

When one comes to sketch the sources of Getulio Vargas' power there are many to point out, some implicit in the outline of his career above. His opportunism, for instance. His slipperiness. The hard driving line of his ambition. And his great good luck.

Then one should also mention his good humor. Vargas is one of the few smiling dictators—Batista of Cuba is the only other one I can think of. Even when he is off guard, he is almost always smiling. And he is one of the few dictators nicknamed by their own people. One nickname is Gêgê. Another is Xuxu, which means a proliferating and tasteless Brazilian weed.

It is difficult for most people to dislike the chubby Vargas, if only because he is himself so friendly. He likes human nature, which has been good to him, and he likes people. He seldom disagrees with anyone. He may delay or equivocate, but he almost never says an outright No. He has very few enemies except on extreme Left and Right, and he seldom bears grudges. No dictator is so little vengeful.

Once proposals were submitted for a new set of coins. Getulio's portrait was on one side of the series, and the state interventor's on the other. Vargas suggested, "Let us name the coins for Victor Hugo." His advisers looked puzzled. Vargas proceeded, "*The Man Who Laughs* is on one side, and *Les Misérables* on the other."

By a decree not too strictly enforced, most places of business in Brazil are supposed to contain Getulio's picture. So a variety of legends has sprung up. One describes the backward peasant who visits all the pubs and cafés of Rio and asks, "Who is the smiling man who owns all these joints?"

Another is a variant of a well-known European story. Mussolini goes to heaven and identifies himself. St. Peter reports his presence to the Almighty. The Almighty says, "I never heard of him. Throw him out." Hitler arrives and the same thing happens. Then Vargas submits himself to the Gates of Heaven. The same thing is about to occur when St. Peter protests to God and says, "You have to let Vargas in, because he's the fellow whose picture is on Your wall."

But, easygoing as he seems to be, Vargas can be cold as snow.

In the early days he consolidated his position by ignoring friends whose usefulness he knew to be outlived. He knows what he wants; he is out to get it, by cold means if warm means fail. He is utterly without nerves. Once he had a serious automobile accident in which one friend was killed and another mangled. When the doctor arrived he checked to see that Vargas was uninjured and found him, a few moments after the crash, with pulse absolutely normal.

Vargas has great common and political sense, which is another source of his power. Shrewd, clever, he never goes into action until he is sure all the cards are up his sleeve. He gives out nicely noosed lengths of rope when he wishes subordinates to hang themselves; he loves to play off rivals against each other. He has not held his promised plebiscite so far because it is a wonderful weapon to hold in reserve in the event of serious domestic trouble, say with the army.

An example of his tactics is the following. He opposes the appointment of a certain politician to a provincial post. Nevertheless he gives the man the job because the army wants him there. Vargas contrives it that the man gets into a terrible mess. He then goes to the Minister of War and General Góes Monteiro and appeals to them to get *him*, Vargas, out of trouble because their man is not doing his job properly.

He is intensely intuitive. One close friend compared him to those lizards which are endowed with protective coloration. Vargas melts into any landscape. Another friend said that he was like a boat without a motor. He sails with the wind, and yet always manages to reach shore. He is not a man of profound original ideas or overwhelming mental capacity or moral grandeur. He loves to compromise. He loves to improvise.

Another source of power is his undoubted courage, which he is never flamboyant about. (There is, indeed, little flamboyance in his nature.) In 1935 he personally led his troops; in 1938 he fired back at the Integralistas, though he might easily have hidden. He walks quite freely on the Rio streets; he has guards, but they are not ostentatious. He is one of the few dictators who never uses an armor-plated car or other such contrivance.

Then, again, there is his industry, a quality almost indispensable to a dictator. He reads most of his mail himself, and answers most letters the day they are received. He writes his own speeches in longhand. His sense of detail is highly marked, and his secretaries say that he never forgets anything. He remembers names and faces of people twenty-five years back.

Another factor is complete personal honesty. He has bossed Brazil for more than ten years, but no one has ever whispered any charge of graft or corruption. No scandal has ever touched him or any member of his family, financial or otherwise.

Again, seemingly a small point, there is his ability to keep his mouth shut—this too among people delightfully notorious for tongue wagging. Vargas talks little. His technique in handling a problem is first to inform himself of the details, then to get technical advice, then to draw his own conclusions, finally to announce a *fait accompli*. He is never in a hurry. He listens to everybody, but no one knows what he himself is thinking. His speeches, which are never stage-managed in advance, are almost always surprises. He is highly reserved in confidences. He has, in short, great sense of reticence, and great fidelity to his own ideas.

In 1930 when he was governor of Rio Grande do Sul, he was conferring one afternoon with his Minister of Interior. Shots were heard outside. The Minister looked up startled and asked what they meant. Vargas chuckled and said, "It is the revolution we have just made." The Minister had heard nothing of it, nor had Vargas' wife.

Another detail is his quite genuine modesty and sense of tolerance and proportion. Once he appointed as minister of justice (!) a man who had been implicated in a plot to murder him. He is almost completely unassuming; he loathes pomp, ceremony, display. He hates to wear formal clothes, and it is almost impossible to get him even into a dinner jacket.

Finally, he is an extremely typical Brazilian, with a profound knowledge of his own people, their merits and defects. In his own peculiar person he epitomizes the national character, which is probably his greatest source of power.

Achievements and Succession

Partisans of Getulio Vargas will tell you that he has done more for Brazil in ten years than any succession of rulers did in a hundred. Enemies of Vargas admit some of his concrete accomplishments, which are indeed considerable. But they say that he has killed democracy and civil liberties in Brazil, that he has destroyed its traditional freedom. To which Vargas adherents reply, (1) that Brazil was certainly not a "democracy" under the Paulista governments that preceded him, (2) that free elections and a free press are no criterion of democracy in Latin America, since elections and press may so easily be purchased, (3) that Brazil is governed with extreme tolerance even though it is a dictatorship (for instance, the death penalty has never once been applied), and (4) that if Vargas were to be overthrown a period of ruthless army control or political chaos would follow.

Social and economic reform under Vargas has been distinct, and the Ministry of Propaganda gives the visitor impressive statistics to prove it. The government has abolished trade unions, but its record in social legislation is probably the most advanced in Latin America, except for Mexico and Uruguay. Ministries of labor, commerce, education, and public health were created for the first time. One massive project, partly accomplished, is the drainage of the Fluminense marches near Rio, which will reclaim many thousands of square kilometers of land and give sustenance to perhaps two million people. Mussolini's similar work of draining the Pontine marches is tiddlywinks by comparison.

The Vargas government has staked 77,471 kilometers of hitherto undefined frontier. It raised the number of consumer's cooperatives from 57 in 1930 to 1,036 in 1940. It reduced the external debt for the first time in 100 years. It promoted the growth of wheat from zero in 1930 to 210,000 tons in 1939. It increased industrial production by 148.5 per cent in ten years, a record surpassed only by the U.S.S.R. It raised the number of students in secondary schools from 60,000 in 1930 to 300,000 in 1940—still a pitiably small figure, of course, for a country of 43,000,000 people. It lifted the number of primary schools from 27,000 to 42,103. It claims to have reduced illiteracy from 79 to 43 per cent, but it is difficult to accept this figure without some question. It increased railway mileage by 10 per cent, and lifted the number of airports from 31 to 512 in ten years. It doubled road mileage and built 56 new radio stations. It has established national parks, drought control, and a public health system.

But the thing that Vargas and his men are proudest of goes beyond this. The regime likes to think that its greatest achievement is in the realm of political unification and stability. Vargas struck at the entrenched rights of the separate states; he burned all the state flags in a public ceremony; he reduced drastically the interstate tariffs (which had grievously hurt the internal economy of the country), and abolished the independent state judiciaries; he is running Brazil with federally appointed interventors, on strictly national principles. He wiped out *Caudilhismo*, that is guerilla banditry by frontier chieftains. He has worked above all to overcome political indifference, to abolish separatism and provincialism, to give the country a true national sense, to give it—his supreme ambition—development, unity, and order.

One curious point is that, uniquely among dictators, Vargas never attempted to build up a political party of his own. The state is called the *Estado Novo*—this derives from Portugal—but no parties exist, not even a government party. There are no shirts in Brazil, no badges, no insignia, no salutes. Several reasons explain this. For one thing, the party system has never flourished in Brazil. For another, Vargas is not particularly interested in the *forms* of political organization. He likes to make politics by playing one group against another, and he thinks creation of a single party might split the country instead of unifying it. Again, the army might frown on a totalitarian party. Finally, there is no real need for one, since almost everyone of consequence is on the Vargas side.

Vargas has made at least tentative arrangements for his succession in the event of his death in office. By a recent decree the presidency is to pass to the president of the Supreme Court, Justice Eduardo Espinola. Until a short time ago the president of the court was chosen by the other justices. In November 1940 Vargas assumed the right to make this appointment himself and saw to it that one of his close friends got the post.

Seeing Vargas Plain

I met Vargas twice. The first time João Alberto brought me to the palace informally. The President had just become a grandfather, and was beaming with pleasure. Then a few days later Lourival Fontes, the propaganda director, drove me to Petrópolis where Vargas had moved for the summer months. The road, one of the loveliest in the world, mounts swiftly to the burnished gardens of the mountain capital.

We had luncheon with Commander Peixoto and his wife, Vargas' daughter Alzira; we loafed in the casino and played roulette for 5¢ stakes; then late in the afternoon I went to the Rio Negro palace. Here the president received me. He sat at the end of a long table, smoked a cigar deliberately, laughed a good deal, and asked more questions than he answered. His daughter made the business of interpreting a delight.

The main thing that Vargas said was that if the United States declares war on Germany, Brazil will co-operate with us in any way possible. He said, "Brazil is a peace-loving nation. Brazil has no taste for foreign wars. Brazil does not intervene in the affairs of Europe. But if the United States goes to war with Germany,

Brazil will stand solidly with the United States in all matters of hemisphere solidarity and defense."

The President was clearly aware of what dangers Brazil might face if Germany should win the war and if the British fleet should disappear; he mentioned how urgently necessary it was that all the Americas should work together.

Chapter XXIV
Behold Brazil

~~~~~~

B RAZIL, which is the fourth largest nation in the world, covers almost half the total area of South America; its frontiers touch every country on the continent except Ecuador and Chile, and it has a variety and diversity of interest unmatched by any other hemisphere republic. It is prodigious, it is multiform, it is unique.

The basic struggle in Brazil is, as in Panama and the Andean states, that of Man versus Nature. The rivalries, the tussles for power, between Vargas and the Paulistas, between Aranha and Góes Monteiro, between industrialists and coffee planters, seem childishly petty by comparison. What counts in Brazil is something as elemental as the tides sweeping the ocean off the great beaches, or the Amazon ineluctably marching 3,900 grayish-green miles to the sea—where, in its delta, resting casually like a pebble, is an island as big as Denmark. Pan American Airways, by grit and skillful engineering, has recently carved an airport out of the steppe-land at Barreiras, so that you may fly comfortably over the bulge of Brazil, from Rio to Belém (Pará) in nine hours. Should that plane ever have a forced landing near Barreiras, the calculation is that a rescue party would take about eight *weeks* to reach it. Yet the region is not even jungle; a plane lost in the Amazonas jungle might well *never* be found. Barreiras looks like Montana or Wyoming, a buff-and-sienna upland patched with short green brush and crooked ravines. For hundred-mile after hundred-mile, it rolls under you unchanged. And for hour after hour of flight, you see no house, no telephone pole, no road, no smallest patch of cultivation, no living human being.

In Brazil the untamed wilderness seeps into the cities, it oozes into the suburbs, it proliferates into the gardens, it crawls into your back yard. Innocently enough I told friends in Rio de Janeiro—sitting at a café as urban, metropolitan, and sophisticated as the Stork Club—that I hoped to see some jungle before I left Brazil. Ten minutes away by taxi I was seeing it.

Overwhelmingly the great problem of Brazil is to harness nature. It is to build roads, tame rivers, establish communications, develop remote regions, and thus begin to tap the country's inordinate, illimitable fountains of hidden wealth. In one part of Brazil or other almost every known crop will grow. It contains almost every known mineral, including some of the greatest strategic importance. Brazil could hold nine hundred *million* people if developed, experts say.

Above all, consider communications. Rio de Janeiro and São Paulo, each a city of over a million, are about 250 miles apart; the train connecting them takes eleven hours; the trip by road is harrowing. It takes a week for a newspaper to get from Rio to Natal. Freight rates are exorbitant. In pre-war days, it was cheaper to ship goods from Porto Alegre to Recife via Hamburg (in Germany!) than direct.

But the confrontation of man versus nature is only one of several struggles in Brazil. Think of the confrontation between races, between black and white. Think of that between the European civilization of the narrow coastal strip and the primitive Amazon Indians of the remote interior. Or the confrontation between the growing volume of industrial production and the older economy based on export of raw materials. Or that between rich and poor. Brazil is replete with social, economic, and national problems of the most staggering—and stimulating—difficulty.

A word on Brazilian history. The country was discovered in 1500 by its own Portuguese Columbus, by name Pedro Alvares Cabral. Colonization began a few years later, and centered on the port of Bahia, which—nowadays predominantly a Negro town— I have heard Brazilians call their "nucleal cell." The Indians along the coast were backward, with no culture like that of Aztecs or

Incas; they were too feeble for hard labor, and the Portuguese began to bring in Negro slaves. The colonists entrenched themselves along the coast, founded settlements like Rio de Janeiro (which was settled partly by French Protestant missionaries), and turned their backs on the opaque green wilderness of the interior. Attempts to push inside did not come till later. In North America our frontiersmen faced westward from the beginning. In Brazil (as in Argentina) the orientation stayed toward Europe.

In 1808 came a cardinal event. Napoleon invaded Portugal, and its ruler, Dom João, fled forthwith to Brazil. Nothing like this ever happened in the Spanish colonies. Brazil not only remained part of an empire, under a king; it assumed leadership over the empire, replacing the mother country. In 1821, when the Napoleonic wars were safely over, Dom João returned to Lisbon, but his son Dom Pedro remained in Brazil as regent. Then the Brazilians declared themselves independent and shook off Portuguese rule; Dom Pedro became Emperor Pedro I. Brazil, uniquely in the hemisphere, acquired a court, imperial paraphernalia, and the like. For years it was far richer and more impressive than the mother court in Lisbon.

During the nineteenth century three issues were dominant, (1) immigration, (2) slavery, (3) republicanism versus monarchy. European immigrants—mostly Portuguese, Italian, and German—poured into the country as they poured into Argentina. The Italians made São Paulo their "capital"; the Germans clustered in the southern cattle districts. There were some five million black slaves in the country, and this phenomenon produced the same kind of struggle that had occurred earlier in the United States; slavery was abolished in Brazil in 1888. A revolution (1889) followed emancipation almost at once, and the empire was liquidated. Pedro II—who had ruled with great decency and moderation for forty-eight years—was dethroned, and the country became a republic, which it has been ever since.

One odd point: the Brazilians decided many years ago to build

a Federal District like Washington, D. C. This was prompted
partly by the example of the United States, partly out of fear
that Rio was too exposed to European invasion. But the Federal
District—which is deep in the interior state of Goiaz—still exists
only on the maps. Nothing is there today, not even a boundary
stone.

The constitution (1891) that governed Brazil until Vargas
was a strongly federalist document, patterned closely on that of
the United States. Its well-meaning authors were much under
the influence of Comte and the philosophy of positivism; it was
unique in the history of Latin America in that it did not mention
God.

The Amiable Brazilians

Brazilians are happy people. This generalization is of the utmost importance. They are also infinitely charming people.

In Brazil the garbage collector sends you a Christmas card;
the mailman may, if bored with work, casually toss your letters
into the sea; it can easily take twenty years to settle a lawsuit;
divorce is illegal and few people worry much about who is or isn't
married; the colloquial phrase for being a little drunk is "out in
the rain." You may telephone your hotel—as a mild joke—and
ask if you yourself are staying there; like as not the answer will
be that it never heard of you. The ministry of propaganda reserves to itself one hour on the radio every evening; no one
dreams of listening and the period is laughingly called the "hour
of silence." It is considered bad form in the extreme to get
drowned in the crashing breakers directly in front of your hotel,
which embarrasses the management; a few hundred yards away it
is quite all right.

Brazilians strikingly resemble the Chinese in some respects
(just as many Argentines so curiously resemble the Japanese),
though they are much milder people. They are apt to be slipshod
about engagements, and they arrive, at last, with fabulously
interesting excuses for being late. They are tolerant, cultivated,

intensely *simpáticos*, and disorderly. Street traffic is anarchic (though not so anarchic as in Buenos Aires); and no one adores anything quite so much as a really gruesome automobile accident. Brazilians, like Chinese, hate to be hurried; their tempo is deliberate; they love good food, good drink, good talk; you can win them with a smile. Like Chinese, they pay comparatively little attention to the color line; like Chinese, they enjoy dilettantism. Almost all the bright young men—as in pre-Japanese Shanghai—keep a government job with one hand, and write poems, edit magazines, or play with sculpture with the other.

What other city but Rio de Janeiro could support such an institution as the annual carnival, when all work stops absolutely for three days, when almost the entire population dances the *Samba* on the black-and-white[1] tessellated sidewalks, when no one sleeps, few get drunk, everybody flirts, no one fights, and everyone has a superlatively carefree time?

Almost everyone in Rio knows everyone else, and it seems that almost everyone—in the upper classes at least—is related. The shortage of surnames is acute—Silva, Cunha, Oliveira, Guimarães, Almeida, Gonçalves are among the common ones— and the telephone book lists people by their *first* as well as their last names! (The telephone girls chuckle banteringly, by the way, when the visitor does not know Portuguese.) No one knows who anybody's grandfather is, and no one asks or cares. Many people simply adopt any name they happen to like.

Never have I known folk more friendly or hospitable. I do not mean merely the aristocrats of Rio. Drive out into the country in Minas Geraes. Stop at any farmer's hut. He will probably ask you to lunch.

I hope my Brazilian friends will not mind, but two jokes about one aspect of the national character enchanted me. Up in Bahia a peasant is reclining happily in a grave. A friend asks him why he is lying there. He replies, "Oh, I'm starving to death, that's all." The friend says, "Get up; I'll give you some

[1] Which are so symbolical of the mixed races of the country.

beans." The peasant looks at him with some faint shade of interest. The friend says, "But you'll have to cook them yourself."
Whereupon the peasant sinks back into the grave again.

The other story describes a farmer in the rich uplands of São
Paulo. But he has no crops. A visitor asks him, "Don't you grow
anything here?" The farmer replies stolidly, "Nothing." The
visitor gazes about and says, "Do you mean to say that if you
planted coffee here, it wouldn't grow?" The farmer says, "Oh,
if you bothered to plant it, of course it would."

No Color Line, More or Less

In theory at least Brazil, which has been justly called the greatest melting pot in the world, has no color line. There are no
political or legal discriminations against Negroes or mulattoes;
even social discrimination is comparatively rare. Anyone who
visits the Copacabana beach any day may see white children
playing with black and brown, with parents of assorted colors
looking on. One President of the country, Nilo Peçanha, was a
dark mulatto; there have been a good many fairly eminent Negro
or mulatto scientists, politicians, and men of affairs.

On the other hand, Brazil is certainly no paradise for the black
man. The Negroes are, by and large, the poorest members of the
population; they do the least pleasant kinds of work; they are
the exploited class, especially in the north. And people in Rio
tell me that a tendency *toward* discrimination has become discernible lately. One thing that caused this was American movies,
with their sharp intimation of the color line. Another is Nazi
propaganda. Incidentally, Brazilian newspapers never print news
of lynchings in the United States, or anything else that might
tend to increase race prejudice.

Those comparatively few Brazilians who are of Indian ancestry
are, as a rule, proud of it. They romanticize their origins and
have what might be called a Pocahontas complex. A famous
Cardinal—the first ever appointed in Latin America—was

descended from an Indian princess, and translated his name, Arcoverde, from an Indian word.

Figures are hard to get. But a semi-official estimate (1922) is that Brazil is 51 per cent white, 14 per cent Negro, 22 per cent mulatto, 11 per cent *mestiço*, and 2 per cent Indian.

Foreign Minister Dr. Aranha

Oswaldo Aranha (pronounced Aranya), the Brazilian Foreign Minister, is one of the great Americans. He is bright-minded, audacious, bland, acquisitive, candid. There is a strong streak of the D'Artagnan in him, as there is in so many Brazilians. I refer not merely to his dash, but to his incredibly winning charm.

Dr. Aranha loves to talk, and his conversation is the best I heard in South America. In the first hour I had with him, the subjects he mentioned included:

The effect of salt on the human body.
Literary dedications.
The state of New York.
Whether Hitler's mind is exclusively political.
A joke about Mussolini.
An anecdote concerning Morris Ernst, the New York lawyer.
What Vargas told Emil Ludwig.
The role of personality in politics.
The tendency of Spaniards to go to extremes, in contrast to the mildness of Portuguese.
Taxation.
The projected federal capital.
The Bragança family.

The Aranha family—it is one of the great Brazilian clans—was Paulista originally, but Oswaldo was born in the *gaucho* country of Rio Grande. The date was 1894. He was the son of a prosperous ranchman, Euclydes Egydio de Souza Aranha, and Luisa de Freitas-Valle Aranha; his mother, in her eighties, is a marvelous old woman who still dominates the family. The story is that, up to a few years ago, she would drop in casually to see

President Vargas in Rio, and berate him soundly if he were not treating her darling Oswaldo well.

Aranha started out to be a military man, and studied three years in the Military Academy. Then he went to Paris—for some years at the École des Hautes Études Sociales—and returned to Brazil to take up law. In 1926 he got his first political job—assistant chief of police in Porto Alegre—and subsequently became a deputy and then a cabinet minister in the Rio Grande state government. He was one of the leaders of the Vargas revolution in 1930. In fact he was more prominent than Vargas at first; he gave way to him generously when it seemed that the compact Getulio would be a better national leader.

Before this Aranha had had some bold and adventurous days. He fought in local revolutionary squabbles in both 1923 and 1926. He was wounded at the battle of Ibyrapuitan, and again— so seriously that he almost lost a leg—at Herval. Once I asked him what had been the most important element in shaping his political life. He answered, "My career was made in bed." He meant that he had spent long months in hospital recuperating from his wounds, and had thus found time for study, reflection, and integration of his ideas.

Since 1930 Aranha has been Vargas' closest friend and collaborator; he is called both the "front and back" door to the President. He became Minister of Justice in Getulio's first government; he wanted to set up a real revolutionary tribunal à la France, but he was dissuaded largely—so the story goes—because everyone he wanted to put up for summary trial had relatives in the new government. In 1931 he became Minister of Finance. He knew nothing whatever about finance; he learned quickly. In 1934 Vargas sent him to Washington as ambassador to the United States—possibly because he was getting too important— and four years later he returned home to become Foreign Minister, which he has been ever since.

Aranha's career in the United States was spectacular. He was probably the most popular Latin American ambassador who ever lived in Washington. He had an enormous salary—$50,000 per year—and he entertained with lavish cleverness and generosity. Also he worked hard. He did not know one word of English when he arrived; he learned it about as fast as any human being ever has. He knows the United States extremely well, and is deeply fond of it. His years in Washington were immensely beneficial in broadening him. The chief *political* source of his power in Brazil today is his closeness to the United States; he is the essential link between his own country and North America.

On the night of the American elections in November 1940 Aranha had a party, so that his friends could hear the election returns. His four beautifully brought up children have all been educated in the United States. They were almost as devoted Roosevelt partisans as their father. Whenever a state came in for F.D.R., they shouted, "We're winning, Daddy."

Aranha is very handsome: tall, supple, graceful, with a mane of graying hair. It is hard to tell the color of his luminous eyes; in some lights they seem hazel, in others gray. He makes anyone in the room feel that he is a friend for life. One of his great qualities is that he is always faithful to his friends. He neither smokes nor drinks. He is one of those lucky people who can get along on four hours' sleep a night. His sense of his own worth is considerable, and his ambition great.

He works in the historic room at the Itamaraty Palace (Foreign Office) where one of his predecessors, Rio Branco,[2] lived and died. The four walls are frescoed with the legend, IN THIS ROOM, WHICH WAS, FOR MANY YEARS, HIS WORKROOM, DIED, ON FEBRUARY 10, 1912, THE GREAT MINISTER OF FOREIGN AFFAIRS OF THE UNITED STATES OF BRAZIL, JOSÉ MARIA DA SILVA PARANHOS, BARON RIO BRANCO. Aranha likes to show it to visitors, wrinkle his nose, and say that there are too many commas.

In Washington a beautiful but somewhat ignorant lady once approached Aranha and said, "Mr. Ambassador, what does your

[2] Branco, not Blanco. In Portuguese "r's" always appear when you expect "l's," just as "m's" appear instead of "n's."

country produce?" He bowed gently and replied, "Diamonds and orchids, madame, for creatures as lovely as yourself."

Brazilian Key to Hemisphere Defense

How does the Vargas government stand in regard to the United States and hemisphere defense? The answer is that Brazil, the country, is overwhelmingly pro-American; Vargas the man is certainly *not* pro-German. But there are strong pro-German influences, as we shall see.

All of Vargas' personal instincts and sympathies—to say nothing of those of Aranha—are pro-United States. This is partly because the United States is the power that can help Brazil most. But like every country Brazil must safeguard its own self-interest; these are dangerous times and it must watch both ways. If Germany should win the war outrightly and overtly, the pressure on Vargas to pro-Germanism would be enormous. If, on the other hand, Great Britain—with United States help—wins the war, Brazil is safe. What Brazil hopes for most is a strong lead from Washington; if the United States should declare war on Germany, it would almost certainly follow at once.

On June 11, 1940, as France was collapsing, Vargas spoke abruptly. He said, "We and all humanity are passing through a historical moment of great repercussions . . . We feel that the old systems have entered into decline. It is not however the end of civilization as the pessimists and die-hard conservatives claim, but the tumultuous and fruitful beginning of a new era . . . Balanced economy no longer has room for a monopoly by privileged classes of the comforts and benefits of civilization . . . For this reason the state should assume the obligation of organizing all productive forces in order to provide the people with everything necessary for collective aggrandisement. *The era of improvident liberalism, sterile demagoguery and useless individualism has passed.* There is no longer room for regimes founded on privilege and class distinction. *Vigorous peoples fit for life must follow the route of their aspirations.*" (Italics mine.)

This speech created much excitement, not least in the United States. One explanation for it is that Vargas thought that the Germans were going to win the war hands down that summer, and was preparing himself for the good graces of the victor. But the Brazilian Ministry of Propaganda promptly issued a statement amplifying the speech, affirming that it presaged no change in Brazilian foreign policy, and promising that Brazil would continue to adhere to the principles of hemisphere solidarity. And on June 16 Vargas added that "Brazil will not fail President Roosevelt in complete loyalty."

As to the American attitude to Vargas and Brazil, it is often asked how we in the United States, standing above all for the principles of political liberty and democracy in the Western Hemisphere, can countenance close friendship with a Brazil that is frankly a dictatorship. There are two answers. The first is that although Brazil is technically a dictatorship it is a benevolent dictatorship. It is a *personal* government, not an officially totalitarian government. There is very little sense of political pressure in Brazil; if you didn't know it was a dictatorship, you would probably never guess it. The second answer involves the kind of decision that realistic politicians must face. We may not like the fact that the country is a dictatorship, but a strong, stable, friendly Brazil is much more important to us than domestic civil liberties there. We play with Vargas because we must.

Now to another point. It is that Brazil is far and away the most important country in South America as regards hemisphere defense. Strategically it is the key to everything.

From Dakar, on the western hump of Africa, it is only some 1,600 nautical miles—say six or seven hours' flight for a fast modern bomber—to Natal on the Atlantic bulge of Brazil. But from New York to Natal is about 3,600 miles; from New York to Rio de Janeiro is 4,770 miles. Europe, in a word, is much closer to Brazil than we are. If Vichy France should give Dakar to Germany, or if Germany should take it otherwise, or if Germany should win the Battle of the Atlantic and gain control of the South Atlantic, then Brazil becomes sharply vulnerable. If the British fleet should be lost before a great American fleet was ready to take its place, the Atlantic barrier between Europe and the Americas would largely disappear. It would become, instead, a passageway for Germany. It would become a channel that Germany could traverse with ease.

A bridge is useless unless it is open at both ends. The best way to close the Dakar-Natal bridge is to make Natal itself an impregnable hemisphere base. Dakar would not be easy to take or defend. But Dakar loses much value if Natal, *the other end of the bridge,* is secured firmly in American hands.

I am speaking somewhat loosely. Recife (often called Pernambuco), which is about 95 miles from Natal, would be a better base than Natal, since it has a deeper harbor, more wharfage, and better communications and mechanical facilities. Belém (Pará) should also be an important base; Pan American Airways is at work now improving and enlarging its landing fields.

Bad communications are the chief defense problem of Brazil. The ports on the bulge—Natal, Recife, Bahia—are only primitively connected by land; there is no communication with Rio except by sea.[3] If the country were better developed, if communications were more adequate, a wonderful air base might be built in the center of Brazil, somewhere near Canudos. It would be more or less equidistant from all parts of Brazil and indeed from most of the continent as a whole; substantial airpower there could dominate all South America. But to build such a base would take years upon years, and cost untold millions; up-river bases on the Amazon might be more practicable. The Amazon is, as everyone knows, navigable for big ocean steamships all the way to Manáos, 930 miles from the sea, and an army based on it would be absolutely secure on both flanks. Nothing but unexplored jungle and desert exist on either side.

[3] For all practical purposes at least. Supplies *could* reach the bulge from Rio by railway to Pirapora, then by boat down the San Francisco River to Joãzeiro, then by railway again to Bahia, then by rail and road—a bad one—to Recife.

The present situation (August 1941) is that the United States and Brazil are co-operating freely to establish effective air facilities on the Atlantic bulge. In June 1941—after many denials and subdenials that any negotiations were going on—the assistant military attaché of the Brazilian embassy in Washington let it out that the United States was preparing to extend credits of $100,000,000 for construction. The "bases" will remain under full Brazilian sovereignty, but they will be "available for the use of United States armed forces in the event of emergency." (New York *Times*, June 17, 1941.) In July, General George C. Marshall, testifying before the military affairs committee of the United States Senate, said that red tape had pushed back for three months "the development of essential air facilities in Brazil, where Pan American Airways have been improving facilities so that we can move with expedition." A little later news leaked out that American planes were using Brazilian fields in transit toward Africa, where the British take them over. A South Atlantic bomber ferry exists similar to the one between Canada and the British Isles, but it is less widely known.[4]

In July 1941 President Vargas authorized Panair do Brasil, the local subsidiary of Pan American Airways, "to build or improve" eight airfields above the Amazon and along the bulge. This immediately followed revelation that the German Condor line was very active in this territory.

General Góes Monteiro and the Army

The most important man in Brazil after Vargas and Aranha is the tough and slippery General Pedro Aurelio de Góes Monteiro, the chief of staff of the army. General Góes (pronounced Goy-es) was born in Alagôas in 1889. He entered the army as a private, and worked himself up rank by rank, slowly; it took him twenty years to become a captain. Then officers of the French military mission then in Brazil noted his ability—General Gamelin

---

[4] News of this ferry became public when President Roosevelt announced it after his meeting with Winston Churchill in August 1941.

thought him one of the most brilliant soldiers he had ever met—
and assigned him to special instruction in the staff school. Thereafter he rose rapidly. He helped Vargas and Aranha make the
1930 revolution—he had married a young woman from Aranha's
home town. In 1932 he put down the Paulista insurrection, though
the story is that he kept telegraphing his São Paulo friends that
he meant them no personal harm. General Góes became chief of
staff in 1937. He has twice visited the United States as a guest
of General Marshall.

It has become almost a byword in Brazil that the redoubtable
Góes is pro-German. In April 1940 he accepted the Grand Cross
of the German Eagle; and his first trip to Washington came
just in time to circumvent an invitation to visit German Europe.
For a time he seemed convinced that Germany was bound to
win the war, and it was he who was largely instrumental in buying Brazilian arms from Germany. But in reality Góes is not pro-
German; he is merely pro-Brazilian. He is not sure what the
United States will do, but he has healthy respect for our power;
he is waiting to see just what lead we make. What Góes wants—
like all Brazilians—is to play the winning side.

Góes and Aranha are good friends—I had an amiable lunch
with them together—but they have sharp tiffs occasionally. In the
summer of 1941 it seemed that Aranha's influence was predomi-
nant, and that of Góes waning. But no one should discount the
General's potential power and prestige. He runs the army, and
the army counts—most definitely. It is the one thing in the
country that people do not joke about. If the army should ever
turn against him, Vargas would be lost.

General Góes is talkative, indulgent, uncouth, and convivial.
He has a wide smile in a big loose mouth. He has not yet quite
recovered from the death of his only son, who was killed in 1936
in an airplane accident. For a time his deep melancholia alarmed
his friends. His wife still wears mourning; the boy's room is kept
as a kind of shrine. One Brazilian friend said, "Góes is like
a boy whose Christmas presents have been stolen."

The Minister of War—who is technically superior to Góes—is General Eurico Gaspar Dutra. He also rose from the ranks; he also holds a high German decoration and is sometimes called pro-German. General Dutra works mostly behind the scenes; he is aloof, inscrutable, hard to know. He was born in an isolated jungle village in the partially unexplored state of Matto Grosso in 1885. He is not so important as Góes, because he has no troops as a personal following. One of his closest associates in the Ministry of War is supposed to be an Integralista.

The Brazilian army is the largest in Latin America, numbering about 110,000 officers and men on the active list, with reserves of some 250,000. It is a well-trained force, with good morale; what hampers it is lack of communications and modern mechanized equipment. The Brazilian air force has about 200 planes. For years the Army was French-trained; the first chief of mission in Brazil was none other than General Gamelin. But an American military mission, specializing in coast artillery and antiaircraft defense, replaced the French in 1934.

A United States naval mission has been on duty in Brazil since 1925, and the Brazilian navy is thoroughly pro-American. Admiral Beauregard, our naval attaché in Rio, was head of the mission for years, and is called the father of the Brazilian navy.

Bagé Incident

In 1938 the Brazilian army ordered about $60,000,000 worth of munitions from the Krupp works at Essen, mostly antiaircraft guns. A purchasing mission went out from Rio, and established itself in Berlin. Came the war and the British blockade. The first shipments of arms were ready; the problem was how to get them to Brazil. In December 1940 a Brazilian merchantman, the *Siqueira Campos*, called at Lisbon and loaded a cargo of the arms worth perhaps $3,000,000. The British stopped the *Siqueira Campos* and took it to Gibraltar. After long discussion the ship was released and permitted to sail for Brazil with its German guns, after Foreign Minister Aranha promised explicitly that the same thing would not occur again.

But another Brazilian ship, the *Bagé*, had meantime called at Lisbon, and began to load with arms. Presumably this was on orders from the military behind Aranha's back. Aranha heard about it, and was furious. The British refused to give the *Bagé* the necessary navicerts, and Aranha could do nothing but order it to unload. As a result, this second shipment of German arms has never reached Brazil. The British did not object so deeply to Brazil getting arms—even if German—as to what the Nazis might do with the cash they would receive. For instance they could buy essential raw materials.

The *Bagé* case caused a grand turmoil in Brazil. The army was wild with indignation, not merely because it had lost its arms, but because its prestige was so badly hurt. Generals Dutra and Góes were blamed for having placed such a big order in Germany when war and blockade were inevitable. It seemed that the loss of the *Bagé* made part of the *Siqueira Campos* shipment value-less, since the *Bagé* carried complementary material. Góes wrote violent letters to such officials as Dr. Lourival Fontes, the director of propaganda, asking whether Brazil was pro-Brazil or pro-British or what.

The pro-ally newspaper *Carioca* then attacked Góes. And the most important paper in Rio, the *Correio da Manhã*, also strongly pro-ally, took sides against him. Góes told Dutra that he was going to close both papers down. Dutra, alarmed, called the palace. Alzirinha Vargas telephoned Góes, and told him that he ought to consult her father before going into such nonmilitary affairs as suppressing newspapers. Vargas then ordered him not to touch the *Correio da Manhã*, but Góes did send a platoon of soldiers to close the *Carioca*, a less conspicuous paper. Two days later it opened again. Everyone—except the unhappy editor of the *Carioca*—seemed satisfied.

As I heard the story in Rio, "General Góes went out after an elephant, and got a mouse."

The Germans in Brazil

The German colony in Brazil, concentrated mostly in the three southern states of Rio Grande do Sul, Santa Catharina, and Paraná, is the largest, richest, and most cohesive in Latin America. Here, as in the Valdivia region in Chile and Misiones in Argentina, whole towns look as German as Dortmund or Kiel. Everything is *echt-Deutsch* from shops to speech. Accurate statistics are impossible to get, but a reliable estimate is that there are 830,000 German-born Germans in Brazil, as well as 1,370,000 more of German descent, which makes a total of 2,200,000, more or less.

The Italian colony is bigger—there are probably at least 3,000,000 Italians in Brazil—but it is not so active politically; even so, São Paulo is almost as Italian a city as Turin. Japanese number about 200,000. Since 1934 they have been limited to about 3,000 immigrants a year, by terms of a new immigration law.[5] Repeatedly the authorities have had to close clandestine Japanese schools.

The Fifth Column in Brazil—incidentally the phrase "Fifth Column" is forbidden in the newspapers—centers naturally in the German districts, but its real heart is the German embassy, and its lifeblood the L.A.T.I., Condor, and other Axis airlines. The Vargas government has taken drastic measures against Nazism in the German districts; it has suppressed the German newspapers, closed down 1,200 schools, outlawed all political activity, and checked propaganda as far as possible. Insignia, parades, societies, and so on, are forbidden. Military barracks have been installed throughout all the "German" territory. No other country has taken such severe steps against racial Germans.

---

[5] This curious law, directed mostly against the Japanese, restricts immigration by each nationality to 2 per cent of the number of immigrants who entered Brazil between 1880 and 1930. It has produced curious anomalies. For instance 0.6 per cent of a Canadian may enter Brazil annually! The Japanese carefully fill their 3,000 quota each year.

Vargas has reputedly said that if his *local* Germans make trouble he "will eat them alive."

The Nazis realize the extreme importance of Brazil, and devote tremendous energy to it. The Reich's embassy has no fewer than 120 employees; the Germans are reputed to spend $2,-500,000 per month on propaganda. Transocean, their news agency, serves twenty-eight newspapers in fifteen Brazilian states; its chief is the "cultural" attaché of the German embassy. The official government newspaper, *A Noite,* takes Transocean, because it must take all foreign agency reports; three of the twenty-four newspapers in Rio de Janeiro are German-controlled. The noisiest is *Meio Dia.*

Brazil was, of course, the country where the Germans—until the war—performed their greatest miracles with barter trade. The technique was based on "compensation marks" and export subsidies. Germany bought Brazilian raw materials, and paid for them with marks frozen in Berlin; with these, Brazil could purchase German manufactured goods. In 1933 Brazil took 12.1 per cent of her total imports from Germany; by 1938 this figure had risen to 25 per cent. In 1933 Brazil sent 8.1 per cent of her total exports to Germany, and by 1938 this percentage rose to 19.1. But the Brazilians were not always pleased with what happened. Often they had to accept from Germany manufactured goods for which they had no use. Their choice was limited. One precious story is of an enormous cargo of glass eyes that reached Rio. Brazil was drowned in expensive cameras and aspirin tablets.

Since the war German trade has, naturally, been drastically cut down. Even so, German freighters occasionally squeeze through the blockade and reach Brazilian harbors; in fact, Germany tries harder to keep up trade with Brazil than with any other neutral state. On March 28, 1941, the German freighter *Dresden* (5,607 tons) slipped out of Santos bound for Vladivostok. On April 9, the *Hermes* (4,416 tons) managed to evade the British and reached Rio with a cargo that included a new plane for Condor. On April 28 the *Lech,* after staying in Brazilian waters for two months, escaped from Rio with 3,876 tons of mica and other strategic raw materials. Early in July, six more Axis ships, three German, three Italian, managed to scrape through.

But more important than ships are airplanes. The L.A.T.I. service, flying across the Atlantic from Dakar to Natal, is as we know the essential Axis link to the Americas. It carries not only mail and passengers and propaganda but cargoes of such freight as gold, platinum and diamonds. By means of L.A.T.I. the Germans reach their agents not merely in Brazil and South America but in the United States; documents and money go from Rio to Santiago de Chile or Lima, and then up the west coast to Panama; thus they escape the British control station at Trinidad. The United States watches communications in Panama carefully, but it has effective control merely in the Zone, not in Panamanian territory.

Why do not the British succeed in cutting off gasoline and oil for L.A.T.I.? Seemingly this could be done easily enough, by tightening the blockade at points like Río de Oro where the big Italian planes refuel. The explanation may be an unspoken understanding that the British will let L.A.T.I. alone, provided that the Germans continue to let the British fly freely from London to Lisbon. German fighters could knock off these Lisbon planes without much trouble, but they have never done so. Such tacit "agreements" occur in modern war.

The Condor line, nominally Brazilian but in actuality a subsidiary of Deutsche Lufthansa, is the biggest and most important German airline on the continent. It flies every inch of the exposed Brazilian bulge, and penetrates deep inland; it goes just where strategical considerations are most pressing. But Condor has had its troubles. At the beginning, about 1927, most Condor pilots were German citizens. But nationalism was rising in Brazil, and the Germans shrewdly had their officials and pilots naturalized. Then in 1934 Vargas issued a decree—which the Germans (and also Pan American) had anticipated, requiring that pilots of

Brazilian-registered planes, whether serving international or domestic routes, must be Brazilian nationals. The Germans, with their pilots duly naturalized, thought they were safe. But in 1940 came a new decree, demanding that all pilots of Brazilian-registered planes be *born* Brazilians. This was aimed directly at Condor, since by that time Panair do Brasil, the Pan American subsidiary, had trained enough native Brazilian pilots. This decree hurt Condor severely—so did the acute shortage of new planes and spare parts—but it is still flying. In June 1941, in fact, it opened a new service from Fortaleza, on the northern coast, to Therezina in the hinterland. According to Harold Callender in the New York *Times* (July 24, 1941), the Brazilians have no passport control at Fortaleza, and a "steady trickle of Germans" arrive there from the south, and then "disappear into the interior."

On the other hand, Brazilian authorities watch Axis aviation carefully. In April 1941, L.A.T.I. was fined $1,000 and threatened with expulsion because an Italian plane left Recife and "flew seven hours and fifteen minutes to an unknown destination on the pretext of testing gasoline consumption." In May the Brazilian Air Ministry denied permission to Air France to resume its service from Rio to Buenos Aires. In June L.A.T.I. asked for a "mother ship" near the Fernando da Noronha Islands to assist navigation; the request was turned down.

Other items in the fight against Fifth Columnism may be summarized. In January 1941 Dr. Fontes issued a statement forbidding attacks on the United States in the Brazilian press. He said, "Brazil considers the United States one of its best friends, and attacks against it will not be permitted, especially wanton attacks." A little later publication of all foreign-language newspapers was forbidden in Brazil. This was obviously aimed at the totalitarians, since there is only one important English-language paper in the country, whereas seventeen German newspapers exist, fourteen Italian, and nine Japanese.

Then, in June, came something of great weight. The United States and Brazil signed a new trade agreement providing that the United States has the *exclusive* right for two years to purchase Brazilian strategic materials. The list includes just those substances mentioned in Chapter I of this book, of which the United States may run short in time of war or prolonged emergency, and which Brazil can easily provide—manganese, titanium, nickel, industrial diamonds, mica crystals, bauxite, chromite, quartz. Rubber is also included, though Brazilian rubber production is very small. This agreement is probably the most important American achievement on the hemisphere front since the war began.

Brazil, it is interesting to recall, is the only Latin American state that has refused credentials to a German ambassador. He was Dr. Karl Ritter, one of the best-known economic experts in the German Foreign Office. Aranha and Ritter began to have trouble in 1937, when Brazil first suppressed the local Nazi organizations. Then came the Integralista coup in 1938; the government accused the Reich's "cultural attaché" of complicity, and arrested several Germans. Ritter protested. Aranha, irritated, told him that he was no longer *persona grata*. Ritter returned to Berlin, ostensibly to attend the Nuremberg rally in September 1938; then the Germans decided to defy Brazil, and Ritter took passage back after the rally. Aranha—a man of character—thereupon said that he would not be received if he returned. Ritter had to leave his boat at Lisbon—while he was actually en route— and has never been in Brazil since.

Another point: Brazil was the only country in South America to declare war on Germany in 1917.

Chapter *XXV*
A Word About Commodities

~~~~~~

THE weirdest thing in the whole realm of hemisphere economics is that Brazil, which produces 69 per cent of the
world's coffee, *burns* part of its coffee crop each year. This is to
check production and keep prices up. In seven years the Brazilians
have destroyed about 70,000,000 sacks of coffee, worth at least
$350,000,000. About 4,000,000 bags—say 15 per cent of the
total crop—are burned each year. In some years the percentage
is a good deal higher. Yet raw coffee accounts for about half
Brazil's total exports.

It is a story with the aroma of lunacy. Coffee, it happens, is
incredibly resistant, one of the toughest, one of the most inde-
structible of substances. At first, in 1934, thinking of ways to
get rid of it, the authorities decided on burial. Then they found
that four million sacks (132 pounds each) take a lot of room,
and that it was necessary to plow up an area practically the size
of Rhode Island. They found, secondly, that the coffee did not
have any fertilizer value; it would not turn into nitrogenous
products; in fact—on the contrary—it destroyed the soil!

The experts put their heads together in consternation. They
decided, instead of burying the wretched stuff, to throw it over-
board. Thousands upon thousands of sacks were piled on barges
at Santos, hauled out to sea, and tossed into the water. What
happened was that the coffee killed the fish and polluted the
beaches for miles around . . .

So, earth and water having failed, Brazil turned to fire.
More complications. Coffee consists 11 per cent of water, and
it won't burn! That is, it won't burn unless artificial fuel is used.
So the authorities had to import kerosene—which is expensive—
to help the flames along. It is calculated that it costs 25 cents a bag
to burn the coffee, in shipping, warehousing, labor, and fuel, quite
aside from the price of the wasted coffee itself. So Brazil pays

about $1,000,000 a year to *get rid* of its 4,000,000-sack surplus crop. Coffee is the country's Frankenstein.

The government owns no coffee land, but controls production by authority over marketing and price; Dr. Jayme Fernandes Guedes, head of the Departamento Nacional do Café, runs the industry. Coffee, a difficult once-a-year crop, is grown mostly on *fazendas* of modest size; there are no huge individual landowners in Brazil like the *estancieros* of Argentina. Nor has Brazil a large landless proletariat in the coffee regions. The coffee workers live on the *fazendas* the year around, with their own houses and gardens; often they are permitted to plant corn or cotton between the coffee trees. They get very little cash. What they get is the right to live on the *fazendas*.

The government determines what the "sacrifice quota" shall be, that is, the amount of the crop to be destroyed. It alone has the right to destroy. Suppose you are a *fazendeiro* with a crop of 1,000 bags. Someone in New York offers to buy it. But you cannot sell it until the government gives you permission, since the law forbids shipment of coffee to any point within sixty miles of the sea, which precludes foreign sales. The government then tells you that your sacrifice quota is 15 per cent. So you send 850 of your 1,000 bags to the nearest port for export, and 150 to the nearest government *armazem* or warehouse. These are scattered all over the coffee country. Your export coffee will not be released until the 15 per cent to be burned is in government hands. The government agents let the sacrifice coffee pile up at the *armazéns* until a good quantity is accumulated, and then burn it.

As it comes off the tree, coffee looks something like a green cherry; in fact, the pod is called a cherry colloquially. You put the cherries in a drying chamber—almost every *fazenda* has one —and let them dry for some weeks; then they are spread on bricks and alternately watered and left in the sun to dry again. The cherries burst open, and the coffee beans pop out; they are green, with no smell or taste. Then comes tasting and classification, which take place after roasting. The beans go into a rotating vat over a gas flame; after a few minutes they crackle, depending on the amount of moisture left. The roasted beans are ground, and the taster pours boiling water over them; he tastes, and spits into a ceremonial cuspidor. What counts is the residual taste. The whole thing is done very ritualistically. Each *fazenda* has its taster, to determine what is its own best coffee; the purchasers—in Rio or Santos—have their tasters too, so that they may choose between the different *fazendeiros*. The coffee is then graded and shipped. Only *green* coffee is sent to the United States, since after roasting it loses flavor.

And now a stimulating development. American chemists—the most conspicuous is Herbert S. Polin of New York—have worked out a system for converting coffee into plastics. Here science plays a useful role in political affairs. Coffee is one of the most intricate compounds known; after exhaustive work, Polin discovered that plastics could be made from it. The Brazilian government, highly interested, bought rights to the process, and built an experimental plant in São Paulo. Already it is handling some 50,000 sacks of coffee per year, turning the stubborn beans into a powder which in turn becomes everything from automobile wheels to fountain pens to radio sets. Eventually, the Brazilians hope, 5,000,000 bags a year will be converted—which will go a long way toward solving Brazil's coffee problem. It may end the insanity of burning.

One of the oddest loans in financial history depends on coffee. During the economic crisis of the early 30's Brazil needed money to finance the *destruction* of its crop. So it borrowed $40,000,000 from the United States—with 9,000,000 bags of coffee as collateral; the actual coffee is kept in warehouses. Thus Brazil, in order to pay for burning its coffee, must permanently keep 9,000,000 bags out of circulation! The administrator of this "coffee loan" is Olavo Egydio de Souza Aranha, one of Oswaldo's cousins.

When Brazil started burning coffee, other countries—notably

Colombia—grabbed the chance to increase their own coffee acre-
age. As a result, Brazil has lost much of its former market, which
it is now difficult to regain, since American buyers have become
accustomed to the milder Colombian blends. United States purchases of coffee are controlled by the April 1941 quoted agreement
between fourteen hemisphere republics. Each country agrees to
limit its exports to the United States to a given figure. The total
for 1941 is 15,900,000 bags; of this Brazil contributes about nine
million.

Rubber, Amazon, and Steel

Let commodities be our cast of characters for another page
or two. Let us turn to rubber.

Fifty or sixty years ago Brazil was the only rubber-producing
country in the world; today, though 300,000,000 rubber trees
grow wild over an area of 1,300,000 square miles (five times the
size of Texas!), production has sunk to practically nothing—a
pittance of 16,000 tons a year, which is about 1 per cent of world
production. In the old days rubber ruled Brazil. Fantastic for-
tunes were carved out of the Amazon jungles. The town of
Manáos, the center of the rubber trade, was one of the most
hectically flourishing in the Americas; it had an opera house
that cost $5,000,000, the largest and one of the most elaborate
in the world. Today the jungle is eating into what is left of
Manáos, and the Opera is a ghostly rat-infested mausoleum.

Why did Brazilian rubber collapse? First, because the Amazon
regions are swarming with malaria and other tropical diseases, and
relatively inaccessible to world markets. Second, the price of rubber dropped enormously, from $3.06 per pound in 1910 to about 21
cents today. Third, extravagance and inefficiency in Brazilian
production. Fourth and most important, British traders *stole*
Amazon seedlings, smuggled them out of the country, transported
them to Malaya, and set up a rival industry there. (*Time,* Nov.
4, 1940.)

A word about the Amazon, the most spectacular river in the

world. Its basin drains an area larger than the United States east of the Rockies, and contains 13,000 miles of navigable waters; along its banks are something like 50,000 different kinds of plants, and snakes that may weigh five tons. Its valley—if developed—could grow not merely profuse quantities of rubber, but rice, other foodstuffs, tropical oils, drugs, almost every known kind of hardwood, and even cattle. Oddly enough, much of the Amazon Valley is not particularly hot. The state of Amazonas, with an area of 731,363 square miles, is about the size of Mexico. Yet its population is only about 450,000, less than that of Washington, D. C.

In October 1940 President Vargas visited Amazonas in an exploratory aerial tour. He wants to see it developed; he wants to open a *Marcha para o Oeste*, march to the West. Also he is profoundly interested in the resuscitation of the rubber industry. So is the United States. Where else would North America get its rubber, if Japan cuts off Malaya and the Indies?

Some years ago Henry Ford bought an enormous Amazon tract—over 3,500,000 acres—near Bõa Vista, and called it Fordlandia. Here some 7,000 workers cleared the jungle, destroyed useless trees, planted new ones, lived behind screens, and sought to produce rubber. But a fungus struck the new trees just as they were beginning to produce; it takes at least seven years for a tree to reach maturity. Fordlandia was abandoned—though this is not officially admitted—and work began all over again at a tract called Belterra, some eighty miles away on the Tapajóz river. Here millions of inferior trees will be cleared out, to make way for seedlings of a healthy type. So far, 3,200,000 new trees have been planted at Belterra. Some 12,000,000 more are to come, and commercial production will begin in 1943—so it is hoped.

Near Belterra is something else American, an odd relic of days gone by. It is the colony called Santarém, settled in the 1860's by Confederate soldiers who refused to accept General Lee's surrender; they moved to Brazil under the protection of Dom Pedro II, and have maintained their distinct community life ever since.

Another similar colony of descendants of U. S. Confederates exists at Villa Americana, in the state of São Paulo.

At Itabira in Minas Geraes, some 200 miles from the coast at Rio, is one of the most extraordinary sights in the Americas, a giant mountain made of iron. It is like the Eisenerz in the old Austria, but bigger; it contains between 12 and 15 *billion* tons of iron ore of the highest grade, ore that is 64-66 per cent pure iron, of a quality far superior to that found in Lorraine, say, and about equal to that of Sweden. This Itabira deposit is the largest in the world.

Neither the Itabira nor other iron mines in Brazil have been extensively worked—largely on account of lack of coal and transportation difficulties—though Belgian and French companies have scraped the surface. It wasn't easy to get Itabira ore to the sea, and Brazil's only coal, of poor quality, is in Santa Catharina, about a week away by rail. But for at least twenty years Brazil has dreamed of building a great steel industry. When the war came, the army demanded that the government do something toward industrializing the country, as an essential factor in national defense. And Brazil got frightened at reported maneuvers by Krupp[1] and other German interests to buy out the small Belgian companies. (Until the war, the Germans tended to *dis-*courage development of Brazilian industry, because they did not want the country to be a future competitor.)

In 1938 Vargas invited the U. S. Steel Corporation to investigate. Its experts were enthusiastic about the quality of Brazilian ore; they said moreover that Santa Catharina coal would be usable if properly treated. But at the last moment U. S. Steel withdrew. Vargas turned to the American government—which by that time was also vitally interested to see that Brazil had a national steel industry. Negotiations, conducted by Jesse Jones and Dr. Guilherme Guinle, were successful; the Export-

[1] One story is that Hitler's agents "offered to transfer the entire Skoda works from Czecho-Slovakia to Brazil." (*Time,* Oct. 7, 1940.)

Import bank will contribute $20,000,000 and the Brazilian government $25,000,000 to building a plant. It will be located at Volta Redonda, in the state of Rio de Janeiro, which has easy access to the sea, and is midway between Rio, São Paulo, and the mines.[2]

Dollars into Decimals

I drank my beer on the terrace overlooking the incomparable Copacabana beach, and looked at my check. I inspected it curiously. As I have said, Brazilian money is written in a language all its own. The check read 00:005$200. Translated into American this means a fraction over 25 cents.

One thousand *reis* equals one *milreis*, which is roughly 5 cents American. The *milreis* is written 1$000; two and a half *milreis* would be 2$500. The *milreis* is the normal unit, since the *real* (the singular of *reis*) is so vestigially small. One hundred *milreis* ($5.00) are written 100$000; one thousand *milreis* ($50.00) are called a *conto* and are written 1:00$000. People talk more in terms of *contos* than in *milreis*—if they can afford it.

Some salaries and wages are as follows, more or less. The poorest type of agrarian worker, in the Bahia district, say, gets about one *milreis* (5 cents) a day. The daily wage for an unskilled industrial worker in São Paulo is about 60-75 cents, that of a skilled worker anything up to $1.20. Ford pays his workers 10 *milreis* a day (50 cents) at Belterra, a rate unheard of for the region. A good cook gets about $5.00 a month, a clerk in the telegraph office about $15, and a policeman about $20. A cabinet minister earns 8 *contos* a month, or $400. Very few officials get much more.

The United States has, through the Export-Import bank, helped greatly to ameliorate Brazil's economic crisis. Recent loans are:

[2] Minas Geraes was unhappy not to have the plant in its own state territory, next to the mines, but its feelings have been assuaged. Contracts were let for $36,000,000 in December 1940, and in July 1941 the O.P.M. in Washington guaranteed Brazil the necessary priorities.

$19,200,000	Loan to the Bank of Brazil for unfreezing American credits
$25,000,000	Rotating exchange credit to the Bank of Brazil
$20,000,000	Steel plant
$10,000,000	Loan to finance purchase of ships, rolling stock, and the like
$74,200,000	Total

Brazil has, like most of Latin America, suffered seriously from the loss of European markets caused by the war, even though the United States is its best customer. Foreign trade is down between 35 and 40 per cent.

City of São Paulo

I have talked often of the Paulistas in these pages, and no word about Brazil could be anywhere near complete without brief mention of São Paulo. It is the third biggest city in Latin America—after Buenos Aires and Rio de Janeiro—and the fastest growing in the hemisphere. Its population was only about 25,000 fifty years ago; it grew to 1,151,249 in 1938, and it is growing now at the rate of about 50,000 a year. In this prodigious rate of increase—as well as other categories—it startlingly resembles Chicago.

São Paulo, with its factories, glittering skyscrapers, hydro-electric development, and intense commercial life, differs as much from bland, beatific, beautiful Rio as does Pittsburgh, say, from Paris. São Paulo, the province, is by far the richest and best developed state in Brazil; it contributes over 50 per cent of the country's total industrial goods, and well over 50 per cent of its federal taxes. It is forward-looking and on-the-make.

A healthy rivalry exists between São Paulo and Rio de Janeiro; São Paulo says it is the lonely locomotive pulling the twenty other Brazilian states. The Cariocas (residents of Rio) don't like to admit this, and they add that every Paulista, no matter how

excessive his provincial pride, has only one real ambition in life—
to die in Rio.

Brazil Needs Things, Too

I asked five Brazilians—a cabinet minister, a taxi driver, an
eminent sociologist, an army officer, and a hotel clerk—what their
country needed most. Their answers: (1) better communications
and industrialization; (2) more to eat; (3) national integration,
cultural development, homogeneity; (4) opening up of the back
country by roads and aviation; (5) communications and education.

Not one of the five mentioned any prevailingly *political* de-
sideratum. Which is another indication that the government of
Getulio Vargas has affairs nicely in hand.

Chapter XXVI
Brazilian Roll Call

$\sim\sim\sim\sim\sim\sim\sim\sim\sim\sim\sim\sim\sim\sim\sim\sim\sim\sim\sim$

A<small>FTER</small> Vargas the two most important men in Brazil are, as we know, Oswaldo Aranha and Góes Monteiro. But near the top are three other worthies who need careful mention. One is the veteran politician João Alberto Lins Bandeira de Barros, who was for some years president of the National Council for Economic Defense and of the Federal Council of Foreign Trade. As such he was near to being economics dictator of the country. He chuckled when people called him "a substitute Schacht."

João Alberto—no one ever dreams of calling him by his full name—is usually thought of as a *gaucho*, but he was born in Recife, in the North. His career of revolutionary activity, intellectual accomplishment, and political vicissitudes would fill a chapter. His charm is almost as great as that of Aranha, his close friend; his dash and hardiness are legendary. Once he had a forced landing in a seaplane in the Plata, when he was an exile in Uruguay. His skull was fractured. Nevertheless he swam five miles to safety.

João Alberto, the son of a middle-class lawyer, joined the army as a boy. In 1924—long before he met Vargas—he was a leader of the celebrated Prestes Column, a revolutionary band that marched thousands of miles through the country, and of which more presently. João Alberto then became one of the group of *Tenentes* (lieutenants) who staged the 1930 coup d'état and helped Vargas into power. It is axiomatic in Brazil that João Alberto is the one man with whom Vargas, that masterful politician, *never* quarrels. Since 1930 he has been interventor in São Paulo, chief of police in Rio, and consular inspector abroad. Recently he was named minister to Canada—a more important job than it sounds, because Brazilian trade with Great Britain proceeds best by Canadian routes.

In João Alberto's house—overlooking the incomparable Rio

harbor near the country club—are a death mask of Beethoven, a lovely Van Gogh print, Persian carpets, Amazonian arrows, Peruvian silver, and bowls of flowering yellow acacia. João Alberto is tall, with a formidable hooked nose and hawklike eyes. His conversation is humorous, animated, confidential. His beautiful blonde wife is his accomplished hostess.

João Alberto can do things that no other man can do. I visited him for lunch. "My house is your house," he smiled in greeting. He asked if I had met Vargas. I replied that I was still waiting for my official interview. He said, "Come along." We drove to the palace and in about seven minutes I was shaking the President's hand.

Dr. Lourival Fontes, the director general of the *Departamento da Imprensa e Propaganda* (known everywhere as D.I.P.) is the explosive young man who is the Goebbels or Brendan Bracken of Brazil. Lourival—everyone calls him by his first name—is ingenious, melodramatic, overworked, and lively. His hair juts up in profuse disorder; his eyes shine with showmanship. He is an exceedingly magnetic character.

Dr. Fontes, who has one of the hardest and most thankless jobs in the country, controls all incoming and outgoing news; his budget for propaganda is about $500,000 a year. The censorship is fairly liberal in some respects, and severe in others. When I was in Brazil no mention whatever was permitted of hemisphere negotiations. Even when Góes Monteiro went to Washington, the censorship shut down on what he said; even the base crisis in Uruguay could not be mentioned in Brazil. Reason: the acute sensitiveness of most Brazilians to matters reflecting on national sovereignty.

Lourival was born in the small northern state of Sergipe. An ambitious youngster with a direct and logical mind, he studied law, worked on a newspaper, edited the magazine *Política e Hierarquia,* and became director general of tourism. His zest for publicity work brought him to the attentive Vargas eye. He has traveled in Europe and in the rest of South America, but he has not yet visited the United States. He hopes soon to do so.

His wife, Senhora Adelgisa Nery, one of the most beautiful women in Brazil, is a well-known poetess. They were married in Aranha's house; Lourival is an Aranha protégé. Senhora Fontes visited the United States in 1939, and is strongly pro-American. But Lourival himself has totalitarian leanings, some of his friends like to say.

One of the most provocative and interesting men in Brazil is Dr. Francisco Campos, the Minister of Justice and Interior. People call him *Chico Sciencia*—"Chico" is the ordinary diminutive for Francisco, and "Sciencia" refers to his erudition. Dr. Campos has a library of 15,000 books; it is called the best private law library on the continent. Two recent works he enjoyed were the *Collected Papers* of Mr. Justice Frankfurter and *Law and the Modern Mind*, by Jerome Frank.

Dr. Campos, in his middle forties, was born in Minas Geraes. For years he has been close to Vargas, and it was he who wrote the 1937 constitution; intellectually he is the "father" of the *Estado Novo*, new state. One of his recent books, *O Estado Nacional*, has been bitterly attacked as pro-totalitarian. It says that democracy is "stagnant," and that all countries are looking for "a man of destiny, a Caesar." John W. White summarized the book in the New York *Times*, whereupon Campos gave to another *Times* correspondent, Frank M. Garcia, an exposé considerably watering down his views. He said that his point of view was "historical," and he denies that he is anti-American.

Dr. Campos told me that he was convinced that economic revolution is the keynote of the twentieth century, just as political revolution was the keynote of the nineteenth. Democracy, he thinks, must be reformed; and sometimes reforms need a strong hand, since people will not give up their vested interests or privileges without a fight. The old ideals are outworn, Dr. Campos feels. The world, in a state of revolution, needs new direction and authority. He said—wistfully—that it was easy enough for the United States to be a democracy, because of our standards of education. But it is not so easy to make democracy work in a country like Brazil, with its huge illiteracy and lack of training for political leadership.

Campos draws red and blue doodles as he talks. He is tousled, informal, aware. He says he joined Vargas because Getulio was so "calm."

Cabinet and Interventors

Of the other cabinet ministers the most interesting is probably 48-year-old Arthur de Souza Costa, the Minister of *Fazenda* (Finance). He has enormous shoulders; his handshake is like that of a professional wrestler. One of the ablest politicians in Brazil, Souza Costa is self-made. He was a poor boy in Rio Grande do Sul, and started work as an office boy in a local bank; at thirty he was its president—an accomplishment of which he is justly proud. Vargas made him president of the Bank of Brazil in 1932, and Minister of Finance in 1934. What interests Souza Costa most is the rapid progress of Brazil toward industrialization. He thinks that in another twenty years his country will be one of the greatest industrial powers in the world—and he may well be right.

General João de Mendonça Lima, the Minister of Communications and Public Works, is one of the original band of *gaucho* revolutionaries.[1] He has had thirty-nine years in and out of the army, mostly as a specialist in military engineering. He is a religious fanatic, and founded a cult of his own when his wife died. He officiated as a "priest" at his son's wedding . . . Admiral Henrique Aristedes Guilhem is the grand old man of the Brazilian navy, and is Minister of Marine. He has been a salt-water sailor for a flat fifty years.

[1] The *gauchos*, as we know, run Brazil, and everybody wants to be one. In the early Vargas days politicians would often move to Rio Grande—conspicuously—so they could return as "*gauchos*" a few months later.

Waldemar Falcão, the Minister of Labor, was born near the Natal bulge in 1895. He has been a lawyer and professor; he is one of the most prominent lay Catholics in Brazil, and has bitterly attacked communism . . . Fernando Costa, the Minister of Agriculture, is the only Paulista in the government. One of his hobbies is development of *gazogenio* trucks and tractors that operate on vegetable charcoal, and thus utilize agricultural products as fuel . . . Gustavo Capanema, who became Minister of Education and Public Health at thirty-four, is a hard-working young intellectual who wants to build more schools.

Of the interventors in Brazil's twenty federal states the most conspicuous is young Commander Ernani do Amaral Peixoto, who married Senhorita Alzira Vargas, as we know. Peixoto is important not merely because he is the President's son-in-law but because of his own distinct abilities. He was named interventor in the state of Rio immediately after the 1937 coup d'état; before that he had been naval adjutant to Getulio. The marriage was a genuine love match. Like his wife, Peixoto is ardently pro-United States.

The interventor in Minas Geraes is Benedicto Valladares, the only governor of a state in his own right, so to speak; he *was* governor at the time of the 1937 coup, and he is the only one whom Vargas kept on. Valladares, a native Minero, was born in 1892; he is a lawyer by profession. He is tremendously proud of his state, which has 8,000,000 people—it is the most populous in Brazil—in an area almost that of Texas. The capital, Belo Horizonte, was built from scratch in this century, and, like Paris or Washington, is something for city planners to be proud of. It dominates Brazil's great mineral deposits.

The ambitious Dr. Adhemar de Barros, a doctor of medicine, was interventor in São Paulo—and thus had one of the most difficult jobs in the republic—until he retired in 1941. He was succeeded by Fernando Costa, the Minister of Agriculture . . . The interventor in the strategic state of Pernambuco is Agamemnon Magalhães, a journalist and professor, whose inclinations are mildly leftist . . . One of the most democratically-minded men in Brazil is the interventor in Rio Grande do Sul, by name Cordeiro de Faria.

There are many other Brazilians in public life about whom we should say a word. Luis Simões Lopes is the head of D.A.S.P. (*Departamento Administrativo dos Serviços Públicos*), or director of the civil service. He is a *gaucho* from Rio Grande who has been close to Getulio for many years. His complete control—under Vargas—of the country's civil servants and functionaries is an important item in the structure and operation of the dictatorship.

Another *gaucho* and Vargas man of long standing is João Neves da Fontoura, the legal adviser to the Bank of Brazil. He is one of the few people in the country who can tell Vargas distasteful truths, and even say No to him if necessary . . . Another influential personality is Mauricio Nabuco, the permanent head of the Foreign Office; he is the beautifully trained and astute Sumner Welles to Aranha's Hull. His father was a famous Brazilian ambassador to Washington, and his sister is the country's foremost novelist.

Rio's Dodsworth and Muller

Dr. Henrique de Toledo Dodsworth, the mayor of the Federal District of Rio de Janerio, bears a sound old English name, but he speaks little English. He is a doctor of medicine by profession, the scion of an old Empire family, and the nephew of Paulo de Frontin, the engineer who built much of Rio. Now Dodsworth has ambitious projects to remodel this most beautiful city in the Americas. His $4,000,000 program includes removal of the San Antonio hill in the heart of the city, excavation for a new tunnel to Copacabana, and building the new eighty-meter-wide, two-mile-long Getulio Vargas boulevard.

Major Felinto Muller, the chief of police in Rio, is one of the most powerful men in Brazil, not merely by virtue of his official position, but because he is so close to Vargas. Muller, of German descent, entered the army at nineteen; he was one of the leaders of the revolutionary Prestes Column; years later he helped put Prestes into jail. He spent several years as a refugee, hiding in his native province, Matto Grosso; for a time he worked as a chauffeur in the Argentine. He is a 100 per cent Vargas man, and some people call him pro-totalitarian. His brother is federal interventor in Matto Grosso.

Opposition to Vargas, Who and Why

We must now tell the strange story of Luíz Carlos Prestes, the "Cavalier of Hope." A young officer and revolutionary, he led a revolt against the government in 1924, long before the Vargas days. With him were such officers as João Alberto and others who have since become famous—and respectable. The movement, which centered on Rio Grande, was suppressed, but Prestes gathered the remnants of his "army" and fled. His column then performed "a long march" that is almost comparable to that of the Red Army in China. It fought fifty-six battles; it made treaties with Indian tribes; it set up shadow "states"; it marched from the extreme south of Brazil—always through back country, always eluding government pursuers—to Bahia in the north, and then down the Amazon to the Bolivian frontier, literally a stupendous feat. Finally, after three years, the column disbanded, and Prestes and his men crossed into Bolivia, where they were interned. Then Prestes moved to Buenos Aires.

Vargas made the 1930 revolution. He got in touch with Prestes, who had formed a Leftist organization called the National Liberation Alliance. For a time the two worked amicably together; then Prestes went to Moscow, and became a full-fledged communist. He returned to Brazil—foolishly—and was arrested after the 1935 so-called communist "revolt." He was charged with sedition and sentenced—a monstrous sentence—to seventeen years in jail.

But this was not all. While Prestes was in jail other communists sought to keep up secret activity. The secretary of the party, Marcel Bomfim, had a friend, a girl named Eliza Fernandes. She often visited Prestes in prison. Early in 1938 six communists called at her home, and one of them strangled her; they thought she was betraying them to the police. Two years later, in 1940, Prestes was hauled out of jail to stand trial for complicity in the Fernandes murder. He, it was charged, ordered his comrades to kill her, though he was in jail at the time. And he was sentenced to *thirty years* more in prison. Which accords ill with Brazil's traditional reputation for tolerance and mercy. The Vargas government should reduce such savage sentences.

Another communist serving an unbelievably shocking prison term—thirty-eight years!—is Honario de Freitas Guimarães; he too is accused of complicity in the Fernandes murder. Guimarães had a remarkable life. He was a son of one of the richest and most aristocratic families in Rio; he went to Eton, where King George V gave him a prize for excellence in French;[2] at Oxford he was a classmate of the Duke of Gloucester. He returned to Brazil, left his family, became a diamond prospector, worked as an overseer on some big *fazendas*, and turned communist after seeing the miserable conditions of the poor. The police did not catch him till late in 1940.

Brazil has four living ex-Presidents, three of whom still reside comfortably in the country. Wenceslau Braz, a wealthy textile manufacturer, was President in 1914-18; he brought Brazil into the war, and retired from politics soon after. Epitacio Pessôa was head of state from 1919 to 1922, and then became Brazilian member of the World Court at The Hague. In 1922 Arthur da Silva Bernardes became President; his regime was one of the most agitated in Brazilian history. Finally Washington (for George Washington) Luíz Pereira de Souza reached the presidency in 1926, and lasted till 1930, when Vargas displaced him. He fled to Portugal, where he stayed until early in 1941, when he came to the United States. Brazilians—even of the Vargas

[2] Cf. Walter Kerr, in the N. Y. *Herald Tribune*, Jan. 3, 1941.

camp—respect Washington Luíz highly, because during his long exile he never told any secrets or raised his voice against the regime that threw him out.

The most prominent Paulista exiles today are Armando de Salles Oliveira, a former governor of the state of São Paulo, and his brother-in-law Julio de Mesquita Filho, former owner of the great newspaper *O Estado de São Paulo*. Oliveira was the anti-Vargas candidate for the presidency in 1937. He was arrested for a brief interval, held in protective custody, and then allowed to leave the country. He and Mesquita live in Buenos Aires, and do what they can against Vargas; they send pamphlets across the frontier and so on, but their influence is not great . . . Another exile—in Uruguay—is General Flores da Cunha, who was a *gaucho* very close to Vargas, and one of the early revolutionaries. Vargas, people say, fears him more than any other Brazilian.

The Integralista leader Plinio Salgado, who in 1938 attempted to overthrow the government with Nazi help, is an exile in Portugal. He is distinguished not merely for his green-shirted insurrectionism, but as the author of several neurotic novels. Vargas once told a very distinguished American friend that the Integralistas had had $1,000,000 to spend, and that if they had had twice that sum, the outcome might have been sadly different. Nowadays the Integralistas have no more than a shadow of their former influence, even though several key politicians once belonged to the movement.

Most political prisoners in Brazil—the government denies that any are purely "political"—are kept in Rio or on Fernando da Noronha Island off Recife. Most are communists, and most serve comparatively short terms; even such an enemy of the regime as Salles Oliveira doubts if there are more than 500-600 in all. What the police like to do is keep all so-called communists or active oppositionists "taped," so that when the government wants a burst of activity, arrests may be quickly made.

More Brazilians

As an indication of the vitality and variety of Brazilian life let us name three more men. This means omitting any but bare mention of many others who might be named: for instance, Afranio de Mello Franco, the grand old man of Brazilian diplomacy, who settled the Letitia dispute between Peru and Colombia; for instance, financiers like Valentim Bouças, Vargas' golf partner, and Guilherme Guinle, who owns the Santos docks; for instance, journalists like Assis Chateaubriand, "the Hearst of Brazil," and Paulo de Bettencourt, the editor of the *Correio da Manhã*; for instance, brilliant sociologists like Dr. Gilberto Freyre and publicists like Austregesilo de Athayde.

My final three are these. First, Dom Pedro de Bragança Orleans, the head of the royal house—to which the country still pays taxes, though they are small. Dom Pedro and his family live in Petrópolis, which in theory still belongs to them; they are well-liked and respected, and the Vargases are their close friends. They live like good Brazilian commoners; there is no faintest hint of a royalist political movement. Dom Pedro's brother, Dom João, was accidentally shot and severely wounded during the Integralista putsch in 1938.

Second, by contrast, take Conte Francisco Matarazzo, who got his title from Mussolini. He was the son of an Italian immigrant to São Paulo, who did a humble business in sausages and spaghetti; today he owns no fewer than 107 industries, and is easily the most powerful industrialist in the hemisphere below the United States. Count Matarazzo's career is strikingly like that of some Detroit or Pittsburgh millionaires. He is close to Italy in sympathies, but he takes little part in politics.

Third and finally there is the Cardinal, Dom Sebastião Leme da Silveira Cintra, who, very close to Vargas, has marked political influence. Archbishop Leme, the second Cardinal in Latin America, is a Paulista by birth; a comparatively young man, he was educated in São Paulo and then Rome. It was Cardinal Leme who persuaded President Washington Luíz to leave the country peaceably when Vargas assumed power in 1930; he personally took Luíz to Fort Copacabana, and stayed with him until a British boat picked him up.

Chapter XXVII
The Coming American "Imperialism"

~~~~~~

THE Caribbean area is a world of its own in this tour of Latin America that we are making. It consists of that group of tropical and subtropical islands known commonly as the West Indies, and more accurately as the Greater and Lesser Antilles. Most of these islands were discovered by Christopher Columbus; they saw the voyages of Raleigh and the piracies of Drake; they knew the exploits of legendary characters like Robinson Crusoe and the depredations of Henry Morgan. In the area are three independent states, Cuba, Haiti, and the Dominican Republic; two United States dependencies, Puerto Rico and the Virgin Islands; a group of British colonies like Jamaica, Trinidad, and Barbados; and small islands belonging to France (Guadeloupe and Martinique) and the Netherlands (Curaçao and Aruba).

In the West Indies are luscious tourist playgrounds, as at Nassau; there are islands ground down by crushing poverty, like Tobago; hidden coves exist where tall galleons once sailed, mellow with romance; behind them may be sugar plantations, coffee *fincas*, banana groves, where negro workers are still virtually slaves. The Caribbean gamut stretches from the austere dignity of Morro Castle to the wretched hovels near the asphalt lake in Trinidad. It includes such diverse items as the oldest negro republic in the world, a modern French aircraft carrier, $250,000,000 in Vichy gold, brand-new American naval bases, one of the prettiest examples of personal despotism known in the western world, and an exciting experiment with the WPA.

One common denominator of the region is that Spanish influence is not so strong as in most of Latin America. Here the writ of the Danes, the Dutch, the French, the British, the Americans has been deeply signed. Another is absence of Indian heritage. The West Indies do not remotely resemble such Indian-based countries as Ecuador or Bolivia or even Mexico. In the Caribbean

411

the Indians were exterminated quickly, and the negroes came in early. The population today is mostly negro and mulatto.

Another common denominator is the vital importance of the area to American defense. The Caribbean is rapidly—and of necessity—becoming an American military and naval lake. This is because, as everyone knows, it commands the eastern or Atlantic approaches to the Panama Canal. In Chapter X, I discussed the essential strategy of the canal in relation to local defenses and approaches from the Pacific. Here I continue the story with consideration of the other and more important approach, that from the east, the Atlantic, the Caribbean.

Our Caribbean Defense System

Geography has been good to the War Plans division of the United States general staff. As a glance at the map will show, the Canal is screened on the east—though not on the west—by a semicircle of islands easily dominated from the United States and where fortified bases may be strongly established.

The gist of our defense problem, as it was explained to me by officers in the area, is to control the entire Caribbean region with sufficient force to block off enemy approach. The Antilles are a natural barrier between the Atlantic and the Canal; our strategy is, in a word, to dominate this barrier. We must sterilize the Canal— by naval and air bases—from any possible attempt at aggression by an unfriendly power. This means (a) that we must prevent any German or Axis occupation of the independent Caribbean states or of the British, French, or Dutch colonies, and (b) we must close the Caribbean entrances to the Canal against possible attack based on aircraft carriers.

As to the first point, our main line of defense must and should be political. By maintaining our present close and friendly relations with the governments of Cuba, the Dominican Republic, and Haiti,[1] the United States does more for effective defense than it can by any other means. We must give economic assistance when

[1] Venezuela and Colombia also, it goes without saying.

it is necessary; we must scrutinize carefully any evidences of Fifth Columnism; we must retain our position as indisputably the dominant power in the area. By speaking softly, if possible. But by speaking loudly if a loud voice is essential.

In regard to the British, French, and Dutch colonies, our position was immeasurably bettered late in 1940 when we acquired base sites from Great Britain in exchange for fifty over-age destroyers. All hemisphere states are privileged to make use of these bases. It goes without saying that we must prevent German occupation of *any* Caribbean island. The whole Caribbean area should be considered as a single giant base, military experts say.

As to the second point, defense of the canal against attack from aircraft carriers, the chief passages where a carrier might slip through are the following:

1. The Straits of Florida between Florida, the Bahamas, and Cuba. This passage is protected by our mainland bases in Miami and by the base soon to be built in the Bahamas.
2. The Windward Passage, which lies between the eastern tip of Cuba and Haiti, and which is the chief commercial route for traffic between the United States and the Canal. It will be protected by new bases in Jamaica and at Mayaguana in the Bahama group.
3. The Mona passage between the Dominican Republic and Puerto Rico. Protected by the formidable new base built by the United States at Borinquen, on the northwestern edge of Puerto Rico.
4. The Anegada passage between the Virgin Islands and the British island of Antigua. It will be protected by our present installations at St. Thomas, on the Virgin Islands, and the Antigua base now authorized.
5. The most southerly area, near the coast of Venezuela, which would be the direction of penetration from South America. This we hope to protect at Trinidad.

Generally experts reckon that the extreme effective range of airplanes launched from a carrier is 650 miles. The nearest entrance through the Antilles to the Canal is the Windward Passage, which is 800 miles distant. The furthest point is Martinique, 1350 miles. If entrance into the Caribbean is absolutely excluded to any hostile ship by means of our circle of new bases, the canal will presumably be safe from carrier attack.

One gap, however, worries naval and military authorities, that between Antigua and St. Lucia. Here is a stretch of 220 miles in which we have no protection. A base might have been established on the British island Dominica, which lies in this gap, but Dominica was not included among the territories we leased—a result of hasty preliminary judgment. It is important to note that the French islands Martinique and Guadeloupe lie in this exposed gap between Antigua and St. Lucia. They are a special and worrying problem of their own.

An air base means more than a hangar and a runway. It should include underground shops, ammunition depots, bomb shelters, machine facilities, and above all safe storage for great quantities of gasoline and oil. It should be vigilantly garrisoned, with several thousand men to each base. Patrols from base to base must be incessant. As I heard it cogently expressed in Puerto Rico, "Unless we defend our new bases properly we are simply building them for Germany."

Each of the new Caribbean bases includes both an army and a navy station, although they do not duplicate activity. The army provides pursuit ships and fighters for defense, antiaircraft installations, and coastal defense fortifications. The navy provides long-range patrol bombers for overocean reconnaissance. The only fighters the navy utilizes are on carriers, and the navy has no antiaircraft, except on ships. But the navy's bomber patrol is already vigorously functioning. Every day, from Miami to Trinidad and back again, navy planes scout the waters of the Caribbean and Atlantic in flights 1200 miles or more out to sea. The big bombers roar over the entire Antilles area.

Some experts think that the Caribbean bases should be only a beginning. They visualize their extension every 400 or 450 miles straight down the coast of South America as far as the River

Plata. The line would run from Georgetown in British Guiana (our most southerly base site at present) to both Paramaribo in Dutch Guiana and Cayenne in French Guiana, and then proceed to such stations in Brazil as Belém, St. Luiz de Maranhõa, Fortaleza, Natal, Recife, Bahia, Victoria, Rio de Janeiro, Santos, Florianapolis, and Porto Alegre, ending finally at Montevideo in Uruguay. This is an extreme conception, perhaps. Such an extension may never be necessary. And we know how difficult it will be to achieve.

The reasoning behind this "extended base" theory is, of course, that the Caribbean area should be fortified not merely to defend the Canal but as a stepping stone for defense against any attack that may come from South America proper. The easiest route of enemy assault—especially since the Caribbean itself will be so well protected—might be across Brazil and the Guianas, and then toward the Canal through Venezuela and Colombia. To meet this potential threat our experts envisage a great "migration" of United States patrol planes and bombers, moving southward step by step. If bases were ready, it is said that we could transfer at least 500 bombers from Florida to the La Plata region in three days.

The New Antilles Bases

Of the eight areas where we acquired base sites in the destroyer deal, *Trinidad* is probably the most important. This island, which Columbus named for the Trinity, is shaped like the profile of a railway tie, and holds about 450,000 people (mostly Negro and *East* Indian) on an area of 1,860 square miles. It has a splendid deep-water harbor, the Gulf of Paria, which can be easily fortified and is big enough to hold the entire British and American fleets, as well as offering shelter for seaplanes and submarines. Trinidad is vital not only because it is the southern pivot of the Caribbean defense system but also because it blocks—or should block—any attack northward from South America.

Our biggest establishment in Trinidad will be the naval base and anchorage in the Gulf of Paria. After various snags, serious work began in the spring of 1941. We have the right not merely to fortify the adjacent hills and the two entrances to the Gulf (called the Dragon's Mouth and the Serpent's Mouth) but to utilize fully the wharves, docks and storage facilities in Port-of-Spain, the island's capital. The United States army is also active in Trinidad, with no fewer than three separate base sites. The main army base is at Cumuto, about 22 miles east of Port-of-Spain, where an airfield and its accessories will be established on 17 square miles of leased territory. Subordinate bases will be at Longdenville (for aircraft) and at Salibia Bay. American troops to garrison Trinidad began arriving soon after the base sites were chosen.

Jamaica is also important, because it lies only 500 miles from the Canal and is situated directly in the Caribbean. Its population is 1,173,000, of whom perhaps 20,000 are white. Here we have leased six different parcels of land, including the approaches to Portland Bight and the shoreline of Manatee Bay. Jamaica has two admirable deep-water harbors, at Kingston and Port Royal; at Port Royal is a naval dockyard that the United States will put to use. In Jamaica we may confront a complex local political situation. Here, as in Trinidad, insufferable poverty and shocking living conditions have caused serious riots. The Jamaica People's Party is a powerful nationalist organization, which on the whole welcomes the American projects, because these may tend to diminish British influence. But the People's Party is demanding safeguards against imported skilled labor and it may provide a headache or two to the American administration before the bases are complete.

To the south of Trinidad is *Georgetown* in British Guiana, where the United States navy has outlined two bases. Georgetown is the southernmost anchor of our present naval patrol. There are considerable deposits of bauxite, the ore from which aluminum is derived, in British Guiana, which both the United States and Great Britain are anxious to protect.

Northward from Trinidad are *Antigua* and *St. Lucia*, islands deep in the slough of economic ruin, with predominantly negro populations producing rum, sugar, and molasses. In Antigua we have leased two small preserves, and in St. Lucia six. Both Antigua and St. Lucia will be subsidiary air bases for assisting naval patrol.

In the *Bahamas*, where the Duke of Windsor is governor, our principal installation will be a base at Mariguana island, at the extreme other end of the archipelago from Nassau. Most Bahaman harbors (there are 20 important islands in the group) are too shallow to be good anchorages, and too reef-ridden for easy use by seaplanes. Mariguana's eventual importance will be in helping to "control" the Windward Passage.

Bermuda, our seventh site, is of prime importance, but it is rather outside the geographical scope of this book. It is an essential link in the route from the Atlantic coast to the Azores and Lisbon; it is an ocean vantage-point which could, if developed, dominate the entire mid-Atlantic. Our projects here are more extensive and ambitious than in any other base site except Puerto Rico and possibly Trinidad. The Bermudian airbase alone is to cost $9,150,000, and the hullabaloo of our preparations has shocked the quiet islanders.

The eighth base acquired by the United States is *Newfoundland,* with which this book cannot deal. The sites in both Bermuda and Newfoundland are, incidentally, "free gifts" of the British government to the United States, not 99-year leases as in the case of the other six. In all base territories we have full sovereignty and extraterritorial rights, according to the agreement signed in London in March 1941. And all Latin American states have full right to use them.

Headaches Over Martinique

Martinique and Guadeloupe are two small islands that have belonged to France since the buccaneering days of the seventeenth century. Since the French collapse in June 1940, they have been desperately poverty-stricken, probably more so than any region in the hemisphere. One reason was the cessation of exports—sugar, coffee, rum, and so on—that normally went to France; another was the inability of the French government to send remittances and pay salaries. Yet, despite conditions approaching starvation, the islands have remained loyal to Vichy, and the French admiral in charge, Henri Robert, is a staunch Pétain man.

In the harbor of Fort-de-France, Martinique, the French aircraft carrier *Béarn* lies at anchor. Close by are a cruiser, the *Émile Bertin*, two auxiliary cruisers, and four smaller ships. On shore are 105 modern American-built airplanes that were sold to France and delivered as far as Martinique—whence the *Béarn* was to carry them home—when France fell. The planes, contrary to general impression, are well kept and are in good condition. They are covered with tarpaulins and their motors are oiled and set working once a week. Among them are Curtiss dive bombers, Curtiss fighters, and Stinson training planes. Also in Martinique is some $250,000,000 in gold, which the French, before their collapse, sent there for safety.

Neither the United States nor Great Britain will permit the *Béarn* and its cargo of first-class fighting ships to reach Europe. They are carefully watched, as are all affairs at Martinique, by a United States naval observer on the spot and by a destroyer patrol which the United States—not Great Britain—maintains outside the harbor, to keep the *Béarn* from slipping out. Moreover, our scouting planes fly over Martinique daily.

In November 1940 the affairs of this island seemed about to provoke a first-class crisis. It was announced suddenly in Washington that units of the United States fleet were visiting the eastern Caribbean on "maneuvers." The story behind this is not merely that we feared than the *Béarn* might escape but that Vichy might announce some change in the status of the colony. Also there had been reports of submarine activity near the Canal and rumors—never confirmed—of German pilots arriving in Martinique from Colombia. In any case it seems clear now that the United States was prepared to take Martinique and Guadeloupe over, and in fact was on the point of doing so. But after a few days of tension the French ambassador to Washington, Gaston Henry-Haye, told the State Department that the Vichy government officially disclaimed any intention of surrendering any French possessions in the western hemisphere to Germany. This statement was accepted by the United States government, and the "maneuvers" were called off.[2]

American army and navy officers would like very much to add Martinique and Guadeloupe to our defense cordon. Certainly we could not countenance their being fortified by anyone else. Guadeloupe is about 400 miles from Puerto Rico, and Martinique about 400 from Trinidad. Thus the two islands stand directly in the widest gap in our chain of bases. The eastern half of Guadeloupe is fairly flat, and could provide a good landing field; Martinique has an excellent harbor, as well as drydock facilities of some value. Admiral Leahy, when he was retiring from the governorship of Puerto Rico to become United States ambassador to France, said quite frankly, "Martinique would make a perfectly splendid base —if we had it."

The Dutch islands Curaçao and Aruba are in a different category from the French possessions, and they present different— but important—problems. They are loyal to the Netherlands government in exile, and they are now garrisoned by British troops. Nor is our navy idle. The islands are only 620 miles from the Canal, and their proximity to the Venezuelan coast gives them strategic value. Also, Curaçao and Aruba, as I have noted in the chapter on Venezuela, possess oil refineries cardinally necessary to British conduct of the war. Venezuelan crude oil goes from Lake Maracaibo—which is too shallow for ocean-going vessels— to the Dutch islands, where it is refined and shipped. About five-sixths of the total immense output of Venezuela's oil is refined in Aruba and Curaçao.

[2] In April 1941 came a similar scare over Martinique, but similarly it died down.

The Future Beckons

The new American bases on British territory and our vital potential interest in the French and Dutch colonies naturally pose serious questions for the future policy of the United States.

Suppose Great Britain should lose the war. It is all but inconceivable that we should permit any island on which we are building bases to leave our possession. Similarly we would be almost certainly bound to take over the French and Dutch areas. Considerations of national defense would make this imperative. In fact, preparations for assuming complete control of the islands are already well advanced in case we have to move quickly. As I heard it said in Washington, "Of course we shall have to take the islands, but we don't know what on earth to do with them when we have them."

So the possibility, even if it is remote, exists that someday the United States may have on its hands some scores of islands with a mixed—largely black—population of several millions, mostly very poor. Some folk will shout that Yankee Imperialism has come again, even though the Act of Havana (1940) specifically provides for our taking over "non-American" territory in certain contingencies. It says: "If a non-American state shall directly or indirectly attempt to replace another non-American state in sovereignty . . . over any territory located in America . . . such territory shall automatically come under the provisions of this convention." Obviously the United States is the only American republic with the power and prestige to take the islands over.

Imperialism is usually unpleasant, but it is not necessarily vicious. It means, in essence, nothing more or less than expansion of power, and nations must often express themselves in terms of power to defend themselves. National survival is, after all, a perfectly worthy and respectable object in policy. What most people resent in imperialism is, of course, its customary intimate connection with exploitation. If you remove the curse of economic *exploitation* from the imperialist idea, you remove much of the stigma from imperialism itself. Therefore, if the United States is forced into formal acquisition of any hemisphere area, we should take the most scrupulous care to do so without profit. We should make it clear that we are not gaining from any transfer of sovereignty, that we do not wish to derive any selfish economic or political advantage from a British defeat, and that we have no intention of establishing a regime of commercial exploitation. It should be the United States that makes the sacrifice, not vice versa.

More than one unpleasantly knotty problem will arise if we are forced to assume sovereignty over Caribbean areas beyond the bases. For one thing, the question of internal political status. We should have to decide whether the islands should be dependencies, territories, or simply occupied areas. Again, consider the complex economic factors involved, whether for instance the Caribbean islands with their low standard of living could afford to be included in the American tariff system. Again, there is the ticklish matter of citizenship and immigration to the United States for populations that are largely underdeveloped socially, diseased, illiterate, and of mixed blood.

One ingenious possibility is that Canada, not the United States, might take over sovereignty. This would of course depend on the outcome of the war and the whereabouts of the British fleet. Another possibility would be the invention of a kind of joint trusteeship on the part of Latin America as a whole, with the United States as the administrator.

Normally an imperialist experiment faces two obstacles or dangers. One is from native oppositionists who resent control by the dominant power from the *socialist* point of view; what they object to is exploitation by capitalism as well as by predominantly political factors, as in some parts of China. The other is traditionally *nationalist* in character, as in Ireland say. Native nationalists resent political domination by another power, because they want complete independence for themselves. Sometimes these parallel currents merge, as in the left wing of the Indian National Congress. But the United States should be able to forestall serious opposition on these scores, first because the Caribbean peoples are on the whole pacific in temperament with no deep nationalist instincts, second because the entire recent trend of our foreign policy has been away from imperialism. Above all, we must make it clear that we do not intend to exploit any territory for private gain.

Finally, if we do have to take any islands over, we should remember closely the lessons of our previous experiments. We should, for instance, keep in mind the example of Puerto Rico—and do a great deal better.

Chapter XXVIII
Our Orphan Island

STRICTLY speaking, Puerto Rico is outside the province of this book, since it is not an American Republic but a dependency of the United States. But after I had spent a few days in San Juan, the island's dingy capital, I decided that it must have a word.

I plodded through the streets of San Juan, and I took a brief trip or two into the countryside. What I found appalled me.

I saw rickety squatter houses perched in garbage-drenched mud within a few miles of the new United States naval base.

I saw native villages steaming with filth—villages dirtier than any I ever saw in the most squalid parts of China.

I saw the smoke of burning refuse near San Juan harbor—and smelt it—a scene that is a shame and disgrace to the United States.

I saw Franco flags flying openly in many villages, since several thousand Puerto Ricans retain Spanish nationality and are Fascist-minded. This on United States soil!

I saw children bitten by disease and on the verge of starvation, in slum dwellings—if you can call them dwellings—that make the hovels of Calcutta look healthy by comparison.

I saw, in short, misery, disease, squalor, filth. It would be lamentable enough to see this anywhere. It would be shocking enough in the remote uplands of Peru or the stinking valleys of the Ganges. But to see it on American territory, among people whom the United States has governed since 1898, in a region for which our federal responsibility has been complete for 43 years, is a paralyzing jolt to anyone who believes in American standards of progress and civilization.

The picture seen by the eye is bad enough. The story heard by the ear is even worse.

I found that in Puerto Rico between 350,000 and 400,000 school children—about 56 per cent of the children of school age—do not go to school, because there are not enough schoolrooms.

I found that in some villages a flat 100 per cent of the population has malaria.

I found that infant mortality in Puerto Rico is the highest in the world, four times that of the United States.

I found that the average income of the *jíbaro* (peasant) is about $135 per year, or less than 40 cents a day.

I found that a pound of meat costs 30 cents in Puerto Rico, whereas in Santo Domingo 45 miles away it is 6 cents.

I found that there is no milk fit to drink, and that even the public water supply—on American territory!—is not safe, because the island cannot afford proper sanitation methods.

Also—and this is the Puerto Rican paradox—I found hope and confidence that a new administration is going to mend many of these things.

Presenting Puerto Rico

Legally Puerto Rico is "an organized but unincorporated territory of the United States," which means that it is a "dependency." We do not use the term "colony," which is too imperial for American taste; but a colony is what the island is, more or less. Its status is lower than that of Alaska (an "incorporated" territory) and is the same as Samoa or the Virgin Islands. Most people think that this represents a temporary condition; therefore the classic issue in Puerto Rican politics is what the island's eventual fate will be.

The technique of government and administration in Puerto Rico is a baffling hodgepodge deriving from a law passed in Washington in 1917, the so-called Organic Act. This gives the island a legislature (19 senators, 39 representatives) elected freely by the Puerto Rican people. Also the island elects a Resident Commissioner to the United States, who is a member of the House of Representatives in Washington, but who cannot vote. Otherwise Puerto Rico is largely governed from Washington, under the aegis of the Department of the Interior. The highest local official is the governor, who is appointed by the President of the

United States for an indeterminate period; the President also appoints the local Attorney General, the Commissioner of Education, and members of the Supreme Court. All Puerto Ricans are United States citizens by right of birth.

The governor, appointed from Washington, is the local boss. But he must co-operate with an elected legislature which often opposes him. The system is roughly—very roughly—that of the provinces of British India. Out of it confusions grow.

The United States took Puerto Rico during the Spanish-American war in 1898. The island had long been known as Spain's stablest, richest, and most conservative colony; yet there was no resistance to the American troops when they landed. Indeed, they were welcomed as deliverers. Puerto Rico fell into the American lap, more by accident than by military or colonial design, and has been wriggling ever since.

From the economic point of view the overwhelming problem of Puerto Rico is the relation of population to the land. The orphan island teems and bristles with crowded thousands. It covers only 3,435 square miles, which is less than the area of Connecticut; yet the population is about 1,800,000. Next to Java, it is the most densely populated region in the world—a fact of which few are aware. The density of population is 520 to the square mile, as against 41 in the United States. The people are about three-quarters white, one-quarter black and mulatto. Among the "whites" there are many grays.

Puerto Rico's poverty is caused first and overwhelmingly by overpopulation, which is in turn caused by several factors—natural fecundity for one thing, the influence of the Roman Catholic Church, and the efficiency of the United States health service. But there are other reasons why the island is so desperately poor.

First, sugar. Puerto Rico lives mostly by sugar, the price of which has drastically fallen in recent years. About 65 per cent of its sugar is controlled by four large American companies, which are absentee-owned. This means that most of the profits leave Puerto Rico, where they might contribute to the common wealth, and go to the United States. I heard it said by one expert that the four chief companies have taken $78,000,000 out of Puerto Rico in the past fifteen years, which is about five times the average annual budget. But this is not the whole story. Sugar was once highly profitable, and so land was given over to sugar—which no longer pays its way—that might have been truck gardens and at least given the people something to eat. Again: the grinding season for cane sugar is very brief; thousands of itinerant workers can count on only a few months' work a year. Again: production costs are very high.

Second, the American tariff. Here is a complicated issue. Puerto Rico is technically part of the United States, and is therefore bound by our tariff schedule. This means that Puerto Ricans pay the same high prices for goods that people in the United States do. They are miserably poor; yet for shoes, manufactured goods, rice and other foodstuffs, tools, textiles, and other consumers' material (there is very little industry on the island) they must pay New York or California prices. They must pay precisely what we pay, though our standard of living is enormously higher.

Third, concentration of land ownership in big estates. These may soon be broken up, however, as we shall see below.

Fourth, the United States coastwise shipping laws, to which Puerto Rico must subscribe. The rates from New York to San Juan are terrific, yet only by this route can the island import most of the goods it needs. Puerto Rico might have built up a flourishing export trade except for the unreasonable cost of shipping, which is a United States monopoly. I was told that it costs 2 cents per bag to ship sugar from Manila to New York, a distance of 10,000 miles. To ship it from San Juan to New York—1,300 miles—costs 18 cents.

These are among the reasons for the island's poverty and its low living standard. A final example: the daily per capita consumption of milk in the United States is three quarters of a pint. In Puerto Rico it is exactly one teaspoonful.

Muñoz Marín and Independence

The most important living Puerto Rican is the President of the Senate and the leader of the Popular Democratic Party, the American-educated Luis Muñoz Marín.

This man has striking quality. Of all the political personages I met in Latin America, I would put him near the top. Powerful physically, contemptuous of formality, careless in appearance, with a vivid imagination and a brilliant critical mind, Muñoz Marín is destined to go far in the affairs of the Western Hemisphere.

I always like physical and mental vitality, but seldom have I seen the example of it Muñoz afforded me. I saw him at 10 P.M. in the home of a friend, where he was living secretly to escape incessant demands on his time. He had recently been ill and had been ordered to rest. Yet he had worked eleven hours without interruption when I saw him. He called for drinks and wrestled with a bottle opener. He is a chain smoker. He began to talk, and when I prepared to leave at 1 :45 A.M. he was still talking. He then summoned a secretary to proceed with work.

Early in the evening he showed me something with great pride —a letter from the White House.

December 16, 1940.

My dear Senator Muñoz Marín:

I wish to thank you for your very kind letter of October 28, extending your congratulations on the results of the recent election.

The purposes of the Popular Democratic Party as you have outlined them are highly praiseworthy and should result in vastly improved social and economic conditions for the Island. I particularly appreciate your pledge of co-operation and assure you that this Administration stands ready to do all in its power to assist in finding a solution for the problems of Puerto Rico.

May I extend to you my best wishes for your success.

Sincerely yours,

FRANKLIN D. ROOSEVELT.

Incidentally, this must be one of the very rare White House letters which contain a typographical slip. Obviously the President meant November 28, not October 28, since Muñoz could not have been congratulating him on the results of the 1940 election on the earlier date.

Of Spanish stock, Muñoz Marín is the son of a distinguished father, the late Luis Muñoz Rivera, who was Puerto Rico's first commissioner to Washington. Young Muñoz was educated at Georgetown University. His first interests were literary. He wrote poems, and his wife is the well-known American poet Muna Lee. In 1920 or thereabouts—when he was in his early twenties—he joined the socialist party, though his father sternly opposed this step. He campaigned for La Follette in 1924, and then returned to San Juan. His life, to the hilt, has been devoted to Puerto Rico ever since.

He gave up official socialism, and by 1932 had risen high in the ranks of what was then called the Liberal Party. He became a senator in the local legislature, and was one of the leading spirits of the PRRA, the Puerto Rican equivalent of the WPA which initiated several big-scale economic projects. But in 1937 he was expelled by the Liberals, because he was attacking the sugar barons bitterly and because he had come out openly for Puerto Rican independence.[1] The Liberals stood merely for statehood. Muñoz wanted complete independence. He spent a year or so out of power. People said he was "finished." But he wasn't finished—not by any means.

In July, 1938, he founded a new party, the Popular Democratic Party, to give expression to his opinions and to fight the 1940 general election. He brought this party from a membership of zero to the largest voting strength on the island in a little over two years. The party is theoretically pledged to independence from the United States. But Muñoz views independence as a "reserved subject." He took into view the new situation caused by the Euro-

[1] Also because the sugar interests refused to continue contributions to the Liberals until he was dismissed.

pean war and the defense problems of the United States, and he dropped—temporarily at least—his major objective out of regard for future contingencies. In a word, he gave up his main plank. He told his people that he absolutely eliminated the question of independence during the electoral campaign, and that he was *not* campaigning on the issue of insular status. As he put it to me, "I refused to make use of the independence issue in the campaign because it would have divided the people on an abstract issue which the election could not possibly settle." His idea now appears to be a kind of "independence"—in the vague future—within some sort of Pan-American federation. Puerto Rico is to be a "link" between the Americas.

Muñoz did some spectacular campaigning. He told me, for instance, that he had made 30,000 speeches in fifty days. My eyebrows lifted. He laughed and explained that he made records— they cost 84 cents each to make—and sent 200 of them into the villages with instructions that each was to be played ten times daily. He put loudspeakers on oxcarts. He traveled by muleback. He visited nearly every community on the island. He went out— himself—and sold advertising for a newspaper called *El Batey*, and got $175 per issue, which was enough to finance a four-page sheet. He ran the circulation from nothing to 100,000 copies— enormous for Puerto Rico. During his campaign he wrote out twenty-two bills—complete to the last comma—for presentation to Congress, so that the people would know that his program was not merely a matter of promises, but actual legislation already drafted. As a result of all this he won the election.

But only by a very narrow margin. Muñoz's campaign was refreshing, he did not win easily. His party got control of the senate, but only by ten out of nineteen seats. In the legislature the result was a tie, 18 for Muñoz, 18 for his opponents. The balance of power in the legislature thus devolved on an independent group called the Unification or *Tripartita* party. But Muñoz persuaded this group of three to vote with him, so that customarily he has a clear—but slight—majority.

The opposition runs him so close partly because it is a coalition, not a single party. It consists of strange bedfellows, the Union Republicans, who are extreme conservatives, and the Socialists. Both these parties believe in statehood as the ultimate solution of the Puerto Rican problem. The cleavage is between the Muñoz belief in independence as an ultimate ideal and the statehooders who will be satisfied if Puerto Rico becomes the forty-ninth state. The leader of the Union Republicans, who represents big business and the middle class, is a picturesque lawyer, Rafael Martínez Nadal. He is a graduate of Johns Hopkins and a former president of the senate. The socialist leader, who is now Resident Commissioner in Washington, is the ex-senator Bolívar Pagán. He succeeded the venerable Santiago Iglesias, a Spanish-born carpenter who created the Puerto Rican labor movement.

Muñoz is now president of the senate. As such he is the leading political power on the island, after the governor. Muñoz carries his taste for the dramatic even into senate halls. In March 1941 he entered the chamber wearing an overcoat, a muffler, and a cap "drawn well over his ears," with an attendant close by to give him medicine (New York *Times*, March 20, 1941). He was recuperating from a recent illness. He named his mother, Doña Amalia Marín, as his political heir, and said that she would take his place if he did not recover.

One group in Puerto Rico goes much further than Muñoz Marín in seeking independence. Muñoz may dislike much that we do, but he does not believe in violence. He has steadily opposed terrorist methods. But the youthful fanatics of what is known as the Nationalist Party are extreme Yankee-haters who want independence at any cost. Muñoz Marín rather resembles Nehru in India, one might say, whereas the Nationalists are roughly comparable to the Calcutta terrorists. The Nationalist leader is, however, out of the picture now, for the good reason that he is in jail. His name is Pedro Albizu Campos. He is a mulatto, and a brilliant graduate of the Harvard Law School. During the Great War he mustered into a Puerto Rican regiment as a negro. and became an excellent officer. He is a fiery and effective orator; he became Nationalist leader about 1930. He stood uncompromisingly for complete independence,[2] but in the 1932 elections he got only 2 per cent of the popular vote. He set about preaching racial freedom, and he tried to create a national "army." In 1936 he was arrested, following the murder of the local police commissioner, E. F. Riggs, and after two stormy trials he was sentenced to ten years in Atlanta penitentiary, for "conspiracy to overthrow the government of Puerto Rico by armed force."

Luis Muñoz Marín is packed with ideas for the future development of Puerto Rico. An idealist first and last—and something of a demagogue—he said to me, "What counts is what a country *wants* to be. The goal is the important thing. If a country wants to be a democracy, it should be treated like one."

He told me that the greatest achievement of his election campaign was educative. He said to the people, "We must get democracy working here *even if we lose.*" And he described how, over and over again, in every corner of the island, by every effort he could muster, he told the ignorant *jíbaros* that they must at least learn to say Yes or No, that they must learn to know what those simple words meant, that they must not merely shout Hurrah and ask $2 for their votes.

His program is based largely on efforts at economic amelioration. He pointed out, for instance, that the island consumes 257,000,000 pounds of rice per year, worth roughly $9,000,000. It costs 4-5 cents a pound to the consumer. Two cents of this comes from the United States tariff, although the rice itself is from Louisiana; but the United States maintains a tariff on foreign rice from Siam, and so on, which lifts the price.

One of his ambitions seems already achieved, on paper—the passage of the Puerto Rico Land Authority Bill, which aims to break up the big sugar estates. The Organic Act of 1917, going back to a resolution passed in 1900, contains what is known as the

[2] "Legally" the Nationalists base their case for independence on the theory that Spain was about to give the island autonomy just before 1898.

"500-Acre Law," which provides that no corporation may hold more than 500 acres of land. Most of the sugar properties are very much larger than 500 acres, and the law was never enforced. The end of this story is not yet, but Muñoz has succeeded in getting a new law to replace the old one. Early in 1941, Rexford G. Tugwell arrived in Puerto Rico to investigate technical problems of land redistribution.[3] Then followed a decision of the United States Supreme Court validating the limitation of estates to 500 acres, as the early law provided.

Muñoz has ambitious schemes for education also, but it remains to be seen if he can get funds to put them through. He promises an end to illiteracy in four years, which seems unduly ambitious, since the present illiteracy rate is no less than 41.4 per cent.

The old-guard conservatives do not like Muñoz, and they fear him. I heard one powerful business man say, "Have you met Muñoz? Is he really going to take our sugar away?"

Muñoz himself thinks of his movement as being a Puerto Rican counterpart of the American New Deal. At long last, he puts it, both the United States and Puerto Rico are attempting to drive ahead on similar basic principles.

Gibraltar to the Canal

As I have indicated in the preceding chapter, Puerto Rico is a vital pivot in United States defense. This is not the result merely of geographical factors; it is not only because Puerto Rico straddles the Antilles and thus helps to block off the eastern approaches to the Panama Canal. Its importance comes mainly from the political fact that it is an outright possession of the United States. It is the only site in the Caribbean (except the Canal itself) where we can go as far as we want in any way we please, since it does belong to us. We can exploit its natural advantages exactly as we choose. Every other Caribbean area is subordinate in importance

[3] Later Mr. Tugwell was named Chancellor of the University and Governor of the island, a good augury for its future.

to Puerto Rico, because the others are not our property (except for base sites), whereas Puerto Rico is.

Puerto Rico is the largest island in the chain of the Lesser Antilles; it is twice as big as Trinidad, for instance. It lies 1,210 miles from the Canal, 1,150 from Miami, and 657 from Trinidad. Thus its key position as the "Gibraltar of the Western Hemisphere."

Our defense efforts in Puerto Rico have been prodigious since the summer of 1939. The complete cost of the installations planned on the island will be at least $50,000,000 and perhaps $75,000,000. San Juan is like an anthill bursting with military activity. To mention only one detail: the garrison of the island was increased from 800 men to 16,000 in the eleven months from March 1940 to February 1941.

Such a vast augmentation brings vexing problems—social, economic, administrative—problems of health control, labor, military and naval priorities, local education, food reserves, air-raid defense, and the like. One result may be economic improvement to some degree. You cannot pour $50,000,000 into a country the size of Puerto Rico without stimulating purchasing power, even though you may risk an artificial boom.

The principal project of the United States army in Puerto Rico is the great air base at Borinquen field, on the extreme northwestern tip of the island. This base is designed to command the deep Mona passage between Puerto Rico and the Dominican Republic next door. It is a thrilling experience to fly over Borinquen and see the hangars, runways, and barracks chopped out of the surrounding jungle. The field lies sheer on top of a tawny cliff; planes take off and skim directly over the blazing blue water. Other army installations on Puerto Rico are the air base at Ponce, on the southern shore, for pursuit and fighter squadrons, and six "satellite" or dispersal fields elsewhere. Altogether the island will garrison some 150 planes, with accommodation for 450 more (which could be quickly flown down from Florida) in case of need.

The chief navy project is the Isla Grande base at San Juan har-

bor, where we are building a 672-foot drydock and where an air
station for six squadrons of patrol bombers is in busy service. Isla
Grande already has a good airport, reclaimed from the mud; it is
used now by Pan American commercial planes, and its facilities
are being steadily augmented. This base will also be the home
station for whatever aircraft carrier—or carriers—we assign to
Caribbean patrol. The navy has plans for another big base in
Puerto Rico, a protected anchorage off the eastern edge of the
island, near Vieques, but the work is just beginning. It will cost
$35,000,000.

To summarize, Puerto Rico is the key to our Caribbean defense system, which means that it is the key to the eastern defense
of the Canal. As such, it is seeing the most strenuous days in its
history.

Fifth Column and Falange

A potentially serious problem in Puerto Rico is that of the
Falange, the organization that has dominated Spain since General
Franco's victory. The Falange is more influential in Puerto Rico
than in any area in the hemisphere except possibly Cuba. It is the
island's Fifth Column.

In Puerto Rico there are about 6,000 citizens of Spanish nationality, those who were permitted to opt for Spanish citizenship
in 1898. This community is small, but it is powerful in business
circles, very close-knit, and profoundly Fascist in sympathy. During the Spanish Civil War its gifts to Franco amounted to more
than $1,000,000. Many young men, reaching maturity in these
Spanish families, hate the United States and so go so far as to
take formal oaths to defend Spain against American "encroach-
ments." On the other hand, many folk in the Spanish community
—seeing how American opinion has swung against fascism, and
fearing our entrance into the war—have begun cautiously to dis-
claim their Falange connections.

An official unit of the Falange exists in San Juan, and has registered with the State Department as the representative of a foreign

principal. But its leaders plead loyalty to the local government, and say that they "take no part in politics." The Federal Bureau of Investigation has nevertheless opened an office in San Juan, and watches the Falange minutely. The organization carefully denies that it wishes to restore Puerto Rico to Spain. But almost any Sunday in San Juan you may see Franco flags brightly flying.

Still Virgin Islands

Unfortunately I did not visit the Virgin Islands, which are close to Puerto Rico and are also United States territory. Pan American Airways serves the islands with one plane each way a week, but I could not match my crowded itinerary to those particular days.

The United States purchased the Virgin Islands from Denmark in 1917 for $25,000,000. The motive was simple, even in those days; apprehension that Denmark might sell them to Germany. The Islands, with an area of 133 square miles and a population of 85,000, confront the same basic problems as Puerto Rico, chiefly poverty. The population is—as it was in Danish days—English not Spanish-speaking. The chief exports are sugar and an admirable variety of rum.

The Virgin Islands are a minor link in the Caribbean defense system. The navy makes use of St. Thomas harbor, and the army maintains a subsidiary air base at St. Croix.

Chapter XXIX

Columbus Called It Hispaniola

O N HIS first voyage to the American Indies shimmering on the western horizon, that imaginative sailor Christopher Columbus discovered a Caribbean island which he called Hispaniola, meaning "Little Spain." He set foot on what is now Haiti on December 6, 1492, shortly after his first landfall at Watling Island in the Bahamas. Hispaniola was—and is—an exceptionally curious place, and it has had as curious a history as any region in the hemisphere. Today it is divided into two independent states strikingly different from one another, Haiti and the Dominican Republic. Haiti occupies the western third, and the Dominican Republic (often called Santo Domingo) the rest.

On the poinsettia-fringed shores of Hispaniola, Columbus— the vainest, the luckiest, and the most persistent sailor the world has ever known—pitched his first camp and built his first fortress, La Navidad. It was in Hispaniola that he lost his caravel the *Santa María*; here that he picked up his first naked Indians and screaming parrots for delivery to Seville; here that his men grumbled and almost mutinied as he lay sick for five months. In Hispaniola Spain created its first colony in the new world— which Columbus still thought to be the kingdom of Cathay— founded its first university, and erected its first cathedral, which still stands. In this cathedral at Ciudad Trujillo Columbus and his son lay buried for some years, after they had been exhumed from Spain. Columbus crossed the Atlantic after his death as well as before.

When he first arrived in Hispaniola it was inhabited by mild-mannered Indians whom his men promptly butchered. Hardly an Indian survived fifty years after his coming. As early as 1512 the Spaniards were bringing in negro slaves to work the new plantations. These slaves proliferated just as did the crops they grew—spices, indigo, tobacco, sugar. The island became rich, and the slaves survived the violently hard labor to which they were subjected. As a result Haiti today is 90 per cent pure negro and 10 per cent mulatto (there are no whites except foreigners)—the only negro republic in the world, Liberia excepted. The Dominican Republic next door has, in contrast, a considerable white population—perhaps 20 per cent. The rest is mulatto, with some Indian admixture. Haiti speaks French and a bastard patois called Creole. Santo Domingo is Spanish-speaking.

The history of Hispaniola until modern times is a complex record of murder, romantic madness, nationalism, greed, ignorance, foreign intervention, and black magic. The basic trend was rivalry between French-speaking Haiti and Spanish-speaking Santo Domingo. At first the Spaniards concentrated on Santo Domingo because it had some gold—not much. Meantime French and British buccaneers and traders got into Haiti and found a better bargain. It turned out to be the richest colony in the new world, and they began to loot it. The French grip on the island grew, and Spain was forced to give up the Dominican end; all of Hispaniola—then called Saint Domingue—formally became French in 1795.

Observe the date. The distant winds of the great French revolution began to reach Haiti. They blew on dark fires and soon produced one of the most exceptional events in history—the revolt of the Haitian negroes against their French masters. A black chieftain whose name is legend, Toussaint L'Ouverture, beat the French and established a free republic in 1801. Napoleon sent troops under his brother-in-law, General Leclerc, to conquer Toussaint and his fighting blacks—the only instance of attempted Napoleonic penetration of the western world. Toussaint was captured. But the revolt went on—blindly, blackly, savagely. Two formidable negro chieftains, Dessalines (who had all the whites on the island exterminated) and Christophe (who built the citadel near Cap Haitien which stuns tourists to this day) continued to fight until independence was confirmed. Dessalines was "Emperor" from 1804 to 1806, and Christophe became "King" of part of the island, as Henri I, in 1811. But Christophe, a man of fantastic quality, killed himself later. Haiti has been a republic ever since.

The affairs of Santo Domingo next door were inextricably entangled with this bloody record. Part of the time it was united to Haiti, despite the difference in language; part of the time it reverted to Spain or had a semi-independence of its own. The Spanish upper classes furiously resented subjection by negro kings, and they joined the French to fight Toussaint and Dessalines. Then the Spanish revolted against the French, and Santo Domingo went back to Spain in 1809. Later, two more remarkable mulatto adventurers—Pétion and Boyer—reconquered the Dominican regions and reunited the island under Haitian rule till 1844. After a revolution in 1861 Santo Domingo reannexed itself to Spain— the only country in Latin America that has ever done so. In 1865 the Dominicans pulled loose from Spain again, and four years later occurred something more curious still. The forlorn little country asked to be incorporated into the United States! A treaty annexing it was negotiated and drawn up; it failed of ratification in the United States Senate by just one vote. Had this vote gone otherwise, the Dominican Republic might be part of the United States today.

During the late nineteenth and early twentieth century both Haiti and the Dominican Republic, now independent states, were tormented by the most vicious kind of civil disorder and revolution. By 1915 Haiti in particular had succumbed to complete political chaos. There had been six Presidents in four years, and three of them were murdered. One President, Guillaume Sam, was torn to pieces by a mob that dragged him from the French legation after he had slaughtered a batch of political opponents. The United States felt compelled to intervene, and the marines took over protection of public order. We had been contemplating intervention for some time.

This was one of the earliest and most celebrated cases of "Yankee Imperialism" on record. Beyond doubt Americans entered Haiti for mixed motives some of them dubious. We wanted to save lives and protect foreign property—yes. But also we wanted to protect private American investors who had an important stake in the country—and what counted more—important friends in Washington. Bloodshed in Haiti was the pretext for intervention, not the real reason. American interests were largely concentrated in the National Bank of Haiti and a railroad concession controlled by the National City Bank of New York. It all makes an unsavory story. The best summary is that of Ernest Gruening in *Foreign Affairs*, January, 1933. Once established in Haiti, the American administration took control of the entire government, wrote a new constitution,[1] ruled through puppet politicians, and forced the country to float a $40,000,000 loan on exorbitant terms.

But—it is important to state—the American occupation turned out to be a good thing for Haiti on the whole. We never intended permanent settlement or conquest; we had no remotest idea of making Haiti a colony in the orthodox imperial way. The occupation lasted for 19 years—until 1934, when the Good Neighbor policy was getting under way—and it ended a year ahead of schedule. Too long, certainly. But American guidance and control grew wiser and more lenient as the years went by. We ended a period of appalling violence and we restored political stability and public order. We contributed to education and public works. The cost to Haitian civil liberties was negligible. As if there had been any "civil liberties" before!

American intervention took place also in the Dominican Republic. Our marines went there in 1916, a year after our entrance into Haiti, but they stayed only until 1924. Intervention in the Dominican Republic never aroused as bitter resentment—either locally or among Villardish liberals in the United States—as did the prolonged Haitian adventure. Anyway the chapter is closed, or closing. No armed forces are maintained by the United States in either country today. Nor do we maintain any direct

[1] President Franklin D. Roosevelt has been quoted in the New York *Times* (August 19, 1920) as saying, "The facts are that I wrote Haiti's constitution myself, and if I do say it, I think it is a pretty good constitution." See Gruening, cited above. Roosevelt was Assistant Secretary of the Navy at the time.

political control. In the Dominican Republic we have gradually unloosed financial strings, though we maintain a lien on Dominican revenues until the outstanding debt is liquidated; in Haiti we still have a Fiscal Representative who superintends local finance and controls the customs in collaboration with Haitian authorities.

The Redoubtable Trujillo

Let me turn now to the Dominican Republic and its contemporary personal and political issues. It is an attractive oddity of a country, smaller than West Virginia and with a population less than that of Los Angeles. In many ways it strikingly resembles Guatemala, although there are very few Indians. A completely ruthless and efficient dictator, Generalissimo Trujillo, rules it with a steam roller, as General Ubico rules Guatemala. He exploits it, too.

The Dominican Republic, like Guatemala, pays somewhat appealing attention to the surface amenities. No beggars are allowed; it is forbidden to walk barefoot; children are permitted in the public parks only if they are properly dressed. The Dominican Republic carefully asks if you are a journalist before giving you a visa—again like Guatemala—and pays close attention to any visitors. And Dominicans are formidably sensitive.

The country has one peculiarity I have never met anywhere else in the world. Whenever the newspapers have a good story, they blow a siren that rings throughout the capital city, Cuidad Trujillo. I heard it early in February 1941, when Colonel Batista in near-by Cuba squelched a coup d'état. This was big news to the Dominicans. But I thought the Dominican siren—merely the equivalent of the old cry of "Extra!" in New York—signified a couple of air raids at least.

The Dominican Republic is run, bossed, awed, bullied, suppressed, frightened, stimulated, made to work, and in general sat upon by one of the smoothest *hombres* in Latin America, General Rafael Leonidas Trujillo Molina. I did not meet General Trujillo. He was in New York when I visited his country.

I regret this very much. He is the archetype of the old-fashioned Latin American despot—though he has some modern ideas—and I wanted to see him and study his coppery face. Though his regime is leather-handed, he is dapper in appearance, suave in manner.

General Trujillo, who was born in 1891, calls himself General-issimo of the Armed Forces, Founder and Supreme Chief of the *Partido Dominicano*, Benefactor of the Fatherland, Restorer of Financial Independence, and First Journalist of the Republic. (This last because he owns the newspaper *La Nación*.) These titles were given him by the Dominican Congress—unanimously. Foreigners in the country discreetly refer to him—when he is not present—as "Mr. Jones" or "Mr. Jackson."

This puissant general, who is a mulatto and proud of it, came of humble stock, like his friend Batista in Cuba. He started life as an errand boy and cattle hand, and then entered the Guardia Nacional; after six years of service he rose to Colonel. This was in the period of American occupation. The United States Marines liked Trujillo, who was a doughty officer, and he built his career largely on their favor. They said, "He thinks just like a marine!" One American officer, a Major Watson, gave him his first chance; Watson "created" Trujillo much as—in a faraway part of the world—the British General Ironside "created" the present Shah of Persia. Trujillo's chief aide today is an ex-marine, Col. C. A. McLaughlin.

Trujillo rose rapidly and in 1930, after the marines were gone, performed the coup d'état that gave him power. The President was Horacio Vázquez; Trujillo was army chief of staff. He made his "revolution" by telling Vázquez that army "reservists" were marching on the capital. The frightened Vázquez promptly re-signed—though the Trujillo troops were still far away. But Trujillo did not at once make himself President. He appointed someone else to the job (a man who is now in jail), and then, a stickler for proper form, superintended "elections" whereby he became "legal" President. He remained President till 1938, serving two terms; then he decided to resign and rule from behind the

scenes. In 1939 he visited Europe briefly—just before the outbreak of war—and saw the United States (for the first time)
en route. He went to the United States again in 1940.

General Trujillo's domination of the Dominican Republic is
complete and rigorous, but occasionally he must take drastic steps
to retain his position. Early in 1940 a group of dissident army
officers disappeared; one is said to have been poisoned while in
jail, the others shot.[2] Later in the same year a group of former
comrades—when reports were current that Trujillo was ill—
determined to seize control in the event of his death, in order
to keep the succession from members of his family. One of these
was General José Estrella, formerly Trujillo's closest friend. The
center of the plot was the Santiago region. But an officer in the
capital betrayed the conspirators, and Estrella and the others were
arrested. Estrella was sentenced to twenty years' imprisonment for
complicity in a murder case ten years old. Estrella admitted the
murder—but said he had performed it on Trujillo's orders!

Late in 1940 the *Partido Dominicano*, the only political organization in the country, was purged and a new group—inside the
Partido Dominicano—came to be formed, called the *Partido
Trujillista*, composed exclusively of intimate adherents of the
dictator. Its leader is Dr. José Enrique Aybar, a professor of
medicine, one of Trujillo's best friends, and his private dentist.

The worst blot on the Trujillo record is the massacre of Haitians
in the autumn of 1937. By the most conservative estimate, at
least 7,000 Haitians were slaughtered in cold blood, cut to pieces
with machetes, and left out in the fields to rot. These Haitians
were absolutely innocent of any political ideas. They were itinerant
farmers and laborers who drifted into Dominican territory each
year to get work cutting sugar cane. What apparently happened
was that Trujillo, with ambitions to control the whole island if
not the whole Caribbean area, had sent agents to Haiti to foment
revolution there. These were caught by the Haitian authorities.

[2] See *The Hemisphere,* December 20, 1940.

Trujillo ordered reprisals. Then Dominican troops got out of hand and went berserk at this convenient opportunity for wholesale slaughter.

This affair made the Generalissimo extremely unpopular in Washington; it was, indeed, one of the most unpleasant Latin American episodes in many years. Trujillo, alarmed, has behaved cautiously ever since. He needs American good will, and he has enough sense to know how important the United States is in Caribbean affairs. Besides he is very pro-American. This is partly because of his training with the marines, partly because of natural instinct. Trujillo would be delighted if we actually established bases in the Dominican Republic—one of the few Latin American leaders to take this point of view. He knows, of course, that United States garrisons and aircraft on his territory would serve to stabilize his regime.

The basic, essential fact to be known about the Dominican Republic may be expressed in one sentence: Trujillo in effect owns and runs it—except for the American sugar properties—as his private estate, almost as Gómez ran Venezuela. He controls the salt and shipping monopolies; he dominates the match monopoly; his dummies have their hands on practically all business enterprises. Trujillo manages this "estate" with considerable efficiency. The budget is balanced, and administration is well handled. But he makes vast sums out of it, while the peasants come near to starving. They do forced labor on the roads; they are lucky if they earn 20 cents a day.

About 60 per cent of Dominican economy depends on sugar. Trujillo—with an eye to approval in the United States—leaves sugar severely alone. Even during the Haitian massacre, the miserable fleeing Haitians who took refuge on American-owned sugar estates were not molested. Trujillo, it seems, is content to let Americans control 60 per cent of the country's business, provided he is free to do what he likes with the remainder.

But hard times are coming to Santo Domingo now. At least

60 per cent of the sugar crop was customarily exported to Great
Britain and Canada. In 1940 British purchases sank to zero—
literally. The British stopped buying because of wartime exigencies, and this threatened to bring complete economic collapse. The
United States has stepped into the breach in several ways. First,
the Export-Import bank lent the Dominican Republic $3,000,000
late in 1940. In theory this was to build a hotel in the capital city
(which, uniquely among world capitals, does not possess one)
and for road development. Second, American experts are working
on a scheme whereby Dominican sugar is transformed into "in-
vert molasses," which in turn becomes alcohol. By importing this
molasses the United States hopes to take about 12 per cent of the
Dominican sugar crop.

Meantime, as a natural development of the Good Neighbor
policy, the United States early in 1941 gave up its control of the
Dominican customs, which had been American-run since 1905.
This agreement followed years of complex negotiation. Our customs control was originally established to provide security for
Dominican bonds sold in the United States. Private American
bondholders protested against the 1941 agreement, which was
made without consulting them, but their protest was ineffective.
The State Department took the view that the United States no
longer collects debts by such mechanisms as direct control of customs. On the other hand, American rights continue to be safeguarded. For instance, we retain a lien on all Dominican revenues,
not just customs, for gradual debt repayment, ending in 1969.
But no one knows what is going to be happening in 1969.

At the age of 50 Generalissimo Trujillo is a perfect picture of
the successful Latin American dictator. He has millions in the
bank, all the gaudy comforts of life, absolute political authority,
an army to back him up, puppet politicians to play with, a peas-
antry to exploit. He has cleaned up Santo Domingo physically; he
has established political stability and maintained friendly relations
with the United States; all his opponents are under the sod, in
prison, or in exile.

Like politicians in other lands, Trujillo likes comfort and display. He maintains five elaborate houses, one of them converted out of a night club called the Sans Souci. He is ambitious, cool, and forceful. An excellent horseman, he enjoys riding. He likes to eat, to drink (especially a kind of brandy called Carlos Primero), to smoke, to dance. His yacht, the *Ramfis*, purchased from the Fleischmann family (it was formerly known as the *Camargo*), is the most splendid in the Caribbean;[3] it has an American skipper, an American engineer, an American chief steward. One of Trujillo's characteristics is an inordinate fondness for clothes. He keeps absolutely complete wardrobes, even a full set of uniforms, in all his five houses. Every trouser leg is pressed to a shiny edge.

He has had several wives—the present Madame Trujillo, whose name was Doña María de los Angeles Martínez Alba, is of pure Spanish descent—and several children. His family sense is very strong; like so many public men in Latin America, he clings close to his own kind. He has four sisters and a number of brothers; all play a role. One brother, Héctor, is chief of staff. One, Virgilio, is minister to Belgium and Switzerland. Of the others—though they have importance—no one talks much, except in whispers. One of his sons, aged ten, is a brigadier general in the national army. This son was recently promoted. At 5 he had become a colonel!

The other Dominican political personalities are—to put it mildly—somewhat overshadowed by the Generalissimo. The President of the Republic, however, is a personage of considerable dignity; he is Dr. Manuel de Jesús Troncoso de la Concha, aged about 60, a lawyer by profession, a scholar of distinction, and a former rector of the university.[4] The Foreign Minister, Dr. Arturo Despradel, is a fluent professional diplomat who knows procedure well. An attractive character is Vaino Pichardo, the

[3] But the Generalissimo is unfortunately a bad sailor.
[4] A unique cabinet post exists in the Dominican Republic, that of Secretary of State for the Presidency. Presumably this is to give Trujillo direct access to the head of state if he needs it. The post is held by one of Trujillo's uncles.

head of the *Partido Dominicano*, who is very close to the Generalissimo.

As to matters of defense in the Dominican Republic, there is
virtually no Fifth Column problem, because no local Fascist party
could exist and Germans are almost unknown. American military
and naval planes use Dominican air fields practically at will. We
could probably make formal arrangements for bases any time
we wanted them, but at the moment they are unnecessary. The
minuscule country is from a military point of view virtually a
dependency of the United States.

Refugees in Sosúa

I have mentioned points in General Trujillo's character and
career that may pain the tender-minded. But one accomplishment
to his credit should perhaps recommend him to their thanks—the
colony for European refugees at Sosúa.

Here is a tract of some 50,000 acres in the northern part of the
island, the personal property of the Generalissimo, which he recently donated to the Dominican Republic Settlement Association.
Originally, becoming interested in the refugee problem, Trujillo
contributed a 26,000-acre estate worth $100,000 which had
formerly belonged to the United Fruit Company. Later he donated additional lands, including a mountain area.

The Sosúa colony derives from the Evian conference to deal
with the plight of Jewish refugees called by President Roosevelt
in 1938. The conference talked piously and did practically nothing.
But out of it came a permanent Intergovernmental Committee on
refugee problems. This committee has so far received an actual
offer of land from only one nation—and of all nations in the
world it happened to be the Dominican Republic. General Trujillo
said that he would be glad to give haven to 100,000 refugees.

Trujillo's motive was, one can imagine, double. First, he was
eager to get favorable mention in the United States—particularly
after the Haitian massacre mentioned above. Second, he had the

long-range idea of improving the quality of Dominican stock by deliberate importation of healthy white blood.

A group of American philanthropists led by James N. Rosenberg of New York followed Trujillo's lead by creating the Dominican Republic Settlement Association. This, working in close conjunction with the American Department of State and the Dominican Republic, organizes the emigration of refugees from Europe and their settlement on Dominican soil. The Association is financed largely by private contributions, and officially the movement is nonsectarian. Most of the refugees who have arrived are Jewish.

The work has been in progress only a year, and only about 300 refugees are so far at work on the 750 acres under cultivation. A thousand more settlers are expected during 1941. Buildings are going up and activity is lively; Mr. Rosenberg and his associates are confident. Various agencies in the United States, including the Brookings Institution, are sending experts in such fields as rural electrification, tropical forestry, and sanitation, to lend technical assistance.

The Sosúa experiment may give answers to several questions of considerable potential interest. First, can white Europeans settle satisfactorily in a tropical Latin American republic; second, can they grow crops to provide more than mere subsistence? A third point will be the future social and political relations between the refugees and the Dominican natives. Something at least remotely akin to the Zionist experiment has moved into the Western Hemisphere. Luckily Dominicans are not Arabs—at least not yet.

Politics and Voodoo

I turn now to Haiti. In this unique little country the picturesque almost obliterates the practical. Take a pair of scissors and cut a mouse in half. Tie a red ribbon around the rear legs and stick a penny in the dead mouth. Cover liberally with parsley and catsup and arrange the whole in a neat symmetrical design. Then deposit on your neighbor's doorstep.

I am exaggerating, of course, but the *wanga* (which may be either a charm or a curse) that I describe plays a vivid role in the life of Haiti. This is the country of *papalois* and *mamalois* (witches), of muffled drumbeats from hillside thickets, and of *zombies*—whom the natives believe to be folk who have been drugged, raised from the "dead," and made to work as slaves.

Voodoo, all nonsense aside, is a kind of animistic cult based on secret ritual and magic; as one friend in Port-au-Prince said to me, it is a religion of propitiation, fear, and hate. The voodoo worshiper seeks to exorcise the forces of nature—mountain torrents, snakes, the parching sun, hurricanes, poisonous weeds— so that they may not destroy him. Similarly he seeks protection from his enemies. The technique is aggressive. You put a curse on your enemy before he can put a curse on you. The witch doctor or priest prescribes the particular charm that will do the job, and makes a certain profit thereon. The prospective victim then buys off trouble by procuring a countercharm. So at least the procedure was described to me. Anyone—not merely the voodoo priest—may utilize *wangas* or charms. Anyone can "put the eye," as I heard it expressed, on anybody else. The priests sometimes are very powerful. If they say to their followers that a certain person is to be removed, that person will have an uncomfortable time. He may not be murdered, but he will be shunned by other Haitians, thoroughly terrorized, and probably forced to leave the community.

Voodoo is thus of considerable political importance. No Haitian government would dare to stamp it out, though one recent President, Louis Borno, a devout Roman Catholic, attempted to discourage it. His successor, Sténio Vincent, gained popularity and thus entrenched himself in power by leaning the other way. "Legally," the practice of voodoo is forbidden, but almost everybody practices it.

Haitians are much milder folk than the Dominicans next door. Gentle, rather timid, ruminative, 90 per cent illiterate, with small national sense despite their heroic past, speaking their strange mixture of French and Creole, they are an attractive and picturesque community. There are about 3,000,000 Haitians, living on 10,204 square miles, the area of Maryland; they occupy only one-third of the island, but their population is about twice that of the Dominican Republic. Most of them are peasants, and most are very poor. The annual budget is only about $6,000,000. The amount of currency in circulation is about 50 cents per head.

Haitian economy depends largely on coffee, and the fall of coffee prices has impoverished the country. The average coffee crop—say 27,000,000 kilograms—was worth around $16,000,000 in 1929; today the same amount brings perhaps $6,000,000. The United States took 56.7 per cent of Haiti's total coffee crop in 1939-40; Haiti was the first country in 1941 to sell its coffee quota. This shows remarkable foresight among the Haitians and their advisers, such as the American fiscal representative, Sidney de la Rue. Until 1934 the United States bought no Haitian coffee at all. But obviously the American market would be of tremendous importance if Europe should be lost. So the Haitians adjusted their coffee blends to American standards of quality and taste. Similarly there has been great development in the sale of bananas to the United States. In 1935 Haiti had scarcely any banana industry. But by 1940 it was producing 3,000,000 stems, all raised by small peasant landowners, and marketed by the Standard Fruit Company, an American concern.

The chief political issue in Haiti since the restoration of political order and the evacuation of the United States marines has been the struggle for power between the mulattos, who comprise about 10 per cent of the population, and the pure blacks. Though greatly outnumbered, the educated mulattos hold practically all power. The blacks resent this—they dislike the mulattos much more than they dislike whites—but there is very little they can do about it. The situation derives from a law early in the nineteenth century which established that pure negroes must go into farming and trade, while mulattos were permitted to enter the professions. Thus the mulatto class—doctors, lawyers, engineers—became intellectually and socially dominant, and economic and political dominance naturally followed.

Haiti is very much off the beaten track from the political point of view. Of all the Latin American countries on which I have filed clippings and information for years, it has the slimmest dossier.

Merci, Papa Vincent

The grand old man of Haiti is Sténio Joseph Vincent, who became President of the republic in 1930, and who served as such until 1941. Robust, vigorous, jovial, he does not look his 67 years. He was a poor boy, but he managed to scrape his way through school; a brilliant student, he got his degree in law at 18. Vincent is a man of deep culture, an intellectual. He is the author of numerous books; he can converse with vivid clarity on almost any subject; his indispensable hobby is reading; he talks French with the purity and grace of a member of the French academy.

I saw him in his modest private villa in the oddly named village of Kenscoff, 4,500 feet above Port-au-Prince, the harbor capital. Walking along the roads were marvelously straight-limbed, firm-breasted women, with trays and bowls balanced on their heads; they march gracefully mile after hilly mile, with their hands swinging, never touching the burdens their heads carry. The road is winding, jagged, and lined with jungle; the valleys dip steeply to the sea, flowering with blazing red poinsettia, bougainvillea, and wild nasturtium.

Dr. Vincent is a gracious host. He commented on the excellent relations between Haiti and the United States, and told a pleasant anecdote about himself and President Roosevelt. They met at Cap Haitien in 1917 when Roosevelt was Assistant Secretary of the Navy and Vincent was Secretary of Interior in Haiti. Both were momentarily disgusted with politics; both swore they would never take public office again. But—Vincent chuckled—it was in the cards for Roosevelt to be President of the United States three times, and himself President of Haiti twice.

Dr. Vincent has spent his whole life in political service. While he was still a law student he worked as a school inspector. Then he went abroad—to both Paris and Berlin—as a diplomatic attaché. Returning to Haiti he became in turn a government commissioner, a judge, a senator, and eventually president of the Senate. He spent ten years, 1920-30, in the political wilderness, poverty-stricken and out of office. In 1930, though he started as a bad third, he managed to win the presidential election by some very complex political strategy. Early in his career—when the marines were in Haiti—he was hotly anti-American; he was the country's severest critic of United States intervention. Later he came to acknowledge Haiti's dependence on the United States politically, economically, and geographically, and he changed his mood and policy. As things stand today he is one of the staunchest pro-Americans in the hemisphere.

There are no political parties in Haiti, and Vincent ruled for ten years by keeping close control of the armed forces (the first duty of every Latin American statesman), and by astute political chessplay. A lone wolf himself, he balanced various groups against one another. His passion and joy was—and is—political maneuver. He sought to build schools, and to organize relief work for the poor. His idea was to make use of individual largesse if necessary, and he maintained a semi-private charity—out of his healthy salary of $25,000 a year—called the Caisse d'Assistance. He likes to go out into the country and distribute coins himself.

Vincent is a bachelor, and his sister is his inscrutable and all-watching hostess. He likes to sip Haitian rum in which peaches have been soaked, and a delicious drink it is. He is a chain smoker of Philip Morris cigarettes. His English—as he put it to me—is good enough so that he can read the *Times*, but not the magazine *Time*. He doesn't like to be called a dictator, and he is very proud that in Haiti—in considerable contrast to the Dominican Republic hard by—there has been no political execution in 17 years.

Early in 1941 Vincent, his friends said, was flirting with the idea of following Roosevelt and getting himself elected for a third term. Unfortunately, it had already been necessary in 1935 to amend the constitution in order to let him run a second time, and a third term was forbidden unless approved by special plebiscite. Vincent could have "arranged" to win this plebiscite, no doubt. For a long interval, he refused, like Roosevelt, to disclose his ultimate intentions. On March 10 the Chamber of Deputies went on record voting to extend his term. Then Vincent suddenly changed his mind. On April 4 he announced that he would not run again, and on April 15 the Haitian minister to Washington, Dr. Élie Lescot, was chosen President as his successor.

Lescot, born in 1883, is a lawyer, administrator, and diplomat of much experience. For some years he was a judge, like Vincent, and he served in various cabinets as Minister of Agriculture, Education, Justice, and Interior. It was Lescot, astute and dignified, who arranged the settlement with the Dominican Republic after the 1937 massacres. Many Haitians thought he behaved too softly on this occasion. But he had little choice.

School children in Haiti have for years sung a tuneful ditty called *Merci, Papa Vincent*. The song became a kind of national anthem in diminutive. Now—perhaps—it will be *Merci, Papa Lescot*.[5]

Fifth Column and Defense

As regards Fifth Columnism and national defense, the position of Haiti is much like that of the Dominican Republic. German commercial influence is stronger in Haiti, but political expression

[5] Other Haitians of importance are Senator Zéphirin, a full-blooded negro who is a former President of the Senate; Dr. Fernandez Dennis who was educated in France and is both Minister of Finance and of Foreign Affairs; the commander of the army Colonel Jules André; the commander of the palace guard, Major Durcé Armand, and the President's personal physician, Dr. Rulx Léon.

is mute. Like its neighbor, Haiti will almost certainly give the United States any facilities it wishes. But neither Haiti nor the Dominican Republic is very important today as a site for a full-fledged base, since our acquisition of British bases makes them superfluous. But Haitian landing fields may be useful as fueling stops for fast fighter planes whose range is too short for direct flights from regular base to base.

Chapter XXX
Cuba's Batista

~~~~~~

THE first thing you notice is his broad puckish smile. Cuba's Batista sits like a panther behind his desk and smiles, chuckles, chortles. This man, like Vargas of Brazil, is a dictator with a sense of humor. Not that there is much to laugh about in Cuba— or elsewhere—these unhappy days. Batista's country faces economic problems as grave as any in its history. Nor do his vivacity and white-toothed laughter represent more than a fraction of his complex personality.

Colonel Fulgencio Batista y Zaldívar, the 40-year-old President of the Republic of Cuba, is of medium height, strongly built, with glossy black hair and an oriental cast of features. His face is vivid and lively. He wears a gray shirt and a beautifully tailored dark gray suit; he stretches his shoulders back and you see the tailor's name—Oscar—inside the jacket. As he talks he laughs, jabs a carefully manicured finger at the interpreter, reaches for documents, stirs around in his chair, grins, writes doodles on big paper charts, and makes you feel thoroughly at home. On his desk are a litter of telegrams, a portable radio, a cluster of telephones, and all the evening papers. On his wrist is a large and complex-looking watch, and on one finger a heavy diamond-studded ring.

The gist of what Batista said to me was this. "I stand for the people. I act only with the authority of the people. My preoccupation is to do everything I can for the people, with the will of the people. When I was merely commander-in-chief of the army the position was somewhat abnormal. I have become President of the Republic, by the choice of the people, so that I may represent more than merely the army, so that I may represent the free will of the entire Cuban nation. When I took off my uniform as commander-in-chief, I told the people, 'I am one of you, I am one of yours.' "

He went on to discuss briefly Cuba's relations with the United States, which have never been more intimate and friendly. He said that if the United States should be forced into actual warfare against Germany, Cuba would of course follow at once. "No matter what happens in the field of economics, our friendship with the United States will remain close and complete," is the way he put it.

It happens that there was a good reason for President Batista's flashing humor when I saw him. The events of February 3 and 4, 1941, had just occurred. No wonder he was good-humored. He had just liquidated bloodlessly an attempt by army colonels to unseat him.

On February 1 Batista had summarily discharged Colonel Bernardo García, the chief of police, a somber and powerful figure in the life of Havana. The President charged him with negligence and other derelictions. What is more, Batista wanted to get rid of him because he smelled trouble from the army. García belonged to the clique headed by Colonel José Pedraza, the commander-in-chief of the army, and Colonel Angel González, the navy chief of staff. These two, Pedraza and González, were among the original group of sergeants who helped Batista seize power in 1933. But now they had come to a parting of the ways. Pedraza and González decided to get rid of Batista and they used the affair of Police Chief García as their pretext.

First Pedraza announced, in clear defiance of the President, that the police belonged to him and that he would continue to keep García on the payroll as his private "secretary." Then, brazen and confident, he telephoned Batista, used insulting language, and threatened to set up a military dictatorship or start civil war.

Batista waited for two days, while the army maneuvered its guns into position. Bloodshed seemed certain. But on midnight of February 3, the President slipped out the back door of the palace, drove to the national barracks at Camp Columbia, and confronted the military at their headquarters, though he was unarmed and accompanied only by one or two loyal officers. He talked all night to the dissidents. At 4 A.M. he was on top. At 9 A.M. he announced that Pedraza, González, and García were under arrest; he proceeded to suspend constitutional guarantees for 15 days; then he made the best speech of his career to the officers and men at Camp Columbia, telling them that irresponsible military interference in civil affairs must never occur again, that the military must finally subordinate themselves to the civil authorities, that Cuba had out-grown its famous addiction to military violence, that the country had, in a word, grown up.

The next day, February 4, 1941, Pedraza and his friends were released—without punishment—and exiled to Miami. Batista abruptly restored constitutional guarantees, announced that the affair was over, and resumed his normal work—sleek and smiling.

The analogy for the United States would be, say, for President Roosevelt to discover Colonel Knox, Mr. Stimson, and J. Edgar Hoover plotting against him, to checkmate the plot neatly, pack the ringleaders off to exile, and lose nothing except one night's sleep.

Not the least remarkable aspect of the affair is that Batista him-self came to power originally by engineering a plot closely similar to the one he squashed.

The Sergeant-Stenographer

Batista's origins are obscure. It is often said that he has some Chinese blood. It appears that he was born in 1901 in a place called Banes, a village controlled by the United Fruit Company in Oriente province. His family was desperately poor, and he was orphaned at 11. He grew up without much formal education. As a child he saw the advantages possessed by American officials of the banana company, their schools and recreation rooms, in con-trast to the wretched circumstances of life forced on the Cuban workers, their suffering and poverty. Batista has never forgotten the harsh lessons of his youth.

At 12 he got a job with a tailor; then he worked in the cane fields for a while; he sold goods in a grocery store, studied to be a barber, and emerged as a brakeman and then a conductor on the local railway line. This was not enough for the young Batista. He had energy and ambition. But he lacked education, and the only way he could get it was to enter the army. He did so, and after 12 years as a private, became a sergeant.

Meantime he went to an army night school, and taught himself to be an expert stenographer. This was a key to his future career. Hitler was a house painter; Mussolini was a school teacher; Stalin studied theology and Vargas practiced law; Batista is the only dictator who launched himself to power with a stenographer's notebook and typewriter keys. He wandered over Cuba—still a sergeant—taking dictation from his superiors. He learned a lot of secrets—and remembered everything. His officers came to trust his clever, adhesive mind, and they permitted him to organize other night schools. Soon he was the best-known sergeant in the army, and he often wrote orders which his officers signed without reading. He made contacts with privates and fellow sergeants all over Cuba, dictation notebook in hand.

On September 4, 1933, came his coup d'état. But first I must sketch the turbulent political scene at that time.

The curse of feudal Spain lay deep on Cuba, even after the island won its independence. After the Spanish-American War and United States withdrawal, a succession of feeble governments attempted to rule. Poverty and squalor; the imprint of decadent clericalism on a partly negroid population; flaming political corruption; vanity, laziness, greed among the rich; revolutionary agitation by the students—this was the background. Then came the Machado tyranny from 1924 to 1933, one of the most vicious governments that ever existed in the Western Hemisphere. Machado was a looter. He was a murderer. He sucked gold— some $80,000,000 of it—from American banks, and he sucked blood from bodies of young students. Machado finally fell in August, 1933, largely as the result of brilliant diplomacy by Sumner Welles, then the American ambassador to Cuba. When Machado went, it was like taking the cover off a boiling sewer. Cuba exploded. Came weeks of turmoil. Passion, brutality, revenge, terrorism, burst steaming over Havana. Then—Sergeant Batista stepped in calmly.

At dawn on September 4, 1933, sergeants in all the Cuban garrisons simply announced that their officers were dismissed. Most of the officers never got up so early; they left the duties of reveille to Batista and his sergeants; they had lost all touch with their men. So the rank and file stood firmly with Batista. He promoted himself to colonel and appointed himself chief of staff. It was as easy as that. His organization—all over Cuba—was perfect. His night school (and the stenographer's notebook!) bore full fruit. There was no bloodshed at all on September 4 or the days immediately following. Later came terrorism and an attempt at a countercoup by officers who locked themselves in the Hotel National, but it was beaten down.

Batista's real career then began. He weeded out the toughest of his sergeants, restored many loyal officers to rank, abolished all ranks above colonel, and proceeded to clean up Cuba. For years he worked mostly from the background; he stood behind the scenes, carefully avoiding conspicuous notice. His revolution was purely political at outset. Later it took on social tinges. Batista grew and expanded greatly. He overtook his fellows and contemporaries. In 1933 he was little more than a conspirator, hard-boiled, tense and lean. The growth to the suave Batista of today, the President of Cuba—with his charm, his qualities of grace and humor—is remarkable.

During the seven years he was chief of staff Colonel Batista made and unmade Presidents practically as he saw fit. Nobody else in the hemisphere has been such a President maker and un-maker.

First, he persuaded President Carlos Manuel de Céspedes, the stopgap successor to Machado, to resign, and appointed a five-man directory to succeed him. This directory ruled for only five days, from September 3 to 9, 1933.

Second, he supervised the election of Dr Ramón Grau San

Martín as President. The United States refused to recognize the Grau administration, and out Grau went, in January, 1934.

Third, Dr. Carlos Hevia, who was a graduate of the U. S. Naval Academy at Annapolis, became President, and stayed President for exactly one day, January 15, 1934.

Fourth came the presidency of Colonel Carlos Mendieta, which lasted till December, 1935. The United States recognized Mendieta, and voluntarily abrogated the Platt amendment, which had given us the right of intervention in Cuban domestic affairs.

Fifth, a puppet named José Barnet ruled for a few uneasy months, but soon Batista tossed him out.

Sixth, Batista decided that the people were ready for an "election," and Dr. Miguel Mariano Gómez became President of the Republic. This was in 1936. But presently Batista saw to it that Gómez was impeached and replaced by Laredo Bru.

Finally, in the summer of 1940, Colonel Batista determined to run for President himself. He judged the time to be finally ripe, and he felt that Washington would not object. Besides, he wanted to legalize the *de facto* situation. The election—to everyone's surprise—was fairly and freely operated, and Batista won. Had he lost, of course, he could easily enough have circumvented the defeat. But he did not lose, and in October, 1940, he became constitutional President of Cuba.

Batista rules because he is the boss. That is the plain fact of the matter. But he must have a parliamentary cloak, a façade, and the coalition that provides this is one of the oddest on record anywhere. It stretches from the extreme right, represented by ex-President Menocal and the *Partido Democrática Republicano*, all the way to the communists—plus one or two splinter parties on the extreme left. Batista resurrected the communist party in 1939, and gave it legal recognition in preparation for the 1940 elections, because he felt the communists might have considerable electoral strength among the people. Cuba is the only country in Latin America, Chile excepted, where the communists support the government in power. But they have very little power themselves. By bringing them into his coalition, Batista hamstrung them.

The Batista coalition begins, then, at farthest right (as if, say, Mr. Roosevelt ruled with the active support of Herbert Hoover), and proceeds through various center parties—to the Cuban equivalent of Earl Browder. The old Liberal party of Machado, which is trying to rehabilitate itself, is included in the coalition; this is odd inasmuch as Batista helped to throw Machado out. The *gap* in the Batista coalition, roughly between right and center, is comprised of representatives of two ex-Presidents, Gómez and Grau—who oppose Batista on personal grounds—and by the remnants of the celebrated A.B.C. This was the student terrorist organization that fought Machado. Two or three years ago the A.B.C. turned legal.

In October 1940, Batista promulgated a new constitution—a heavy document, 286 articles long. When I saw him he picked up a red-bound copy, weighed it in his fingers, and chuckled amiably. The new constitution strengthens the powers of the central government, sketches a program of land reform, makes voting in elections obligatory, and—in theory anyway—subordinates ownership of property and operation of commercial enterprises to the "social and economic interests of the state."

So far has the lithe, slippery, smiling sergeant-stenographer advanced. There may be more to come.

Personal Qualities of Batista

Like all men, Batista has defects. He would be the last person to proclaim himself a paragon. For one thing, he is more successful as a politician—a showman—than as an administrator. He is apt to build things too expensively for the Cuban purse, out of desire to make them flamboyant enough for the Cuban nature. One of his favorite projects, a million-dollar tuberculosis sanitarium near Trinidad, in Santa Clara province, is a case in point. So is the grandiose children's playground on the Malecón in Havana. Of course, Batista is paying debt to his own starved childhood with such extravagance. His brother, whom he adored, died of tuberculosis for want of medical care. As a youth he never so much as saw a playground.

He has good ideas, but he may be lax in enforcing them. Partly as a result, Cuba suffers from a traditional malady (though things are infinitely better than under Machado, for instance), that of inflated pay rolls, *relajo* (relaxation) in morale, corruption by minor officials, nepotism. One reason for Batista's stern action in February of this year was a realization, at long last, that Cuba *was* poor, that the government must have money, that corruption had to stop, that officials like Pedraza were too expensive by far.

Another point is that the President customarily surrounds himself with Yes-men. He likes to be among people who do not make him uncomfortable, like his notorious secretary Jaime Mariné, who drives around Havana in an orchid-colored Buick. He is a much better man than any of his friends. But he is, in a way, the product of a gang, and many of the old cronies are still powerful, and think wistfully of gambling rackets in the old days and spoils to divide. Few people—except these cronies—dare approach him.

But the most important of Batista's defects—so friends told me in Havana—is that he learned too much late in life. He is still voracious for education; for instance, he began to teach himself English two years ago, and now speaks it fairly well; and this is all to the good. But he has the familiar shortcomings of a man who obtained most of his education as an adult. He may suddenly be knocked off balance by too rapid digestion of a new idea. He lacks perspective and proportion. Think of reading Karl Marx, Spengler, or Pareto—to say nothing of Plato or Darwin—for the first time at thirty-eight or nine!

On the positive side Batista's qualities are many and considerable. First, one must mention his ambitious intelligence, his great skill as a politician, and his good humor.

He hates cruelty. This is a quite genuine trait, and it is important because Cuban politics—until Batista—have been spattered with blood. Batista has never killed anybody. Both his coups were bloodless. There has not been a single execution in his seven years of power. Nor is there a single political prisoner in Cuba. Far cry from the Machado days!

Again, consider his even temper, his sense of moderation, unusual qualities in a person of complex racial heritage. He can get honestly angry, but he has no fits of futile temperament. He works easily and well, and he is easy to work with. In this he resembles Vargas of Brazil.

Batista is full of common sense, and he has very little vanity or sensitiveness. He is one of the few Latin American heads of state who are freely—and sometimes brutally—caricatured in their own newspapers.

He has great vitality and industriousness. When he visited New York in 1938, he worked so hard all day that his aides would virtually collapse; then he would pick up the long-distance telephone and govern Cuba most of the night, and be up at 6 the next morning, fresh and bright.

Another quality, and perhaps the most important of them all, is his sense of kinship with the common people, the humble underpossessed—which means 90 per cent of the Cuban population. This is not merely good politics. It is emotional conviction arising out of the miseries of his own youth. Batista, like Cárdenas in Mexico, has a deep-rooted mistrust of the upper classes. He hates the rich. His ambition is to educate the masses, elevate them, improve their living standards, incorporate them decently into the life of the community. He is, first and last, a people's man.

Batista's personal life is quite normal. He likes to smoke cigarettes from a long holder. He is fond of both gambling and alcohol, but he seldom indulges in either because he thinks it sets a bad example. He doesn't go to church often. He plays squash for exercise. His hobby is locomotives—perhaps because he was a brakeman once.

When he wishes to bestow high favor on a friend, he gives him a heavy gold ring. In the center is a large amethyst, flanked by two diamonds on each side. Inscribed are Batista's initials and those of the friend, and the date of the friend's birthday. Most regimental commanders in Cuba get these rings, and many other officials are proud of having them.

Batista married a young woman of humble origin a good many years ago, and his married life has been happy. There are three children, Mirta aged 11, Rubén 8, and a little girl, Elisa, born early in 1941. Batista is deeply fond of the children, especially the boy. He has decked him out with a sergeant's uniform, and calls him the "Little Sergeant." Batista once told a friend, "No one knows who my family was, but anybody in the world can hear my boy say, '*My* father is Batista!'"

The Batistas are not particularly interested in money—he is no looter like most of his predecessors—and they live fairly modest lives. The official residence is the Presidential Palace, owned by the Cuban government. Privately, Batista has bought a bright-colored plaster villa near the sea in the Miramar district, and he still maintains the house in Camp Columbia where he lived when he was chief of staff. The Batistas entertain little, and seldom go out into Cuban "society."

In 1938 Batista was preparing to visit General Malin Craig, the American chief of staff, in the United States—which was his first trip outside Cuba. He looked at the blazing rows of medals on his uniform and cautiously asked, "How many decorations does General Craig wear?" "Only one," came the reply. Batista roared, "Name of God!" and said to his orderly, "I will not go to Washington like a monkey on a stick. Rip off all my medals but the two top rows."

Sugar Daddyism

Neither military affairs nor the new constitution nor political juggling is the major preoccupation facing President Fulgencio Batista just now. One problem is so big that all the others fade into insignificance. That problem is sugar.

Cuba lives at least 75 per cent on sugar, and the price of sugar utterly dominates the economic life of the island. When sugar rose steeply in 1920—to the fantastic figure of 22½ cents a pound—Cuba voluptuated in crazy wealth. When it fell later—to the equally fantastic price of 3½ cents—the island rocked in poverty and panic. For twenty years various schemes have been launched, both in the United States and Cuba, to control sugar production and keep prices stable. Cuba is the second sugar-producing country in the world.

About 85 per cent of Cuban sugar mills are American-owned, and two-thirds of Cuba's sugar crop goes to the United States. In return for selling us sugar, Cuba buys our manufactured goods— some $80,000,000 worth in a good year—which means that Cuba is a very important customer. The American investment in Cuba amounts probably to $1,200,000,000—the largest American invest-ment in any country in the hemisphere, Canada excepted. To gauge the importance of this sum, recall that it is about four times the total American investment in all the Far East.

By terms of a trade agreement signed in 1934 Cuban sugar is given a quota in the United States exactly as is beet or cane sugar from domestic producers. From this point of view the country is part of the American internal sugar system. But Cuban sugar pays a stiff duty to enter the United States, 90 cents per 100 pounds. This was, however, regarded as a concession to Cuba, not as a dis-crimination against her, since other foreign countries pay a duty of $1.85. As a result, such sugar exporting states as the Dominican Republic think that Cuba, a kind of kept woman of the United States, is being unduly favored. But the Cubans—who are abso-lutely dependent on the United States market—say on the contrary that we take advantage of them. They feel that the domestic sugar industry in the United States is a hothouse phenomenon, too highly subsidized and too expensive to the American taxpayer. They point out that their sugar is natural, not artificial, and that they could produce infinitely more than the quota—about 2,000,000 long tons a year—allows them. (Indeed, most Cuban mills are only running to about 50 per cent capacity; they grind only about three months a year.) What Cubans want is a bigger quota, and—as an ideal—entry of their sugar duty free.

Early in 1941 the Export-Import Bank came to Cuba's rescue with a $12,000,000 loan, which is expected to finance the 400,000-ton surplus of the present crop. Were it not for American beet-sugar senators who want to protect their own local industry, such loans—inevitably there will be more of them—might be unnecessary.

Sugar plays an enormous role in Cuba's domestic economy and finance, it goes without saying. It is taxed in various ways. One tax of 9 cents per bag pays for the military schools which Batista has scattered over the island.

Cuban Fifth Column

We come now to the question of defense and of Cuba's political relations to the United States. From the official point of view, the State Department looks on Cuban internal politics exactly as if they were the politics of Bulgaria. We do not interfere. In fact, we lean over backward not to interfere, if only because Cuba is so close. There has been no American intervention in the country since the Good Neighbor policy began. Nevertheless, our indirect influence is profound. It is almost inconceivable that President Batista would take any important step without first consulting George S. Messersmith, the tactful, able American ambassador.

In the realm of national defense Cuba is regarded by our general staff practically as Florida is. The island covers 800 miles of vitally important Caribbean frontier—vital for the defense of the Panama Canal, vital in our chain of Antilles bases. A stable, peaceful, friendly Cuba is essential to our defense system. We could under no circumstances permit any foreign power to get a foothold there.

At Guantánamo, at the southeastern tip of the island, we maintain an important naval station; we reserved the right to utilize this when we abandoned the Platt Amendment. So far, American military and naval authorities do not consider that we need any other bases in Cuba. But every Cuban air field is ready to receive our pursuit ships or bombers any time we send them. Everything is prepared.

"The United States asks much of Cuba," I heard it said in Havana. "In military affairs we take it for granted that the island is an integral part of the United States. Yet we adopt an official hands-off policy in political affairs and in economics we treat Cuba as a foreign country, though we favor it."

The Batista government has taken as strong action against Fifth Columnism as any other Latin American state. Early in 1941 a decree was issued flatly barring all totalitarian propaganda on the island. Organizations affiliated with foreign powers were ordered suppressed (with the exception that the communist party remains legal, it being assumed that the Cuban communists are independent of Moscow), and the flags, uniforms, and insignia of totalitarian powers were forbidden. All political meetings expressing totalitarian ideas were banned, as well as any use of the mails, telegraph, or radio to disseminate them. The President was given authority to deport any undesirable foreigners of totalitarian sympathies, and even foreign diplomats who overstep their normal duties are subject to expulsion. Finally, the decree specifically prohibits "talking or writing about the United States or any other democracy with disrespect."

The heart of Fifth Columnism in Cuba was the Spanish Falange organization. There are about 300,000 Spanish *citizens* in Cuba— those who opted for retention of Spanish citizenship after 1898— and they constitute an influential community. Yet Batista has had the courage to include the Falange in his anti-Fifth Column measures. Spanish flags no longer fly in Cuba—though in the American territory of Puerto Rico they are common. And Batista refused recently to accept the appointment of a man named Genaro Riestra as Spanish consul general to Cuba, because he was a prominent Falangist.

The fact that the Cuban *army*—for years the real repository of political power on the island—has been generally pro-American has, of course, helped Batista greatly. Usually Fifth Columnism is dangerous only if it takes root in the military or air forces of a country. In Cuba, this never happened, and as a result the Germans—despite their usual attempts to buy minor newspapers and distribute pamphlets—have never been important.

The Cuban Nazi party, which existed legally until the 1941 decrees, is the only one in Latin America that frankly sought to change its name to "Fifth Column party." But no one did much but laugh. In July 1941, all Axis consulates in the country were ordered closed, following similar action by the United States.

Prime Minister and Others

Second to Batista in the structure of Cuban government is the Prime Minister. Uniquely among Latin American states, Cuba has one. He is Dr. Carlos Saladrigas, a vigorous lawyer in his middle 40's; he was one of the authors of the coup against Machado, and he has been fairly close to Batista for some years. The President, however, keeps most of his cabinet ministers rather at arm's length; he doesn't want them to be too important. Dr. Saladrigas is very friendly to the United States—he spent some time in America as an exile—and is a close friend of Sumner Welles. When I saw him in February 1941 he said that Cuba would enter the war immediately if the United States did.

The foreign minister, Dr. José Manuel Cortina, is a well-known scholar and orator, a wealthy landowner, and a parliamentarian of much experience. Cortina was born at San Diego de Núñez in 1880. He was educated as a doctor of law at the University of Havana, and has been active in public life for many years. He has written several dozen books, and was president of the Pan-American conference at Buenos Aires. His capacity to express himself in literary work or conversation is notable. He is a good friend of the United States.

Other cabinet ministers reasonably close to Batista—though they are not cronies—are Dr. Juan José Remos, the Minister of Education, and Dr. Domingo Ramos, the Minister of Defense.

Closer to the President—indeed closer than anyone outside the immediate circle of army friends and cronies—is Amadeo López Castro, a former Minister of both Agriculture and Finance. López Castro is of humble origin, a man of the people. He is the person whom Batista calls when he wants a serious job done, and he is called the brains of the civilian administration.

The leader of the Rightists in the Batista coalition, old General Mario Menocal, an ex-President before Machado, was one of the heroes of the Cuban revolution against Spain. His administration as President was distinguished by some remarkably liberal spending. He is a representative of the upper-class élite in Cuban society, which normally pays scant attention to politics and despises the parliamentarians. The Menocals are an exception. Menocal's son, attractive and unassuming, is mayor of Havana—traditionally the second most important job in the country.

Among the important left-wingers—at the other end of the coalition—are Blas Roca, a mulatto and a former cobbler, who is one variety of communist, and Juan Marinello, a member of what is called the *Unión Revolucionaria Comunista*. Members of this group worked together—with the army!—to bring out the Batista vote among the poor. The chief Cuban labor organization, the *Confederación de Trabajadores Cubanos*, has never been legally recognized, but it functions more or less openly. Another Leftist leader is García Agüero, a negro schoolteacher.

Among oppositionists the most conspicuous is Dr. Ramón Grau San Martín, a President after Machado and the defeated candidate against Batista in 1940. Dr. Grau is a distinguished doctor and professor of medicine, gaunt, bearded, amiable, a bachelor. For a time he was thought to be very radical, but now he leads a center group, the *Auténticos*. The United States refused to recognize Grau's government, but he is tolerably friendly. He spent some time in jail during the Machado tyranny.

The leader of the ABC's, Joaquín Martínez Sáenz, is one of the ablest men in Cuba. Nowadays the ABC—formerly the stu-

dent revolutionist group—represents the upper middle class, professional men, people of good family, and nonpolitical folk who
think that politics should be purified and improved. The ABC has
no great following these days, either in the chamber or among the
public, but it stands for much that is healthy in the life of Cuba.

One should also mention ex-President Miguel Mariano Gómez,
who was deposed by Batista when he refused to agree to the
9-cent sugar law. Gómez leads the opposition group called the
Acción Republicana. He is a comparatively young man, the son of
a famous former President; he was mayor of Havana under
Machado, and he gave the city as good an administration as the
corrupt Machado would permit. Gómez is fairly rich, and is land-
lord to the offices of the American embassy in Havana.

Batista's Accomplishment

Finally, let us inspect the achievements of Fulgencio Batista,
which are considerable. He has built hundreds of schools and put
the army to work teaching in them. His program for rural rehabilitation is ambitious. He has organized health clinics, orphan-
ages, and so on. His sugar co-ordination law aims to improve the
status of the *colono* (poor farmer), by breaking up the big estates. Constantly he has sought to reduce the disequilibrium
between rich and poor.

But his main accomplishment is something bigger—he has restored civil authority to Cuba. Though an army man himself, he
has ended military control of the island and is giving it what
promises to be reasonable political stability. By becoming constitutional President, he hopes to end forever buccaneering by the
army—always Cuba's most pressing danger. If his luck holds
good, Batista will have solved "the Cuban problem."

Chapter XXXI
What to Do About It

~~~~~~

S O NOW this long journey is complete. We have seen twenty countries in this political circumnavigation of a continent. We have seen Latin America in all its intricate and complex variety from the ochre uplands of Mexico to the glittering islands of the Caribbean. We have met enigmatic democrats like Cárdenas and not-so-enigmatic dictators like Vargas. We have looked at meat in Argentina, Indians in Peru, poverty in Puerto Rico, bases in Uruguay, and nationalism almost everywhere.

Here then is Latin America. Here is an area more than twice the size of the United States, here are 125,000,000 people in the brisk daylight of the Western Hemisphere. Here are broad reservoirs of wealth virtually untapped, here are unexampled opportunities for economic and political evolution. Here is a North American stake of almost $4,500,000,000. Here is our vulnerable continental frontier.

I don't want to add the weight of a formal summary to a book that is already long enough. Besides, I wrote most of my summary at the beginning—in Chapters I and II. Twenty independent republics have arisen from the mists of feudalism and are facing the turbulent realities of this century. Behind them—a complex Indo-Spanish heritage and colonial slavery. Before them—free collaboration for hemisphere solidarity and development.

But, very briefly, it is perhaps admissible to outline again several embracing trends:

First and foremost, the Good Neighbor policy is working well. Relations between the United States and Latin America are better, closer, than they have ever been before—which ought to be good news for all concerned.

Second, what might be called a gradual "Americanization" of the continent is taking place. United States movies and radio are stimulating this movement, and it will increase as commercial, political, and cultural relations develop.

Third, the root problems of Latin America remain bad transportation, social underdevelopment, insufferable poverty, and illiteracy. To raise the standard of living, to raise the standard of education— these are issues which should dominate the future.

Fourth, Latin America remains tenaciously conscious of its nationalisms, though these are not nearly so mutually antagonistic, so internecine, as those in Europe or Asia. Frontiers still mean something. But Latin America has a genuine hemisphere sense. A leading politician from almost any country may be a spokesman for the entire continent.

Fifth, many Latin American countries are dictatorships or semidictatorships, but as education advances, as the influence of the United States is more and more intimately felt, a *gradual* trend toward democracy is manifest.

Sixth, the great socio-economic struggle that dominates so much of the world is comparatively inconspicuous in Latin America, though it is growing. Only in Mexico has a genuine social revolution taken place, though Uruguay and Chile have experimented successfully with paternalist reforms. One reason for this quiescence on the class front—to date—is the primitive economy of most of the hemisphere. Another is the influence of the Catholic church.

Seventh, Latin America watches the development of the European war with aware apprehension. Almost every country is menaced by Axis propaganda and Fifth Columnism. It is meantime protected by the British fleet exactly as is the United States. If Germany should win the war, the future is unpredictable. The United States might lose everything.

A Last Look South

Here then are these twenty independent neighbors of ours. Here then is Latin America. What are we going to do about it?

First, as regards matters of *defense*. The United States should, with every means at its command, continue to pursue negotiations for the use of naval and air facilities at such points as Acapulco, Valparaiso, Montevideo, and especially Natal or Recife on the bulge of Brazil. Such facilities, as I have pointed out several times in this book, might be leased by the United States in the name of the hemisphere as a whole. We need not infringe on local sovereignties. We do not need exclusive jurisdiction. All we want—and all we have negotiated for—is the use of facilities, nothing more.

During the past year military and naval chiefs of staff of most of the American republics have visited the United States, accompanied by leading officers. These visits serve a useful purpose, and they should be augmented. Also we should make it possible for more young officers to come to the United States for military, aeronautic, and naval training. We should be able to honor distinguished Latin American military folk with proper decorations, which is impossible now without congressional action.

At present the United States maintains military or military aviation missions—for technical advice and training—in Argentina, Brazil, Chile, Colombia, Ecuador, and several of the Central American republics, and naval missions in Brazil, Colombia, Peru, and Venezuela. Also United States officers are directors of military training in Guatemala, El Salvador, and Nicaragua. These services might well be extended. Any hemisphere state that wants American officers as instructors should have them for the asking. Meantime, it was announced in August 1941 that 404 Latin American pilots and technicians are coming to the United States for training.

The Gallup poll contained the following question recently: "If Brazil, Argentina, Chile, or any other Central or South American country is actually attacked by any European power, do you think the United States should fight to keep that European power out?" In March 1938, the answers were: Yes, 33 per cent; No, 67 per cent. But by February 1941, the answers were: Yes, 86 per cent; No, 14 per cent. Which shows the way the wind is shifting.

For a time the "Quartersphere" idea was popular in the United

States; that is, that we should drop our military interest in Latin America below the Brazilian bulge, and concentrate our efforts on Mexico, the Caribbean area, and the countries immediately adjacent to the Canal. But the Quartersphere policy is impossible. It would probably work out as an invitation to an aggressor, who would then be in a better position to attack. The United States must defend all of Latin America—despite the tremendous technical difficulties—or nothing.

Finally, by close and intimate political and diplomatic contacts, we should continue to guard against any *internal* revolution fomented by an unfriendly power.

Second, *economics*. Here the chief problem is that of mounting surpluses, as we well know. Latin America is, as it has been nicely put, "commodity rich and consumption poor"; its economy, depending on the export of raw materials, is dangerously "exposed."

For the United States to purchase *all* the Latin American raw materials that customarily went to Europe would, of course, be ruinously expensive. It would cost well over a billion dollars a year, and it is politically as well as economically out of the question. Think what our beef and cotton senators would say! But, particularly on the crucial question of Argentine beef, some sort of token purchases might be made.

Also the United States might extend its hemisphere purchases of commodities that we must in any case buy somewhere, but which at the moment we obtain largely from other sources. We should promote Latin American production of quinine, rubber, manganese. Take such a commodity as wool. We take only 28.7 per cent of our total imports of wool from the hemisphere; this percentage could easily be increased. The same thing is true, with varying percentages, of cacao, diamonds, various tropical nuts and oils, binding twine, and several metals like platinum and zinc.

United States purchases from Latin America jumped enormously when the American defense program got under way. This was partly because of our effort to build up stocks of essential raw materials like mercury and tin. As this book goes to press, statistics have become available[1] showing that the United States bought $340,000,000 worth of Latin American goods in January-April, 1941. This is a 50 per cent increase over 1940 and a 200 per cent increase over 1939. For the first time in years, the American republics sold to us more than we sold to them, in other words had a favorable trade balance *vis-à-vis* the United States. If this trend continues, it will mean that we are replacing Europe as Latin America's most important customer.

South America is poor. How does a continent—or a country—get rich? First, by virtue of political stability and enlightenment. Second, by industrialization. Everything that the United States can do to promote the growth of industry in the hemisphere—as for instance by stimulating steel production in Brazil—will be of value.

The so-called "cartel idea" has meantime, it seems, been shelved. This was a plan whereby the United States would buy Latin American surpluses through a kind of international purchasing agency, on which each country would be represented, and sell them in the name of the hemisphere as a whole. We could thus find the best available market—if any—on the broadest possible basis, and give emergency help to whatever producer needed it most. Also, Germany for instance would be obliged to trade with the international agency rather than with individual countries, which would be advantageous to our political policy. But the cartel plan bristled with so many technical difficulties that, temporarily at least, it has been dropped.

It was, however, an interesting attempt to face squarely a basic problem, which, in the words of Stuart Chase, is "to make the real wealth of the whole hemisphere available to all."

Meantime the Export-Import Bank, with $500,000,000 to play with, stands by. By March 31, 1941, it had lent $220,737,000 to 16 Latin American states, mostly to relieve pressure on local currencies or to promote industrial projects or road building.

[1] New York *Times*, June 28, 1941.

Argentina got $60,000,000 to hold up the sagging peso, Cuba $12,000,000 to finance the current sugar crop, Chile $12,000,000 for the purchase of American airplanes and industrial equipment, Costa Rica $4,600,000 for work on the Pan-American Highway, the Dominican Republic $3,000,000 to build hotels and roads, Ecuador $150,000 for checking the cocoa blight, and so on.

Third, *aviation*. Here the problem is double-edged. The United States government should continue strenuous help to Pan American Airways in maintaining its splendid Latin American services, and if possible augment them. It is difficult nowadays to get short-notice passage on several Pan American routes because of the increasing shortage of planes and personnel. At the same time we should watch with wary attention the activities of the German airlines still flying in the hemisphere.

Fourth, general *cultural* relations. In this category the root problem is probably social. Latin Americans are, one should always remember, highly sensitive folk—so sensitive that it may be an affront in Brazil to say that it is a hot day when the temperature is 101, because Brazilians may consider this a derogation of their climate. Also Latin Americans consider themselves rather definitely superior culturally to the *norteamericano*. Our program is totally off-key when we send emissaries to Buenos Aires, for instance, to expatiate on *our* cultural or social virtues. In fact, this is fatal. Latin Americans don't like uplift any more than we do. The approach should be the opposite. We should try to convince the Peruvians and Argentinians and so on that, somehow, in spite of everything, we are not *all* gringo savages. We should make it clear—if possible—that *we* are nice people too.

Meantime the Nelson Rockefeller organization has much onerous work on hand. One good job already done was investigation of United States exporting companies which for years did business in Latin America through German agents. In other words, American big business was helping to finance the Nazi Fifth Column. Some 1800 agents were blacklisted, as we know.

The field for cultural development is obviously enormous, but it must be fertilized with great tact as well as energy. More Latin American students should come to the United States; the difficulty is that most cannot afford the trip. But steamship costs might be reduced, and a really extensive series of scholarships established, so that thousands of the best young men and women in Latin America could have a year of university training here. Also, there should be an American school in every hemisphere country; the difficulty here is the opposition the Church might furnish. On our side great opportunity awaits United States students visiting Latin America, for instance in the fields of anthropology, tropical medicine, tropical economics, sociology.

One additional point: an increase in the availability of American books to Spanish readers. I do not mean merely books by Hemingway or Steinbeck or O'Neill, but textbooks, vocational books, manuals of engineering and the like. American books are, on the whole, not very widely translated in Latin America; in English they are prohibitively expensive.

Finally, Latin American newspapers are woefully inadequate in their handling of North American news—just as we are woefully inadequate in handling Latin American news—and there might be mutual improvement in this direction.

The Good Neighbor policy, as I have several times pointed out, should work both ways. One small thing the Latin Americans, on their side, could do to improve the hemisphere spirit, would be to build some tolerable hotels. Also they might take time out and master the grim and grisly business of spelling North American names. I have seen Mr. Sumner Welles described as "Wells," "Weeles," and "Wlles." And no one who has read *The Donkey Inside* can forget how Ludwig Bemelmans came out Bnelemaas in Ecuador—under a picture of James Cromwell.

Fifth, *radio*. In this field the United States has cardinally neglected a tremendous responsibility and opportunity, at least till recently. Our private short-wave stations, however well-meaning and agreeable, are pitted against the massive totalitarian efficiency of Dr. Goebbels. German broadcasts to Latin America are, of course, incessant, and when our southern neighbors listen to Germany—on some 2,000,000 short-wave sets—they hear the official voice of the German nation. But when they listen to North American programs, they get a lamentable hodgepodge of advertising talk, incomprehensible jokes, commercial announcements, band music. News reports are as a rule inadequate in themselves, and moreover they do not represent any unified attempt to outline broad United States policy. American broadcasting companies are thoroughly alive to the unpleasantness of this situation, and the State Department is now helping to co-ordinate their programs. But much more needs to be done.

Sixth, *propaganda and political relations.* It is always, of course, much pleasanter to fight fire with water than with fire. But propaganda has become a political weapon of such formidable potency that, if the United States wishes to combat Fifth Columnism successfully, it must develop a positive, aggressive program of its own. For one thing, we should encourage visits to the United States by leading Latin American dignitaries. The best propaganda is the truth. Let Avila Camacho, Aguirre Cerda, Getulio Vargas visit the United States and see for themselves what we are—and how powerful we are. Of the twenty American Presidents, only five have ever seen New York. A conference—say in Washington—of all the hemisphere heads of state might be invaluable.

Another point relates to the extreme importance of prestige in Latin American affairs. The American military attachés in the hemisphere should outrank the military representatives of every other power, even if we have to make our officers lieutenant generals. In one country—until recently—the American attaché was a mere major, whereas the Germans and Italians had colonels, and the Japanese a general. Similarly every American head of a diplomatic mission should be a full ambassador, even if he holds this status only temporarily. A press attaché—to direct and correlate propaganda work—should be established in each of our embassies and legations.

Finally, I asked every Foreign Minister I met how he envisaged the development of hemisphere relations. The answer was the same in almost every country, that these relations must continue to improve, since we are all in the same boat together. The living future of Latin America is bound to that of the United States. What is more, the future of the United States is indissolubly bound to that of Latin America. We need Latin America just as much as it needs us.

Acknowledgments and Bibliography

I HAVE several hundred people to thank for their generous help in preparing this book. The sources for most of it, except the historical passages, are personal—what I saw with my own eyes, what I heard with my own ears. In New York and Washington, and then in each Latin American capital, I saw dozens of friendly experts, of all categories and varieties. I listened to what they said, accepted their information gratefully, and tried to write it all down. I took notes on conversations with 338 people, usually as soon as the talks were finished.

I want particularly to thank the Heads of State and the Foreign Ministers whom I saw (I hope they will not dislike too much what I have written), as well as other cabinet officers; my newspaper colleagues in various capitals; the officials and pilots of Pan American Airways, who extended many favors never to be forgotten; and the splendid corps of American diplomatic and consular officials throughout the continent, whose services were inestimably helpful. I also want to thank Mr. Cordell Hull, the Secretary of State, Mr. Sumner Welles, the Under Secretary, and Mr. Laurence Duggan, who was in charge of Latin American affairs in the State Department when I took my trip, for giving me much useful advice and opening doors for me in every capital.

On the other hand, it is strictly to be understood that no American official, in any manner whatsoever, has any responsibility direct or indirect for anything I say. This is not an "official" book. The State Department gave me every possible help—most generously—but the book is altogether my own show. No one in the Department asked to see the manuscript officially, and for all I know it may be horrified at much that I have written.

On returning from my five months in Latin America I read fairly widely. For historical matters I depended mostly on the *Encyclopædia Britannica* and the *Columbia Encyclopedia*, as well as several of the books listed below. I found various reports of the Foreign Policy Association valuable, especially those by Howard J. Trueblood and Charles A. Thomson. Two pamphlets in the Headline Book series, also published by the Foreign Policy Association, were particularly useful, *Challenge to the Americas* by John I. B. McCulloch and *Look at Latin America* by Joan Raushenbush. As to periodicals, I have read most of the recent articles on the hemisphere in *Foreign Affairs, Fortune, Time, Harper's,* the *Nation,* and the *New Republic.* The *Fortune* series on Latin America, published during 1938, was very stimulating and illuminating, and I think that the articles on Argentina and Chile, both by Archibald MacLeish, set a standard for this kind of job that has never been excelled. Other writers whom I have followed in periodicals are Lewis Hanke, Stuart Chase, Hubert Herring, and Hanson W. Baldwin for military affairs. As to newspapers, I have clipped and read all Latin American news in the New York *Times* and New York *Herald Tribune* for the past year.

The following books were helpful in varying degrees:

Aikman, Duncan: *The All-American Front,* New York, 1940.

Baldwin, Hanson W.: *United We Stand,* New York, 1941.

Beals, Carleton: *America South,* London, 1938.

Beals, Carleton: *Pan America,* Boston, 1940.

Beals, Carleton: *The Coming Struggle for Latin America,* New York, 1940.

Bird, Esteban: *Report on the Sugar Industry in Relation to the Social and Economic System of Puerto Rico,* San Juan, 1937.

Calderón de la Barca, Madame: *Life in Mexico,* New York, 1937.

Carr, Katherine: *South American Primer,* New York, 1939.

Chase, Stuart: *Mexico,* New York, 1937.

Chase, Stuart: *The New Western Front,* New York, 1939.

Díaz del Castillo, Bernal: *The Discovery and Conquest of Mexico,* London, 1939.

Fergusson, Erna: *Guatemala,* New York, 1938.

Foreman, Clark, and Raushenbush, Joan: *Total Defense,* New York, 1940.

Gaither, Roscoe B.: *Expropriation in Mexico, The Facts and the Law,* New York, 1940.

Government of Mexico: *The True Facts About the Expropriation of the Oil Properties in Mexico,* Mexico City, 1940.

Gruening, Ernest: *Mexico and its Heritage,* New York, 1940.

Hanson, Earl P.: *Chile, Land of Progress,* New York, 1941.

Hanson, S. G.: *Utopia in Uruguay,* New York, 1938.

Inman, Samuel Guy: *Latin America, Its Place in World Life,* New York, 1937.

Interamerican Statistical Yearbook, New York, 1940.

Kelsey, Vera: *Seven Keys to Brazil,* New York, 1940.

Kirkpatrick, F. A.: *Latin America,* New York, 1939.

Martin, Percy Alvin: *Who's Who in Latin America,* Stanford University, 1940.

McBride, George McCutcheon: *Chile, Land and Society,* New York, 1936.

Millan, Verna Carleton: *Mexico Reborn,* Boston, 1939.

Muñoz, Joaquín, and Ward, Anna Bell: *Guatemala,* New York, 1940.

Munro, Dana G.: *The Five Republics of Central America,* New York, 1918.

Parkes, Henry Bamford: *A History of Mexico,* Boston, 1938.

Phelps, Dudley Maynard: *Migration of Industry to South America,* New York, 1936.

Prescott, William H.: *History of the Conquest of·Mexico,* New York, 1936.

Prescott, William H.: *History of the Conquest of Peru,* New York, 1936.

Rourke, Thomas: *Gómez,* New York, 1936.

Rourke, Thomas: *Man of Glory, Simón Bolívar,* New York, 1939.

Royal Institute of International Affairs: *The Republics of South America,* London, 1937.

Santamaría de Paredes, Don Vicente: *Study of the Question of Boundaries between the Republics of Peru and Ecuador,* Washington, 1910.

Seabrook, W. B.: *The Magic Island,* New York, 1929.

Seaton, George W.: *Let's Go to the West Indies,* New York, 1938.

Siegfried, André: *Suez and Panama,* New York, 1940.

Simpson, Eyler N.: *The Ejido: Mexico's Way Out*, Chapel Hill, 1937.

Strode, Hudson: *The Pageant of Cuba*, New York, 1936.

Tannenbaum, Frank: *Peace by Revolution*, New York, 1933.

The South American Handbook, London, 1940.

Thompson, Wallace: *The Mexican Mind*, Boston, 1922.

Tomlinson, Edward: *New Roads to Riches*, New York, 1940.

Townsend, W. Cameron: *The Truth About Mexico's Oil*, Los Angeles, 1940.

United States Tariff Commission: *The Foreign Trade of Latin America*, Washington, 1940.

Vandercook, John W.: *Black Majesty*, New York, 1928.

Waugh, Evelyn: *Mexico, An Object Lesson*, Boston, 1939.

Weddell, Alexander Wilbourne: *Introduction to Argentina*, New York, 1939.

Wertenbaker, Charles: *A New Doctrine for the Americas*, New York, 1940.

Whitaker, John T.: *Americas to the South*, New York, 1939.

Whitbeck, R. H., and Williams, Frank E.: *Economic Geography of South America*, New York, 1940.

Wilgus, A. Curtis, and d'Eca, Raul: *Outline History of Latin America*, New York, 1939.

Wilson, Charles Morrow: *Central America*, New York, 1941.

Ybarra, T. R.: *America Faces South*, New York, 1940.

Several chapters of this book appeared in tentative style in various magazines, and I have the editors of *Readers' Digest, Cosmopolitan, Look, Foreign Affairs, Town and Country, Harpers'*, and *Current History* to thank for permission to reprint them. Above all, my thanks go to Mr. DeWitt Wallace, editor of *The Reader's Digest*, who helped to make my trip possible, and who has printed part of the manuscript in abbreviated form.

J. G.

Index

A.B.C., informal understanding of three nations, 264
Acción Argentina, anti-totalitarian movement, 312
Acción Católica, in Mexico, 114
Acción Nacional, in Mexico, 114
Acevedo, Blanco, 341
Acknowledgments, 479
Act of Havana, 29, 313
Aeroposta Argentina, 19
Agrupacion Civico Bolivariano, 184
Aguilar, Cándido, 91
Aguilar, General Francisco, 103
Aguilar, Marqués de, 22
Aguirre Cerda, Pedro, 234-236, 241-244, 255, 258
Aikman, Duncan, 7
Airways in Central America, 145-146
Albert, King of the Belgians, 357
Alberto, João, 353, 362, 368, 400-401
Albizu Campos, Pedro, 430
Alemán, Miguel, 47, 91, 92
Alessandri Palma, Arturo, 239-241, 245-247
Alexander VI, Pope, 6
Alianza Popular Libertadora, Chile, 248
Alianza Popular Revolucionaria Americana, 201
All-American Front, by Duncan Aikman, 7, 200
Almazán, General Juan Andreu, 37-40, 41-42, 101, 102
Almeida, José Americo de, 355
Alvarado, Pedro de, 7
Alvear, Dr. Marcelo T. de, 290, 321-322
Alzaga Unzué, Rodolfo, 295
Amadeo, Octavio, 320
Amaro, General Joaquín, 98-99
Amazon River, 191-192, 350, 381, 394-395
America South, by Carleton Beals, 6, 181
American colony in Mexico City, 47
American Export Lines, 145
Anaconda Copper Company, 261
Anderson, Dr. Luis, 136
Andes Mountains, 161, 182, 197, 207, 238
Andrade Marín, Carlos, 196
André, Colonel Jules, 452
A New Doctrine for the Americas, 25

Anglophobia, aid to Nazis in Mexico, 111
A Noite, Rio newspaper, 387
Antarctic claims of Chile, 265
Anticlericalism, 10
  in Ecuador, 189
  in Mexico, 71
Antonio Rios, Juan, 258
Aprista movement, Peru, 201, 208-214
Aramayo, Carlos Víctor, 223
Aranha, Oswaldo, 362, 376-379, 385
Araucanian Indians, 237
Araujo, Dr. Alfonso, 170
Araujo, Dr. Miguel, 129
Archbishop of Durango, 10
Arco air line, 174
Argaña, Dr. Luis A., 277
Argentina, 282-300, 301-318, 319-334
  area and population, 285
  army and navy, 322-325
  attitude to its neighbors, 3, 316-317
    to Monroe Doctrine, 24
    to United States, 284, 304-305, 312, 326, 328
  beef industry, 296-300, 301-304
  British influence, 305-306
  country with two Presidents, 284-292
  democracy of, 2-3
  divorce forbidden, 10
  foreign and war policy, 312-315, 316-319
  gripped by profound crisis, 282-289
  interventor system of government, 319-320
  pampas and their wealthy owners, 296-300
  political leaders, 284-292, 321-334
  solidarity and defense, 312-315
  trade, 12, 301, 303, 304, 328-330
  traits and characteristics, 292-295
Argentinisches Tageblatt (anti-Nazi), 308
Arias, Dr. Arnulfo, 147-150
Arias, Dr. Harmodio, 147
Armand, Major Durcé, 452
Arriba, Madrid, 348
Arroyo, Augustín, 79
Arroyo del Río, Dr. Carlos Alberto, 194
Artigas, José Gervasio, 335
Arze, José Antonio, 225
Associated Press, 318
Atahualpa, Inca king, 199

Athayde, Austregesilo de, 409
Author, distance traveled, ix
Avianca air line, 20, 174, 175
Avila Camacho, Captain Gabriel, 46
Avila Camacho, General Manuel, 34-52
  attitude to religion, 45-46
  cabinet personnel, 91-96
  domestic policy, 48-51
  how he became President, 34-42
  interview with, 42-46
  personal life, 43-46
  reform measures, 50-51
Avila Camacho, General Maximino,
  46, 48
Axis influence, 16-33
  in Argentina, 306-311
    Bolivia, 229-232
    Brazil, 386-390
    Colombia, 166-167
    Costa Rica, 137
    Cuba, 467
    Ecuador, 191-194
    El Salvador, 129-130
    Guatemala, 124-125
    Honduras, 144
    Mexico, 109-115
    Nicaragua, 141-142
    Panama, 147-151
    Paraguay, 278
    Peru, 205-206, 215-216
    Uruguay, 341, 343-347
Aybar, Dr. José Enrique, 442
Aymará Indians, 198, 220
Aztecs, 60, 64-65, 199

Baldomir, General Alfredo, 339, 342,
  349
Baldwin, Hanson W., 480
Banana trade, 11, 135, 141, 144, 170, 449
Banco Germánico, Paraguay, 278
Banco Italiano, Lima, 207, 216
Bandeira de Barros, João Alberto Lins,
  400-401
Barandon, Paul, 347
Barber, Charles H., 68
Barceló, Alberto, 331
Barco oil concession, 170
Barnet, José, 459
Barros, Dr. Adhemar de, 404
Bases, naval and air, 31, 153-159
  Argentine opposition, 314-316
  Antilles bases, 415-417, 420-422
  Chile, 269
  Costa Rica, 137
  Dominican Republic, 443, 446
  Galápagos Islands, 194
  Haiti, 453

Bases—(Continued)
  Mexico, 115, 116
  Nicaragua, 141
  Panama, 150-151
  Paraguay, 278-279
  Uruguay, 342, 343, 347-348
  Venezuela, 186
Bassols, Narciso, 104
Batista y Zaldívar, Colonel Fulgencio,
  44, 454-463
  achievements, 469
  personal qualities, 460-463
  squashing a hostile plot, 455-456
  the sergeant-stenographer, 456-460
Batlle y Ordóñez, José, 336, 338, 340-
  341
Bauer, Paul von, 174
Bayer, Karl, 137
Baz, Dr. Gustavo, 49, 94-95
Beagle Island, 265
Beals, Carleton, 6, 181
Béarn, French aircraft carrier, 418
Beery, Wallace, 56
Belém, as an air base, 381
Belize (British Honduras), 24, 123-124
Belo Horizonte, capital of Minas
  Geraes, 404
Belterra rubber plantation, 395
Bemelmans, Ludwig, 477
Benavides, General Oscar, 201, 202,
  203, 204
Bernardes, Arthur da Silva, 407
Beteta, Ignacio, 79
Beteta, Ramón, 49, 79, 96-97
Bettencourt, Paolo de, 409
Bibliography, 480-482
Blacklist, British, 142, 216
Blacklist, United States, 163, 227
  in all Latin America, 475
    Argentina, 309
    Mexico, 116
    Nicaragua, 142
Blas Corral, General, 49
Block, Harry, 72
Blum, Leon, 242
Bocke, General Carlos von der, 324
Boehmer, Imro, 142
Boettger, Walter, 266
Bogarín, Archbishop Sinforiano, 279
Bogotá, Colombia's cultured capital,
  160, 161, 168
Bohnstadt, Colonel von, 130
Boletín de Unidad, Mexico, 113
Bolívar, Simón, 9, 164, 180-181, 190,
  285
Bolivarismo y Monroismo, by Vascon-
  celos, 104

Bolivia, 219-233
  army and politicos, 224-225
  attitude to United States, 225
  German airline ousted, 229-230
  size and population, 219
  the emperor of tin, 221-223
Bomfim, Marcel, 407
Books, American, in Latin America, 476
Bouças, Valentim, 409
Bowers, Claude G., 235
Boyacá, Bolívar's victory at, 181
Braden, Spruille, 174, 233
Bragança Orleans, Dom João, 356
Bragança Orleans, Dom Pedro de, 409
Bravo, Dr. Mario, 332
Braz, Wenceslau, 407
Brazil, 370-390
  amiable traits, 373-375
  area and population, 350, 370, 376
  army, navy, and air force, 384-386
  attitude to United States, 351, 362, 368, 378, 379, 389-390
  Bagé incident, 384-386
  coffee and its problems, 391-394
  color line absent, 375
  foreign policy, 379-382
  German designs on, 30
  historical sketch, 371-373
  political leaders, 400-410
  rubber: its rise and fall, 394
  status of air lines, 388-390
  struggle with nature, 370-371
  three dominant issues, 372
  trade, 387
  what the country needs, 399
Brazilians, sensitiveness of, 475
Briand, Aristide, 245
British fleet, first line of defense, 32
British Honduras, dispute over, 123-124
Brookings Institution, 447
Bryan-Chamorro Treaty, 141
Buenos Aires, 282, 319, 320, 321
Buenos Aires Conference, 28-29, 467
Buenrostro, Efraín, 49
Bulge of Brazil, air service from Berlin, 19, 370, 380, 381, 472-473
Busch, General Germán, 225-227
Butler, Nicholas Murray, 258, 333
Byrd, Admiral, 265

Caballero, Dr. Nieto, 168
Cabot, Sebastian, 305
Cabral, Pedro Alvares, 371
Cabrera, Luis, 103
Cacho, Manuel, 46

Calderón Guardia, Francisco, 134
Calderón Guardia, Dr. Rafael Angel, 134-135
Calderón Muñoz, Dr. Rafael, 134
Callender, Harold, 196
Calles, Plutarco Elías, 47, 55, 64, 101
Camacho (*see* Avila Camacho)
Camacho Montoya, Guillermo, 172
Campos, Dr. Francisco, 402
Canal Zone, 26, 27, 142, 143-148, 152, 153-159, 217, 218
  annual rent and pay roll, 152
  building roads and airports, 156
  building third set of locks, 157-159
  cost of sea-level canal, 159
  cost of whole project, 158
  defense problems, 19, 153-159, 411-422, 432-434
  garrison and safeguards, 155-159
  no road across isthmus, 158
  treaty handicaps, 152
Canning, George, 23
Cantilo, José María, 326
Capanema, Gustavo, 404
Caproni Company in Peru, 215
Caracas, birthplace of Bolívar, 180-181
  high prices in, 177-178
Cárdenas, Dámaso, 83
Cárdenas y del Rio, General Lázaro, 37-40, 55, 73-74, 75, 78-86
  intimate view of the man, 78-86
  most important living Mexican, 86
  sample of his courage, 82
  what he gave to Mexico, 84-86
Carias, General Tiburcio, 143-144
Caribbean, American military and naval lake, 412-422
Carioca, Rio newspaper, 385
Carr, Katherine, 197, 287
Carranza, Venustiano, 55, 63, 107
Carrasco airport, Uruguay, 349
Carrillo, Alejandro, 88
Cartel plan, 474
Casa Rosada, Argentine White House, 287, 291
Casado, Carlos, owns 56,000,000 acres, 278
Castillo, Ramón S., 287-291
Castillo Nájera, Dr. Francisco, 49, 79
Catholicism, profound influence of, 9-11
  in Colombia, 166, 167, 172-173
  in Mexico, 114
Cattete Palace, Vargas' business office, 357
Cedillo, General, revolt of, 81, 83, 100, 112

Central American federation, obstacles to, 122-123
Central Railway, Peru, 207
Cerro de Pasco, copper center, 198
Cerro de Pasco Corporation, 207
Céspedes, Carlos Manuel de, 458
Chaco War, 221, 224, 226, 228, 231-233, 275, 333
Chacras, Ecuador, attacked by Peru, 187
Chaplin, Charlie, 309-310
Chapultepec Castle, 44
Charlone, César, 342
Chase, Stuart, quoted, 60, 474, 480
Chateaubriand, Assis, 409
Chibcha Indians, 164
Chichén Itzá, 59
Chicle, sources of, 14
Chile, 234-259, 260-270
  attitude to United States, 235, 269
  democracy of, 2-3
  industrial and New Deal measures, 262-265
  landed oligarchy, 238
  Popular Front government, 234-259
  size, shape, and population, 236
  social welfare system, 262-264
  tangled tale of Chilean politics, 239-257
  three Chiles, 237-238
Chile, Land and Society, 238
Chilean Wine Growers' Association, 235
Chileno-Spanish War, 237
Chinantec language, 65
Chuquicamata copper mine, 261
Church, influence of, 6, 9-11
  in Argentina, 291
  Brazil, 359
  Ecuador, 189
  Mexico, 50-51, 58, 61, 62, 68, 71-72
  Paraguay, 279
  Puerto Rico, 425
  South America, 162
Churchill, Winston, 350, 382
Ciudad Trujillo, 440
Civil Aeronautics Board, 20
Clark, Foreman, 28
Clericalism, a political problem, 10, 11
Clubs of Urraca, in Panama, 149
Cocoa, in Ecuador, 11, 190
Coffee, in Brazil, 350, 391-393
  in Colombia, 170
    Costa Rica, 135-136
    El Salvador, 128
    Haiti, 11, 449

Cohen, Benjamin, 257
Collected Papers, by Justice Frankfurter, 402
Colombia, 160-175
  area and population, 161
  attitude to United States, 166, 172, 175
  climate and its effect, 164
  dispute over the canal, 25, 26
  diversified export trade, 170
  Fifth Column activities, 171-175
  political leaders, 165-170
  why a democratic country, 164
Colonial period, 7-9
"Colossus of the North," 25
Columbus, Christopher, 6, 411, 436
Communism, in Argentina, 332
  in Chile, 256-257
  in Cuba, 459
  in Mexican labor unions, 88, 89
Compagnie Aramayo des Mines en Bolivie, 223
Condor, German air line, 19, 386, 387, 388
Confederación Nacional de Campesinos, 38
Confederación Regional Obrera Mexicana, 89
Confederación de Trabajadores de Mexico, 38, 88, 89
Confederate soldiers in Brazil, 395
Confederation of Latin American Workers, 88
Conquistadores, 5, 6, 9, 58, 198
Consolidated Oil Corporation, 74
Contre l'Un, by Etienne de la Boetie, 92
Contreras Labarca, Carlos, 256
Contreras de Schnake, Señora Graciela, 253
Coolidge, Calvin, 27
Copello, Cardinal Santiago Luis, 331
Copper, 11, 207, 261
Cordeiro de Faria, 405
Corn Islands, 141
Cornejo, Dr. Lino, 217
Correio da Manhã, Rio newspaper, 385, 409
Cortés, Hernán, 6, 53, 58-61
Cortéz Castro, León, 132
Cortina, José Manuel, 467
Corumbá, a vital air link, 230
Cosach, Guggenheim corporation, 247
Cosmopolitan, 482
Costa, Fernando, 404

Costa Gama, Commander Ruy da, 361
Costa Rica, 131-137
  area and population, 131
  attitude to United States, 136-137
  high degree of literacy, 133
  pure democracy, 2-3, 131-133
Cotton, in Colombia, 170
Council of the Indies, 22
Craig, General Malin, 463
Creoles, Spaniards born in Latin America, 8, 9, 61
Crisol, Nazi organ, 308
Cristeros, rebellion of, 10, 71, 114
Crónica, Buenos Aires, 254
Crónica, Lima, 206
Cruchaga Tocornal, Miguel, 257,258
Cruz-Coke, Dr. Eduardo, 257
Cuauhtémoc, 58, 78
Cuba, 454-469
  as American protectorate, 25
  attitude to United States, 465-467
  last to be freed, 9
  sugar problem, 463-465
Cuernavaca, 44
Cuhne, Alfredo E., 192-193
Culaciati, Dr. Miguel J., 327
Cultural relations with Latin America, 475-476
Cuña Indians, 152
Cunha, General Flores da, 408
Current History, 482
Customs examinations in Argentina, 295
Cuzco, Inca capital, 199, 203

Dakar-Natal bridge, 18, 30, 31, 361, 380, 388
Dalldorff, Julius, 344
Damonte Taborda, Raúl, 310-311
Daniels, Josephus, 47
Dasso, David, 205
Dawson, William, 155
Dávila, Don Carlos, 240, 248-249
Death rate, in Mexico, 58
DeBayle, Dr. Henri, 140
DeBayle, Dr. León, 140
DeBayle, Colonel Luis Manuel, 140
Declaration of Lima, 313
"Declaration of the Principles of the Solidarity of America," 29
Defense system for the Caribbean, 411-422
Delgado, General Nicolás, 275, 277
Democracies, number in Latin America, 2-3, 20

Democracy, in Argentina, 311
  in Brazil, 402
  Chile, 259
  Costa Rica, 131-133
  Peru, 203-204
  Uruguay, 336-338, 340-341
  Venezuela, 183-185
Denby, Alfred, 120
Dennis, Dr. Fernandez, 452
Der Adler, printed in Irún, Spain, 172
Despradel, Dr. Arturo, 445
Deutsche La Plata Zeitung, 308
Deutsche Lufthansa, 19, 388
Deutsche Zeitung von Mexico, 111
Diario de la Guerra, Mexican Nazi organ, 111
Díaz, Porfirio, 35, 62, 68
Dictatorship, in Brazil, 351, 355, 366, 379-380
  in Chile, 240-241
  Cuba, 454, 457
  Dominican Republic, 442-443
  El Salvador, 126
  Guatemala, 118-130
  Nicaragua, 140
  Paraguay, 273-274
  Venezuela, 182-183
Dictatorships in Latin America, 2
Dietrich, Arthur, 109
Dodsworth, Dr. Henrique de Toledo, 405
"Dollar diplomacy," 26
Dominican Republic, 438-447
  dictatorship in, 2
  loss of trade, 12
  massacre of Haitians, 442
  United States relations with, 2
Dominican Republic Settlement Association, 447
Dom Pedro I, 372
Dom Pedro II, 357, 372
Drake, Sir Francis, 411
Dresden, German freighter, 387
Duggan, Lawrence, 479
Dulles, Allen W., 229
Dutra, General Eurico Gaspar, 384, 385

Echandi, Alberto, 136
Economics: chief products of each country, 11
  summary of pre-war trade, 11
Ecuador, 187-196
  attitude to United States, 193-194
  frontier dispute, 187-188

Ecuador—(*Continued*)
  how it differs from Peru, 188-189
  low prices and salaries, 190
  political leaders, 194-196
  size and population, 189-190
  United States mediation, 188
  war with Peru, 187-188
Education, status in Mexico, 10, 50-51
Eguiguren, Dr. Luis, 202
Ejidal Bank, in Mexicó, 69
El Batey, Puerto Rico, 429
El Comercio, Lima, 205, 206
El Día, Uruguay, 336
El Diario de la Costa, Cartagena, 172
El Diario, La Paz, 225
El Deber, Bucaramanga, 172
El Dorado, still sought in Ecuador, 191
El Norte, Nazi paper in Cúcuta, 172
El Pampero, Argentine Nazi organ, 307
El Popular, Mexico, 88
El Salvador, 126-130
  attitude to United States, 130
  loans and gifts rejected, 128
  peasant insurrection, 127
  population and area, 128
El Siglo, Bogotá, 167, 172
El Siglo, Santiago, 256
El Sol, Madrid, 225
El Tiempo, Bogotá, 165, 173
El Verdadero Sandino, by General Somoza, 139
Encina, Dionisio, 89
Engling, Otto, 109
Equator, visited in a sweater, 191
Ernesto Tornquist & Co., 290
Ernst, Morris, 376
Escalante, Dr. Diógenes, 185
Escurra, C. Massini, 327
Espada, Joaquin, 229
Espinola, Justice Eduardo, 368
Espionage, German, in Mexico, 112
Estigarribia, Marshal José Félix, 275, 278
Estrella, General José, 442
Europe, statistics of trade with, 11
European colonies in Latin America, 29-30
Export-Import Bank, 135, 141, 146, 229, 396-397, 465, 474
Exports of Latin America, 11
Expropriation, in Bolivia, 228-229
  in Colombia, 171
  in Panama, 148

Fairbanks, Douglas, Jr., 294

Falange, Spanish, 10, 21-23, 348-349
  in Argentina, 310
  Chile, 252
  Colombia, 171, 172
  Cuba, 466
  Mexico, 102, 112-113
  Nicaragua, 141
  Puerto Rico, 434
Falcão, Waldemar, 404
Falkenheim, Baron von, 109
Falkland Islands, 24, 305
Fascism, among clergy, 10
  anti-Fascist Italians, 16
  in Argentina, 324
  financed by Germans, 17
  in Peru, 205-206
F.B.I. in Latin America, 175
Feng Yu-Hsiang, Chinese general, 100
Fernándes, Eliza, 407
Fernández Artucio, Professor Hugo, 344
Fernández Manero, Dr. Víctor, 95
Feudalism, of landed oligarchs, 21
Feudal system in Mexico, 68-70
Fifth Column, 16-33
  in Argentina, 306-311
  Bolivia, 229-231
  Brazil, 386-390
  Chile, 265-268
  Colombia, 171-175
  Costa Rica, 137
  Cuba, 465-467
  Ecuador, 191-193
  El Salvador, 129-130
  Guatemala, 124-125
  Mexico, 43, 92, 102, 109-115
  Nicaragua, 141-142
  Paraguay, 279
  Peru, 215-218
  Puerto Rico, 434
  Uruguay, 339, 343-347
  Venezuela, 185
Fifth Column, organization and methods, 109-115
Figueroa, General Andrés, 38
Fincati, Admiral Mario, 325
Flores, Luis, 206
Fomento Corporation, Chile, 261
Fonseca, Gulf of, 141
Fontes, Dr. Lourival, 368, 385, 401
Ford, Henry, 312, 395
Fordlandia rubber plantation, 395
Foreign Affairs, 20, 107, 439, 480, 482
Foreign Agriculture, 68
Foreign policy, American, 30-33, 107
  British, 20, 23, 111

ऺreign policy—(*Continued*)
German, 16-27, 30-33
Mexican: causes of change in, 108
Foreign Policy Association, 11
Foreign Policy Reports, 15, 28, 70
Fortune, 57, 206, 208, 260, 296, 480
Francisco Sarabia air line, 114
Franco, Afranio de Mello, 409
Franco, Colonel Rafael, 275, 276, 277
Franco, General (of Spain), 22, 130,
 252, 310, 330, 434
Frank, Jerome, 402
Frank, Waldo, 82, 160
Frankfurter, Justice, 402
Fresco, Dr. Manuel A., 320
Frescoes of Rivera and Orozco, 104-
 106
Freyre, Dr. Gilberto, 409
Friburgo, Baron do Nova, 357
Frigorificos of Buenos Aires, 299
Frontin, Paolo de, 405
Fuente, General César de la, 217
Fuhrmann, Arnulf, 344

Gachupines, "men with spurs," 7, 9, 61
Gaitán, Dr. Jorge, 170
Galápagos Islands, desirable base site,
 155, 194
Gallup poll, 472
Galo Plaza, leading Ecuadorean, 196
Gamelin, General, 382
Gandhi, resemblance of Cardenas to,
 81
García, Colonel Bernardo, 455
Garcia, Frank M., 402
García Agüero, 468
García Téllez, Ignacio, 49, 95
Garité Island, Uruguay, 349
Garrido Canábal, General, 81
Garza, General Jesús de la, 49
Georgetown University, 196, 428
German airways, 18-20, 174-175, 388-
 389
Germans, number in each country, 16
 (*see also* Fifth Column)
 in Argentina, 306-311
 Bolivia, 229
 Brazil, 386-390
 Chile, 265-268
 Colombia, 171
 Ecuador, 192-194
 Guatemala, 116-117, **124-126**
 Honduras, 144
 Mexico, 108-114
 Panama, 157
 Paraguay, 278
 Peru, 16, 207, 216

Gerónimo Pietri, Dr. Luis, 185
Gestapo, in Mexico, 111
Ghioldi, Américo, 332
Gil Borges, Dr. Esteban, 185
Gildemeister family, Peru, 207, 216
Goés Monteiro, General Pedro Au-
 relio, 382-383, 384
Goethals, General, 153
Gold, in Peru, 207
Gómez, Juan Vicente, 176, 182-183
Gómez, Dr. Laureano, 166-167, 172,
 195
Gómez, Marte R., 47, 94
Gómez, Dr. Miguel Mariano, 459, 469
Gómez, by Thomas Rourke, 183
González, Colonel Angel, 455
González Campo, Guatemala, 125
González Gallo, Jesús, 48
González Garza, Roque, 55
González von Marées, Jorge, 241, 246,
 249
Good Neighbor policy, 25-32
 defensive value of, 31-32
 demonstrated in Mexico, 75
 first official mention, 28
 shaped by Hull and Welles, 25, 27-30
 success of, 470, 476
 in Bolivia, 221
 Chile, 251
 Cuba, 465
 Dominican Republic, 444
 Mexico, 107-109
 Panama, 151
 Peru, 213
Graf Spee, crew a thorny problem, 267,
 347
Graft, in Mexican affairs, 75-77
Graham Island, 265
Grau San Martín, Dr. Ramón, 458-
 459, 468
"Great Dictator" suppressed, 310, 333
"Gringos," origin of the word, 108
Grove Vallejo, Colonel Marmaduque,
 241, 254-256
Gruening, Ernest, 59, 439
Grumbach, Edgardo, 328
Guanbara Palace, Brazilian White
 House, 355, 357
Guani, Dr. Alberto, 339, 345
Guano, Peru's valuable crop, 208
Guantánamo, naval base, 25, 465
Guaraní Indians, 272, 277
Guatemala, 118-130
 attitude to United States, 2, **126**
 bad communications, 123
 dictatorship in, 2

Guatemala—(*Continued*)
  how General Ubico rules, 118-122
  population, 122
Guatemala City, 119, 123, 124
Guayaquil, rivalry with Quito, 190
Guedes, Dr. Jayme Fernandes, 392
Guilhem, Admiral Henrique Aristides, 403
Guimarães, Honorio de Freitas, 407
Guinle, Dr. Guilherme, 396, 409
Gulf-Mellon oil interests, 74
Gulf Oil Company, 179
Gundlach, C. F., 227

Haber, Fritz, 260
Haciendas, fantastic size of, 68
Haiti, 437-439, 447-453
  area and population, 449
  attitude to United States, 451
  intervention in, 26
  loss of trade, 12
  Negro population, 437
  voodoo and its persistence, 448
Hall, Melvin, 20
Halperin, Maurice, 107
Hanke, Lewis, 480
Harper's Magazine, 480, 482
Harte, Robert S., death, 105-106
Harvard University, 147
Havana Conference, 29, 94, 125, 322
Hay, General Eduardo, 93
Hay, John, 24
Haya de la Torre, Víctor Raúl, 198, 201, 208-214
  becomes a revolutionary, 201
  organizes his Apristas, 201
Hayes, Rutherford B., 271
Hearst, William Randolph, 48, 409
Hellerman, Hans, 109
Hemisphere, quoted, 132
Hemisphere defense, 30-33, 150, 153-159, 473
  Argentina's attitude, 312-315, 316-318
  Avila Camacho on, 43
  Brazilian key to, 379-382
  Chile's part in, 268-269
  Fifth Column, 16-33
  Uruguay, 347-349
  Venezuela, 186
  West Indies, 411-422
Hemisphere solidarity, 3, 108, 180, 334, 471, 478
Henríquez, General Miguel, 79
Herald Tribune, New York, quoted, 48, 74, 109, 242, 290, 294, 309, 407, 480

Hermes, German freighter, 387
Herrera, General Ariosto, 252
Herrera, Dr. Luis Alberto de, 341, 348
Herring, Hubert, 480
Hertzhauser, Fritz, 174
Hevia, Dr. Carlos, 459
Heynitz, Richard von, 129
Hidalgo, Father, 61
Hillman, Sidney, 312
Hispanidad, 349
Hispanidad Council, 22
Hispaniola, 436-440
History of Mexico, by H. B. Parkes, 54, 61
Hitler, Adolf, 18, 21, 22, 30, 110, 124, 125, 167, 192, 213, 246, 251, 311, 313, 327, 330, 341, 350, 359
Hitler Jugend in South America, 17, 110, 112, 125, 149, 307
Hochschild, Mauricio, 223
Hoffman, Hans D., 174
Hoffmann, Irving, 192
Holusa, Arno, 194
Holzer, Julius, 344
Honduras, 143-144
  area and population, 143
  attitude to United States, 144
  banana republic par excellence, 144
  modified dictatorship, 2
Hoof-and-mouth disease, 301-304
Hornblower, Captain Horatio, 141
Howard, Findley, 276
Huerta, Victoriano, 63
Hull, Cordell, 326, 333, 479
  and Good Neighbor policy, 27
  on Mexican expropriation, 74
  warning to Axis powers, 24
Hundelhausen, Baron von, 129

Ibáñez del Campo, General Carlos, 240, 248
Icaza, Dr. Xavier, 49
Iceland, effect of occupation, 163
Ichazo, General Antenor, 224
Iglesias, Santiago, 430
Illiteracy, 8-9, 58, 64-65, 219, 448
Imperialism, Argentine, 2, 221, 279-281, 293, 320
  British, 20, 23
  Chilean, 220
  Yankee, 25-27, 31-32, 213, 304, 315, 342, 411-422, 438-439
Imperial Oil of Canada, 207
Imports of Latin America, 11
Incas, their civilization, 199

Indians, number in Latin America, 5-7
  in Bolivia, 220
    Brazil, 375
    Chile, 237
    Colombia, 161
    Costa Rica, 132
    Ecuador, 188, 189, 190
    El Salvador, 126, 128
    Guatemala, 122, 126
    Mexico, 57, 58, 59, 60, 65
    Panama, 152
    Paraguay, 272
    Peru, 198-200
    West Indies, 411
Inman, Samuel Guy, 10
Insfran, Pablo Max, 275
Inside Asia, ix, 124
Inside Europe, ix, 124
Inside Latin America, comments on
    title, x
International Labor Office, 87
International Petroleum Corporation,
    207
International Petroleum of Canada, 170
International Petroleum of Peru, 191
International Telephone and Telegraph
    Co., 207, 289
Intervention by United States, 24, 25,
    27
  in Dominican Republic, 439
    Haiti, 438
    Mexico, 107
    Nicaragua, 139-140
Intra-American relations, 27-30
Investments, American, amount of, 14,
    470 (*see also* Trade, United
    States)
  in Argentina, 290, 329
    Chile, 261-262
    Colombia, 171
    Cuba, 464
    Mexico, 57
Investments, British, in Argentina, 283,
    299, 306
  in Mexico, 57
Iquitos, 189, 197, 214, 218
Irigoyen, Hipólito, 286, 287
Isaza, Dr. Antonio, 147
Itabira iron mountain, 396
Italians, early assimilation of, 16
  in Argentina, 309
    Brazil, 386
    Honduras, 144
    Panama, 157
    Peru, 207, 216

Japanese, in Brazil, 386
  in Panama, 157
  in Peru, 187, 208, 216
Jara, General Heriberto, 49, 94
Jarman, General Sanderford, 155
Jaywalking, forbidden in Guatemala
    City, 122
Jíbaro Indians, still head hunters, 191
Jijón y Caamaño, Jacinto, 195
Jiménez, Ricardo, 135
Johns Hopkins University, 360, 430
Jones, Jesse, 396
Juárez, Benito, 61, 62
Jungle, of the Amazon, 350, 370
Jungle, part of Panama defenses, 151-
    155
Justo, General Don Augustín, 284, 292-
    295, 322, 357

Karibischer Beobachter, Barranquilla,
    172
Kennecott Copper Company, 261
Kerr, Walter, 242, 407
Klein, Otto, 344
Kundt, General Hans, 224

Labarca Hubertson, Guillermo, 257
Lafferte, Elías, 257
LaFollette, Robert, 312
La Libertad, socialist paper, 306
La Nación, Buenos Aires, 317-318
La Nación, Dominican Republic, 441
Land problems, in Argentina, 296-299
  in Chile, 262-263
    Mexico, 9, 10, 57, 62-63, 67-70
    Paraguay, 278
    Puerto Rico, 431-432
La Paz, capital of Bolivia, 219, 227, 229
La Plata, Viceroyalty of, 7
La Prensa, Buenos Aires, 317-318
La Prensa, Nicaragua, 141
Larco Herrera, Rafael, 206
Laredo Bru, 459
Larraín García Moreno, Jaime, 258
Lascurain, Pedro, 55
L.A.T.I., Italian airway, 19, 309, 361,
    388, 389
La Tierra de Chicle, by Ramon Beteta,
    97
"Latin America," defects of the phrase,
    1, 200
Latin America, by Samuel Guy Inman,
    10
La Tribuna, Paraguay, 278
Law and the Modern Mind, by Jerome
    Frank, 402
Lease-Lend Bill, 21

Lech, German freighter, 387
Leguía, Augusto B., 200-201, **206**
Leguía, Juan, 201
Leighton, Bernardo, 252
Leisewitz, Dr. George, 266
Leme da Silveira Cintra, **Cardinal** Dom Sebastião, 409
Leñero, Augustín, 79
León, Dr. Rulx, 452
Lescot, Dr. Elie, 452
Leticia dispute, 4, 197, **217**
Life, 44, 359
Liga Latina Americana pro Defensa Continental, 113
Lima, City of Kings, 197
Lima Conference, 29, 326
Limón, General Gilberto, 47
Lindberg, Irving, 141
Lloyd Aero Boliviano, 19, **229**
Loans, U. S., to Latin America, **474-475**
  to Brazil, 382, 393, 397, 398
  Bolivia, 228-229
  Chile, 248
  Costa Rica, **135, 146**
  Cuba, 465
  Haiti, 439
  Mexico, 115
  Nicaragua, 141
  Paraguay, 278
  Peru, 200-201
  Venezuela, 179-180
Lombardo Toledano, Vicente, 87-89
Long, Dr. John S., 234
Look, 482
Look at Latin America, by Joan Rauschenbush, 11
Lópes, Luis Simon, 405
López, Alfonso, 167, 168
López, Carlos Antonio, **271**
López, Francisco Solano; **271**
López, General Héctor F., **41**
López, Miguel, 168
López Castro, Amadeo, 468
López Contreras, General Eleázar, **183-184**
López de Mesa, Dr. **Luis**, interview with, 169
Lozano y Lozano, Dr. Carlos, **170**
Lubinus, Gustavo, **172**
Ludwig, Emil, 376
Lufthansa Peru, 19

Machado, tyranny of, 457
Macias Valenzuela, General Pablo E., 97-98
McBride, George McC., 238

McCoy, Colonel Gordon, 98
McCulloch, John I. B., 480
McLaughlin, Colonel C. A., 441
MacLeish, Archibald, 260, 296, 480
Madero, Francisco, 62
Magalhães, Agamemnon, 404
Magellan, Straits of, 19, 182, 268-269
Managua, 140
Manchukuo, recognized by El Salvador, 130
"Manifest destiny," 25
Manini Rios, Pedro, 342, 345
Marín, Doña Amalia, 430
Marín Quirós, Manuel, 132
Marinello, Juan, 468
Marines, *not* sent to protect Standard Oil, 75
Marines, United States, in Cuba, 26
  in Dominican Republic, 439
  Nicaragua, 26, 27, 139-140
  Peru, 215
Márquez, General Carlos D., 324
Marshall, General George C., 325, 382, 383
Marshall, John, 93
Martínez, General Maximiliano, 126-128
Martínez Alba, Doña María de los Angeles, 445
Martínez Nadal, Rafael, 430
Martínez Pita, General, 323
Martínez Sáenz, Joaquín, 468
Martinique, problem of, 29-30, 417-419
Marx, Groucho, 93
Massachusetts Institute of Technology, 205
Matarazzo, Conte Francisco, 409
Matushka, Henry Graf von, 194
Maximilian, Emperor, 24
Mayas, empire of, 59-60
Medina Angarita, General Isaías, 184
Mein Kampf, 101, 124
Meio Dia, Rio newspaper, 387
Melo, Dr. Leopoldo, 322
Mendieta, Colonel Carlos, 459
Mendonça Lima, General João de, 403
Menocal, General Mario, 468
Merino Reyes, Rolando, 256
Mesquita Filho, Julio de, 408
Messersmith, George S., 465
Mestizos, 6, 8, 58, 59
Mexican Eagle Corporation, 74
Mexican Labor Board, 73
Mexican Revolution, 35, 62-72
Mexican War, 107
Mexicans, resemblance to Chinese, 53-55

Mexico, 34-117
American oil interests, 72-75
area and population, 56-57
army peculiarities, 100-101
attitude to United States, 43, 88, 93, 94, 96, 98, 113-115
British oil interests, 72-75
Cardenas days and years, 78-86
collectivist program, 90
diplomatic break with Britain, 74
ejido land reform system, 65-70
expropriation, 69-70, 73-75
first to disestablish the Church, 71
foreign policy and Axis influence, 107-117
German designs on, 30
labor's present status in, 50
leaders, Left and Right, 87-106
Mexicans at close range, 65-70
object of the revolution, 69
oil under Avila Camacho, 50, 57
political leaders, 34-52, 53-77
vast size, 56, 57
what the country needs, 77
Mexico and Its Heritage, 59
Mexico: A Study of Two Americas, 60
Mihanovich Company, 280
Milreis, monetary unit, 397
Miró Quesada, Antonio, assassinated, 206
Miró Quesada Laos, Carlos, 205
Missions, military and aviation, in Latin America, 472
Mitre family, owners of *La Nacion*, 317-318
Mitteilungen der Deutschen Volksgemeinschaft, Mexican Nazi organ, 111
Mixed Agrarian Commission, 69
Mohr, General Guillermo José, 325
Molina, General Juan Bautista, 323
Mondragón, Dr. Octavio, 47
Monroe, President James, 23
Monroe Doctrine, 23-24, 27-30
Monteiro, General Góes, 356, 364
Montes de Oca, 103
Montevideo, Uruguay, 315, 335, 339, 342, 345
Montezuma, 56, 57, 59, 62
Moore, Colonel James T., 215
Moore Montero, Eduardo, 258
Mora Miranda, Marcial, 258
Morelos, Father, 82
Morgan, Henry, 411
Morgenthau, Secretary, 312

Morínigo, General Don Higinio, 272-274, 276
Morones, Luis, 89
Morrow, Dwight, 27, 72, 107
Movimiento de Emancipación de las Mujeres Chilenas, 253
Múgica, General Francisco José, 99-100
Muller, Major Felinto, 405
Mullins, General, 141
Muñoz Marín, Luis, 427-429
Muñoz, Rivera, Luis, 428
Mussolini, Benito, 330, 341, 363, 409
Muzi Falcone, Baron Filippo, 129

Nabuco, Mauricio, 405
Nájera, Dr. Francisco Castillo, 79, 103
Natal, essential hemisphere base, 380-381
Nation, 480
National City Bank, New York, 180, 439
National Socialist Herald, 111
Nationalism, in Argentina, 282, 284, 285, 293, 334
  in Brazil, 388-389
  Chile, 247
  Guatemala, 123
  Latin America, 18
  Mexico, 116
  Panama, 147-150
  Paraguay, 272
Navarro, José, 48
Nazi organization and agitation, 17, 31, 109-115, 307-308
Nazis en Uruguay, 344
Nelson, Lord, 142
Nelson Rockefeller Committee, 163, 475
Negroes, 5, 372
Nery, Senhora Adelgesa, 402
Neutrality zone at sea, 29
Neves da Fontoura, João, 405
New Granada, Viceroyalty, 7
New Spain, Viceroyalty, 7
New Republic, 480
Nicaragua, 137-143
  area and population, 140
  attitude to United States, 137-138, 139
  barge and canal projects, 142-143
  modified dictatorship, 2
  problem of poverty, 140
  Sandino incident, 139-140
Nicholson, Mrs. Meredith, 138
Niedenfuhr, General, 323

493

Nikumatzu Okada, Peru, 208
Nitrate, in Chile, 11, 237, 260
Norris, Senator George W., 312
North Americans, Latin American name for us, 3
Northe, Dr. Heinrich, 109
N.S.D.A.P. Landesgruppe Mexico, Nazi party, 110

Obregón, General Alvaro, 55, 63
O'Brine, Jack, 109
Ochoa Moreno, Colonel Maximino, 48
O Debate, Vargas newspaper, 352
O Estado Nacional, by Dr. Campos, 402
O Estado de São Paulo, 408
O'Higgins, General Bernardo, 9, 237
Oil industry, in Colombia, 170
  in Mexico, 50, 57, 72-75
  Peru, 207
  Uruguay, 337
  Venezuela, 11, 178-180
Olavarría, Arturo, 244
Olaya Herrera, President, 170
Oliveira, Armando de Salles, 355, 408
Olney, Richard, 25, 27
Open Door policy, origin of, 24
Oranha, Oswaldo, 353
Orozco, José Clemente, artist, 105
Orozco, Soledad, wife of Avila Camacho, 46
Ortiz, Dr. Roberto Marcelino, 284, 289-291
Ortiz, Rubio, Pascual, 55
Oses, Enrique, 308
Ossorio, Adolfo León, 95, 114
Ostria Gutiérrez, Dr. Alberto, 225
Oxford University Press, 10

Pacheco, Pedro, 257
"Pacific Bloc," Bolivia, Ecuador, Peru, 265
Pacini, Regina, 322
Padilla, Dr. Ezequiel, 92-93
Páez, General, 193
Paetz, Julius, 344
Pagán, Bolívar, 430
Palacios, Dr. Alfredo L., 312, 331
Pampas, description of, 296
Panagra (*see* Pan American-Grace)
Panair do Brasil, 20, 230, 361, 389
Panama American, 148, 149, 150
Panama Canal (*see* Canal Zone)
Panama Canal Administration, 154
Panama Railway, 158

Panama Republic, 147-153
  area and population, 151
  attitude to United States, 147-150
  Vichy government's interest in, 157
Pan American Airways, 20, 123, 131, 145, 174, 186, 361, 370, 381, 382, 388, 435, 475, 479
Pan-American Bank, 29
Pan-American Conference, 27
Pan American-Grace Airways, 20, 191, 192, 207, 219, 230
Pan-American Highway, 135, 140, 145-146, 152, 475
Pan-Americanism, creators of, 3, 24, 27, 180, 336
Pan-American Union, 185
Parades, Colonel Ramón, 275
Paraguay, 271-281
  area and population, 272
  attitude to United States, 278-279
  characteristics that make it unique, 271
  decimated by wars, 272
  political leaders, 274-281
  program of the dictator, 272-274
Parkes, Henry B., 54, 61
Partido Nacional Revolucionario, 147
Partido Nacional Socialista Mexicano, 113
Party of the Mexican Revolution, 38, 55, 147
Patiño, Antenor, 222
Patiño, Simón, tin baron, 221-223
Patron Costas, Dr. Robustiano, 331
Paz, Dr. Ezequiel P., 317
Paz, José C., 317
Paz de Anchorena, Señora Z., 318
Peçanha, Nilo, 375
Peck, Walker, 20
Pedraza, Colonel José, 455
Pedrigal, Guillermo del, 258
Peons, 8, 64-65
Peixoto, Commander Ernani do Amaral, 362, 404
Peñaranda de Castillo, General Enrique, 224-225
Pereira de Souza, Washington Luiz, 407-410
Pershing, General, in Mexico, 107
Pertine, General Basilio R., 323
Pessôa, Epitacio, 407
Peru, 197-218
  attitude to United States, 206, 213, 215-216
  border war with Ecuador, 4, 187-188

494

Peru—(*Continued*)
Haya and his Apristas, 201-203
liberalism of President Prado, 203-
204
motor trip up the Andes, 197
political leaders, 200-214
serious Indian problem, 198-200
size and population, 197-198
three different Perus, 197
Peruvian Corporation, 207
Petroleum (*see* Oil)
Petrópolis, mountain capital of Brazil,
357, 368
Philip II of Spain, 249
Phoenix, U. S. cruiser, 308
Pichardo, Vaino, 445
Pinedo, Dr. Federico, 312, 327-329
Pinto, General Francisco, 362
Pistarini, General Juan, 323
Pito, Carlos A., 312
Pizarro, Francisco, 6
conquest of Peru, 199-200
mummied remains in Lima, 198, 199
Plastics from coffee, 393
Platt Amendment, 25, 28, 465
Pochhammer, Wilhelm von, 266
Polin, Herbert S., 393
Popular Front in Chile, 234-259
in Mexico, 88
Popular Socialist Vanguard, Chile, 243
Population, total, of Latin America,
5-6
Porter, Russell B., 173
Portes Gil, Emilio, 47, 55, 94, 101-102
Portuguese, language of Brazil, 1, 350
Post, New York, 307
Poverty, in Argentina, 288
in Bolivia, 219
Chile, 237, 263
Ecuador, 190-191, 193
Puerto Rico, 423-424, 425-426
Prado, Jorge, 202, 212
Prado y Ugarteche, Dr. Manuel, 203-
205
Prebisch, Dr. Paul, 328
Prestes, Luíz Carlos, 354, 406-407
Prestige, diplomatic, 477
Preufert, Emil, 171
Pro-German sentiment, causes, 20-21
Propaganda, suggestions on, 477
Proust, Marcel, 160
Public Roads Administration, 159
Puerto Rico, our orphan island, 25,
423-435
area and population, 425
Gibraltar to Panama Canal, 432-434
technique of government, 424-426

Pueyrredón, Carlos Alberto, 333
Pueyrredón, Dr. Honorio, 321, 332

Quechua Indians, 198, 220
Queiroz, Dr. Andrade, 362
Quetzalcoatl, 59
Quevedo, General Rodrigo M., 38, 47
Quigley, Captain William M., 216
Quincy, American cruiser, 30, 345
Quintanilla, Carlos, 229
Quito, attractiveness of, 188, 189

Race, difficult problems of, 5-6
Argentine sensitiveness on, 293-294
in Brazil, 371, 375
causes fear of Nazi domination, 18
in Costa Rica, 132
in Mexico not an issue, 64
Negro problem in Panama, 148-149
Radio, defects of our broadcasts, 477
Raleigh, Sir Walter, 411
Ramos, Dr. Domingo, 467
Ramos, Dr. Juan José, 467
Rauschenbush, Joan, 11, 28, 480
Rauschning, Hermann, 30
Raw materials, list of important, 15
Readers' Digest, 482
Recife, desirable base site, 381
Reconquest of Mexico, 80
Reinebeck, Dr. Otto, 125
Religion, bearing on social progress, 6
Repetto, Nicolás, 332
Revolution, advent of, 8-9
Reyes, General José, 125
Rieth, Dr. Kurt, 268
Riggs, E. F., 431
Rio Branco, Baron, 378
Rio de Janeiro, 357, 371, 372, 398
Ritter, Dr. Karl, 390
Rivadavia, Bernardino, 285
Rivera, Diego, 43, 63, 104-105
Roca, Blas, 468
Roca, Dr. Julio A., 285, 325-326
Rodríguez, Abelardo, 47, 55, 64, 96
Rodríguez de Francia, Gaspar, 271
Roehm, Captain Ernst, 224
Roman Catholic Church (*see* Church)
Romo Castro, Major Waldo, 48
Roosevelt, Franklin D., 20, 139, 150,
159, 167, 203, 213, 235, 251,
292, 303, 315, 322, 330, 337,
359, 378, 380, 427, 439, 450
Roosevelt, Theodore, 25, 26, 27, 287
Root, Elihu, 258
Rosas, Juan Manuel de, 285
Rosenberg, James N., 447

495

Ross, Gustavo, 241
Ross Santa Maria, Gustavo, 241, 247
Rossetti, Juan B., 258
Royal Dutch Shell Corporation, 74, 179
Rue, Sidney de la, 449
Ruiz Guiñazú, Dr. Enrique, 326
Russell, Bertrand, 160

Saavedra, General Cornelio, 333
Saavedra Lamas, Carlos, 316, 333
Sacasa, Dr., 139
Sáenz, Professor Moisés, 103, 212
Sáenz Peña, President, 333
Sáenz de Tejada, Guatemala, 125
Saladrigas, Dr. Carlos, 467
Salazar, Dr. Carlos, 125
Salgado, Plinio, 408
Salocchi, Gino, 207, 216
Salvador Allende, Dr., 256
Sam, Guillaume, 438
Sánchez Cerro, 201, 204, 212
Sánchez, Graciano, 103
Sánchez Pontón, Dr. Luis, 95
Sánchez Sorondo, Dr. Matías Guillermo, 324, 330-331
Sandino, Augusto César, revolt of, 139-140
Sandstede, Gottfried, 307
Sanitary Convention with Argentina, 303
San Blas Indians, 152
San José, capital of Costa Rica, 131, 132, 135
San José-Limón Railway, 135
San Marcos University, 198, 204
San Martín, General José de, 9, 181, 285
San Salvador, 128
Santa Anna, General, 61
Santa Catharina, German enclave in Brazil, 16
Santamarina, Dr. Antonio, 312, 331
Santander, Francisco, 164
Santiago, Chile, 234, 235
Santo Domingo, (see Dominican Republic)
Santos, Dr. Eduardo, 165-166
Santos, Enrique, 165-166
São Paulo, city and province, 371, 372, 398
Sarmanho, Darcy, now Senhora Vargas, 360
Scadta, German airline, 174, 191
Schleebrugge, Baron Karl Frederick von, 109

Schlubach, Jurgen, 171
Schmitt, Gottfried, 171
Schnake Vergara, Oscar, 253-254
Scott, Edward W., 148
Second Socialist International, 88
Sedta, German airline, 20, 191, 192
Serrano Suñer, Ramón, 22, 252
Servicio Informativo, forbidden, 125
Shaw, Bernard, 160
Shipping laws, effects on Puerto Rico, 426
Ships, Axis, Argentine action on, 314
expropriation by Mexico, 116
by Peru, 215
by Venezuela, 185
Sigatoka disease, 171
Silva Herzog, Professor Jesús, 103
Silver, 57, 207
Simon, Sir John, 185
Sinarquistas, in Mexico, 114
Sinclair oil interests, 74
Siqueira Campos, Brazilian ship, 384
Siqueiros, David Alfaro, 105-106
Sixth Column, 93, 218, 312
Social taboos in Argentina, 295
Socialism, Mexican style, 90
Socony-Vacuum Oil Company, 171
Solf y Muro, Dr. Alfredo, 204-205
Somoza, General Anastasio, 137-140
Sosa Valdés, Colonel Dámaso, 276
Sosúa, haven for Jewish refugees, 446
South America, some general traits, 162-163
South American Primer, 197, 287
South Shetland Islands, 265
Souza Costa, Arthur de, 403
Spain, oppression of its colonies, 7-8
Spain, influence of, in Argentina, 310
in Colombia, 166-167, 172-173
Cuba, 466
Mexico, 112-113
Panama, 149
West Indies, 411
Spaniards, number of conquerors, 7
intermarriage with Negroes, 5
Spanish, where spoken, 1
Spanish-American War, 457
Standard Fruit Company, 449
Standard Oil Company of New Jersey, 74, 75, 170, 179, 207, 227-229, 289
Statue of Christ, symbol of peace between Argentina and Chile, 316
Steer, Carlos, 206
Stella, German ship, 141

Stimson, Henry L., 27
"Strategic materials" that we lack, 14-15
Strobelt, Paul Ernst, 142
Suárez, Eduardo, 49, 93-94
Sucre, General Antonio José de, 9, 181, 190
Sucre, capital of Bolivia, 219
Sugar, in Cuba, 11, 463-465
  in Dominican Republic, 443-444
  in Peru, 207
  in Puerto Rico, 425-426
Sulzberger, Arthur, 165
Sumner, Charles, 25
Sun Yat-sen, Dr., 55

Taboga and Taboguilla Islands, 153
Taca air service, 145
Tacna-Arica dispute, 4
Tamayo, Dr., 195
Tamborini, Dr. José P., 322
Tariff, effects in Puerto Rico, 426
Tegucigalpa, without a railroad, 143, 144
Tehuantepec, Isthmus of, 56, 114, 155
Tejeda, Colonel Adalberto, 103
Ten Haeff, Inga Elizabeth Anita, 360
Terra, Gabriel, 341
Terraza family, owners of thirty million acres, 68
Texas Oil Company, 171
Teziutlán, Mexico, 34, 35, 44
The Grapes of Wrath forbidden, 200
The Hemisphere, 442
The Republics of South America, quoted, 10, 199, 219
Thermann, Baron Edmund von, 267, 306, 311
Thomas, Norman, 312
Thomson, Charles A., 480
Time, 121, 286, 308, 394, 396, 480
Times, London, 317
Times, New York, 22, 45, 142, 165, 173, 196, 261, 267, 310, 317, 344, 347, 349, 382, 402, 430, 439, 474, 480
Timon, Mexican Nazi organ, 111
Tin, chief product of Bolivia, 221-223
Tinoco, Federico, 132-133
Tlaxcalan Indians, 59
Tobago Island, 411
Tobar Donoso, Dr. Julio, 195
Tonazzi, General Juan N., 324
Toro, Colonel José David, 224, 225
Total Defense, quoted, 28
Totalitarianism, reasons for, 20-21

Toussaint L'Ouverture, 437
Town and Country, 482
Townsend, Dr. W. Cameron, 82
Trade, British, 207, 328, 329
Trade, geared intimately with Europe, 8, 11-14
Trade, United States, with Argentina, 301, 328-330
  with Bolivia, 223-224, 227-229
    Brazil, 351, 389-390
    Chile, 261-262
    Colombia, 170
    Costa Rica, 135
    Cuba, 464-465
    Ecuador, 190, 192
    El Salvador, 128
    Haiti, 449
    Latin America, 473-474
    Mexico, 108
    Nicaragua, 141
    Peru, 207, 217
    Venezuela, 179-180
Transocean News Agency, 17, 172 215, 307, 318, 387
Transportes Aereos Centroamericanos, 145
Trends, summary of, 470-471
Tribune, Chicago, 206
Troncoso de la Concha, Dr. Manuel de Jesús, 445
Tropical Oil Company, 170
Trotsky, Leon, 84, 105-106
Trueblood, Howard J., 15, 480
Trujillo Molina, Héctor, 445
Trujillo Molina, General Rafael Leonidas, 440-447
Trujillo Molina, Virgilio, 445
Tugwell, Rexford G., 432
Tungsten, in Bolivia, 223
Turbay, Dr. Gabriel, 169

Ubico y Castañeda, General Jorge, 118-121
"Unidenses," Argentine name for us, 3
Union Popular Alemana, 307
United Fruit Company, 123, 135, 144, 170, 171, 446, 456
United Press, 311, 315, 318
United States, commercial aviation, 20
  exports to Latin America, 13
  foreign policy, 23-24
  Marine Corps Mission, 215
  trade with Latin America, 12, 14-15
United States-Mexican Claims Commission, 93

497

United States Steel Corporation, 396
University of California, 196
University of Chicago, 147
University of Córdoba, 209
University of Illinois, 205
Uriburu, General, 287, 322
Uruguay, 335-349
   area and population, 335
   attitude to United States, 336, 341, 345
   Axis activities, 343-347
   democracy of, 2-3
   Fifth Column scare, 30
   indictment against Nazi plotters, 345-347
   political leaders, 339-342
   trade, 343
Uxmal, 59

Valdivia, German enclave, 16, 265-266
Valdivia, Pedro, 7, 237
Valladares, Benedicto, 404
Vanadium Corporation, 207
Vanguardia Liberal, Bucaramanga, 172
Vargas, Alzarinha, 361, 362
Vargas, Colonel Benjamin, 362
Vargas, Getulio Dornelles, 350-369, 395
   achievements, 366-367
   attitude to religion, 359
   aviation exploits, 358
   crises in his career, 353-356
   family life, 360-362
   interviews with, 368-369
   plans for succession, 368
   qualities and sources of power, 362-366
   story of his life, 351-357
Vargas, Getulio, Jr., 360
Vargas, Dr. Luthero, 360
Vargas, Manoel, 361
Vargas, Spartacus, 362
Vasconcelos, José, 103, 111, 211
Vásquez, Horacio, 441
Vega, José de la, 172
Velázquez, Fidel, 89
Venezuela, 176-186
   area and population, 176
   attitude to United States, 184, 185
   boundary dispute with Britain, 24, 25
   exports, 179
   high cost of living, 176-178
   no taxes: oil pays all, 178-180
   Simón Bolívar: his career, 180-181
   typical monthly budget, 177
Veracruz, bombardment of, 26, 107
Vergara, Dr. Luis, 362

Viceroyalty of New Spain, 61
"Victory of the West," propaganda movie, 268
Villa, Pancho, 26, 36, 48, 63, 107
Villaseñor, Eduardo, 97
Vincent, Sténio Joseph, 450-452
Virgin Islands, 435
Voice of Destruction, by Rauschning, 124, 359
Volio, Alfredo, 136
Von Schoen, German ambassador to Chile, 266

Wakerbacker, Baron von, 109
Walker, American filibuster, 131
Walker Larraín, Senator Horacio, 258
Wallace, DeWitt, 482
Wallace, Henry, 42, 102, 304
War, European: its effect on Latin America, 12, 32, 261, 283-284, 407-410, 471
"War of the Pacific," 237
Washington Luiz Pereira de Souza, 407-410
Welles, Sumner, 25, 27-30, 134, 231, 246, 476, 479
Wendler, Ernst, 230, 268
Wertenbaker, Charles, 25
Western Hemisphere, conference of republics, 27
   police power over, 26
West Indies, defense system for, 411-422
Weyl, Nathaniel and Sylvia, 80
White, John W., 344, 402
Who's Who in Latin America, 223, 333
Wichita, American cruiser, 345
Wilson, Edwin C., 345
Wilson, Woodrow, 26, 133
Wirts, Wilhelm, Mexican Führer, 110
Witchbroom disease in Ecuador, 190
Wolf, Colonel, 323
Workers' University, Mexico City, 89
W. R. Grace Company, 207

Xavier Gaxiola, Francisco, 47, 96

Yaqui Indians, 65
Yerex, Lowell, 145
Yocupicio, General Román, 100

Zapata, Emiliano, 36, 63
Zapotec language, 65
Zéphirin, Senator, 452
Zinsser, Christian, 144
Zipellius, Otto von, 266